Personnel Administration In Education

Leadership for Instructional Improvement

Third Edition

BEN M. HARRIS
University of Texas at Austin

BETTY JO MONK
Baylor University

In collaboration with

KENNETH E. McINTYRE
University of Texas at Austin

DANIEL F. LONG
University of Texas at Austin

ALLYN AND BACON
Boston London Toronto Sydney Tokyo Singapore

To Mary Lee for guidance,
help, and enduring support.

And to J.D. for understanding
and support.

Series Editor: Ray Short
Series Editorial Assistant: Jo Ellen Caffrey
Production Administrator: Susan McIntyre
Editorial-Production Service: Ruttle, Shaw & Wetherill, Inc.
Cover Administrator: Linda Dickinson
Manufacturing Buyer: Megan Cochran

Copyright © 1992, 1985, 1979 by Allyn and Bacon
A Division of Simon & Schuster, Inc.
160 Gould Street
Needham Heights, MA 02194

Library of Congress Cataloging-in-Publication

Personnel administration in education : leadership for instructional
    improvement / Ben M. Harris . . . [et. al.].
        p.   cm.
    Includes bibliographical references.
    ISBN 0-205-13342-8
    1. School personnel management—United States.   I. Harris, Ben M.
    LB2831.58.P47   1992
    371.2'01'0973—dc20   91-39050
                                                                CIP

Printed in the United States

10 9 8 7 6 5 4 3 2   96 95 94 93

— CONTENTS ——————

— LIST OF EXHIBITS ——

—— LIST OF APPENDICES ——

PREFACE

This volume was designed to mark still another era of change and ferment in education, to meet a set of persistent needs, and to anticipate the emergence of demands for excellence in education for all students. During the turbulent 1980s, the persistent and anticipated needs for improving programs and personnel were often frustrated, superficial "reforms" dominated educational decision making, and fundamental structural changes, especially in staffing and instruction, were *not* in vogue.

This book was originally written as an attempt to respond to pressures for personnel administration to adopt new ways of working to enhance the human resource capabilities of our schools. There was also a special focus on instructional personnel. As in past editions, there is a central concern for instructional improvement. Two developments, however, caused us to refocus our attention in some ways. First, the politicalization of change of the 1980s has created many programs that require fundamental restructuring in the 1990s. Second, the impending vacancies and shortages of high-quality personnel of all kinds in our schools force us to give much more attention to the traditional tasks of personnel work, such as recruiting, selecting, assigning, and balancing.

In an era when all of our institutions are being challenged by individuals and groups from all walks of life, we believe that our nation's free public schools, under local leadership, have demonstrated a remarkable level of responsiveness to the needs of a changing society. Were our prisons, hospitals, corporations, and governmental institutions as socially productive and cautiously responsive as the public schools, our children would face a less chaotic world in the twenty-first century. However, past accomplishments and adherence to time-tested educational values do not suffice. The 1990s seem certain to continue toward the electronification of our society, with simultaneous globalization of many aspects of life. These conditions make it more urgent that our schools move to higher levels of excellence. High-quality education for all is needed for our nation to prosper in the twenty-first century.

School personnel have made and will continue to make the difference in moving from mediocrity to quality to excellence. Those involved in personnel administration need to respond now to the needs that extend beyond the usual.

Ben M. Harris
Austin, Texas
and Betty Jo Monk
Waco, Texas

1

Staffing Schools: Challenge for Change

Schools are organizations formed to help people learn. Learning may not be a uniquely human process, but teaching certainly is. In this respect, the educational enterprise tends to be distinctly different from most industrial enterprises. In schools, the facilities, materials, and equipment are important but less crucial to the productive processes of teaching and learning than the *quality of personnel* involved (Gage and Berliner 1989).

This book's concern is with the tasks to be accomplished in getting the right persons in the right positions with the competencies required to perform effectively and efficiently. Thus, recruitment, selection, assignment, and evaluation of personnel are the central concerns of this book. The *improvement of instruction* through staffing is emphasized rather than the maintenance of existing programs with existing staffing patterns. Similarly stressed is the staffing of instructional programs rather than various auxiliary service programs, as important as they are.

A Set of Assumptions

Assumptions underlie nearly everything we do in the name of "professional practice." They predetermine what we regard as appropriate or inappropriate. Certain assumptions may gain credence from a body of supporting research and theory. More often than not, however, they are based on logic, experience, or tradition and are open to serious challenge even if widely accepted in current practice.

The assumptions that follow have been carefully selected to form the framework upon which other chapters are based. Because they are explicit, the reader can test each against the wisdom of his or her own experience.

1

The Humane Character of Education

Personnel practices are especially influential in determining the character and quality of instructional programs because of the essentially humane character of the educational enterprise. Unlike most corporate organizations, a school's products, clients, and workers are all human. The school is an essentially humane institution, not because of any philosophical bias but because of the dominance of human interactions in all facets of its operation. The school's instructional programs, even more than some supporting services programs, are highly humane in the sense that we are using this term. Technology, along with its associated hardware and software, plays a part in the teaching-learning process, of course. Certain instructional programs rely more heavily on materials and equipment than others, but almost without exception, the human element is crucial to the quality of learning that takes place in schools.

Instructional Staff Centrality

A school's instructional staff is central to its productivity, and the quality of that staff's performance is the major factor influencing the teaching-learning process (Benne 1990; Glatthorn 1990). This assumption is often verbalized in our society, especially in connection with campaigns for pay raises and, less often, at evaluation and contract times. Nonetheless, it is difficult to escape the position that those who directly influence the experiences of students—call them teachers, counselors, principals, supervisors, or superintendents—inevitably influence the learning process, too. It is important, however, not to equate *instructional staff* with the position of the *teacher*, for quality schools utilize complex staffing patterns.

Under traditional, self-contained classroom arrangements at the elementary school levels, "the teacher" is, in fact, the dominant member of the instructional staff; only the principal and parents are likely to have much influence other than the teacher. In traditional secondary schools, with their highly departmentalized structures, no staff member is likely to be closely associated with the individual student. Under such conditions the peers, parents, and larger society are probably the dominant learning influences. However, at all levels, emerging programs emphasize individualization of instruction, team teaching, block-of-time arrangements, career education, work experience, parental involvement, and special resource personnel (Cohen 1988; Lewis 1989b). These developments are placing new importance on the instructional staff as *a group of individuals* influencing the learning of students. This detracts not at all from the centrality of the instructional staff, but makes the staffing task much more sensitive and difficult. It is the rediscovery in the 1980s of the need for fundamental *restructuring* of schooling, in contrast with minor reforms, that should guide personnel practices in the years ahead (Hart 1989; Louis and Miles 1990; Wayson 1988).

Flexible, Adaptable Staffing

The changing character of instructional programs demands flexible patterns of staffing and creative adaptations in recruitment, selection, assignment, and evaluation. How simple it would be if every opening needed only to be "filled" like a cavity in a healthy, permanent tooth. Personnel offices have often functioned in this simplistic way in the past; some may continue to do so. However, staffing for improvement of instruction can be very dynamic (Harris 1985). Every opening can be viewed as an opportunity to improve instruction. New programs can be staffed with an eye to the new elements in the program that may call for new positions, new roles in old positions, and new relationships among incumbents. Current effort to move away from "tinkering" educational reforms toward restructuring of schools, programs, and systems places renewed emphasis on flexible, adaptive staffing (Cuban 1990; Miller 1988). Old programs reaching maturity and becoming outdated can be revitalized through reassignments and restructuring of staff relationships. Programs under fire for whatever reason offer opportunities for improvements that can be facilitated by flexible, adaptable, imaginative staffing practices.

Functional Competence

The ability to function effectively and efficiently is the essential basis for recruitment, selection, assignment, and evaluation practices. While objective measures of functional competence in complex professional areas of performance are still limited, estimates and approximations can and should guide staffing practices (Harris 1986, 77–95; Medley et al. 1984). The reliance upon degrees, transcripts, letters of recommendation, years of experience, and certificates as indices of competence has reduced personnel administration to a set of clerical routines in many instances. An even more serious effect of this substitution of paper for performance has been widespread acceptance of mediocrity within the teaching profession (Task Force on Teaching as a Profession 1986), disillusionment and distrust among the school's publics—both pupil and adult—and a tragic neglect in recognizing those who are genuinely competent.

Cooperative Involvement

Staffing for instruction is a task area of such importance and complexity that the involvement of many people both within and without the school system should be arranged. This effort would hardly be necessary if personnel practice were to continue as a parts-replacement operation in which every opening called for a specific replacement. The use of staff personnel practices as part of the improvement process, however, calls for the cooperative participation of many who are concerned also with improvement of instruction. Supervisors, consultants, coordinators, and directors are some of the staff personnel who are often closely associated with planning and implementing new programs and, hence, are vitally concerned with the selection and assignment of personnel.

The school principal is always greatly concerned about the personnel assigned to his or her building and needs to be involved not only because of that concern, but also because of the insights and aspirations a good principal has concerning the improvement of the instructional program. As "site-based management" proposals become operating realities to some extent, the involvement of principals and teachers in personnel decisions will be required, and the roles of parents will also need consideration (Barth 1990). Teacher interest in new personnel selected and assigned to a school stems also from their need to work together and share responsibility for the learning outcomes expected from any school or program. Hence, teachers have a responsible stake in personnel decisions.

It can be argued that cooperative involvement should be an integral part of personnel practice because it is "democratic." The guiding principle in this argument is that those who are affected by a decision should be involved in making that decision. This principle is indeed sound, but it is not a sufficient guide or reason for involvement. The essential criteria for involvement vary with the staffing task, the emphasis given to change, and specific situational factors (Conley and Bacharach 1990). In general, however, the following principles seem to apply:

1. Personnel most directly affected should be most directly involved.
2. Personnel with relevant expertise should be involved to the extent and in ways that assure full utilization of their expertise.
3. Personnel with responsibilities for planning change should be involved in ways that assure that plans will be implemented.
4. Personnel with responsibilities for implementing and operating instructional programs should be involved in ways that assure efficient operations.
5. Personnel with responsibilities for evaluating programs and developing policies to guide instructional change should be involved in ways that assure implementation of policy guidelines and responsiveness to assessed needs.

Human Resources Sought

Educationally useful human resources exist in a great variety of places and among diverse kinds of people; hence, staffing practices should be concerned more with human capabilities and less with traditional titles, certificates, and degrees. Just as staffing patterns are rapidly changing and becoming more flexible and diverse, so the sources of personnel need to be made more diverse in recognition of the fact that human resources are where you find them. College preparatory programs have no monopoly on producing professional competence. Experience in one school situation is not always a predictor of the quality of performance in other situations. Experience cautions against relying too heavily on promotions from within and ignoring other sources of personnel. The certification process in most states appears to be less a guarantor of competence than an authorization to seek a position to demonstrate possible competence. In fact, it seems clear that so-called reforms in some states have substantially weakened teacher preparation programs (Task Force on Teaching as a Profession 1986), making the "paper credentials" even less valid than in the past.

The nontraditional sources of human talent are numerous. The military services have contributed many ex-officers and ex-enlisted men and women to school and college staffs, many of whom have functioned well even without traditional qualifications. The extreme teacher shortage of the 1940s and early 1950s resulted in the employment of thousands of technically unqualified personnel who demonstrated the ability to function long before they met formal requirements. Reports of the success of black students in collegiate programs for which these students were not "qualified" are numerous and well documented. Teacher Corps programs have demonstrated the unique capacity of dedicated individuals, given some technical support and professional guidance, to function at high levels in unusually difficult situations in which the performance of traditionally qualified individuals has tended toward mediocrity. Even more dramatic are the results produced by Peace Corps volunteers in many parts of the world.

There is not a strong argument to be made for replacing professional or technical training with dedication, nor is there a case to be made for the proposition that anybody can teach. The view expressed here is that competence to perform effectively is essential in all such personnel. Competencies are largely learned, but they are present in all kinds of people with all kinds of educational and experiential backgrounds. Just as too much reliance on *paper* instead of performance criteria is ineffective in personnel selection and assignment, so it is unproductive to recruit and select from a manpower pool that is narrowly circumscribed by degree, certificate, experience, and other requirements.

Influence and Control Patterns

The changing character of our society is reflected in a complex pattern of influences and controls on staffing practices (Schlechty 1990). Legal and pressure-group influences and controls offer new and more difficult challenges in personnel administration. The rapidly changing society offers many opportunities for improving instructional practices, but conflicts within society offer also a bewildering array of new forces and barriers to the improvement process.

The school reform efforts of the early 1980s added many new "prescriptions" for personnel practice. New evaluation schemes, career-ladder promotion plans, alternative certification programs, and extensive teacher testing were but a few of these "reforms." The current excitement over "restructuring" schools and districts and emphasizing site-based management (Hart 1989), curriculum revisions (Cuban 1990), and parental involvement in policy decisions (Cohen 1988) will challenge personnel practices more than ever before (Conley and Bacharach 1990).

So much ferment in educational affairs can be frustrating and chaotic as well as challenging. Anne Lewis, discussing the "Education Summit" of September 1989 with governors of the states formulating national goals for education, expresses a concern shared by other thoughtful educators who are sometimes forced into observer roles when major decisions are made: "What the summit failed to do was reflect any semblance of true leadership—the kind that can inspire people . . . " (1989a, 180).

The older social issues continue to have their influence on personnel practices even as new ones emerge. This book deals specifically with civil rights, collective bargaining, and legal liability issues that relate to instructional staffing. It suffices at this point to say that effective staffing for instructional improvement will come only with dramatic changes in current practices in the direction of making instructional program needs at least as compelling as the need for personal rights, economic well-being, job security, and personal status.

School Clients Served

The client groups to be served by the public schools are numerous. Personnel administration cannot be conducted without some kind of priority system. Much of the current political debate over education affairs would give a naive citizen the impression that the clients to be served with exclusive top priority are business establishments or the government itself. We submit that *students* are the clients with top priority. Parents, too, must be considered a priority client group. These assumptions do not ignore the interests of business, government, and society and the economy in the broadest terms, in the quality and character of the education provided to children and youth. However, democratic traditions in the United States have been strengthened and reaffirmed, supporting students' rights to an education, supporting parental rights vis-à-vis the treatment of their children, requiring the school to act in loco parentis, and reinforcing local control. While none of these traditions are unassailable, they support the assumption that students and their parents deserve a special place in the minds of educators as preferred clients. Federal legislation supporting educational opportunities for the handicapped (H.B. 94–142), combined with recent efforts of the U.S. Congress in support of early childhood education, parental involvement in the education of their children, and unprecedented nationwide concern for dropout prevention, supports the assumption that our top-priority clients are children, youth, and parents.

From the point of view of the practice of personnel administration, the assumption that students and parents are our clients to be served with fidelity means that our recruitment, selection, assignment, and evaluation of personnel gain significance far beyond the usual considerations. Are we recruiting those who can be committed to children and youth? Are selective criteria and processes rigorous enough to assure the best applicants opportunities to serve in our schools? Do assignment and evaluation practices assure optimum opportunities for students with a steadily improving instructional program?

The assumptions discussed above are assumptions only, but they have been carefully considered. Subsequent chapters present ideas and suggestions for practice on the basis of these assumptions. The reader may want to challenge some of them; hence, they are made explicit here.

Exhibit 1.1 was developed by Richard W. Clark (1988) in elaborating on the problem of "overlapping and interdependent relationships"

EXHIBIT 1.1   The "Active" Personnel Administration Program

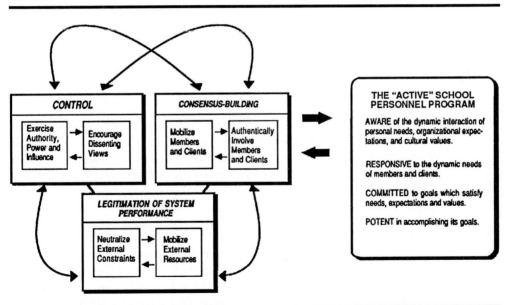

Adapted from Richard W. Clark (1988) "Who Decides? The Basic Policy Issue," Chapter 8 in Tanner, Laurel N., ed. *Critical Issues in Curriculum*, Part I. 87th Yearbook of the National Society for the Study of Education. Chicago: University of Chicago Press. Figure 1. The Active School, p. 192. Reprinted by permission.

(pp. 192–193) in curriculum policy decision making. It serves, however, to address a number of our assumptions. The "active" personnel administration program can give meaningfulness to our assumptions by utilizing such an interactive model.

The Instructional Activities of Schools

Instructional processes make schools unique among the humane institutions of our society. Instructional staffing is, therefore, the unique concern of personnel administration in school settings. The degree of its importance is evident in the large proportion of school budgets generally allocated to instructional staff salaries. It is reflected in public opinion by persistent demands for better teachers and better instructional programs. Curiously, it is not always exemplified by the rigor or sophistication of our recruitment, selection, assignment, and evaluation practices.

The concept of the school as a place where the activities of the staff are primarily instructional is so commonplace that the policymaking and organizational ramifications of the idea are sometimes overlooked. We sometimes forget to think carefully and clearly about those ideas we have already accepted and tend to take for granted.

The Nature of Teaching

Personnel administration gives most of its attention to teaching, for teaching is at the heart of the operation of schools. Schooling is uniquely characterized by formally organized teaching. Learning of many kinds goes on in many places in and out of schools, but *teaching* makes schools unique social institutions.

Teaching is an ancient craft that has been the focus of scholarly interest at least since the times of Socrates and Plato. The Socratic method of teaching continues to interest practitioners some 2,000 years later. Plato, worried about too much emphasis on writing rather than on memorizing (Harris, W.V. 1989), argued, "Writing weakens the memory and fosters forgetfulness."

In modern times, the work of philosophers, social scientists, and statesmen in Europe and America added substantially to the ancient notions about teaching and learning. It has been left to the twentieth century for teaching to become more than a craft or trade, building on psychological principles (Gagne 1976), and a genuine professional, "scientific basis" for teaching effectiveness now exists (Gage 1985; Gage and Berliner 1989).

With a growing body of research and theoretical models of effective teaching practice (Joyce and Weil 1980) clearly established, teaching is now recognized by experienced practitioners and scholars alike as among the most complex of all human endeavors. Teaching is both art and science, built on research in psychology, sociology, anthropology, and human development and learning. The research on teaching has addressed questions of teacher effects as an applied science. Early studies concentrated on input-outcome relationships, attempting to identify traits, experiences, attitudes, or personality types that differentiate "good" from "poor" teachers. These studies have had little success in predicting teaching effectiveness.

The focus of research and theory on teaching shifted dramatically following World War II to process-outcome relationships. Ryans studied behavior patterns of teachers in the classroom (1955); Bales (1950) and Flanders (1970) studied verbal interactions between teacher and students; Dunn and Dunn (1977) were leaders in studying teaching styles; and other researchers have addressed lesson design, classroom climate, classroom management, and time on task. Such studies have generated a whole array of fairly solid findings about generic teaching behaviors that can predictably enhance learning. They have also revealed the severe limits of our knowledge. Teaching is now recognized as so much more complex than previously thought (Dodl 1972) that some even raise serious questions about the worth of further scientific inquiry (Hansgen 1991).

Despite enormous complexities, some generalizations are now available as rather reliable guides to thoughtful practitioners. Exhibit 1.2 lists some of these, elaborating on the research cited above. There seems to be little doubt from a research and scholarly view that teachers make a big difference in the learning that results from classroom instruction. Learning occurs above and beyond classroom teaching, of course, but formal teaching "works," at least for many kinds of learning (Barth 1990; Dunkin and Biddle 1974; Gage 1985; Wittrock 1986). Of course, it is "good" teaching that "works," for teaching makes both positive and negative differences.

That teaching must promote active student involvement or engagement with the objectives of the lesson, unit, or course is another generalization that is well documented if not fully accepted in practice. Some teachers and many laypersons persist in viewing learning as a passive process limited to listening, memorizing, and regurgitating. The most effective teaching stimulates interactions verbally, visually, kinesthetically, intellectually, and affectively. Such teaching provides opportunities for and guidance in using content in solving real problems in real-life situations. Active learning can be offered by teaching in many styles and forms (Joyce and Weil 1980). Stodolsky reports, however, what many classroom observers already know: "Intellectual activity in classrooms is impoverished . . . mundane and mediocre . . . " (1988, 98).

EXHIBIT 1.2   Generalizations about Teaching

1. Teaching makes a big difference in what is and is not learned.
2. Teaching requires active student involvement in an interactive process.
3. Teaching is so complex that it is never mastered, can't be simply characterized, and is at best only crudely assessed.
4. Teaching can be effective in a variety of forms, styles, models, and lesson designs.
5. Teaching practices of generic kinds consistently relate to student learning.
6. Teaching practices are invented and learned; they do not develop naturally.
7. Teaching is both art and science, like any professional endeavor—music, medicine, writing, or managing.
8. Teaching in schools is only one source of influence of student learning; others include parents, peers, and media.
9. Teaching that is organized, systematic, and sequenced promotes more learning.
10. Teaching that is creative, imaginative, and varied promotes more learning.
11. Teaching that utilizes multisensory experiences promotes more learning.
12. Teaching that students perceive as meaningful, purposeful, interesting, and satisfying promotes more learning.
13. Teaching that recognizes and adapts to individual differences promotes more learning, because each person learns differently.
14. Teaching that is personal, empathetic, and friendly promotes more learning.
15. Teaching that starts with motivation, stimulation, and purposefulness requires little discipline and control.

Instructional Support Activities

The essential product toward which most staff efforts and, hence, most funds are directed is student learning. The assumption all school programs make is that something happens to students *in school* to help them learn—something that probably would not happen out of school. These direct interventions of the school staff to foster pupil learning are "teaching" activities. Obviously, learning occurs in the absence of teaching. However, the responsibility of the school is to influence the student toward certain learning outcomes. Accordingly, teaching is the central task or function of the school.

Certain direct instructional support activities are needed in relation to teaching, leading to learning. These are activities directed toward teachers or others working with students. They are direct instructional activities in the sense that they relate to and affect the learning process. They are support activities, as distinguished from teaching activities, in that they influence learning through teaching rather than directly influencing the student (Glatthorn 1990, 105–6). Some of the distinctions between teaching, learning, instruction, and support services may appear inconsequential, but they can help to shape our thinking about staff assignments, roles, and competency requirements.

Teaching is what a responsible official does with one or more others, designated as students or pupils in learner roles, to facilitate, direct, expedite, encourage, influence, or otherwise directly promote specified learning outcomes. Accordingly, many people teach, including teachers, counselors, librarians, principals, and parents.

Instruction is any and all activity carried on within an organized context that directly relates to the learning process that is occurring or being projected, whether it relates directly to the student or to adults, materials, facilities, schedules, and so on. Hence, instruction may continue when teaching ceases, as in homework or self-instructional situations.

Curriculum is any formal guideline for teaching and instruction, designating goals, objectives, activities, sequences, materials, or conditions for learning. A unit outline, a textbook, a course of study, a syllabus, and a law are all *curricula* to the extent that they can and do direct, guide, or influence teaching and instruction.

Education is the process of learning, wherever and however it may occur. Education does not require teaching, instruction, or curricula as defined above, but, of course, in formal educational contexts they are all included as part of the "educational process."

Schooling is the process of organizing and operating a special environment for special kinds of selected learning. Hence, schooling distinguishes formal from informal education, although it is conceivable that formal education in on-the-job situations might lack the formalities of schooling.

Direct services are the activities that directly influence the product sought. Hence, teaching is a direct service in relation to learning. Vision testing is a direct service in relation to health.

Supporting services are the activities that facilitate, expedite, enhance, coordinate, or otherwise make direct services more efficient and/or effective. Hence, purchasing services are supportive to teaching when they assure the availability of instructional supplies. In-service training is a support service to teaching when it facilitates the use of new media or techniques.

Instructional support services essential to the best teaching that can be provided include media services, curriculum planning, program evaluation, counseling, testing, and even extracurricular activities when properly provided to motivate and supplement. Still other forms of instructional support involve induction programs for new teachers, peer or supervisory coaching, in-service training, and other forms of clinical supervision.

Noninstructional Support Activities

It would be naive to assume that instructional activity is all there is. Several types of work that are required of schools are different from what we think of as instruction. Activities associated with supporting services, developmental services, and business services are all a part of the duties of many staff personnel. Noninstructional duties as responsibilities of the instructional staff have come to be widely accepted. This is work associated with the *entertainment* of the students and other segments of the community.

Whereas staffing for noninstructional support is not primarily a concern of this book, these activities cannot be forgotten or ignored. Noninstructional products are expected in most school communities. These noninstructional products are also *potentially* supportive of good instruction and might be defended or even expanded for the sake of capitalizing on that potential. Athletic programs that are not excessively competitive could be utilized to promote physical and health education. Social services can enhance a pupil's opportunity to learn and can build family support for pupil learning. Entertainment programs properly conceived can foster curriculum development, community support, and parental involvement.

The extensive studies of relationships between learning and nutritional status, mental health, self-concept, family relationships, and economic well-being cannot forever be ignored by schools seeking to serve children and youth (Wagstaff and Gallagher 1990).

Hungry children do not learn well, even with an excellent teacher; food services and more direct social services are essential. Weary children, awake all night in a brawling household or local pool hall do not study well the next morning; family services must support the frustrated teacher. Sick children lacking both preventive and routine medical treatment miss school and come to class unable to concentrate; the new programs of school reform or teacher empowerment may make little difference to these students. The young person unable to buy snacks, books, and clothes and to pay lab fees is apt to feel like an outsider and leave school very early intellectually and as soon as possible physically.

Supporting social services may be the most significant challenge for personnel staffing in the 1990s (Reed and Sautter 1990).

Innovative Educational Programs

Instructional support services can be very immediate in their effects on the teaching-learning process, or they can be rather long-range. *New programs,* as a product, are quite distinct from learning. Services associated with new and innovative programs include program evaluation, curricula development, staffing, and in-service training.

The activities leading to these innovative or new programs are instructional in character but are developmental, as distinguished from operational. They result in products and services that, in turn, change instruction. These activities are largely carried on at the staff-services level, with little direct involvement of students. When they do involve students, such participation tends to be incidental to the product, in the sense that the activities are not designed to *serve* the student. The student is a resource used in the development process. On the other hand, innovative programs cannot be developed in a vacuum, so regular staff members are usually very much involved at one stage or another in instructional developmental activities. Unfortunately, this involvement tends to be disruptive of both normal, routine teaching and direct support activities.

Proposals for innovations are frequently presented to practitioners and officials at all levels. Commissions, associations, scholars, politicians, the U.S. Congress, state legislatures, and governors now regularly initiate proposals for change in school operations. Occasionally, even practitioners have their opportunities. Fortunately, most proposals die as quickly as they are formulated. Some are purely political window dressing, not intended for serious development. Others are impractical or even counterproductive and are soon recognized as such. Others are resisted by special interests within and outside the field, regardless of educational merit (Bacharach, 1990).

Personnel administration is always affected by serious efforts to implement innovative programs. Innovations require changes in recruitment, altered job descriptions, and sometimes new assignments and reassignments. Responding too quickly to innovative proposals may be wasteful and produce staff balance problems; responding too slowly to changing needs may jeopardize effective implementation.

Our schools are caught on the horns of a dilemma with respect to innovations. Justly we can criticize existing practices, as do some who argue that "The Horse Is Dead" (Hart 1989). These critics call for major restructuring of our schools—the way we organize, teach, staff, and involve students, teachers, and parents (Schlechty 1990). Others lament the monotonous "recurring waves" of school reform and innovations (Cuban 1990) emerging and receding in 15-year cycles (Schlesinger 1986). Still others are concerned that so many "innovations" are, in fact, very old ideas that have not prospered in the past and have little real promise for the future (Doyle 1989; Gibboney, 1991).

The multiple dilemmas of innovations or changes that are too much and too little, too slow and too rapid, too numerous and too limited, too radical and too outmoded, too sound and yet impractical, are probably with us to stay (Peters 1987). The task of managing such a bewildering array of forces and cross-currents, while providing imaginative leadership and a sense of direction, yet maintaining a steady process of change and innovation, is the challenge of school administration for many years to come.

Resource Allocation by Product and Service

Resources are always scarce. Even in recent decades, as expenditures for education have increased dramatically, the needs for expanded instructional, support, and noninstructional services have grown even more. Innovations, reforms, and restructuring efforts add still more demands for resources of all kinds.

Resource allocation is largely a personnel matter in schools. A set of generalizations can be posited about the allocation of resources.

1. Resources tend to be concentrated on direct services.
2. Resources tend to be allocated very meagerly to indirect or support services.
3. Resources tend to be allocated more heavily on student services than on staff services.
4. Resources for indirect, developmental services tend to be least valued by practitioners concerned with direct services.
5. Budget cuts or reallocations of resources tend to fall most heavily on indirect, developmental services.
6. Hence, indirect, developmental services are constantly threatened and need protection.

These generalizations are tendencies, not absolutes, and they are subject to empirical investigation. To the extent that they hold true, these tendencies have significant implications for staffing practices and especially for instructional staffing. In humane institutions most resources are devoted to staff. In schools most resources are devoted to instructional staff, but noninstructional programs compete constantly for always scarce resources. On the other hand, the unique instructional development activities, which are essential to the improvement of the instruction process, also compete for scarce resources. In the interplay of these competing forces, innovative programs suffer from several detractions:

1. These services tend to be intangible in their effect.
2. These services are intermediate- and long-range in nature and do not easily prove their worth in the short run.
3. These services are usually not perceived as directly pertinent to students' lives and immediate needs.
4. These services disrupt (temporarily) the operation of the regular instructional program and are therefore often perceived as a nuisance.

Those who desire to improve instruction through staffing programs must be fully cognizant of these detractions and take vigorous and persistent steps to compensate for them. A law of organizational life seems to operate to the advantage of direct service programs, both instructional and noninstructional, to the disadvantage of instructional development services. It is analogous to Gresham's law in economic life: cheap money drives out "good" money. In organizations, it appears that routine drives out creativity; immediate needs and demands get maximum response while long-range requirements languish in neglect. As with all such laws or principles of life, this one describes tendencies rather than inevitabilities. There is a persistent, ever-present tendency for routine demands to monopolize staffing practices. This reality must be recognized and dealt with as a serious threat to efforts for the improvement of instruction, even when disguised in catchy terms like "accountability," "results-oriented management," and "back to basics."

Basic Tasks of Instructional Staffing

Four essential tasks of instructional staffing have been mentioned, and these tasks should be clearly designated and defined. They are recruitment, selection, assignment, and evaluation. Taken together, they constitute the core of a personnel administration program. Staff development activities associated with personnel administration include in-service education and personnel resources planning. Each of these tasks receives some attention throughout this volume.

Recruitment

This task concerns the availability of personnel resources from which to make selections and assignments. Recruitment involves identification of various manpower pools from which to select. More than that, recruitment involves cultivating new and more abundant or higher-quality resource pools. The building of communication channels with individuals and groups who offer talent is an important part of the recruitment process. Maintaining a competitive position in the job market so as to attract both the number and the quality of applicants needed is part of the recruitment task.

Recruitment is often treated in a rather casual or routine manner, except for a limited number of highly specialized fields. For instance, physics teachers are often in very scarce supply and recruiting may be intense because of the perception that only a graduate physicist will do. However, in other assignments, such as biology, English, or fourth grade teaching, a "make-do" attitude may prevail.

A long and unfortunate tradition in the United States is to respond to serious shortages of qualified school personnel by lowering standards, issuing emergency credentials, resorting to on-the-job training, and looking the other way when the quality of performance begins to suffer. In fact, one of the little-recognized causes of serious educational problems throughout the 1960s and 1970s was the failure of public officials at all levels of government to recognize the simple facts about the post-World War II "baby boom." Unprecedented numbers of births demand unprecedented efforts to train, recruit, and select new teachers. In the absence of a concerted national program, teacher shortages remained serious and widespread for thirty years, and the quality of teaching inevitably suffered.

The emphasis of this book on improving instruction dictates that recruitment be considered from a dynamic perspective regardless of the conditions in the job market. The growing complexity of staffing patterns, the pressures for equalization of educational opportunities within and among school systems, the increasing rates of retirement, and growing pressure for quality education make competition for personnel more severe in the 1990s and beyond. Certainly, recruitment cannot be viewed as unimportant even in a relatively static manpower market, given the urgent need to upgrade the quality of instructional personnel serving children and youth (Task Force on Teaching as a Profession 1986).

Will the disastrous neglect of the past continue? Teacher recruitment and training for the new "baby boom" generation is once again at issue. Approximately four million babies were born in the United States each year throughout the 1980s. A full-scale teacher shortage is on our doorsteps, with more than 200,000 new teachers required each year from 1990 to 2000 (Ogle 1990, 92). This time the problem is even more alarming than in the past, for several reasons:

1. *Class size norms* nationwide have declined steadily since the 1950s to commonly accepted levels of twenty to twenty-five or less.
2. *Early childhood education* programs for two- to five-year-old children are becoming clearly recognized as essential to a top-quality educational system, and these programs create entirely new demands for teachers.
3. *The young adult college graduating classes* have been declining in size for over ten years. Hence, competition for these graduates has intensified.
4. *The technological/computerization revolution* sweeping the United States is intensifying the competition for college graduates with the technical abilities needed for science, mathematics, business, and various other non-teaching positions.
5. *Teacher training programs* were cut back in size during the 1980s and are neither adequately funded nor adequately staffed for increasing enrollments.

6. Retirement rates are skyrocketing as the young teachers of the 1950s, '60s, and '70s complete twenty- to forty-year careers.

Selection

Securing the best qualified personnel for service in each assignment in each school or office involves predicting the performance capabilities of people and comparing them with job requirements. Both of these are perplexingly difficult responsibilities. Job requirements must be carefully specified, and this task is complicated by changing conditions. But the ability to *predict* the performance of an individual who is little-known to the predictors and who will be assigned to a new situation seems to defy rationality (Snow 1989). Even so, that is the task of selection.

Fortunately, sufficient research has been done to guide practitioners away from common malpractices. New approaches and developments hold the promise of much more rationality in the future and thus better predictions and better matching of person to position (Webb et al. 1987).

Assignment

Providing the best person for the right assignment of responsibilities at the right place and at the right time means not only assigning new personnel but also reassigning and balancing personnel as problems emerge, conditions change, needs are redefined, and individuals change. The assignment task requires attention to changes in situations, problems, and people themselves to assure that staff members serving instruction have opportunities to maximize their contributions wherever possible.

A new staff member with outstanding capabilities or potential may not be best utilized in the position or positions currently open. Openings may need to be created by reassignment to assure fully efficient utilization of a new person on the staff. Similarly, changes in community characteristics, curriculum, or faculty composition may make reassignment essential to reconstitute a staff of a school or office for optimum effectiveness. Changes in people also influence assignments. People grow older and more proficient and need opportunities for reassignment. Health problems—physical and emotional—create conditions calling for reassignment. Even the emergence of cliques, intergroup conflicts, and political alliances may call for reassignments.

One of the neglected aspects of personnel practice has been the assignment task. The facts about stagnation within faculty groups are well known. Extremes of inequality between faculty groups, even in the same school district, have been readily apparent. The dangers to morale and productivity of a system that offers no variety or diversity in assignments are well recognized. Even so, little use of a host of alternative assignment practices has been made in our schools. The nearly universal practice is to make seemingly appropriate assignments with no consideration of changes short of an emergency. Personnel administration for the future cannot enjoy the simplicity of this tradition, because people cry out for new opportunities and instructional programs need to make optimum use of all available talents.

Evaluation

This task involves determining the extent to which instructionally relevant performances of staff personnel meet performance expectations and needs. Evaluation of personnel is part of a larger task domain concerned with evaluation of the instructional program. However, personnel administration must be primarily concerned with the performance of individual staff members. Evaluation of instructional personnel involves measuring and describing performances in operation that are clearly related to the instructional program in some way. This, too, is an enormously complex task because it includes not only the difficulty of measuring human behaviors but also the difficulty of verifying the relationships between those behaviors and the learning process.

Basic to the evaluation task is securing objective, reliable, and relevant information about staff performance. In addition, there are problems of decision making regarding the uses of such information. Decisions need to be guided by evaluative information so that alternative and concomitant courses of action are wisely selected. Dismissals must not occur without due process and high-quality remedial efforts; hence, diagnostic evaluations are essential. Reassignments must serve as constructive improvement efforts rather than as a way to remedy a bad situation. In-service training programs need to be better targeted on essential needs; hence, evaluation efforts must achieve scope as well as depth. Promotions ought to be based on objective assessment of past performance as well as projection into the future; therefore, evaluations need to be cumulative and multidimensional.

It would indeed be reassuring to find evidence that a typical twenty-item rating scale completed in March on all teachers is an effective evaluation of personnel. The truth is that such scales are largely a useless exercise in meaningless data gathering (Medley et al. 1984).

Personnel is where the money goes. It is the agent of instruction, the agent of change. It is in the more rigorous pursuit of the personnel evaluation task that more effective decisions concerning improvement of instruction are to be found.

Other Tasks

Tasks of other kinds, if less basic, are nonetheless important in school personnel administration. The induction of new employees, the reassignment and balancing of staff groups, the management of personnel services, and the provision of staff development opportunities are a few of the tasks addressed in later chapters.

The induction of new employees, especially those in first-time positions as teachers or administrators, has largely been neglected. Because professional lives are very complex, situational factors vary widely; because educational expectations are rapidly changing, the induction into a specific position, site, and role demands assistance. The costs of poor induction are frustration and inefficiency, at least; at worst, poor induction can lead to dismissals, resignations, and serious staff conflicts.

The management of an array of personnel services involves tasks that extend well beyond those outlined here. Various writers emphasize salary management (Castetter 1986), personnel record keeping (National School Boards Association 1982), and coordination of negotiations and union contract management (Ramsey 1984), as a few examples of personnel management tasks that require constant attention in schools.

Staff development program planning is still another task of growing import that may well be neglected. Whether this aspect of the instructional improvement process properly belongs to supervision, general administration, or personnel administration is a continuing issue, but probably it must be a shared responsibility. The special contributions to be made in assuring appropriate opportunities for continuing professional growth and development by personnel practices are numerous. Staff development programs should be related to assignment, reassignment, promotion, and job enrichment, as well as to morale and personnel evaluation.

Dynamic Staffing for Change

The distinction between staffing for change and staffing to maintain the status quo has special significance. Obviously, schools must operate in a reasonably normal manner. When a teacher resigns, a replacement must at least be considered. When a serious discipline problem erupts in a classroom, some response is called for: it might be dismissal, reassignment, or emergency remediation in the form of teacher retraining or reorganization of the class. A new law mandating a new course or a new program obviously may call for additional staff or reassignment. The program of staff personnel administration must deal with these realities of daily life in the operation of schools. The distinction to be drawn, however, is between these routine, urgent, and normal concerns of instructional staffing and a set of dynamic, programmatic, change-oriented concerns.

Concerns for the operational must be distinguished from concerns for the developmental in providing instructional staffing services. The former is tractive (Harris 1985), in the sense that the practices are directed toward the maintenance of the status quo, toward routine, toward coping, toward reducing dissonance in the system, and toward making existing practices more efficient. The developmental concerns of a program of instructional staffing are dynamic in nature. The practices that result from this orientation to staffing are directed toward change, innovation, creative problem-solving, increasing dissonance—if needed—and the replacement of existing conditions with some that may be more effective as well as more efficient.

Both aspects of staffing practice must be present in a program of personnel administration. However, preoccupation with the tractive is seductive. Tractive as compared to dynamic practices are more simplistic, encounter less resistance, cost less, demand less creativity, can be delegated more easily, and are less demanding of both time and emotional energy. In the short run, a personnel administration program dominated by a tractive orientation and preoccupied with the operational will seem quite effective. In the long run, however, a program that neglects the developmental needs of instructional staffing will be beset with problems. Problems grow, situations change, and people's needs are unfulfilled. Haskew's report to the president of the United States from the National Advisory Council on Education Professions Development (1969, 2) makes explicit these same concerns on a national level: "There is also an absence of any bold planning to meet the problems of tomorrow. . . . We find the . . . plans no match for the needs. In fact, the so-called plans are timid and token. . . . These decisions and actions add up to default on the proclaimed responsibility of the Federal Government . . . in supporting the nation's educational enterprise." Such timidity is often reinforced at local levels, even more than two decades later.

Humane Personnel Practices

Of the factors determining the quality of the services delivered to students in educational institutions, one of the most important is the employee's relationship to the institution. The efforts of people determine whether a social institution achieves its goals. In fact, organizations of all types— whether industrial, governmental, philanthropic, or other—depend for their success ultimately on the skills and abilities of the people who comprise them. No technology yet developed can substitute for the uniquely human qualities that all of us bring to the workplace. As a consequence, ideally the individual employee should perceive the institution as a positive element in his or her life.

The humane character of a school organization cannot be established by the personnel department alone, but it can be promoted if the personnel operation gives humaneness top priority. The very nature of personnel administration services offers both opportunities and problems in promoting the humaneness of an organization. From the initial contact with a candidate, through the routines of day-to-day operations, to termination of employment, the personnel administration staff is building an image. If these services are provided in a manner that is supportive of the employee, efficient in operation, and cognizant of the intrinsic worth of the employee, an image of humaneness will emerge. Such an image, however, must be developed by a consistent set of relationships among staff throughout the system. Needless to say, creating a humane institution is not an end in itself. The purpose for seeking to maintain, emulate, and enhance humaneness among staff personnel is to ensure that students will benefit from better learning within such a school environment.

Summary

The proper staffing of schools is a crucial leadership task. Instructional staffing is, of course, most important because the essential business of a school is to provide instructional programs that facilitate learning for children and youth. The changing character of the educational scene demands a responsive program of personnel administration in which the emphasis shifts from filling positions to providing staff members who are increasingly competent and doing so in ways that stimulate the instructional improvement process. A dual emphasis on staffing for change and staffing for quality instruction is advocated to capitalize fully on the unique character of the school as an institution that is essentially humane.

The basic tasks of staffing for instruction can be designated as recruitment, selection, assignment, and evaluation of instructional personnel. In the direction of these tasks, the character of staff personnel administration as a leadership program can be given a professional form that avoids some of the overly simple and nearly clerical forms it has assumed in some school settings.

The definitions of these four tasks of staffing for instruction are deceptive unless each one is seen as a rather complex array of activities that need to be carefully planned and organized with a balanced emphasis upon both tractive and dynamic orientations to instruction. This book is primarily concerned with improvement practices of the more dynamic kind.

Suggested Study Sources

Bacharach, Samuel B., ed. 1990. *Education Reform: Making Sense of It All*. Boston: Allyn and Bacon.

> *This is a thorough analysis of the "reform" movement of the early 1980s. Outstanding chapters by distinguished individuals such as Passow, Boyer, Cuban, Shanker, and Wise provide perspectives and critical analyses that were previously unavailable. Of special interest are the first three chapters overviewing the "movement." Chapters 10–19 provide many perspectives on defining and redefining "good education" in a politically charged atmosphere.*

Castetter, William B. 1986. *The Personnel Function in Educational Administration* (4th ed.). New York: Macmillan.

The classic treatment of school personnel administration (1st ed., 1962), this book provides an interesting perspective on the evolving field of practice as well as offering a comprehensive treatment. Considerable attention is given to collective bargaining, performance appraisal, and employee compensation.

Gage, N. L. 1985. *Hard Gains in the Soft Sciences: The Case for Pedagogy.* Bloomington, IN: Center on Evaluation Development and Research, Phi Delta Kappa.

This a brief but rigorous case for pedagogy. The author, a distinguished elder researcher-statesman, systematically reviews the progress made in recent decades in developing a solid scientific basis for professionally responsible teaching practice. He devotes a full chapter to "improving the gains" by addressing researchers as well as practitioners.

Gage, N. L., and D. C. Berliner. 1989. "Nurturing the Critical, Practical and Artistic Thinking of Teachers." *Phi Delta Kappan* 71 (November):212.

Two distinguished scholars, researchers, and statesmen review briefly their arguments for taking the research on teaching methods seriously without abdicating responsibility for making professional judgments. They emphasize similarities among professions involving "thoughtful practitioner(s)" . . . who can intelligently evaluate research . . . reconcile [it] with practical knowledge, and use artistry in taking the context into consideration" (p. 212).

Harris, Ben M. 1985. *Supervisory Behavior in Education* (3rd ed.). Englewood Cliffs, NJ: Prentice-Hall.

As a comprehensive treatment of instructional supervisory practice, much of this volume has implications for personnel practice that is directed to improving instruction. The first three chapters present theoretical perspectives on functions of the school operations, process of change, and tasks of improving education. The definition of "staffing for instruction" is especially pertinent.

Hart, Leslie A. 1989. "The Horse Is Dead." *Phi Delta Kappan* 71:3 (November):237–42.

The author argues that our basic concept of "school" and the way we organize schools are outmoded, indefensible, and doomed to ineffectiveness. The problem, he says, is that while expert practitioners and scholars alike have known the "horse is dead," all "blue ribbon" commissions and others continue to suggest "reforms" or "restructuring" that retain the old structures. He proceeds to discuss mission, organization, and "reconceiving learning."

Lewis, Anne C. 1989. *Restructuring America's Schools.* Arlington, VA: American Association of School Administrators.

A thoughtful analytical treatment of the concepts, proposals, and implications for change embodied in the late 1980s fever over "restructuring." Distinctions are made between "reforms" of various types. Chapter 1 gives an historical perspective on reforms and restructuring proposals.

National School Boards Association. 1982. *The School Personnel Management System.* Alexandria, VA: The National School Boards Association.

A fairly comprehensive manual of ideas for personnel management from the point of view of the local school board. Ten chapters offer practical ideas about policy, job analysis, personnel record keeping, personnel appraisal, etc. A special feature, comprising nearly half of the volume, is an alphabetical listing of position titles, cross-referenced to five levels of job function.

Reed, Sally, and R. Craig Sautter. 1990. "Children of Poverty: The Status of 12 Million Young Americans," *Phi Delta Kappan* 71(June):K–12.

Published as a special report, this article documents in rigorous fashion the growing problem of poverty as it relates to schools and society. This report is full of factual detail and has great value in providing an historical perspective on 25 years of child neglect since the exemplary work of the 1960s. The authors go beyond raising the issues and documenting the problems to suggest educational responses.

Wagstaff, Lonnie H., and K. S. Gallagher. 1990. "Schools, Families and Communities, Idealized Images and New Realities." Chapter 5 in Mitchell, Brad, and LuVern L. Cunningham, eds., *Educational Leadership and Changing Contexts of Families, Communities, and Schools*, Part II. National Society for the Study of Education. 89th Yearbook. Chicago, IL: University of Chicago Press.

Review of statistics on family. "The most obvious generalizations from these indicators is that pluralistic America possesses no dominant form of family . . . poverty has increasingly become black, female and youthful . . . " (p. 104). The authors argue that traditional responses to changing family will not work: "school personnel work closely (in effective schools) with families and community agencies to identify and ameliorate family problems . . . " (p. 113).

Wayson, William W., et al. 1988. *Up from Excellence: The Impact of the Excellence Movement on Schools*. Bloomington, IN: Phi Delta Kappa Educational Foundation.

This book grew out of a commission for the authors to analyze and interpret the flood of reports of the early 1980s criticizing and proposing reforms for U.S. public schools. The authors are highly critical of nearly all of the critics—not for criticizing, but for confusing excellence with test scores, failing to recognize strengths, and generally for politically slanting recommendations. Chapter 10 makes useful proposals.

Webb, L. Dean, et al. 1987. *Personnel Administration in Education: New Issues and New Needs in Human Resource Management*. Columbus, OH: Merrill.

Six "issues" are identified in the early pages; while they are not really new, the author provides a valuable review. The issue relating to compensation of educational personnel provides a useful perspective by comparing 1974 and 1984 data on salaries. Chapter 5 provides a useful review of Bolton's position analysis outline.

Wittrock, M. C., ed. 1986. *Handbook of Research on Teaching*. (3rd ed.). New York: Macmillan.

An update of research on teaching that includes chapters on various aspects of teaching by distinguished scholars, such as Brophy and Good, on teaching behavior; Clark and Peterson, on teacher thinking; Doyle, on class management; and Rosenshine and Stevens, on teaching functions.

_2

Functions of Staff Personnel

"Form follows function," according to an old adage. This saying has meaning for the professional architect who contemplates the intended uses of a proposed structure before putting the drawing pencil to work. The hack architect, on the other hand, may begin sketching a favorite design right away. Personnel administration, like general administration, is largely concerned with the whole of the educational enterprise. People are the substance from which human organizations such as schools are built; hence, administrative and supervisory endeavors tend to be dominated by concern for people. But just as the skilled architect considers function first and physical structures second, so staffing decisions must be similarly sequenced to consider first how people are to function, determining structural arrangements later. Greenfield (1976, 5) cautions against the tendency to think of organizations as real and distinct from the actions of people: "It is an ill-founded dualism which separates people and organizations."

Activities and Services

The essential and distinctive activities of people in the school operation are those of instruction. All other activities should be, from a logical point of view, supportive of the instructional process, regardless of how that process is characterized in any given school or program. In fact, of course, many activities closely associated with school operations are not supportive of instruction, or their supportive effects are so limited or indirect as to be difficult to defend logically. Nevertheless, remotely instruction-related activities, such as food service and athletic events, are well established and accepted for their own sake in most schools, regardless of their relationship to instructional program goals and objectives.

However, many commonly recognized activities of school operations are clearly supportive of instruction even though they are not instructional in nature. Student immunizations, vision testing, parent counseling, and pupil transportation are but a few examples. Immunizations reduce illnesses among individual children and prevent epidemics that could have devastating effects on pupil attendance, to say nothing about the effects on pupil health status. Vision testing identifies students whose vision may impair efforts to learn and, hence, often stimulates corrective actions by home, school, or other community agencies. Parent counseling, in some forms at least, offers parents instruction in stimulating pupils to learn.

Whether in the form of better attendance, better health, better study conditions, a better emotional climate, or a better sense of personal worth, a wide array of noninstructional support activities directly aims to make pupils more responsive to instruction and, therefore, more likely to learn. The relationship between a bus transportation system and support for instruction hardly needs elaboration.

Service Relationships

Exhibit 2.1 on page 26 is a representative listing of the kinds of activities that are associated with each of five categories of services. This exhibit also emphasizes the distinction between development services and services directed toward more immediate needs of students or staff.

Multiplicity of Activities

The enormous variety of staff activities that characterize the operation of the educational enterprise cannot be managed or staffed as isolated entities. It is not feasible, efficient, or economical to try to approach educational staffing one activity at a time. The operation is too complex and multifaceted, and too many activities are shared among staff members while others are necessarily aggregated into a single staff assignment. For example, a counselor cannot be assigned to a single teaching activity such as advising, because instructional support activities such as testing, grading, and course scheduling may need to be combined in this staff member's assignment to ensure efficient pupil allocation. On the other hand, it may not be feasible, efficient, or economical to assign all counseling activities exclusively to counselors, because funds may not be available for a sufficient number of positions, and other personnel (teachers, for instance) may have responsibility for much of the routine counseling needed. Furthermore,

EXHIBIT 2.1 Five Catgories of Functionally Related Services, by Clients Served

	Students A. Teaching	Staff B. Direct Instructional Support	Development C. Research and Development
Instructional Services			
	advising presenting turtoring diagnosing guiding arraying planning	delivering materials ordering supplies repairing equipment scheduling classes employing staff testing and scoring grading papers	in-service training program evaluation curriculum design materials development manpower planning project monitoring
Noninstructional Services	D. Special Pupil Support	E. Noninstructional Support	
	food serving home visiting physical examining disciplining hall monitoring bus loading playground directing	tax collecting budgeting purchasing bookkeeping cleaning	

the disruption of schedules incident to an intensive counseling effort might reduce instructional efficiency rather than enhance it.

Overspecialization

An approach to this dilemma of staffing for a myriad of distinctive activities, without excessive overspecialization and disruptively uncoordinated division of labor, is to focus on the *functions* to be performed, subsuming activities within functions. This approach involves clearly defining functions to be served by the school operations, differentially allocating resources to each function, and then staffing within each functional allocation to provide a staff with the competence necessary to maintain all required activities.

The dangers of specialization are gradually coming to be recognized in education as they have been in other disciplines, such as medicine. Economist John Kenneth Galbraith (1971) cautions, "But we must remind ourselves that specialization is a . . . convenience, not a . . . virtue. It allows . . . the use of a wider spectrum of talent" (p. 405). Hence, we have created grade levels, subject-centered departments, and specialized certificates. The numerous tasks, services, and activities to be provided by school personnel will not neatly fit into discrete positions. But broad functional categories may well be more suitable than traditional categories of positions such as "teacher," "administrator," and "supervisor," even though we must ultimately select and assign a person, give him or her a title, and ensure that the individual will neither be in a straitjacket of performance restrictions nor feel "underemployed."

Defining Five Service Functions

One of the advantages of staffing in terms of services within functional categories is the focus on instruction and teaching. On the other hand, the noninstructional functions are not ignored. Services to *both* students and staff are shown in Exhibit 2.1, where the highly neglected instructional development services are fully recognized. The five kinds of services included in the exhibit are elaborations on the five functions of the school operation described by Harris (1985): (1) teaching, (2) general administration, (3) supervision of instruction, (4) special pupil services, and (5) management (auxiliary services). These groupings very closely parallel services A–E in the exhibit. As originally defined, Harris's five functions utilized two essential dimensions: instruction-relatedness and pupil-relatedness. Custodial care and entertainment functions were recognized but not included, since these activities are not really related to instruction.

Redefining the five basic functions of a school operation as clusters of service activities provides a relatively simple, yet realistic, way of viewing staff needs in broad perspective. Each service within a functional area should be reasonably distinct from those provided within other functions. Services should be defined so that outcomes from each are also relatively distinctive. It follows that each service could be readily delegated. Exhibit 2.2 defines functional relationships as staff assignment decisions, but, more important, they make relationships operational and emphasize outcomes.

Interrelationships

Many things are more complicated than they seem. In this instance, interrelationships need to be viewed both within functions and *between* functions. Also, service delivery is rarely on a one-at-a-time basis, so a service to

EXHIBIT 2.2   Functional Relationships

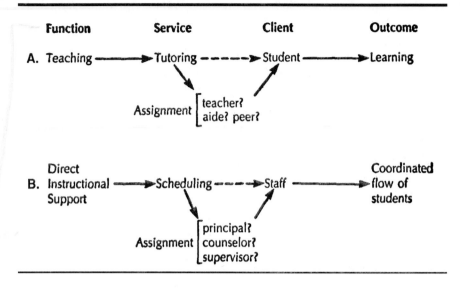

multiple clients, multiple services to single clients, and multiple services to multiple clients are all part of a complicated staffing picture.

The people in any set of relationships can be viewed as either those served (clients) or those serving (staff). Once again, it is not always possible to categorize people so neatly. For instance, a teacher may be the client in an in-service training context but the staff member in the classroom. This classification system becomes untenable when the in-service training moves into the classroom and the teacher is *both* client and staff member simultaneously. This is just one of the very difficult problems that clinical-supervision and coaching services face. Even so, each situation or problem requires that the relationships between staff and client be made fairly clear and distinct.

Staff-Client Relationships

There are many ways of characterizing staff-client relationships. From the view of persons assigned functional responsibilities in schools, the relationships are not usually hard to describe:

1. Teacher arranges to test students.
2. Nurse conducts vision screening for students.
3. Librarian organizes books in school library for easy use by students.
4. Principal schedules students for different classes, class periods, and classrooms.
5. Supervisor conducts training sessions for teachers who need to learn new skills.

These few examples indicate the beginning of a problem, however. Notice how many different staff persons are providing services to the same client. Notice that the services may or may not be functionally compatible, even though the ultimate outcome might be the same for all services. The principal's scheduling may conflict with the students' use of the library, which may also conflict with the nurse's vision-screening program, and all of these services may conflict with the supervisor's training sessions.

Of course, problems of coordination in complex organizations are widely recognized, but they have a bearing on staffing patterns and on the way personnel administration procedures can serve to improve school operations. If we could return to the days of the little red schoolhouse, many of those problems would disappear. The lone classroom teacher would schedule, do vision screening, and maintain his or her own room-library collection; the principal would be nonexistent; and the rural supervisor would wait for an "institute day" at the county courthouse to conduct a training session. But specialization and organizational complexities are with us. We will not be returning to the "glories" of the past, so personnel administrators must carefully analyze interrelationships among staff and clients and assist in the coordination process. More important, careful function-related staffing can prevent coordination problems.

Three sets of relationships are likely to emerge:

1. The same client is served by a number of staff persons who provide different services.
2. Different clients are served by a number of staff persons who provide different services.
3. Different clients are served by the same staff person who provides different services.

There are other possible combinations of those three factors, but three serve to highlight the problem. Exhibit 2.3 on page 30 illustrates these three cases and suggests staffing considerations implied in each one.

Competitive Relationships

The last set of relationships—competition among clients for the same scarce services provided by a staff person—is most difficult to handle. In the illustration offered in Exhibit 2.3, the competition is likely to take the form of conflict between the expectation that personal problems will be addressed and the pressure from the faculty for students to be served. The psychologist is caught in a squeeze unless priorities are clearly designated and conflicts can be resolved. It may be, however, that these two assignments are so competitive that different staff persons should receive them. Another approach would be to eliminate one of the service offerings entirely.

Competitive relationships confront staff personnel in numerous situations. The home economics teacher teaches cooking but is also expected to

EXHIBIT 2.3 Three Illustrations of Client-Staff-Services Relationships

1. *Same Client, Different Services (Coordinate Relationship)*
   Example: A student from across town is bussed to another middle school for an opportunity to participate in the instrumental music program, which is not available in the neighborhood of residence.
   Services to Be Coordinated: Are the same people involved in both sets of activities? If not, are they assigned to the same work group? If not, how are schedules coordinated?

2. *Different Clients, Different Services (Independent Relationship)*
   Example: Teacher organizes students into tutoring-study teams to assist each other in their assignments. Principal schedules the teacher for bus duty.
   Services Involved: Teaching through tutorial arrangements and special pupil support services in bus loading.
   Staffing Considerations: These are relatively independent. Time frames do not overlap. Both services are under the direction of the principal.

3. *Different Clients, Same Services (Competitive Relationship)*
   Example: School psychologist is assigned to students who are emotionally disturbed. Faculty counseling is also provided for staff members who have difficulty coping with minority students.
   Services Competing: Teaching through specialized counseling services and instructional development through faculty counseling.
   Staffing Considerations: How is a lone psychologist to respond to needs of two large, different client groups (students and staff)? How will priorities be assigned? Will resistance of faculty lead to student counseling dominating the job?

provide desserts for PTA meetings; this teacher faces a competitive demand for cooking services. The coach who is expected to teach physical education and win football games has students and sports addicts competing for his or her services. The supervisor who is expected to plan and direct an ongoing program of in-service education but also to be on call for every teaching crisis that arises faces competition.

Staff personnel practices can resolve some competitive relationships and ensure more independent and coordinate relationships if they call for careful consideration of each job assignment and position in terms of functional relationships between clients and services. Whenever possible, a limited number of clients should be assigned for a set of services to be provided. When services are diverse, client groups should be more limited in variety or number or both. On the other hand, those who must serve numerous clients (either in variety or number) should be allowed to give priority to a very limited array of services.

Whenever competitive relationships are unavoidable, the diverse clients and the staff member must have a clearly designated mediator. For instance, the supervisor responsible to the principal whenever crises occur in the classroom must have a director of instruction or assistant superintendent who can resolve conflicts. Otherwise, both the principal and the

EXHIBIT 2.4   Functions of School Operations

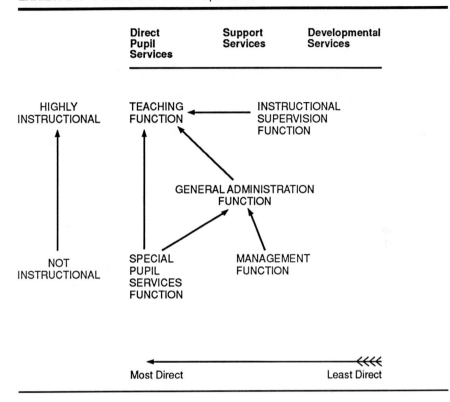

supervisor feel neglected. If the principal gets directions from one administrator and the supervisor receives them from another, conflicts will not be easily resolved.

Functions of School Operations

The functions that require staffing are both instructional and noninstructional, as indicated above and in Exhibit 2.4. The major functions are briefly reviewed here to define each more clearly and to give focus to the personnel positions involved.

The Teaching Function

Traditionally, the teaching function has been central to all others of the school as an educational institution, and it will undoubtedly remain so. Technology in instruction is changing teaching activities but not altering teaching's

EXHIBIT 2.5   Job-Related Definition of Teaching

Classroom Teacher: Any individual assigned to a specific grade, level, and/or curriculum area with one or more regularly assigned student groups

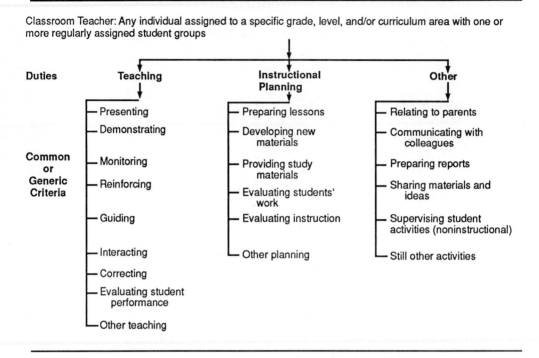

Source: Harris, Ben M. 1986. *Developmental Teacher Evaluation*. Boston: Allyn and Bacon, p. 59.

central position in the school operation. Teaching, as a function, consists of instruction-related activities that directly promote student learning and have a direct impact on the learner. By this definition, teaching activities are restricted in scope, but the variety of personnel involved in the teaching function extends beyond those persons commonly associated with teaching as illustrated in Exhibit 2.1.

Classroom teacher, librarian, diagnostician, and counselor are the more obvious positions included in the teaching function. Less obvious are those held by principals, psychologists, and aides who work directly with students. Teaching activities include presenting information, tutoring, advising, diagnosing, directing learning activities, questioning, and reinforcing behavior.

Harris (1986, 59) illustrates job-related aspects of teaching that emphasize the distinction between direct services, which focus on the student as client and as learner, and support services, for which the client may be staff, parent, or other that gives support to teaching activities.

Exhibit 2.5 represents the larger job of teaching as three distinctive service strands—teaching, planning, and other. Hence, instructional support activities include planning lessons, selecting materials, arranging the learning environment, securing resource personnel, scheduling events, evaluating pupils' work, scoring tests, conferring with parents, and many more. These activities are directly supportive of teaching activities but have no direct impact on the learner. They are all, however, instructional in nature, undertaken with the pupil as client in mind, and intended to promote learning.

The Special Pupil-Services Function

Highly pupil-related endeavors that are not very instructional in nature are important to the efficiency and effectiveness of educational institutions. Services in this functional area are numerous and diverse. A difficult staffing problem stems from this diversity because the services—as varied as pupil transportation, food services, health service, and recreation—produce demands for personnel from diverse sources with highly unrelated competencies. The assignment and training of these personnel to ensure support for instruction are among the most perplexing problems personnel administrators face. The one thing these problems share is the need to make the pupil-client more amenable to teaching and better able to learn.

An inventory of the activities of this function would be difficult to produce. Many are obvious from the position title. The key concern of personnel administration in regard to these staff members is the *support characteristics* of the services. Food services are not an end in themselves but a means of overcoming hunger, expediting feeding, and improving pupil nutrition. Each of these outcomes or services of the cafeteria staff of a school is presumed to improve the conditions under which learning occurs. Similarly, health services—immunizations, vision testing, physical examinations—are offered as support to the teaching function and are presumed to promote learning. Obviously, bus transportation service for a field trip is an instructional-support service, but, similarly, bus transportation is also presumed to lead to more regular attendance and greater punctuality for those students who might otherwise not be able to secure transportation. Thus transportation services are supportive of teaching and learning.

Because special pupil services often have social value independent of their value as support services, they tend to be expanded beyond the needs of the student at school. They also tend to be extended to pupils for whom they are not really needed. From a standpoint of social policy, such expansions and extensions of special pupil services might be desirable. From the standpoint of educational policy and the problem of allocating scarce resources, such extensions or expansions have serious implications for staffing. For instance, most transportation systems discourage or prohibit riders who live within easy walking distance. This is a financially based decision. Those might be the students with the most erratic attendance patterns, and, hence, the teaching function would be better served by transporting them than by carrying students of affluent parents more as a convenience than as a supporting service. On the other hand, extensive medical services, including provision of examinations, medicines, therapeutic treatment, glasses, hearing aids, and so on, might be readily justified for some pupils whose parents are both financially and educationally disadvantaged, to the extent that their children would not be physically fit to learn without such services. Various federal programs directed at assisting such pupils to become better learners have funded such services. However, these services are usually believed to be beyond the scope of those needed by most students for effective functioning in schools, and far more limited services are provided by these health maintenance personnel.

Special pupil services that are urgently needed by some pupils are often overlooked; that is, no staff is assigned to provide them. Mental health problems are widely recognized as among the most serious negative influences on pupil learning, yet psychological services are only gradually being accepted as a school responsibility, and staffing is generally inadequate or nonexistent. Financial needs of youth are often very urgent for clothes, recreation, and other personal items. Job placement and loan services are rarely offered below collegiate levels in systematic ways, and staff members assigned to provide such services are often ill-equipped for such responsibilities. Too often, an unprepared assistant principal, vocational teacher, or counselor assumes job placement responsibilities.

The problem for personnel administration in this area of special pupil services is perplexing. These services must be extended to meet urgent needs that have not been traditionally recognized. Service offerings must be tailored to the unique needs of individual pupils and their parents. However, different community agencies can and often should relieve the school of responsibility for some of these services. But most stubborn of all is the problem of extending services to those most in need rather than having them monopolized by other students with less urgent need but more influential parents. The solution to such a dilemma may often require extending such services to all.

The Instructional Supervision Function

The most comprehensive view of instructional supervision defines it as all of those highly instruction-related activities that are *not* highly pupil-related (Harris 1985). The most limited view is associated with teacher evaluation involving a supervisor or administrator visiting classrooms and providing evaluative feedback to teachers and others. The latter concept not only is too restrictive in scope of activities but also implies practices that are neither efficient nor effective. Modern clinical supervision concepts are somewhat less limiting and much more professionally justifiable. However, nearly all concepts of supervision in current thought and practice emphasize the improvement of an array of instructional services (Glatthorn 1990; Glickman 1985; Pajak 1989).

Accordingly, the supervision function involves services related to instructional development as well as direct instructional support. Services of supervision include developing curriculum and materials, evaluating programs, and providing for in-service training (Harris 1989).

Supervisory services are offered by staff personnel with various titles and competencies, as is true in all functional areas of school operation. Key types of positions directly responsible for these services include directors of instruction, principals, program coordinators, technical consultants, trainers, designers, and evaluators (Bailey 1985). The many position titles that have been utilized for supervision service delivery reflect the confusion regarding this function, the ambivalence over the value of these services, and the lack of clarity of assignments. Once again, some definitions of terms might be helpful. The term "supervisor" is not a position title in most instances; it is a generic term referring to several positions that are responsible for supervisory services. Hence, *director, coordinator, consultant, specialist,* and *general supervisor* are commonly used titles for supervisors. Increasingly, titles being used by school districts for supervisors are descriptive of the major kinds of service the position holder is to deliver. Accordingly, titles like *director of inservice training, media consultant,* or *specialist, coordinator of evaluation,* and *supervisor of staff development* are now in common use (Pajak 1989). A countertrend in supervisory position titles may be developing from the practice of utilizing supervisors in a team with task or project assignments that do not lend themselves to specialization. Titles under such staffing plans may be restricted to *consultant, supervisor* or *coordinator,* without specialties being designated even though they are possessed by individual position holders.

Many activities for the improvement of instruction have been specified in some detail by Harris (1985, 70–86) and by many other scholars and practitioners. Pajak's (1986) survey of supervisory skills reflects the most recent judgments of practitioners. Competency specifications for supervisors regardless of title are discussed in chapter 4, using the nine task areas originally designated by Harris (1963). Bailey's (1985) and Pajak's (1986) studies provide support for utilizing such descriptors in defining the supervision function.

Glickman (1985) and Glatthorn (1984) emphasize supervisory services as approaches to teacher development. As such, they tend to support practicing supervisors in schools that report extensive use of demonstrations, intervisitations, film and videos, discussion groups, and directed practice activities, as well as curriculum development and formative evaluation.

The Management Function

The services associated with the management function are designated as noninstructional support in Exhibit 2.1. These are sometimes referred to as auxiliary services. Like special pupil services, they tend to be noninstructional and of numerous kinds. Tax collecting, purchasing, accounting, printing, warehousing, equipment maintenance, and cleaning are but a few of the services for which a school must either contract with private firms or provide specialized personnel. Because this book is essentially concerned with instructional staffing, little further attention will be given to personnel office responsibilities in this functional area. Obviously, it deserves much fuller consideration.

A preliminary set of tasks associated with this function has been developed and validated in a study by Pringle (1989).

The Administration Function

The services associated with administrative personamnel tend to be coordinative—communicating, controlling, scheduling, monitoring, resource allocating. Competencies of principals are supervisory in nature and consequently do not provide a full picture of the noninstructional and instructional services provided. The central position of administrators in coordinating the various services of schools makes staffing decisions regarding such personnel extremely important. Just as supervisors are especially important for the developmental services for which they are uniquely responsible, so administrators are uniquely responsible for the smoothly coordinated operations of programs. Principals, program directors, superintendents, and other administrators must be competent as organizers, communicators, and resource allocators. They must be able to monitor, schedule, and evaluate a host of interrelated services to minimize conflicts and facilitate goal accomplishment.

Resource Allocations by Function

The school is a humane institution described as relying very heavily on people in all aspects of its operations. Unlike labor-intensive industrial organizations, schools and other humane institutions are people-centered in terms of goals, processes, products, and clients. This distinguishes the school from the steel factory or the petroleum refinery in no uncertain way. On the other hand, the "people" characteristics of schools in many ways make their operation like that of hospitals, prisons, and insurance companies. Staff personnel administration is especially important to the success of such enterprises for two reasons:

1. Effectiveness is inevitably dependent on the people on the staff, not on the clients, technology, or raw material employed.
2. Production costs are primarily associated with people's salaries rather than with capital investment or the cost of raw material.

EXHIBIT 2.6 Functional Comparison of a Regular Classroom with a Team Operation

Activities	A Regular Classroom (% of Time)	B Team Classroom (% of Time)				
		T_1	T_2	A_1	A_2	Total
Teaching						
Planning	5	15	10	—	5	30
Presenting	25	20	5	5	5	35
Diagnosing	5	5	20	—	—	25
Guiding	5	10	20	10	10	50
Directing	15	5	5	20	15	45
Interacting	5	15	20	5	5	45
Arranging	1	—	—	15	5	20
Reinforcing	4	20	10	10	10	50
Monitoring	10	5	5	5	15	30
Clerical	20	—	—	15	20	35
Special Pupil Servce	5	5	5	15	10	35
TOTAL	100	100	100	100	100	400

Note: Dashes indicate no time allocated to the corresponding activity.

These two points of distinction are so obvious that it seems needless to stress them. However, these are the facts that give urgency to the need for the highest quality of staffing practices in recruitment, selection, as - signment, reassignment, and evaluation. These facts also argue for relating costs to personnel rather than to pupils, as educators usually do. Per-pupil cost figures tend to focus on neither product nor process. The pupil is treated as an input into the system—a client. Per-pupil costs, therefore, tell us almost nothing about the character of the school operation except in a very gross way. High per-pupil costs mean that staff costs are high. Beyond this, we gain little from monitoring such figures. By way of contrast, human-resource accounting procedures (Paperman and Martin 1980) may hold greater promise for schools than for business organizations.

Studies of the way staff members utilize their time are much more informative because these studies relate costs to function. A team arrangement, for example, involves some assumptions about the ability of a team to serve as well as an equivalent staff of separate teachers; more economical use of text, time, and other resources in the team situation is also assumed. Functionally and positionally, teams are different and require a different approach to recruitment, selection, and assignment than is traditionally employed (Stolze 1989).

A further analysis of a team-teaching situation to determine how the different staff members function in terms of various teaching, clerical, and special-service activities can be most revealing.

The time allocations associated with the teaching services in Exhibit 2.6 furnish another way of assessing a school operation. For instance, in

Situation A, presenting activities cost the same as for Teacher 1 and Teacher 2 in Situation B, although there would be an additional cost for each teacher's aide in the latter situation.

Such detailed function/cost analyses are undertaken only under special circumstances. However, the illustration does indicate the kind of thinking that personnel administrators can and should contribute to program planning, evaluation, and policymaking endeavors in school systems that are trying to improve instruction by means of cost-effective programs. The utility of functional compared to positional analysis also is illustrated by the team teaching-regular classroom comparison. Obviously, such comparisons would be very difficult to make using positional categories, because unlike positions are involved. The functions and activities provide the common elements for analysis (Coleman 1979, 86–8).

Exhibit 2.7 illustrates still another use for function-analysis techniques. In this instance, the total administrative staff of a particular school was analyzed to determine how well the four nonteaching functions were being provided. Similar analyses for each of the other staff groups assigned

EXHIBIT 2.7   Illustrations of a Time[a]-Function Analysis for an Administrative Staff Group

| Function | Positions | | | |
	Principal	Assistant Principal	Coordinator	Total
Teaching	0	0	30	30
Supervision				
Curriculum	100	0	35	135
Materials	20	0	0	20
In-service	570	60	415	1,045
Evaluation	200	15	55	270
Special Pupil Services				
Health	50	0	0	50
Welfare	75	10	105	190
Psychological	0	0	0	0
Discipline	30	10	0	40
Management				
Reports	85	135	430	650
Finances	95	5	15	115
Maintenance	0	140	410	550
Transportation	10	10	30	50
General Administration	275	990	0	1,265
Miscellaneous	65	10	55	130
TOTAL (ALL FUNCTIONS)	1,575	1,385	1,580	4,540

[a]Hours reported in logs.

to the same school provided the basis for identifying overlapping and neglected services. Analyses of this kind are based on logs maintained by individual staff members, by estimates, or both. Once again, the use of functional categories that are relatively independent of the specific position in which the staff member serves permits focusing on the services provided. Obviously, this is also a useful technique for reality testing of job descriptions.

Summary

The function of staff personnel activity is viewed in this chapter as persistently instructional in orientation. Staffing should reflect function rather than form wherever possible. Exhibit 2.4 attempts to show functional relationships in terms of instructional emphases, on the one hand, and the directness of services, on the other. Services to be provided—instructional or noninstructional—and clients to be served—students or staff—provide a framework for functional analysis of personnel in action. Special attention to staffing for development is often required, because clients are only indirectly served. As staffing patterns reflect functional responsibilities and interrelationships among staff groups, problems of overspecialization and resource allocation persist, but more useful ways of analyzing staff performances emerge. The rigidities of traditional positional assignments can be avoided, in part, as services within broad functional areas become the focus for cost analyses and related staffing decisions.

Suggested Study Sources

Aft, Lawrence S. 1985. *Wage and Salary Administration: A Guide to Job Evaluation.* Reston, VA: Reston Publishing.

> *Chapters 2–4 focus on job analysis, job descriptions, and job evaluation. The author describes simple, practical procedures for analyzing jobs in functional ways. The case material presented is in a college setting, but the variety of positions analyzed is useful for application to school settings.*

Castetter, William B. 1986. *Personnel Function in Educational Administration* (4th ed.). New York: Macmillan.

> *This is one of the most comprehensive treatments of human resource management. The author is an authority on personnel administration in education, and his defining of the nature and scope of the field provides an invaluable frame of reference based on long-term perspectives and up-to-date insights.*

Coleman, Charles J. 1979. *Personnel: An Open System Approach.* Cambridge, MA: Winthrop Publishers.

> *Chapter 4 provides a useful treatment of the author's views on defining positions. This is largely a business and government point of view that may have implications for better school practices.*

Gael, Sidney, ed. 1988. *The Job Analysis Handbook for Business, Industry and Government.* Vol. II. New York: John Wiley & Sons.

This comprehensive volume provides chapters on nearly every aspect of job analysis. This book is a valuable resource for any effort at writing job descriptions or restructuring roles and relationships in the school setting.

Grootings, Peter, et al., eds. 1989. *New Forms of Work Organization in Europe.* New Brunswick, NJ: Transaction.

This work contains reports from many countries depicting the movement toward reform and restructuring of work in industrialized Europe during the post-World War II era. The dramatic rebuilding of many nations is depicted in case reports, including reports from both western- and eastern-European countries on efforts to humanize and democratize work in industrial settings. The overview chapter by Gustavsen and Hethy is basic reading.

Harris, Ben M. 1986. *Developmental Teacher Evaluation.* Boston: Allyn and Bacon.

Chapters 1 and 2 provide detailed discussions of current practices and basic concepts of personnel evaluation as related to teachers. Later chapters focus on linkages between personnel evaluation and merit pay, incentives, and other personnel functions.

Harris, Ben M. 1985. *Supervisory Behavior in Education* (3rd ed.). Englewood Cliffs, NJ: Prentice-Hall.

This book defines supervision of instruction in rather broad terms, embracing staffing for instruction and personnel evaluation as major tasks of instructional leadership. Several early chapters focus on the nature of supervision as leadership, change process, the tasks of instructional improvement, and staffing patterns.

Howarth, Christine 1984. *The Way People Work: Job Satisfaction and the Challenge of Change.* Oxford: Oxford University Press.

This is a brief but pointed review of work organization problems and prospects for improvements in industrial organizations. It includes discussion on why employees lack motivation, resist change, and become nonproductive and presents illustrative case reports. Chapter 7 identifies practical ways of improving work organizations. The emphasis is on changing the environment, the job, and its technology as well as on salary and incentives.

Pajak, Edward. 1989. *The Central Office Supervisor of Curriculum and Instruction: Setting the Stage for Success.* Boston: Allyn and Bacon.

One of the recent efforts to analyze central staff functions with respect to improving instruction, this volume is based on a survey of current practices. This book is especially valuable for its focus on a much-ignored staff group.

Smith, Stuart C., and J. J. Scott. 1990. *The Collaborative School: A Work Environment for Effective Instruction.* Eugene, OR: Eric Clearinghouse of Educational Management.

This is a brief review of concepts and practices supporting collaboration in school operations. Written in collaboration with the National Association of Secondary School Principals, the book emphasizes teacher-principal collaboration. Chapter 2 cites evidence that collaboration among teachers promotes student learning. Other chapters include a survey of collaborative practices and suggestions for introducing them. Although little attention is given to district- or community-wide collaboration, many of the ideas have broader application.

___3___

Innovations and Traditions in Staffing

The manner in which schools and colleges are staffed is greatly influenced by past practices and the assumptions and traditions associated with such practices. Obviously, when assumptions of the past are still valid, some of the same practices are justifiable. Traditions that have withstood the test of time and continue to serve the updated goals of education should be continued. But educational change comes about slowly even in a rapidly changing society, and staffing patterns seem more stable and unchanging in some ways than instructional materials, course offerings, special services, and school buildings. The changes that are being or have been reflected in staffing patterns of schools in the United States have been characterized for the most part as *additions* to traditional staff groups or as *special program* staffs (Ogle 1990, 88). To be sure, there are isolated examples of departures from tradition that can be shown to include changes in staffing patterns, such as some magnet schools (Boyd and Walberg 1990), drop-out prevention programs (Slavin et al. 1989), special education alternatives (Biklen et al. 1989, 256), and "distance learning" projects (Office of Technology Assessment 1990). However, the enormous array of modifications in instructional programs undertaken in schools in the United States often seem neither to result in nor to be assisted by basic changes in the school staff. In part, this failure is another example of the chicken-and-the-egg phenomenon. Programs cannot be implemented in innovative ways without staffing patterns that reflect the needs of such programs; however, the needs are not clearly known until after the staff is employed and patterns established, so the new programs tend not to flourish; they are abandoned or corrupted (Harris 1985), and thus new staffing patterns become unnecessary (Herriott and Gross 1979, 25–30).

This chapter reviews the origins of our current practices, identifies the innovative programs that should lead to changes in staffing, and suggests future directions that can give personnel administration a more dynamic role in fostering change for the improvement of instruction.

Curricular and Organizational Traditions

The dominance of self-contained elementary school classrooms over the years reflects rural school traditions more than a commitment to curricular integration. Departmentalized secondary school programs have developed as near carbon copies of collegiate structures and have gradually been extended downward as urbanization and the consolidation of rural schools evolved. While some medical and dental schools and teachers' colleges have experimented with a variety of staffing patterns, schools for the most part remain staffed and organized much as they were more than a hundred years ago. Even the newer community and two-year colleges, which have more freedom to innovate, tend to follow traditions established in four-year colleges, although they have made some substantial changes in course offerings, admissions criteria, and evaluative processes.

Self-contained or Departmentalized Organizations

Staffing patterns in most educational institutions reflect either self-contained or departmentalized organizations for instruction. Teacher-training programs remain bifurcated in reflection of these two distinct organizational patterns. Grade-sequenced formal course structures; extensive reliance on a textbook for every course; a quarter, semester, or year-long time frame for instruction; and rigidly controlled sequences and expected rates of progress are nearly universal characteristics of educational institutions in the United States. All of these traditions derive in part at least from rural realities of the past and collegiate traditions of the Middle Ages.

Highly departmentalized school organizations also reflect a growing emphasis on specialization of staff function under the influence of the industrialization of society. It is widely observed that specialization produces a paradox of greater efficiency within the limited scope of the specialty, with neglect for the broader range of outcomes. Even so, schools have increasingly used specialized personnel with differentiated responsibilities that tend to extend departmentalization at all school levels, creating more rigidly scheduled program fragments and reducing communications flow in nearly all directions.

Influence of Traditions on Staffing

Each of these traditions influences staffing practices in direct as well as subtle ways. Reliance on a textbook as the primary curriculum guide and the essential teaching material offers articulation and content control; hence, teachers who have extensive knowledge of subject matter or curriculum design capabilities are not essential and close supervision to guarantee proper content is not required. Likewise, the need for curriculum specialists on the local staff tends to be less apparent under conditions of ready-made curricula in textbook format. The self-contained classroom combines with the textbook to offer each community some comfort in making use of its local residents as elementary school teachers, even though their qualifications may be clearly less than ideal.

Similarly, the departmentalized program structure in nearly all secondary schools calls for staff competence in primarily a single subject field. This situation tends to inhibit flexible uses of teaching personnel and gives each such school a staff that has more allegiance to subject matter than to serving students or the community. This emphasis on the disciplines or the subjects being taught offers substantial opportunity for colleges and universities to influence (if not control) the secondary school curriculum, while dominating teacher training. If assessment of teaching competence in a broad sense were to become a reality, training, certification, selection, and assignment of teaching personnel would have to change drastically. That these innovations would seriously threaten the control mechanisms operated by colleges and state agencies is probably one of the reasons that there has been fierce resistance to the competency-based teacher education programs of recent years.

The formal course structures and sequences of nearly all secondary school programs are convenient for giving each staff person a sense of autonomy, encouraging full use of specialized knowledge, allocating students' and teachers' time, balancing teaching loads, and sequencing learning experiences. Only slightly less formal sequences of units of instruction dominate the graded elementary school program. However, such formal, rigid instructional sequences are highly ineffective vehicles for providing certain learning experiences; they also induce rigidities in time allocations and rates of learning and encourage artificial sequencing. Such sequencing has been widely criticized by many specialists in curriculum and educational administration, including Tyler (1981), Schlechty (1990), Wayson (1988), and Cuban (1990). Nevertheless, the staffing pattern that emerges is simple. A single teacher is assigned to each instructional segment, and students' use of time and the activities they pursue in the learning process are restricted and prescribed (Tyler 1981, 601).

Flexible schedules have threatened these static features of school life very little, since they generally accommodate only minor variations on the same basic themes, with identical operating rules. Potentially, of course, mini-courses, independent self-paced instruction, nongradedness, large blocks of time, field experience, and team teaching, which were advocated most widely during the 1960s, are all threats to the simple staffing patterns characterizing both departmentalized and self-contained classrooms.

Consequences of Traditions

The overriding fact is that both kinds of traditional organization tend to be highly rigid, to oversimplify the real requirements for staff competence, and to lead to professional frustrations on the part of teachers seeking job satisfaction. Concurrently, both traditional structures foster selection and assignment procedures that are mechanistic rather than diagnostic or personalized. Efforts to hold the secondary staff accountable are frustrated by the fragmenting of responsibilities among many individuals working relatively alone within a special subject field. Conversely, the elementary school teacher tends to be excessively accountable and vulnerable to criticism and pressures to which he or she cannot realistically respond, given the severe limitations of time, talent, and material resources available to serve students whose needs, interests, and abilities range widely. Further limiting the self-contained-classroom teachers' efforts are the working conditions of solitude and the absence of adult feedback or professionally relevant collaboration. These conditions make teachers' responses to criticism highly defensive, promote standardization instead of improvisation, and leave the teacher inevitably defensive, tending toward closed-mindedness and maintaining a closed learning environment that rarely excites either teacher or student. These are certainly conditions that promote neuroses and other forms of mental health problems. Yet scholars and practitioners alike continue to attend more to class size than to basic structural and staffing problems (Robinson 1990).

Variations within Traditions

Many forces play upon the school staff in ways that encourage the adoption of variations that are still essentially departmentalized or self-contained arrangements for instruction. Most of these variants can be seen as efforts to cope with some of the seriously limiting features of traditional organizations.

Vocational-technical programs in secondary schools have been quite successfully organized to avoid many of the severe limitations of departmentalization. Blocks of time, laboratory simulations, field experiences, and flexible use of formal course experiences are but a few of the departures from academic traditions found in many vocational-technical programs. The price of such quality programming has been, among other things, to force students and teachers alike to live in one world or the other. The incompatibilities are great, and separate programs tend to emerge even within the same physical facilities of the school. Students are forced to make unrealistic choices between college prep, vocational, and general programs, as if all were not important to most students. For those students choosing vocational programs, staffing practices of different kinds are involved. Practical experience qualifications for teachers of auto mechanics or printing are emphasized over college degrees, but not so for the teacher of government. Small class groups and low student-teacher ratios are accepted as policy or imposed by law. Citizen involvement in the instructional program becomes an important component of the staffing pattern in many vocational programs.

Science programs offer interesting examples of efforts to utilize laboratory simulations and larger time blocks to effect better learning. But these programs share the traditions of academia, have remained closely tied to departmentalization, and have not separated themselves from rigid schedules. Exceptions to this are found in some medical and dental schools where innovative programming, organizational arrangements, and staffing patterns have emerged, but nearly always under conditions of separation or insulation from the academic parent organizations.

The *partially departmentalized* organizations of the upper elementary grades are curious mixtures of the two traditional approaches to program structure. These modified school segments generally reflect expedient responses to pressures or cross-pressures and rarely reflect careful efforts to design for instructional efficiency. Pressures for specialized content offerings that self-contained-classroom teachers cannot (or do not wish to) teach commonly result in the employment of music, physical education, or art teachers. These specialist teachers often organize formal courses scheduled periodically throughout the day in patterns commonly found in secondary schools or colleges. Self-contained-classroom teachers are then forced to departmentalize in substantial degree to accommodate the rigid characteristics of the special teachers' course schedules. Sometimes partial departmentalization stems less from pressure for a special content offering and more from pressures for release time for the teachers of self-contained classrooms. The rigidities of departmental structures serve teachers well in guaranteeing them at least one free period. This is sometimes called a "planning period," though the time is often spent doing things other than planning.

The *departmentalized self-contained classroom* is quite a common organization for instruction. The lack of staff competence in using time efficiently, in planning for intraclass groupings, in organizing for independent study, and in integrating content often promotes departmentalization in the guise of a self-contained classroom. Quite frequently, each "period" of the day is clearly structured to be a specified length of time regardless of need: it is scheduled daily; it is specified for a given subject and no other; and it engages all students uniformly, regardless of individual needs. Such regimented classrooms, while controlled by a single teacher, avoid most of the complications of periodic bells, hall passing, and locker banging. They are, nevertheless, departmentalized organizations in most respects. They are perhaps the least efficient of all because they share the weaknesses of departmentalization without sharing many of the advantages of specialization.

Innovations and Changes in Perspective

Just as curricular and organizational traditions have tended to establish staffing patterns, so have innovations and other changes in instruction modified staffing needs and created new problems for personnel administrators. A great number of innovative instructional practices have had some influence on instructional staffing. The rapid emergence and hasty decline of many new programs (Herriott and Gross 1979; Bloom 1981, 217) in recent decades have perplexed administrators, teachers, supervisors, and parents—to say nothing of the bewildered students (Cohen 1988, 32).

One Hundred Years of Change

The hundred-year period following the Civil War coincided with the industrialization and urbanization of our society. Quite naturally, it was an era of rapid change and innovation in education too. A host of post-Civil War events set in motion many of the forces that shaped the educational system of this country. However, the years after World War I can also be seen as a time frame within which fast-changing societal forces had great impact on educational structures and practices (Tyler 1981, 599). Similarly, the unprecedented variety of social change in the 1950s and 1960s can be unmistakably associated with the changes in education in the years that followed World War II.

The *platoon system* became famous in post-Civil War industrial cities in the United States as immigrants and black and white farmers from the South went to work in the new factories and mines. School enrollments soared. There was a need for a cheap form of education for factory workers' children. The platoon system provided for large classes, limited the need for additional classroom teachers, and made normal school training of teachers a reasonably satisfactory program of drill and recitation under highly regimented conditions. That the system of instruction was inefficient mattered less in hectic times of industrial expansion than the fact that it was cheap and available.

Kindergarten education emerged as a downward extension of elementary education under the dual influences of early studies and writings of John Dewey, Froebel, and Pestalozzi, and the vast numbers of women to enter the labor market during every war. Society's reluctance to provide education for early childhood has persisted to the present, as depressions, wars, and governmental whims add and delete these programs decade after decade. Nevertheless, the long-range trend appears to be in the direction of one or more years of schooling for all children prior to six years of age. Three- to five-year-old children enrolled in schools were estimated to total nearly five million in 1981 and are expected to increase in subsequent years, even with low birth rates.

This trend was given impetus in the 1960s as the Great Society programs of the Johnson presidency began to offer new opportunities for poor mothers to work, while Headstart, nursery schools, and child-care centers were established with federal funds to look after the children and provide learning opportunities for them at the same time (Michel 1990).

Headstart and other early childhood educational programs continue to be debated in legislative circles, confused with day care, and complicated by political advocacy of private and church-related funding. Hence, highly successful programs are being expanded only gradually, and most children younger than six years of age were still unserved in 1990 (Ogle 1990).

Ungraded programs were developed as studies of individuality decreased the emphasis on a uniform standard of achievement. Goodlad and Anderson (1962) were among the most eloquent and rationally forceful advocates of nongraded schools. Even more persuasive was the baby boom of the 1950s, which made it almost impossible for administrators to match enrollments with available rooms and the ages of the students. The formal graded patterns in neighborhood elementary schools could not be maintained. At the secondary level, we responded to the pressure of increasing numbers of students by building new, larger, centralized schools. Grade patterns became diverse and unstable. School desegregation added still further to these grade-structure changes, as separate schools for minorities were closed or converted. The 8–4 pattern so widely adopted at the turn of the twentieth century became increasingly 6–3–3 after World War I, but after World War II, grade patterns of many kinds emerged. Increasing population mobility during and after World War II, accentuated by industrial decentralization and the invention of the mobile home, seriously complicated efforts of supervisors to maintain some rational pattern of age groups, curricular offerings, and organization for instruction. Administrators and school boards responded, of course, by building new schools in all kinds of expedient forms—temporary bungalows or Quonset huts left over from military installations, "portables," remodeled structures, and even open-space schools. Grade structures of every conceivable kind became common. The innovative Nova schools in Florida adopted the old K–6, 7–12 plan. But a seventh-grade school at San Angelo, Texas, was established in the early 1960s, and desegregating school districts all through the South found the single-grade school a court-pleasing arrangement. In the midst of all this turmoil in grade structures, the nongraded school emerged as a rational, instructionally defensible alternative. It has gained considerable recognition but has had little acceptance among teachers, administrators, and parents.

The *middle school program* of instruction developed many advocates in the late 1960s, partially as a response to the grade-structure dilemmas described above. William Alexander (1974) was one of many educators who developed and promoted the implementation of middle school programs throughout the nation. This movement was initially well received as a response to overcrowding in traditional elementary and junior high schools. Student alienation and protests, liberalized sex norms, drug abuse, and desegregation were all social problems gaining attention in the 1960s, and they aroused strong public support for moving young adolescents out of the elementary schools and keeping them separated from older secondary school students. These influences were largely sociological and psychological, but the rationale of the middle school advocates was instructional. A new kind of program for a distinctive stage of development of the learner was the central theme. Along with this theme, of course, went clear expectations that the middle school staff would have special competencies, different from those of other elementary or secondary school teachers.

Differentiated staffing patterns of several kinds emerged in the 1960s as postwar teacher shortages persisted. Team teaching arrangements were advocated by Shaplin and Olds (1964) and others, who emphasized the hierarchical nature of the team to provide leadership for teachers with less experience or more limited skills and competencies. This concept of team structure was perceived realistically in teacher union circles as a threat to the sanctity of the lone, autonomous professional teacher and the single salary schedule. Fenwick English (English and Sharpes 1972) was one of the pioneering administrators and supervisors who implemented differentiated staffing programs that emphasized increasing teacher autonomy, recognition, and scope of responsibilities.

More recent consideration of differentiated staffing for classroom teaching purposes has been limited. The use of teacher aides, paraprofessionals, parent volunteers, and visiting specialists has grown slowly. Advocates of a teaching hierarchy, utilizing "master teachers" for quasi-supervisory duties, coaching, and shared decision making are numerous, but strong trends seem lacking.

Many *other new programs* have emerged, especially over the past fifty years. Vocational training, driver education, open-space schools, large-group instruction, instructional television, individually prescribed instruction, bilingual education, core curriculum, community schools, flexible modular scheduling, mainstreaming for the handicapped, interdisciplinary teaching, language laboratories, 16-mm sound study films, supervised correspondence study, peer tutoring, simulation and gaming, computer-assisted and computer-managed instruction, programmed learning, teaching machines, cooperative learning, interactive video, and still more innovations have all made at least fleeting appearances on the school scene. Because of accelerated rates of technological and social change and broad-based public acceptance of new ideas in education, most of the terms used here to suggest instructional changes have come into existence in only the last twenty-five years. There is some reason to believe that this proliferation of instructional program fragments is abating. Professional judgment, and research and theory on the change process are nearly unanimous in the view that this approach is not the way to improve instruction (Boyd 1987; Cohen 1988; Cuban 1990; Hart 1989; Latham 1988; Miller 1988; Wayson 1988).

Well-intentioned and useful as some of the changes have been, evaluations of promising innovations often reveal either no change or less effectiveness. Herriott and Gross report numerous cases of failures in program innovations based on "inept management" rather than on poor design (1979, 25–30). Even more fundamental are problems associated with the emphasis on the "wave of the future" which our industrial society promotes and schools emulate. Such change may well be misguided simply because no benefits result.

Cohen (1988) provides a compelling historical perspective involving "ancient inheritance," incentives, and high risk as but a few of the unique constraints on educational change and reform (39). Schlesinger (1986) also suggests that historical cycles may greatly limit the direction of changes.

Various studies of recent efforts to develop new programs give us good reason to pause and reflect on Rivlin's (1971) distinction between "random innovation" and more systematic endeavors, called "planned variation" (Fullan 1982). The most effective, best designed innovations have suffered from abandonment and corruption as readily as have the ill-conceived: ungradedness, peer tutoring, continuous promotions, and individualized instruction have all suffered despite their soundness (Shepard and Smith 1990).

The immediate future demands a slower pace of more carefully designed and selected implemented innovations, with less fragmentation. Total systems redevelopment can and should be the wave of the future. Obviously, staffing for such changes must also be more systemic, fundamentally more rational, and based on better diagnoses of performance capabilities (competence) and much longer-range planning.

Reform and Restructuring

The dismal record of accomplishment of innovations was clearly recognized by both scholars and practitioners in the 1970s, preparing the way for the "reform movement" of the early 1980s. These so-called reforms were clearly a reflection of conservative and reactionary political and economic events in the United States (Wirt and Kirst 1989). With rare exceptions, the reforms of the early 1980s were mandated and retrogressive. For the most part they were old ideas, known to make little if any contribution to improving teaching and learning (Cuban 1990; Miller 1988; Wayson 1988). Wayson provided a detailed analysis of more than eighty specific reform recommendations emphasized by various groups within a few years of the 1983 report *The Nation at Risk*, a few of which are highlighted below.

> *Testing programs* were extended, mandated in state after state, made more standardized, narrowly focused on "basics," rigidly administered, and widely used for political purposes (Murphy 1990).
>
> *Curricular changes* emphasized tracking via "honors" programs, magnet schools, and special "academies"; more rigid time allocations for basic skills; narrower curricular objectives, to match the new tests; textbook teaching; and more courses in English, mathematics, and science, while other content areas were largely ignored (Honig 1989).
>
> *Accountability for learning* as measured in the most simplistic ways became the rule, with students pressured to score high or lose privileges and teachers' evaluations often based in part on test scores. Retaining students in their current grade returned as common practice, despite extensive research-based contraindications (Ogle 1990, 18; Shepard and Smith 1990). Annual press releases on declines in SAT score were widely publicized. Teachers learned to teach for the test, and higher-order thinking and application skills were given low priority (Lewis 1989, 12; Ogle 1990, 28,30).
>
> *Early education programs* for three- to five-year-old children stagnated in the 1980s, with only 51 percent of this age group in any program in 1981 and 54.5 percent enrolled by 1987. Public prekindergarten enrollments declined from 1983 to 1987. However, part-time program enrollments have increased steadily since 1984 (Ogle 1990, 56). The political rhetoric of these years was about a mythical land of "choice" and "day care," rather than children yearning for a chance to learn.

Rethinking Reforms

Most of the early efforts of the reform movement in the early 1980s came to be viewed as too limited at best by scholars and practitioners alike. The trends identified above continue to be seen as inappropriate or inadequate, but they may persist with greater long-term effects than innovations of earlier times did. The combined power and influence of national commissions, political leaders, and mass media attention have resulted in legal structural changes and public perceptions that may not disappear readily. Unfortunately, the long-delayed effects of some statewide mandates may create problems for the future, as new and more soundly conceived solutions to improving education emerge.

Unanticipated consequences, both positive and negative, are nearly always associated with the process of change. The reforms of the early 1980s are largely being rejected, however, because the consequences are clear. Mandated programs from state legislative bodies are often ill-conceived, not in their intent so much as in the micromanaging often involved (Wise 1988). Adding courses and credit requirements for high school graduation by bureaucratic decree fails in its honorable intent, while having little effect on the many pervasive problems of a terribly inadequate curriculum (Brandt 1988). Testing teachers for basic "literacy" is not a bad thing to require by law or regulation, but it symbolizes serious concern for the elimination of incompetent teachers, which it fails to pursue (Boyd 1987). In addition, used indiscriminately, it produces serious problems in recruiting handicapped and minority teachers (Leonard et al. 1988).

Restructuring Proposals

The mid-1980s produced a revival of interest in the structural defects in the educational system (Lewis 1989). Scholars and practitioners in public education can be proud of their long history of openness to changes in educational structures that go beyond the merely trivial (Miller 1988). Mikhail Gorbachev's slogans and plans for *glasnost* (openness) and *perestroika* (restructuring) captured the attention of educators as well as the general public.

An enormous number of structural changes in education are being widely advocated and, gradually, each is getting some chance for trial and implementation. Years may pass before the effects of any such change can be fully assessed. Unfortunately, most are subject to threats such as the bandwagon effect, corruption, and bureaucratic/political micromanagement (Harris 1985; Latham 1988).

Lewis (1989) surveyed teachers and school administrators regarding their views on various restructuring proposals she calls "the new reforms." These proposals are quite different in both scope and substance, and they are seen generally to have support among practitioners. Briefly, they are:

1. Reorganizing district structures and governance
2. Requiring more teacher accountability
3. Providing more individualized instruction to students
4. Reorganizing faculty practices (staffing and scheduling)
5. Establishing restructuring experiments
6. Restructuring teaching methods
7. Restructuring curricula
8. Giving greater authority to the school
9. Giving greater authority to teachers
10. Improving teacher education
11. Providing more support for teachers

These eleven proposals tend to be broader and more "structural" in nature than many changes of either the innovations era or the reform movement. Within this broad effort to restructure in many ways to produce a fundamentally new kind of education are several vigorous efforts that are especially important to personnel administration (Brandt 1990).

Site-based management is gaining the momentum of a national movement. It calls for decentralization of many decisions, greater autonomy for the school principal, and, often, teacher involvement in school management. Strong arguments are also made for parental involvement, even in decision making (Aronstein et al. 1990).

Teacher credentialing is being restructured in some places. No clear movement seems to be preeminent—only widespread efforts to change preservice education of teachers in fundamental ways. Some states, such as Texas and New Jersey, have severely limited the professional education component, relying on a degree in an academic field as evidence of qualifications to teach. Other institutions are moving again toward fifth-year internship programs to place more emphasis on professional skills in application (Schwab 1990). "Alternative" certification programs are developing, which place teacher preparation in the hands of local school administrators and supervisors, employing adaptations of vocational and military on-the-job training.

School organization restructuring of numerous kinds is in vogue. Magnet schools have helped to spawn a variety of proposals for "parental choice," ranging from voucher plans to open enrollment to government-subsidized private schools (Boyd and Walberg 1990; Urbanski 1990).

Curricular revisions are gaining attention once again. A return to a highly classical education is supported by "cultural literacy" advocates, placing great emphasis on a designated list of sources of wisdom and culture (Hirsch 1987). More thoughtful advocates of dramatic change in curriculum and instruction include Boyer (Brandt 1988) and Sizer (1988), who promote restructuring in fundamental ways, especially the secondary school.

Other major efforts to change the curriculum in schools are represented by the new California social studies curriculum (California State Board of Education 1988), periodic attention to arts education as more than a "frill" (Chen and Granger 1988), and growing attention to global education (O'Neil 1989).

Persistent Trends in Program Development

Staffing for instruction can be, as it has been, largely reactive. It can also be substantially *proactive*. Programs of instruction can hardly rise above the staffs that direct them. Children and youth have opportunities for quality education in direct relation to the quality of the staff directly concerned with instruction. To ensure quality in both respects is the reason for staff personnel services, above all else. To organize such services to react to fads, passing fancies of private foundations, government agencies, and political or economic pressures under a rationale of expediency is detrimental to the educational rights of children and youth. To promote instructional staffing with more attention to long-range trends and theoretically sound curricular, organizational, and instructional realities offers some relief from pressures, and much more promise of improvements that will take root and grow, to the emerging satisfaction of many interests.

Selected Trends

Genuine trends in program changes are few, but they do exist. Individualization of instruction, diversity of both curricula and learning resources, increased emphasis on meeting current life needs, and growing openness of the school to influences from students and parents all seem to be reasonably persistent and educationally defensible trends. They have been reflected in many major innovative efforts over long periods of time. They are defensible in terms of research and theories related to human growth, learning, and teaching. They are consistent with the basic values most widely held by democratic societies. They are even consistent with the need for educational developments that can help Western industrial societies face the uncertain future.

Staffing Support

Each trend makes somewhat different demands on staff competencies. In turn, each trend can be enhanced by staffing policies and practices that anticipate trend developments and competency needs. *Individualization of instruction,* for instance, develops as a complex variety of arrangements, practices, and materials. Consequently, priorities tend to be placed on diagnostic competencies, nonauthoritarian attitudes and values, versatility in teaching style, creativity in approaches to teaching, high threshold of frustration, tolerance for turbulence (Harris 1985), competence in behavior measurement, and empathy for human diversity. The trend toward *diverse uses of curriculum and learning resources* calls for some very similar priorities in staff competencies but also gives importance to competence in organizing, coordinating, facilitating, communicating, designing curricula, and utilizing materials of instruction. The trend toward *meeting current life needs* calls for utilizing staff personnel drawn from a broad spectrum of society, in addition to utilizing volunteers, part-time employees, parents, and retired citizens for delegated instructional tasks. The trend toward *openness of the school* similarly calls for many of the same staffing competencies but highlights others related to social services and political action. Extensive use of peer tutoring causes a teacher to become more a trainer and coordinator and less a presenter. In a community-school operation, staff skills in communicating with culturally diverse peoples, working collaboratively with laypersons, and identifying nonacademic talents and abilities become important to an extent not required in the traditional school.

Trends in the larger society will very probably influence the needs that emerge within these persistent educational trends. Children and youth who are non-English-speaking, culturally different, intellectually limited, or creatively endowed will demand better programming, and that can be provided only by more appropriate staffing. Instructional management systems associated with these several trends will necessitate a broader variety of school staff personnel who have the requisite technical skills, such as diagnostic testing, student record keeping, and computer-managed information processing. Needless to say, the regular classroom teacher will need a higher order of management skills as well as basic teaching skills.

Trends, too, should not be thought of as unchanging any more than a growing plant should be viewed as just getting bigger. A trend toward greater individualization of instruction can and should undergo developmental changes, which should pose demands for staffing. Staff continuity, which gives perspective to a program of instruction, enhances the developmental process, provided that there is continuing leadership with a broader perspective on the change process. Excessive staff turnover is disruptive of the process of change, but stability in the absence of leadership produces ossification in operations. Rigid concepts of program design produce resistance and confusion. But a purely reactive stance to real needs for change in structure, content, and methods leads only to chaos and ineffectiveness (Seif 1990).

Community Support

Community access to and influence on the school operation has multiple implications for staffing practices. On the one hand, increases in community involvement require new school personnel and new competencies because of the increasing public contact. However, all efforts at program development must ultimately receive public support for survival. Personnel administrators, like other school leaders, need to be cognizant of community expectations and concerns. The staffing implications of any given attitude or point of view within the community may be more directly influential because the public tends to respond to its schools in terms of the people who represent them. Similarly, programs of instruction tend to be supported or opposed depending on the image projected by someone on the staff. Secondhand experience with that staff member may be quite influential. A child's report to a parent may convey an image. A neighbor may report on a visit to school. The local news media may describe programs or practices in ways that heavily influence community attitudes and opinions. Yet national polls continue to reflect strong public support even when criticisms persist (Elam 1989, 41–55).

Support for a program is often verbalized in terms that clearly designate individual staff members. "Miss Jones sure knows how to keep those kids' interest and attention" illustrates one type of verbal support. Another form is less direct: "Well, my kids seem to have done well under this new team setup." However, when problems arise the public becomes negative or apprehensive.

Increasingly, patrons grow both more critical and more supportive of the schools as their own level of educational attainment rises. A well-informed patron can be more discerning in both critical and supportive endeavors. However, to the extent that critical reactions may be less explicitly focused upon individual staff members, it is easy to underestimate the extent to which individual staff actions contribute to school criticism. Programs often gain acceptance or rejection on the basis of the staff's competence to implement them effectively and on the staff's ability to communicate what they are doing for students. Those concerned with personnel administration must be directly involved with surveys, public meetings, advisory groups, and community agencies to ensure a steady flow of information from the public regarding the school's instructional programs as perceived by the consumers.

There is, of course, a larger perspective on public support for education. Commitment to education as a vehicle for promoting the general welfare has never been higher or more widespread, but this has also raised the stakes. That which is more clearly perceived as valuable is also subject to increased attention by various interest groups. Public education has become a prize to be won in the minds of some—a multibillion-dollar enterprise with little "privatization," and an exciting target for venture capital. Educational leaders should be sensitive to the growing propaganda campaign being waged over control of the national education agenda. Some groups appear eager to undermine the institution of free, universal, public education for all. Others are eager, it would seem, to exert much more control over educational policy. Still others hope for massive reallocations of resources from the public to the private sectors of education.

Community relations must involve, then, attention to the state and national scene as well as to the local public.

Positive Developments

It has become accepted, even fashionable, to refer to education and schools in negative terms. Educators feel compelled to confess the failings and shortcomings of public education. However, there is much that is very positive that should be stated. For instance, in 1988 more doctorates were granted in education than in any other field, and education was the only field in which more women than men received doctorates. The percentage of teachers who are college graduates increased from fifty-seven percent in the 1960s to seventy-nine percent in the 1980s (National Research Council

1989). Despite criticisms of industrial leaders, the long-term pattern (1970–1985) has shown an upward trend in wage premiums for both high school graduates and college graduates in the work force (Murphy and Welch 1989, 24).

More directly, there are numerous educational developments that continue to prosper and contribute to quality education in our public schools, including:

Declines in the use of drugs in schools

Extensive mainstreaming of handicapped students

Acceptance of sex education as a part of the school program

Widespread implementation of computer literacy and applications programs

Increasing emphasis on problem solving in many programs

Growing use of cooperative learning arrangements in classrooms

Extensive improvements in teacher evaluation procedures, making them more objective, fair, and useful

Continuing professional staff development as a standard practice across the United States

Citing positive developments or continuing trends hardly does justice to public education, because much that is good about our schools has a long history and has evolved very slowly. Much of the responsibility of educational leaders throughout the 1990s will necessarily involve protecting the best aspects of a model system of education that is the envy of the world. Exhibit 3.1 identifies just a few of the long-term accomplishments of public education that educators and citizens can take pride in maintaining.

EXHIBIT 3.1   Long-Term Progress in U.S. Public Schools

From	*To*
1. Costly education that many could not afford beyond primary grades	Essentially "free," tax-supported education for all—even through high school
2. Students walking long distances to school	Free, safe bus transportation for students living beyond safe walking distances
3. High school programs restricted to serving the few most academically able students	High school graduation available to nearly all as dropout rates decline decade after decade.
4. Virtually no educational opportunity for the handicapped students	Special programs and nearly universal access for all handicapped students, with widespread "mainstreaming"

From	*To*
5. Sack lunches with cold food, eaten in classrooms or playgrounds	Cafeteria services, hot lunches, free or part-pay lunches for the poor families, and subsidized lunches for all
6. Teachers commonly with only a high school diploma or a few months of "normal school" training	Bachelor's degree teacher graduates in virtually all schools, with half holding graduate degrees
7. Schools without libraries except for small book collections, mostly in high schools	Libraries in both elementary and secondary schools, with extensive collections in many, and professional librarians in charge
8. Classes of all sizes, from mixed grades to fifty or more students in many urban centers	Steadily declining class sizes, with wide acceptance of twenty-five or fewer students as "normal," and pupil-teacher ratios nationwide in the upper teens
9. Little or no use of special support personnel	An array of counselors, nurses, teacher aides, clerical assistants, and parent volunteers serving students in many schools
10. Teachers' salaries set at the whim of the local board	Established salary schedules restrict discrimination against women, minorities, and elementary school teachers
11. Highly segregated schools with inferior teachers, buildings, and programs for black, Hispanic, Native American and impoverished students	Substantially desegregated schools, with steady progress toward equality of educational opportunity within communities and states
12. Teachers' jobs subject to political influence, with "at-will" dismissals and virtually no contractual safeguards	Very high levels of teacher job security, with formal contracts, clear probationary and tenure provisions in some states, and extensive case law guarantees
13. Dull, rote memorizing as the characteristic teaching practice in most classrooms	Widespread use of a variety of teaching practices and media in use to stimulate interests and motivate for more learning
14. Harsh, rigid control and disciplinary procedures, with extensive use of ruler slapping, whipping, verbal abuse, and other physical punishments in wide use	Almost complete elimination of physical abuse in classroom settings and steady decline in verbal abuse, along with various forms of corporal punishment
15. Narrow, rigidly defined curricula for students on both the elementary and secondary levels	Expansive curricula embracing science, health, art, music, and vocations and various electives

Other improvements easily forgotten: Science laboratory facilities, extracurricular activities, principals with advanced degrees, curriculum specialists, computers in classrooms, field trips, playgrounds safely equipped, crossing guards, teachers' lounges, word processing and copying equipment.

Summary

Traditional patterns of school organization and the curricular traditions that accompany them are deeply rooted in the "establishment" of education and in the history of the past one hundred years. While some important traditions go back much further, the structure we have is essentially one that has evolved since the beginning of the twentieth century as a tool of an industrial, urbanizing society. It is not surprising, then, that few "innovations" have really taken hold. A few trends do seem to be clearly long-term in nature. These trends are responses more to demands of the society than to grand designs by educational development specialists. Even so, the rate of development and the quality of the programs that emerge will be greatly influenced by the leadership for change that administrators, supervisors, teachers, and citizens exert. Personnel administrators must contribute in crucial ways to the improvement process. There is nothing so powerful as an idea whose time has come. But there is nothing so fragile, apparently, as a new program if the school staff is not adequate to implement new ideas. Personnel administrators must be part of the system for program development as well as part of the system for filling vacancies.

Suggested Study Sources

Bacharach, Samuel B., ed. 1990. *Education Reform: Making Sense of It All*. Boston: Allyn and Bacon.

This volume provides thirty-three critical statements on many facets of the "reform" movements of the 1980s. While numerous writers take rather critical positions, each brings scholarly and practical expertise to bear on such varied topics as site-level management, community involvement, school choice, and testing and evaluation. The subtitle, "Making Sense of It All," reflects the tone of this volume.

Brandt, Ron, ed. 1990. "Restructuring: What Is It?" *Educational Leadership* 47(April).

This issue is almost entirely devoted to reports and opinions related to school restructuring. Site-based management articles are included, but a much broader view is reflected.

Jackson, Phillip W., ed. 1988. *Contributing to Educational Change: Perspectives on Research and Practice*. Berkeley, CA: McCutchan Publishing.

This publication includes chapters of unusually thoughtful analysis of both historical and current developments in education. Cuban's chapter provides a historical view of educational change since 1880. Cohen's chapter on teaching practices puts the problem of resistance to change in perspective from the classroom level. Other chapters are equally stimulating analyses of other movements for change.

Fullan, Michael. 1982. *The Meaning of Educational Change*. New York: Teachers College Press.

A rigorous review with critical analyses of numerous efforts at innovations in the 1960s and 1970s. The author uses federally sponsored programs to illustrate the complexities of the implementation process when large-scale efforts are undertaken.

Lewis, Anne. 1989. *Restructuring America's Schools*. Arlington, VA: American Association of School Administrators.

> *This book is a wide-ranging review of the need for change in education and the distinction between superficial reforms and more fundamental changes. Of special value are the chapters that address restructuring in state control and in school districts as well as school-level changes. Chapter 3, on the "basics of restructuring," is especially valuable, as Lewis reviews radically different views about the nature of schooling advocated by Adler, Goodlad, Boyer, Sizer, and others.*

Murphy, Joseph, ed. 1990. *The Educational Reform Movement of the 1980s: Perspectives and Cases*. Berkeley, CA: McCutchan.

> *This book examines a wide array of reform initiatives. Its authors take rather critical stances in most instances. In addition to a historical review of reforms in the United States, chapters focus on such specific aspects as teacher testing, career ladder, student achievement testing, changes in courses for high school students, and school consolidation.*

Wayson, William W., et al. 1988. *Up from Excellence: The Impact of the Excellence Movement on Schools*. Bloomington, IN: Phi Delta Kappa.

> *Much of this volume traces, analyzes, and criticizes the reform efforts of the early 1980s. This careful documentation of change dilemmas, diverse panaceas, top-down mandates, public unrest, etc., is a significant contribution. Chapter 10, "Guidelines for Achieving True Excellence," is a masterful effort to synthesize the lessons of this era with a positive view toward future progress.*

4

Competency Specifications for Personnel

The public call for accountability in public education, as in other public services, is often credited with fostering the recent strong interest in competency specification. In fact, the accountability movement and other developments in and out of the public school arena have converged to focus attention on people's actual performance in contrast to credentials or other artifacts of performance. The natural evolution of any professional specialization seems to be to give more attention to standards of performance and less to rituals and superficial image-building activities associated with more primitive specialties. We can hope that this pattern will also evolve in education in the years ahead. Attention to the techniques for specifying and using competencies in personnel decisions can contribute to the emergence of personnel administration as a profession.

The Meaning of Competency

Controversial as competency-based teacher education programs have been, halting as their development has been, and limited as the research on them still is, it seems wise to view the entire movement of concern for competence and competency specifications in education as one that will persist and one that can produce improved educational staffing. Preservice preparation programs, dominated by rather autonomous colleges and universities and monitored from afar by state education authorities, will undoubtedly continue to give more emphasis to courses, credit hours, and degrees completed (Goodlad et al. 1990). To the extent that competency specifications tend to replace these artifacts, schools will have more reliable information to use in recruiting and selecting new personnel. However, even in the absence of a major revolution in preservice programming and licensing, the concepts, specifications, and assessment techniques associated with competency-based programs can serve to improve staffing practices within elementary and secondary schools if we focus on the use of competency specifications in recruitment, selection, assignment, and evaluation of personnel in service.

Competencies as Behavior Descriptions

Many problems remain, no matter what approach is taken to evaluation or assessment of performance. However, a major step is to focus on performances rather than artifacts of performance or largely unrelated evidence.

Competencies, when specified as performances in realistic task-relevant situations, assist in focusing on behavior. When competency statements describe the behaviors associated with performances desired and also describe the on-the-job context within which such behaviors need to be manifest, expectations for performance become clear. When competencies are specified as performances out of context, they may still help to focus on training needs, but they have limited utility in defining roles, differentiating responsibilities, or balancing staff groups. Whether we are concerned with developing training programs, evaluating in-service performance, or selecting and assigning personnel, the use of competencies as descriptions of anticipated performance has value. To the extent that these descriptions are broad and general in character, they may fail to differentiate one kind of performance from another. To the extent that the competencies are descriptions of small fragments of larger performance patterns, they will fail to define expected performance and will encourage excessive attention to minutiae.

It may be important to consider examples of competency statements that are not particularly useful in guiding staffing practices. Fragments of performance patterns are sometimes proposed; at the other extreme, broad and general performances are often described as competencies.

A *fragment* of performance can be illustrated as follows: "Recalls Flanders' ten categories of verbal interaction without omission." Such a statement is a description of behavior, but it fails as a competency statement in that it describes only cognitive behavior and is out of context in terms of functional task or purpose. Similarly, a behavior description such as "correctly computes ratios of indirect to direct verbal frequencies using the designated formula" falls short of a statement of a competency even though a specific computational *skill* is described. Again, such a statement is out of context and might well relate to a purely clerical situation, research endeavors, or a hobby, for that matter. Both of these behaviors could be important fragments of a larger pattern of performance: "S/he can accurately record and analyze verbal interaction in the classroom, using Flanders' categories and using matrix analysis techniques; can provide feedback to teachers in terms of most and least frequent events, i/d ratios, and extended indirect behaviors." Such a statement of performance qualifies as a competency with functional utility. It calls for the demonstration of closely related knowledges and skills and specifies where the performance is to be utilized. It suggests, at least, the purpose to be served. Despite the complexity of the behavior pattern, the description communicates rather clear and explicit expectations.

A common fragmentation problem found in competency lists for preservice teacher education is the designation of factual information as competencies, such as "demonstrates an understanding of due process" or "knowledge of the State Department of Education." Still other fragments are deceptively simple: "to recognize staff differences." Simple as it sounds, many complex skill-knowledge relationships are implied but not made explicit.

Overly broad and general statements of performance are enticing for the simplicity they seem to offer the user. This value is usually deceptive, however, because the price of simplicity is loss of both specificity and perspective. Consider a statement like this: "Can work with students in ways that produce effective learning outcomes." What more do we need? This says it all! We can just forget about describing "how" the outcomes are produced! Of course, *if* good measures of "effective learning outcomes" are readily available, if we don't care how they are produced, and if we can be sure that the undefined "work" of the unspecified teacher was responsible for these outcomes, *then* there is some merit in such competency statements. In fact, few of these conditions tend to prevail in the real world of the school or college, and even when they do, it might still be helpful to specify what the "ways" are so they can be reinforced, rewarded, recruited, trained for, and shared with others.

The following statement also is overly general and broad: "Is knowledgeable about the subject being taught." While the form in which the knowledge is to be displayed is not clear and the specific knowledge content is vague, this statement does suggest something that is measurable in behavioral terms by testing. It fails to have utility as a statement of a competency, even though it suggests a task to which it applies. The task is very general—"the subject being taught." Furthermore, it does not describe a behavior pattern for utilizing the knowledge in functional ways in a given situation. The ease with which pseudocompetencies such as this one can be measured is a snare to be avoided. To measure with precision and ease knowledges or skills that are not clearly relevant to on-the-job realities offers little advantage. It is better to have clear descriptions of obviously relevant and important performances, even if measurement poses continuing problems.

Still another highly general kind of statement is this: "Provides students with positive reinforcements and expresses enthusiasm about the learning tasks." Although the two kinds of behaviors are designated and the situation and task are easy to infer, the statement lacks the specificity needed for greater utility as a competency statement.

Each of the overly general statements examined could become useful competencies at some level with careful revision to make the behaviors, situations, and tasks more explicit. Possible restatements might take the following forms:

> Works systematically with students during study periods, giving individual consultations regularly, praising and redirecting, while clarifying anticipated learning outcomes to keep students actively and purposefully involved in assigned learning activities.

> Utilizes knowledge of subject matter being taught to assist students in clarifying misconceptions, guiding them to reliable sources of information, and challenging them to do independent study beyond the textbook assignments.

> When dealing with students who lack interest or express frustration, is able to employ a variety of positive reinforcement techniques, withhold negative reinforcements, and verbalize enthusiasm for the learning task to stimulate student effort and prevent failure.

Distinction between Competence and Competency

The special terms associated with competency specifications and competency-based programs are numerous and not well defined or standardized in use. Two basic terms—competence and competency—need to be distinguished. *Competence* can be regarded as the demonstrated capacity to perform in ways that are regarded as satisfactory. As such, this term refers to actual performance at a measured level of quality. *Competencies*, on the other hand, can be thought of as descriptions of the performances anticipated. To the extent that the description of a performance matches the actual, demonstrated, observable performance, no problem exists. Often, however, descriptions—competencies—are not identical with actual performance. In fact, we have to describe competencies in the absence of a specific performer! Competencies are efforts to describe what is expected, hoped for, desired, anticipated, recruited, being trained for, and so on. Carefully specified statements of competencies are useful, then, to communicate what might be.

Competence, on the other hand, exists within the individual person. As the capability to perform, it refers to actual patterns of behavior that are observable, at least under certain conditions and at certain times. Assessing competence calls for attention to a specific individual and the demonstration of a performance capability. Competence for which no competency is stated may exist. Competencies may be stated even when such competence does not exist among a given staff. These two terms are related but differ in meaning in numerous ways (Sternberg and Kolligian 1990).

Still another subtle but important consideration in defining competence and competency is *capability*. No person is competent under all conceivable conditions. A teacher who is competent in some aspects of teaching young children might not be competent in that same aspect of teaching when the students are adults. The competence demonstrated under a given set of conditions—for example, young children, reading lesson, formal classroom setting, "typical" students, and known basal reading materials—may be drastically reduced when slow-learning, nonreading adolescents with "emotional problems" are elements of the situation. Conversely, if situational factors are drastically different, as illustrated by non-English-speaking students and nontraditional instructional materials, the person's former competence might not be demonstrable as a pattern of behavior at all.

Competencies invariably refer only to individuals, and competence is observed in individuals. However, descriptions of task-relevant activity can define more than an individual's behavior. They can specify relations among people, problems addressed, and situations as they are actually faced in real-world settings. For these reasons, job descriptions are necessarily more than competency listings. However, competency specifications have a unique place in the improvement of job descriptions.

Specification of Professional Competencies

Because professional competencies tend to be very complex and the outcomes may be difficult to describe clearly, efforts to specify such competencies must be carefully undertaken and subjected to critical review before being finalized. Competency statements should focus on professional performance, vividly describe expectations, and relate to real problems and situations on the job. More specifically, a competency statement should:

1. Be a complex performance pattern.
2. Have utility represented by a service or product.
3. Be reality-oriented.
4. Be predictably demanded now and in the future.
5. Have a high priority among performance expectations.
6. Be a synthesized pattern of performance.

Few competency statements measure up to these criteria.

To provide specifications for complex performance patterns, simple listings of knowledge, skill, duties, or responsibilities will not suffice; carefully applied job analysis techniques that sort, separate, and clarify components of performance are required. In such a process, critical, essential, priority tasks are identified, then patterns of behaviors for accomplishing such tasks are specified. Hence, job analysis techniques (Gael 1988) identify tasks, but competencies make performance explicit.

Job Analysis and Competencies

Job analysis is served well by advances in competency specification, because jobs are described more precisely as patterns of people's performance with explicit reference to tasks in view and products or services anticipated. However, jobs, tasks, and competencies are not synonymous when complex human performances are involved. Routine jobs can be described as simple tasks to be accomplished when such tasks are common practice. Then more detailed competency specifications are superfluous. But most jobs, in most situations, require detailed explications to reflect competency expectations fully.

Simple routine performance expectations can be specified as a set of concrete behavior descriptions. For instance, a teacher's aide's competency for preparing handouts and worksheets might be specified as follows:

> Copying Materials. *The aide prepares copies of materials for use by classroom teachers.*
>
> - *Schedules copying activities according to due date and size of job.*
> - *Prepares copies utilizing master copy provided by the teacher, returning both to the teacher on schedule.*
> - *Requests retyped or rewritten original when legible copies cannot be produced.*
> - *Utilizes darkening procedures to ensure that copies are legible.*
> - *Enlarges or reduces original when appropriate, to size material to fit the page or to make copies legible.*

This listing of behaviors or activities, put into the context of a job situation in a school, is not a full job description, but a set of specifications for a portion of a job. It represents a clearly assigned task with a service outcome. It does not detail the knowledge and skills needed for operating copying machines but implies such competency as a prerequisite to this pattern of performance. Another set of specifications for operating a copier is required to make that pattern explicit.

Complex professional patterns of behavior are not easily depicted as a simple listing of procedures, steps, or skills. In such instances, the task to be accomplished is specified, subtasks logically involved are indicated, and specific competencies and behaviors are described. Such detailed performance specifications are illustrated in Exhibits 4.1 and 4.2.

EXHIBIT 4.1 Synthesis of Teaching Variables Established by Researchers Relating to Teacher Effectiveness

Variable Names Commonly Used	*Research Sources*
I. ORGANIZES classroom activities by:	
1. *Structuring* plans, procedures, and expectations	1, 9, 10,
2. Making *preparations,* providing materials	1, 9
3. *Organizing* content, groups, and activities	1, 9
4. *Sequencing* events to facilitate learning	1, 9
II. DIRECTS students in learning activities by:	
5. *Communicating* with *clarity* and *specificity*	3, 8, 9,10
6. Maintaining *flexibility* in plans and sequences	1, 3, 8, 10
7. Providing *task orientation*	1, 3, 8, 10
8. *Allocating time* to learning tasks	9, 11
9. *Pacing* activities according to schedule and need	9
III. INTERACTS with students by:	
10. *Praising* and *encouraging* efforts	1, 2, 3, 9
11. *Reinforcing* and supporting accomplishments	1, 3, 9
12. *Cooperating* and *collaborating*	3, 8, 10, 12
13. *Avoiding criticism* and sarcasm	1–3, 10, 11
IV. STIMULATES student interest and engagement by:	
14. Exhibiting *enthusiasm* for content and activity	1, 3, 9, 10
15. Providing a *variety* of activities for learning	1, 8, 9
16. Using games and simulations	5, 7–9
17. Avoiding dull, monotonous routines	1
V. PROMOTES VERBALIZATION in the learning process by:	
18. Arranging for group *discussions*, teacher- and student-led	4, 9, 10
19. Encouraging *spontaneous expression* of ideas	2, 4
20. *Using student-expressed ideas* as lesson content	2, 8
21. Responding to students with *indirectness*	2, 8, 10
22. Using a *variety of questioning* strategies	3, 4, 9–11
23. *Cueing* students to encourage recall	9, 10
24. Providing ample "wait time" for responses	8, 11
VI. PERSONALIZES teaching for individuals by:	
25. *Tutoring individuals* and arranging for peer and cross-age tutoring	6, 9, 10
26. *Guiding* the activities of small groups	
27. *Differentiating* learning objectives	8, 9
28. *Differentiating activities* and expectations	8, 9
29. *Maximizing* academic engaged time	10
30. Differentiating the amount of *time on task*	9

Sources: 1: Ryans, David G. 1960; 2: Flanders, Ned A. 1970; 3: Rosenshine, Barak 1976; 4: Gall, Meredith D. and J. P. Gall 1976; 5: Seidner, Constance J. 1976; 6: Ellson, Douglas 1976; 7: Leifer, Aimee D. 1976; 8: Pearson, Delmer 1980; 9: Harris, Ben M. and J. Hill 1982; 10: Walberg, Herbert J. 1986; 11: Brophy, Jere and T. Good 1986.

EXHIBIT 4.2   Illustration of Competency Specifications as Three Levels of Specificity

Performance Area 1: Businesslike

The teacher is organized, systematic, goal-oriented, and prepared.

The teacher performs in a variety of ways that clearly reflect planning, goal orientation, prioritization, and detailed consideration of relationships between purpose, activity, sequence, materials, delegation, time constraints, and space utilization. In essence, the teacher clearly knows what is intended and facilitates its realization.

1a—Organizes Classroom Activities

The teacher organizes classroom activities to produce a smooth flow of events with minimum confusion or waste of time.

The activities of the classroom are sequenced. Directions are given to facilitate engagement in activities in a clearly understood fashion. Arrangements are made to avoid waste of time with space, materials and assignments, since they have been preplanned. Individuals are given opportunities to move ahead without wasting time. Events are coordinated by the teacher (and others) to ensure quick and easy transitions from one activity to another. On the other hand, activities have been timed to prevent rushing about or hasty actions.

The teacher—

1a(1) Gives directions for shifting from one activity to another with clarity and simplicity.
    (a) Students are given private directions and assistance, if needed, when others need not be concerned.
    (b) The attention of the student group is secured before giving directions for change.
    (c) Directions are kept brief and only essential details verbalized.
    (d) Individuals who appear confused or reluctant to respond are given prompt, personal attention.

1a(2) Initiates changes in activity for individuals who are ready while others are still busy with prior assignments.
    [(a) through (g) not shown]

1a(3) Arranges all materials for easy distribution as needed during the activity.
    [(a) through (g) not shown]

1a(4) Makes prompt use of supplemental activities of plans modifications to ensure full use of all available time.
    [(a) through (f) not shown]

1a(5) Organizes and directs clerical and housekeeping chores to prevent waste of time by teacher and students.
    [(a) through (e) not shown]

*Adapted from Ben M. Harris and Jane Hill, 1982. *Developmental Teacher Education Kit* (DeTEK). Austin, TX: Southwest Educational Developmental Laboratory.

Job descriptions generally identify only the most important tasks assigned to a person in a position. They are highly abbreviated descriptions and rarely detail the competencies required. For recruitment and general communications they serve very well (Redfern 1984), but the dangers involved in using such descriptions without more explicit job analysis and competency detail are serious. Salary determinations, performance evaluations, selection decisions, and staff development activities all require more detailed description.

Uses of Competency Specifications

Personnel Selection

The discriminating selection of personnel requires that needed competencies be identified and that persons possessing those competencies be recruited and chosen. Although it is true that organizational requirements are sometimes such that a candidate's "promise" or "potential" for outstanding performance becomes the main criterion, the question still arises: What is the candidate able to do that indicates "promise" or "potential"? Normally, however, serious consideration of a school's purposes and an assessment of need in relation to those purposes will suggest that certain competencies have high priority and should be diligently sought.

Job descriptions and screening procedures often are *not* clearly keyed to competencies. Obviously, some criteria, such as intelligence, academic aptitude, and knowledge of subject material to be taught are important, even though not given top priority in competency form. However, job descriptions should clearly identify competency areas, if not specific competency requirements. Interviews, letters, and rating forms employed for gathering selection data should all be explicit in estimating competence. This stipulation may necessitate the use of alternate forms that reflect various competencies for different positions to guide the data-gathering process.

Profile analysis techniques are especially useful for matching individual applicants to positions (Owen 1984). Profiles are compiled using interviews, transcripts, recommendations, demonstrations, and other data sources. However, personnel must be guided by clearly specified competencies when the data are secured and again when scoring such information on a profile (Pigford 1989).

Even when promising persons must be selected without attention to a full array of competencies, as in the case of minority candidates or women who are not readily available on a "fully qualified" basis, *basic* competencies should be specified to allow for the development of new competence with experience and in-service training. The "most-qualified-candidate" concept and traineeships can still be based on explicit competency analyses.

Training and Retraining

Too many training programs are based on the trainers' satisfaction or convenience, rather than on the trainees' goal-related needs. The sensible strategy is to decide what purposes to achieve, to state the competencies needed to achieve the purposes, to select personnel having the competencies, if possible, and to design programs to produce the competencies still needed.

The improvement of performance of personnel is so dependent on clearly defined tasks and competencies that entire chapters on personnel evaluation and staff development focus on these relationships. However, it is also important to consider the role of competency specifications as a vehicle for clarifying ideas and giving real meaning to terms like *quality* and *excellence*.

Task specifications do not change dramatically with new technology or social, economic, and educational developments; hence, competency specifications can and should set high standards for performance, thus serving to guide preservice and in-service training or retraining of high-quality personnel over extended periods of time.

Competency specifications such as those illustrated in Exhibit 4.2 are especially useful in planning for the training, retraining, and upgrading of performances of individuals because they make explicit the behaviors desired. This helps the employee understand what is to be learned and helps superiors to focus on planning training opportunities most helpful to each individual.

Assignment and Reassignment

The assignment and reassignment of personnel are additional responsibilities that could well be based on the competency approach. It seems obvious that the most rational way to match people with work is to try to find people who can do what the job requires. Yet we often see assignments that seem to have been based on "good-old-boy-ism," seniority, administrative convenience, personal preference, or blind faith.

Competency specifications are useful for matching people to job assignments under a broad array of conditions. *New teachers* have special problems because of their inexperience and lack of familiarity with the school and the district, but they also have unique strengths and needs that should be addressed as assignments are made (Bunker 1975).

Reassignments of personnel can build morale, broaden perspectives, and enhance the skills of individual employees by improving the balance of competencies in a school, program, or office. Such changes involve a matching between what the individual brings to the new situation and what he or she can gain from it (Coil 1984).

Promotions to positions such as lead teacher, assistant principal, or department head require careful attention to matching personnel competence to the needs of the job as specified in competency terms (Moore, K. W. 1988).

A special application of the competency approach to assigning personnel is called for when working teams are organized. The orchestration of competencies possessed by two or more people can produce results that some people could never attain by working individually. A special project staff can readily be created with a full array of competencies specified and staff applicants reviewed to determine the "best fit." A spectrum of competency criteria permits the screening and selection of volunteers to form well-balanced teams.

New forms of work organization can be developed to enrich individuals' jobs and produce more effective operations, greater job satisfaction, and a stronger sense of affiliation (Grootings et al. 1989; Howarth 1984). It is no longer wise to conceive of each job as a one-person assignment; rather, teams, work groups, task groups, and other organizing concepts can be used, with the help of competency-based analyses (Gustavsen and Hethy 1989). For example, teaching teams composed of aides, volunteer parents, student teachers, interns, and fully qualified teachers may be employed. Job sharing among two or three highly qualified individuals who are not available or affordable on a full-time basis is another possibility.

In the *amplified project team* approach to the implementation of new programs and projects, proposed by Harris, demanding staffing requirements are served by matching competence to specific portions of a job and utilizing a team of carefully chosen personnel (1985, 136–43). The staffing follows the phases of the implementation process. Hence, a broader array of specialized competencies can be utilized, work load can be spread over more individuals, and a broader base of involvement is provided.

Performance Evaluation

If needed competencies serve as the basis for selecting, training, and assigning personnel, it is logical that the same competencies should be the basis for evaluating performance. For example, if an instructional supervisor is expected to plan in-service training programs that are clearly related to purposes of the school system, then the evaluation of that supervisor's performance should include the processes and products of such planning.

Subsequent sections of this chapter discuss performance specifications of special significance for individuals in teaching and in administrative or supervisory positions. Evaluations that are effective for improving performance in these positions must be formative and diagnostic in nature (Harris 1986, 18, 156; McGreal 1983). Each position requires detailed sets of carefully specified competencies that may also need to be tailored to the individual.

The clear identification of *generic competencies* for teachers or principals still leaves open the question of priorities, which may be quite different for different individuals in different settings. *Diagnostic evaluation* goes beyond a survey of problems and concerns to focus on strengths and the details of specific needs for improvement (Harris 1989, 121–23). These efforts must be guided by highly detailed competency specifications. *Diagnostic feedback* can guide on-the-job improvement efforts, situations in which time is scarce and the context of the job offers the best opportunity for improvement.

Summative evaluations often rely on the availability of an extensive array of evidence, even if detailed specifications are not utilized. In schools, some tasks lend themselves to results-oriented evaluation. This is not always the case in the humane professions where complex, specialized performances still result in mixed outcomes: people die even with the finest medical treatment; outstanding lawyers lose some cases; program administrators and supervisors experience some failures; and not all students learn all that is intended, even under the tutelage of the finest teacher. Summative decision making about the overall competence and worth of a particular employee is still necessarily a process of specifying the best known practices and comparing actual performance to such standards.

Salary Determinations

There is a growing interest in applying business management approaches to school personnel to establish salary classifications. Where appropriate, similar approaches can be utilized in school settings, involving job evaluations (Manese 1988). Specialists in this field recommend identifying the major duties of a position and assigning the percentage of time devoted to each duty (Aft 1985, 55–66). Manese describes a job classification/evaluation approach involving four components (22):

1. Describing and documenting the work.
2. Determining the compensable factors.
3. Determining how much of the work involves compensable factors.
4. Translating the results into wages.

As logical as this appears to be, it is also full of complications. Describing and documenting the work is essentially what we advocate in this chapter as specifying competencies. However, determining compensable factors and translating the results into wages are largely subjective acts.

If such job evaluation procedures have merit in certain educational contexts, their utility and acceptance will depend primarily on the rigor with which competency specifications were detailed in advance. Vague descriptions of duties such as "filing," "processing transcripts," or "assisting with the purchase of supplies" would surely not suffice (Aft 1985, 57).

Salary determinations based on rigorous analysis of very detailed descriptions of performance expectations have promise for more rational and fair wage differentials. Currently, much consideration is given to titles, formal schooling, years of experience, and external wage patterns, but these factors have little direct relationship to competence, responsibility, scarcity, or value-added economics. Substantial improvements in performance specifications can contribute substantially to the quality of differential salary determinations.

Teaching Competencies

Research on teaching has not always provided clear answers to questions about effective teaching practices. Such questions are at the core of good personnel administration. Despite much that is not clearly understood, the research, theory, and professional consensus of the past few decades provide many clear notions regarding the relationship of teaching behavior to student learning (Gage 1985; Gage and Berliner 1989; Kleine 1982, 1929; Mitzel 1983; Rosenshine 1976; Scriven 1990; Walberg 1986; Wittrock 1986). Kleine's 1982 statement is overly cautious compared to syntheses of researchers supported by practitioners in recent years: "The vigorous research on teacher effectiveness . . . has yielded a small but growing number of firm connections between reasonably well defined teacher behaviors and pupil outcomes. . . . "

It is on the basis of extensive, if imperfect, research that practitioners can proceed with due caution to specify desirable teaching practices and utilize carefully detailed descriptions of such practices for teacher selection, assignment, balancing, evaluation, and staff development purposes.

Despite the growing interest in other aspects of teaching, the substantial base of understanding of teaching behavior as generic practice can and should be utilized.

Other aspects of teaching practice may well become more important in the future as the research on thought processes (Clandinin 1986; Clarke and Patterson 1990; Elbaz 1983), knowledge bases for teaching (Leinhardt 1990; Shulman 1986; Stodolsky 1988), creative artistry (Eisner 1985), and a host of other perspectives (Glatthorn 1990, 106–16) associated with the complicated business of teaching become more clearly understood. For the present, however, the most useful and highly reliable tools for improving teaching in the classroom can be based on teacher effectiveness research findings (Pittman and Slate 1989, 45), combined with the wisdom of thoughtful, experienced practitioners.

Generic Teaching Competencies

Research suggesting highly generic teaching behaviors extends at least from the work of Ryans (1955), who established clearly distinguishable behavior patterns common to both elementary and secondary school teachers. The extensive studies over more than a decade, utilizing Flanders's (1970) interaction analysis categories of verbal bahavior in the classroom, demonstrated both the generic character of verbal interaction across levels and subjects and the relationship of selected behavior patterns to student learning (Soar and Soar 1976). The more recent studies of many researchers have become almost repetitious in supporting relationships between twenty to thirty generic behaviors and wide varieties of student learnings (Brophy and Good 1986; Dunkin and Biddle 1974; Gage 1984; Harris 1986; Medley et al. 1984; Wittrock 1986). Exhibit 4.3 presents a synthesis of some of these

EXHIBIT 4.3   Illustration of Competency Specifications at Multiple Levels of Specificity

---

Performance Area IA: Recognizes and Respects Students
   General descriptor: The teacher recognizes and shows respect for each student's individuality, ability, worth, and dignity.

Descriptive paragraph:
   The teacher recognizes that each student is an individual whose learning style and needs must be considered when planning learning experiences. The teacher recognizes the positive relationship between a student's self-concept and his/her ability to achieve. The teacher values and builds upon any abilities which students reveal recognizing the worth of all students regardless of capabilities. The teacher strives to provide emotional support to all students, refraining from imposing or supporting feelings of guilt. The teacher strives to meet needs of students, offering dignity and self-respect to all.

Behavior IA-1: The teacher gives recognition to each student as a worthy and uniquely different person whose learning style and needs are carefully considered in planning and implementing lessons and units of instruction.

Indicator of Illustrative Events:
   IA-1 (a): The teacher verbalizes his/her belief in students as worthy individuals.
   • Responds to students' ideas in positive, praising terms.
   • Avoids using sarcastic remarks toward individuals or the class group.
   • Discusses interesting ideas or products of individual students before the class.
   • Accepts and makes direct use of students' ideas in developing the content of the lesson.
   • (Other?)
   IA-1 (b): The teacher openly and objectively refers to differences among individual students, accentuating the positive, avoiding invidious comparisons, and identifying differences as strengths.
   • Mentions creative talents of individual student when relevant to classroom events.
   • Explains preferences given to certain students in terms of their unique "needs" or strengths.
   • Asks students to verbalize their special interests, abilities, and needs.
   • Openly refers to ethnic, religious, and cultural differences among students, faculty, and other citizens.

Source: Ben M. Harris. 1986. *Developmental Teacher Evaluation.* Boston: Allyn and Bacon, p. 93.

researcher-reported findings with practitioner judgments. Over the past thirty years, thirty teaching variables have been identified as supported by two or more research reviewers. They seem to fall into six patterns of teaching practice.

Performance specifications for practical utilization of generic behaviors have suffered from the abuses discussed earlier in this chapter as well as from the inconsistent, sometimes strange language used by researchers. To be truly useful for communicating to a wide audience of policy-makers, administrators, supervisors, parents, teacher educators, evalua-tors, curriculum specialists, trainers, and, of course, teachers themselves, specifications of teaching behaviors must be both explicit and descriptive of readily observable events. The thirty variables synthesized in Exhibit 4.3 are, therefore, only a beginning framework for more systematic detailing of performance.

Competency Explication

Utilizing a category system developed originally by Dodl (1972), Harris and Burks (1982) identified more than one thousand descriptors of good teach-ing practice, as perceived and reported in research or practitioner reports. These practices were organized to depict, describe, or give some illustrative meaning to seventy-five competencies within Dodl's seven categories of teaching performance.

The categories of classroom practice reflected in this analysis were not unlike those in common use: assessing student performance, communicat-ing and interacting, implementing instruction, and so on. However, each of the seventy-five competencies was described briefly within a category and explicated as an array of practices. For instance, within category two, relat-ing to planning for instruction, thirteen competencies were designated. Competency 2.01 was described as "developing and using curriculum guides and lesson plans." This brief statement was explicated with eighteen behaviors or indicators, such as:

> Has lessons well planned
> Utilizes text as only one resource
> Sequences activities logically

The explication of such brief competency statements as more specific behaviors or indicators of teaching practice is still rather general in nature. In Exhibit 4.1, one of twenty-two categories of teaching practice is shown in explicated form. The category itself is described in a narrative, then one of five competency statements is detailed in narrative form and specific behaviors are explicated for each competency. This rather elaborate use of narrative description at each of three levels of explication is utilized in the

DeTEK system developed by Harris and Hill (1982) as 6 performance areas, 22 behaviors, and 101 indicators.

Other Formats

A somewhat more elaborate format for explicating an array of generic behaviors is illustrated in Exhibit 4.2. What makes this format unique is the use of fairly elaborate descriptions of behavior at each level of specificity. Each behavior is described in more detail than in Exhibit 4.1, and indicators are explicated as "illustrative events." Such four-level explications help to reveal the complexities inherent in a pattern of teaching practice. They also provide vivid mental images of the forms the desired behaviors can take and offer some safeguards against mechanistic or overly simplistic uses of the criteria.

Competency specifications explained in such elaborate detail may appear overwhelming to those familiar only with simple listings of very abbreviated competencies. For instance, performance criteria widely utilized by school districts in the past for teacher evaluation have often designated only two levels—ten to twelve general categories, explicated by a few indicators—with little detailing of actual events at either level (Baltimore City Public Schools 1980; DeKalb County Schools 1975; Denver Public Schools 1971; Texas Education Agency 1985). These appealingly brief lists of competencies are seriously lacking in the ability to communicate explicitly about performance.

In sharp contrast to too much simplicity and brevity in identifying teaching practices is the list developed by Pearson (1980) on the basis of a rigorous review of the research and professional literature and a field validation study involving teachers and administrators. Eighty behaviors were identified, which effectively discriminate between outstanding teachers and others. Appendix D provides a list of Pearson's most discriminating behaviors, organized into eight general categories.

The DeTEK Performance Criteria developed by Harris and Hill (1982) and field-tested in diagnostic sessions with teachers, students, and observers are shown in Appendix A. This is a rather complete set of performance specifications for classroom teaching, with an emphasis on generic teaching practices. Non-classroom behaviors of teachers are not included in the DeTEK system, nor are specialized behaviors that might be important in certain situations.

Leadership Competencies

The many lists of leadership competencies that have been developed in recent years range from collections of opinions having no visible means of support to well-developed statements backed by painstaking research and validation efforts. The authors draw upon their experience with the development of leadership competencies to illustrate the kind of effort that is required to produce worthwhile competency statements in several fields.

Competencies of Principals

Concern for the capabilities of school principals has persisted in various forms since the 1950s at least, when the Kellogg Foundation made large grants to various universities to promote both in-service training and improved graduate preparation. The University Council on Educational Administration devoted much of its energies in the 1960s to studies and proposals for improving the principalship. The emphasis on performance-based competency "programming" for school administrators continued to gain much attention into the 1970s (Craigmile and Kerr 1974; Culbertson et al. 1974; Hilston 1970; Wochner 1976). Renewed interest in the assessment of principal performance was generated by the Assessment Center Project of the National Association of Secondary School Principals (Hersey 1977). However, the 1980s also produced a dramatic shift in focus from detailing and assessing specific competencies to general "characteristics of principals in effective schools" (Cohen 1983; Hagar and Scarr 1983, 39; Ubben and Hughes 1987, 4–6). Leadership styles have persisted over the years as still another focus on the principalship. This focus was initiated in early studies of the elementary school principal (Hemphill 1964) and was stimulated further by the work of Blake and Mouton (1964) in business training. It has continued to gain attention with the influence of organizational theorists like Reddin (1970) and Hersey and Blanchard (1977).

The NASSP Assessment Center program focuses on the assessment of secondary school principals to predict success in the principalship (Schmitt 1983). The elaborate system of simulations and other activities that is utilized focuses on a set of twelve dimensions (Schmitt and Cohen 1990, 205). Details of the specific skills and behaviors have not been made public because of the summative uses intended for the system, but it is interesting that the twelve major categories and their limited published explications suggest widely applicable human and general leadership skills, rather than those particularly required for success in the principalship. The dimensions include communication, personal motivation, judgment, and sensitivity, and the explications, too, are rather general, for example: "Ability to recognize when a group requires direction . . . to effectively interact with a group. . . . "

The University of Washington Assessment Center, under the direction of Dale Bolton, has developed an assessment system focusing on the school principal that is in operation in Seattle. Unlike the NASSP system, this system includes explications of an extensive array of competencies and skills explicitly related to the tasks of the school principal. Simplified activities and scoring procedures have been developed to minimize

EXHIBIT 4.4   Illustration of Castleberry's Explication of Principal Behaviors

---

Category: *Evaluation, Planning, and Development of Curriculum and Instruction*

The Principal—

(1) Analyzes information and issues before decisions are made about curriculum and instruction. (2) Influences the direction of planning among both colleagues and outside groups. (3) Involves teachers as collaborators in formative teacher evaluation. (4) Involves teachers in the evaluation of the programs. (5) Establishes a plan for continuous evaluation of curriculum and instruction. (6) Provides for both short- and long-range curriculum planning.

Evaluation Behaviors:

Collects, organizes, analyzes, and interprets data concerning the performance of students

Designs reliable and valid evaluative procedures for identifying both strengths and weaknesses in existing curricula

Involves teachers in the evaluation of programs

Establishes a plan for continuous evaluation of curriculum and instruction

Involves teachers as collaborators in all aspects of formative teacher evaluation

Planning Behaviors:

Analyzes information and issues before decisions are made about curriculum or instruction

Provides both short-range and long-range curriculum planning

Influences the direction of planning among both colleagues and outside groups

Sets priorities with regard to the curriculum

Developmental Behaviors:

Guides the development of instructional units to implement unique goals and objectives

Supervises the instructional staff in the development of curriculum

Supervises the instructional staff in the implementation of curriculum

---

Adapted from Castleberry, Judy M. 1983.*"Development of a Forced-Choice Principal Behavior Rating Scale"*, Unpublished doctoral dissertation, Austin, TX: The Univ. of Texas at Austin

time and personnel requirements. Furthermore, this system is primarily formative and diagnostic; hence, it could have more general uses, such as personnel recruitment, assignment, and improvement purposes.

Castleberry's Principal's Behavior Profile has one of the most useful sets of performance criteria for the principalship (Exhibit 4.4). A forced-choice set of ninety-six principal behaviors is used to explicate eight categories of performance (Castleberry 1983, 209–13). An original array of 194 descriptors and 156 teachers and administrators was used to validate the behaviors for discriminating between effective and less effective principals. The final set of discriminating behaviors includes twelve in each of eight categories, as illustrated in Exhibit 4.4. The categories that explicitly relate to the work of the school principal:

Community services and relations
Evaluation, planning, and development of curriculum
Financial management
Personnel improvement
Pupil personnel administration
Research and development: innovation and change
School plant management

Competencies of Instructional Supervisors

The work of instructional supervisors has tended to be neglected even more than that of the principal. The numerous titles conferred on central office, intermediate unit, and state- and county-level supervisors has complicated efforts to identify clearly tasks, competencies, and skills for these positions. The largely illusory distinctions between the work and capabilities of "curriculum workers," supervisors, and subject specialists have postponed the reaching of a consensus and discouraged research on supervisory practices. Harris (1963) was among those who proposed a set of tasks of instructional improvement as a framework within which the performance expectations of a variety of supervisory positions could be explicated (Exhibit 4.5). These ten task areas were explicated as thirty-six tasks or competencies and later specified in greater detail as eighty competencies to provide a job description for a director of secondary education (Harris 1985, 325–32). In a partial validation study by Bailey (1985), an extensive array of explicit behaviors were utilized to determine acceptance of competencies in just five task areas. Harris' Developmental Supervisory Competency Assessment System (1980) contains explications of 237 behaviors in all 36 tasks. An example of a single task explicated in detail follows.

Task Area A—Developing Curriculum

   Designing or redesigning that which is to be taught, by whom, when, where, and in what pattern. Developing curriculum guides, establishing standards, planning instructional units, and instituting new courses are examples.

Task A-2—Designing Instructional Units

   The supervisor can design instructional units that specify performance objectives, instructional sequences, a variety of appropriate teaching/learning activities, materials, and evaluative procedures.

1. *Writes statements of performance objectives at varying levels of complexity to guide sequencing of activities and selecting materials for a unit.*
2. *Selects, describes, and sequences a variety of instructional activities for ensuring active involvement by all students in the learning process.*
3. *Designs tests for instructional units that relate to objectives and assess both cognition and application.*
4. *Selects and describes a rationale for the strategy on which an instructional unit is developed.*

EXHIBIT 4.5   Abbreviated List of Professional Supervisory Competencies©

A. *Developing Curriculum*
   A-1   Setting instructional goals
   A-2   Designing instructional units
   A-3   Developing and adapting curricula

B. *Providing Materials*
   B-1   Evaluating and selecting learning materials
   B-2   Producing learning materials
   B-3   Evaluating the utilization of learning resources

C. *Providing Staff for Instruction*
   C-1   Developing a staffing plan
   C-2   Recruiting and selecting personnel
   C-3   Assigning personnel

D. *Organizing for Instruction*
   D-1   Revising existing structures
   D-2   Assimilating programs
   D-3   Monitoring new arrangements

E. *Relating Special Pupil Services*
   E-1   Analyzing and securing services
   E-2   Orienting and utilizing special personnel
   E-3   Scheduling services
   E-4   Evaluating the utilization of services

F. *Arranging for In-service Education*
   F-1   Supervising in a clinical mode
   F-2   Planning for individual growth
   F-3   Designing in-service training sessions
   F-4   Conducting in-service training sessions
   F-5   Training for leadership roles
   F-6   Assessing needs for in-service education
   F-7   Developing a master plan
   F-8   Writing a project proposal
   F-9   Designing a self-instructional packet
   F-10 Designing a training Program

G. *Developing Public Relations*
   G-1   Informing the public
   G-2   Involving the public
   G-3   Utilizing public opinion

H. *Providing Facilities for Instruction*
   H-1   Developing educational specifications
   H-2   Planning for remodeling
   H-3   Outfitting a facility

I. *Evaluating Instruction*
   I-1   Observing and analyzing teaching
   I-2   Designing a questionnaire
   I-3   Interviewing in depth
   I-4   Analyzing and interpreting data

ASCD's Supervisory Practices Study provides the most recent and most comprehensive effort to define current practice and scholarly consensus. Under the direction of Pajak (1986), a nationwide survey of over one thousand outstanding supervisors was completed. Twelve dimensions of supervisory practice were verified and detailed as skills.

The twelve dimensions are shown in Exhibit 4.6, along with the percentage of practitioners and scholars who agreed that the dimensions are important to the work of outstanding supervisors. In only two cases did the respondents disagree. Further support for the acceptance of these general categories as a valid framework for detailing competencies is reflected in their coverage in half or more of the eighteen scholarly works Pajak analyzed.

Executive-Level Competencies

The reality of leadership in local school districts for sixteen thousand superintendents and their assistants is one of the nation's best kept secrets.

EXHIBIT 4.6 Dimensions of Supervisory Practice Supported by Pajak's Study

	Percentage of Agreement	
Dimensions of Practice	*Practitioners* *(n=1,075)*	*Scholars* *(n=18)*
Communications	89	67
Staff Development	88	83
Instructional Program	86	67
Planning and Change	83	78
Motivating and Organizing	80	83
Observation and Conferencing	77	94
Curriculum	73	67
Problem Solving and Decision Making	73	55
Service to Teachers	72	78
Personal Development	71	55
Community Relations	64	50
Research and Program Evaluation	57	72

Source: Pajak, Edward, 1986. "Identification of Supervisory Proficiencies Project." Athens, GA; University of Georgia, and Pajak, Edward, 1989. "A Report on the Nationwide Survey of Outstanding Supervisors and University Professors." A paper presented at the Annual Meeting of the Council of Professors of Instructional Supervision, at Pennsylvania State University, (November 10–12).

Despite a few blind political attacks, such as a high government official's recent references to "the administrative blob," there is a growing interest in the approximately fifty thousand executives who direct the nation's third largest enterprise—public elementary and secondary education.

Interest in the superintendency, the administrative team, and the superintendency team has surfaced in scholarly circles from time to time over the past forty years (American Association of School Administrators 1971; Fensch and Wilson 1964; Halpin 1959). However, the central staff executive functions, tasks, competencies, and skills have usually been subsumed under studies of school administration as though administrative practices in all positions were similar if not identical (Blumberg 1989).

Recent studies of school superintendents have been numerous in comparison with earlier decades. Boles (1975) refocused on the concept of the administrative team, but it was Cunningham and Henges (1982) who stimulated new interest in the superintendency among practitioners. Hoyle et al. (1990) focused their study on the position of the local district superintendent. This was followed by studies of roles and functions of superintendents (Sclafani 1987; Peterson et al. 1987), career patterns (Burnham 1989), critical problems and issues (Kennedy 1989), and many others.

The Executive Leadership Program in Texas has undertaken a series of studies and development efforts focusing on executive performance, going beyond the single position of the superintendent and emphasizing instructional leadership. With funding from the Meadows Foundation, the American Association of School Administrators, and the Danforth Foundation, this program has been explicating instructional leadership competencies to guide research and training and to provide a framework for diagnostic assessment of executives in various high-level positions in public schools.

An AASA-sponsored consortium of universities and professional associations* developed a comprehensive framework for examining and improving the work of school executives. Six domains of knowledge and skill were identified as:

1. General education
2. Instructional leadership
3. Administrative leadership

*The consortium involved scholars and practitioners from AASA, New England School Development Council, California School Administrators Association, Arizona State University, Iowa State University, University of Pittsburgh, and the University of Texas at Austin.

4. Human/interpersonal leadership
5. Personal capabilities
6. Multicultural perspectives

The instructional leadership domain was the focus of the Executive Leadership Program. Initially, five task areas were identified within this one domain. These were explicated as forty-two specific instructional leadership tasks. Following exhaustive reviews of the literature and a series of field studies by practitioners and scholars, validations were undertaken. Finally, each of the forty-two tasks was systematically explicated as subtasks and competencies. Exhibit 4.7 provides an example of the logical reduction process utilized for the explication of each task.

More rigorous validation studies are still in progress (Harris and Wilson 1990; Hord 1990) in efforts to assure practitioners and the public that the work of school executives is well described.

Appendix C provides a complete list of abbreviated task and subtask statements for all five task areas for instructional leadership. A complete listing of all performance criteria for executive instructional leadership is in press (Harris and Wan 1992).

Validation of the instructional leadership task statements by Hord (1990) analyzed both self-reports of 102 executives and reports by their colleagues. Both importance ratings and estimates of individual capability were studied. Exhibit 4.8 on page 84 lists the most important tasks, as reported by both the executives and their colleagues. While all of the forty-two tasks are supported by relatively high importance ratings, the highest and most consistently rated tasks tend to fall in the area of instructional planning and organizing for instruction.

Common and Specialized Competencies

In personnel selection, job descriptions include both common and specialized competencies. For example, a personnel department may want as a common competency in all school principals the ability to lead a constituency in setting goals for the school and, as a specialized competency, the ability to converse fluently in Spanish in order to communicate with people in a particular attendance area. Other personnel would need to possess such competence too. An instructional supervisor called upon to engage in curriculum development in communities with Spanish-speaking patrons and the team leader in a team-teaching endeavor that was a pilot for a multicultural education program would also need such competence.

Problems stemming from the specification of both common and specialized competencies plague the preservice training, selection, assignment, in-service training, and evaluation of school personnel. The problems inherent in the training—especially preservice training—of personnel for both

EXHIBIT 4.7   The Logical Reduction of a Leadership Domain to Tasks, Subtasks, and Competencies

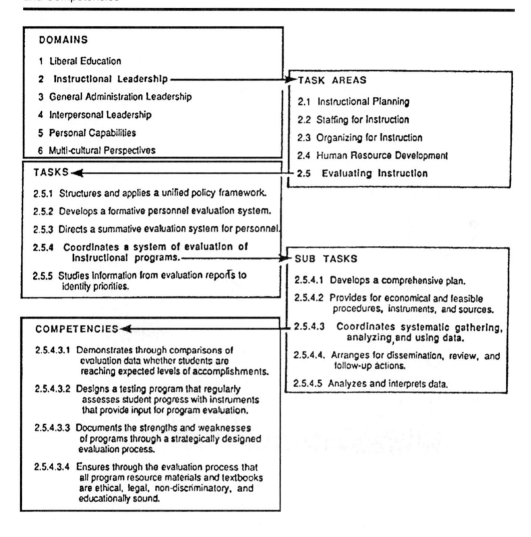

DOMAINS

1 Liberal Education

2 Instructional Leadership

3 General Administration Leadership

4 Interpersonal Leadership

5 Personal Capabilities

6 Multi-cultural Perspectives

TASK AREAS

2.1 Instructional Planning

2.2 Staffing for Instruction

2.3 Organizing for Instruction

2.4 Human Resource Development

2.5 Evaluating Instruction

TASKS

2.5.1 Structures and applies a unified policy framework.

2.5.2 Develops a formative personnel evaluation system.

2.5.3 Directs a summative evaluation system for personnel.

2.5.4 Coordinates a system of evaluation of Instructional programs.

2.5.5 Studies information from evaluation reports to identify priorities.

SUB TASKS

2.5.4.1 Develops a comprehensive plan.

2.5.4.2 Provides for economical and feasible procedures, instruments, and sources.

2.5.4.3 Coordinates systematic gathering, analyzing, and using data.

2.5.4.4. Arranges for dissemination, review, and follow-up actions.

2.5.4.5 Analyzes and interprets data.

COMPETENCIES

2.5.4.3.1 Demonstrates through comparisons of evaluation data whether students are reaching expected levels of accomplishments.

2.5.4.3.2 Designs a testing program that regularly assesses student progress with instruments that provide input for program evaluation.

2.5.4.3.3 Documents the strengths and weaknesses of programs through a strategically designed evaluation process.

2.5.4.3.4 Ensures through the evaluation process that all program resource materials and textbooks are ethical, legal, non-discriminatory, and educationally sound.

common and specialized competencies are formidable. Training institutions seldom know the specific situations into which their graduates will go, nor do they usually know what the job requirements, expectations, or even job titles will be, since these tend to vary widely from one employer

EXHIBIT 4.8 Executives' Tasks of Instructional Leadership Rated Highest in Importance

Task Number	Abbreviated Task Statements	Task Area	Importance Ratings*	Capability Estimates**
1	Identifies federal and state curriculum mandates related to the local district	Instructional planning	8.4	42
3	Understands instructional design	Organizing instruction	8.6	34
4	Exhibits a positive attitude toward staff development	Human resource development	8.7	47
8	Establishes priorities among the district's instructional goals	Organizing instruction	8.6	71
11	Ensures that goals and objectives satisfy the needs of the community	Instructional planning	8.7	67
16	Supervises . . . and updates goals to ensure the philosophy is served	Instructional planning	8.5	64
21	Promotes the development and acceptance of a sound educational philosophy	Instructional planning	8.6	53
23	Develops goals and objectives guided by the district's philosophy	Organizing instruction	8.4	35
33	Monitors student achievement through feedback from program evaluations	Organizing instruction	8.6	46
35	Ensures that curricular needs of all student populations are met	Instructional planning	8.4	45
36	Maintains a system of instructional improvement that seeks to upgrade student learning	Organizing instruction	8.5	40

*Mean importance ratings for both executives and colleagues on ten-point scale.
**Percentage of all possible choices on a forced-choice inventory as most clearly descriptive of capabilities of individual executives.

to another. Hence, specialized competencies tend to be ignored in the educational training process in favor of common ones, or are taught at a superficial knowledge-awareness level without being developed to the level of application.

In-service training gains enormous significance in school operations because of the very problems being discussed. Personnel must be selected and assigned largely on the basis of general competencies, and the employer must rely on in-service programs to develop the unique pattern of specialized competencies needed in a given assignment.

Recruitment and selection tasks need to be approached realistically, without expectations for specialized competency among applicants that cannot be met or can be met only at a great sacrifice. More commonly, recruitment and selection procedures overemphasize specialized competencies to the neglect of common ones or of even basic personal characteristics that may be of overwhelming importance. The teacher employed because of competence in diagnostic-prescriptive approaches to teaching reading whose human relations skills are such that no parent, child, or staff group can work with him or her effectively represents a poor selection decision. The counselor employed because of highly developed competence in personal, therapeutic counseling techniques who has no capacity for working in group settings may be less useful than another counselor with a lower level of one competence and more of the other. The librarian with enormous competence in cataloging, selecting, and organizing library resources who rails against the instructional-media-center concept may be a detriment, on balance, to the school's program.

Assignment and reassignment decisions also must be made with due attention to both common and specialized competencies. If an assignment request urgently calls for a particular specialized competency, then a broader view of competence possessed by the assignee is not essential. However, as conditions change, such a specialized assignment may no longer be appropriate, and reassignment will be in order. Now, if we begin to stereotype personnel as "specialists" or "generalists" or as "math teacher," "counselor," or "primary teacher," we may be creating problems for the program and denying people opportunities to exercise the assortment of talents nearly all possess.

The evaluation of personnel or program tasks is greatly influenced, or should be, by the common *and* specialized competencies required and provided in a given program or job assignment. A teacher who has been assigned to a team to assure media competence as a specialized resource within that team cannot fairly be evaluated as an individual on a broad spectrum of competency criteria. In such instances, the team is the better unit for evaluative analysis to ensure that the sum of competences being demonstrated, in fact, does suffice to produce an effective teaching-learning situation. Curiously, however, this method makes it difficult to ensure accountability. Unless the team is a well-integrated one with clearly accepted, differentiated, and shared responsibilities, deficiencies are likely to be ignored and regarded as someone else's problem.

The best of all possible worlds would provide a school with a full array of personnel, each with a complete range of both common and specialized competencies. Such a world is not likely to emerge; hence organizational arrangements permitting more flexible use of competences in the least restrictive contexts are most promising. The least restrictive alternative in staff personnel work calls for giving top priority to the basic personal characteristics of intelligence, empathy, emotional stability, drive, and energy reserve, as well as to a variety of common competences during the processes of recruiting, selecting, assigning, training, and evaluating. Such priorities would tend to ensure acceptable performance levels regardless of changing conditions and to provide the basis for continuing growth and retraining whenever specialized competencies are clearly demanded.

Summary

The concern for competence will not go away, and it should not. In fact, it is and must continue to be the central concern of all who would claim professional status in our schools. Certainly, the entire profession associated with public schools has been shadow-boxing, not really struggling, with the hard realities surrounding concern for competence. Grades, credits, letters of recommendation, years of experience, tests, interviews, and the like have little to offer in the way of predicting performance or certifying competence. This chapter has suggested ways of relating performance expectations to descriptions of competencies.

Initial efforts to specify competencies in systematic ways give clear indications that we can at least communicate more precisely about competency expectations. Assessing competence continues to be a very difficult problem. Personnel administration will be broadening the emphasis from recruitment and selection to assigning, reassigning, balancing, and evaluating personnel in the years ahead. Competency specifications will inevitably become important tools for performing these tasks.

Suggested Study Sources

Cohen, David K. 1988. "Teaching Practice: Plus Que Ça Change . . . " in Phillip W. Jackson, ed., *Contributing to Educational Change: Perspectives on Research and Practice*, Berkeley, CA: McCutchan Publishing.

The author presents a case for being rather skeptical about many change-oriented programs and argues for much more attention to the teaching components of change process.

Gael, Sidney, ed. 1988. *The Job Analysis Handbook for Business, Industry, and Government*. Vol. II. New York: John Wiley & Sons.

This comprehensive reference book depicts numerous aspects of job analysis as promoted in business and government settings. It includes many illustrations of applications as well as technical analysis.

Gage, N.L., and D.C. Berliner. 1989. "Nurturing the Critical, Practical, and Artistic Thinking of Teachers," *Phi Delta Kappan* 71(November):212–14.

Two distinguished researcher-scholars in the field of effective teaching practices argue for teachers who can "intelligently evaluate research . . . ; reconcile [it] with practical knowledge, and use artistry in taking the context into consideration" (212). The exciting comments on teaching as involving critical thinking with research, artistry, and practical thinking are amplified with illustrations from other fields as well as teaching. These scholars also assert that knowledge about teaching is not at all weak by comparison with medicine.

Harris, Ben M. 1986. "Teaching Criteria," chapter 4 in *Developmental Teacher Evaluation*. Boston: Allyn and Bacon.

A systematic analysis of teaching criteria based on research on teaching effectiveness, but also emphasizing theoretical and practical knowledge, is provided in this chapter. Detailed proposals for selecing and specifiy criteria in performance terms are included.

Leinhardt, Gaea. 1990. "Capturing Craft Knowledge in Teaching," *Educational Researcher* 19(March): 18–25.

The author reports on preliminary efforts to define and measure sophisticated teaching practice as part of proposals for "board certification" in teaching. Problems with testing procedures that are not easily supported by "performance verification" are discussed. Many problems are acknowledged relating to "capturing the craft" (p. 23).

Manese, Wilfredo R. 1988. *Occupational Job Evaluation: A Research-Based Approach to Job Classification*. New York: Quorum Books.

This author presents a four-component job classification/evaluation approach as used at Northwestern Bell Telephone. The four components are detailed and logically analyzed. The emphasis on task analysis as the basis for job documentation appears most appropriate in the field of education.

Owen, D.E. 1984. "Profile Analysis: Matching Positions and Personnel," *Supervisory Management* 29(11):14–20.

The author reports on a useful application of job analysis techniques in the selection and assignment of personnel. The profile technique is worth further development.

Pajak, Edward. 1989. *The Central Office Supervisor of Curriculum and Instruction: Setting the Stage for Success*. Boston: Allyn and Bacon.

This book represents one of the few efforts to focus rigorously on the character of central office supervisory practice as it has developed in the last few decades. The author utilizes both theoretical and practical perspectives in reporting on the culture, leadership performance, and service roles of this very diverse group of supervisors.

Richardson, Virginia. 1990. "Significant and Worthwhile Change in Teaching Practice," *Educational Researcher* 19(October):10–18.

In this review of teacher change and learning to teach, the author suggests the need to combine warranted practice based on research and teachers' practical knowledge to promote change in practice. The rationale for such a suggestion is based mostly on change process theory, but it supports the growing interest in "professional wisdom" beyond research.

Sternberg, R.J., and J. Kolligian, Jr. 1990. *Competence Considered*. New Haven, CT: Yale University Press.

These authors review research from various sources on competence and incompetence at various levels—childhood and adult alike. It is one of the few sources dealing with the topic in detail. Distinctions are made, among others, between actual and perceived competence.

Wittrock, Merlin C., ed. 1986. *Handbook of Research on Teaching*. 3d ed. Washington, DC: American Educational Research Association.

This is a most recent and comprehensive volume with numerous articles reviewing many aspects of research on teaching. Chapter 12, by Brophy and Good, relates teaching behavior to student achievement. Walberg attempts a most useful synthesis of research on teaching (214–29).

5

Recruiting Competent Personnel

Undoubtedly the most important influence on the quality of an instructional program is the collective competency of the professional staff, and the recruitment and selection of able personnel are the sine qua non of the development of a competent staff. It is the caliber of the people in a school district, not procedures or handbooks or regulations or curriculum guides, that is the most important tool a district has to work with when seeking to improve (Meek 1988, 15). A mutt cannot be transformed into a show dog, regardless of the training, grooming, and love that are lavished upon it, and neither can basically weak personnel be "in-serviced" out of their ineptitude. The disappointing records of many training programs are probably due as much to limitations in the trainability of the personnel as to inadequacies in training.

Throughout this book the position is taken that educational programs can make a significant difference in shaping the lives of people and that all aspects of those programs should be consistently dynamic, goal-oriented, and humane. A commitment to such purposes carries with it important implications for all the major subsystems of a school district or school, including organizational patterns, facilities, staff development, and the type of personnel recruited and selected. The first four chapters of this text examine the critical topics of assumptions, staff functions, staffing patterns, and competency as these topics relate to the role staffing plays in instructional improvement. The chapters in this section address recruitment, selection, assignment, evaluation, and staff development as specific activities of the personnel staffing function. These activities are depicted in Exhibit 5.1 as a cyclical, ongoing set of multidimensional activities. Each activity logically leads to another, and the success of the each is tied to the success of previous activities. Undeniably, the success of the selection

EXHIBIT 5.1   The Personnel Staffing Function

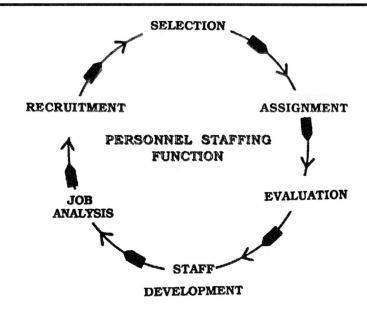

process, discussed in chapter 6, is tied to the success of the recruiting program, because only individuals who have been attracted to the organization and who have actually become applicants are eligible for selection consideration. The caliber and competence of those selected for employment become strong determining factors in the development of performance evaluation and staff development programs. This chapter addresses recruitment of competent personnel as one of the multidimensional and continuous staffing activities affecting the ultimate success of the instructional improvement effort.

As a staffing activity, the recruitment process operates within certain organizational, legal, and financial constraints. The development of a large pool of highly qualified applicants available for selection consideration is the primary goal of the recruitment program. How many applicants are needed and what is meant by *highly qualified* applicants are elements of the recruiting program that must be in harmony with the overall goals established for the personnel staffing function specifically and the total organization, ultimately. The processes related to recruitment of personnel, crucial as they are, constitute only a part of a complex design for instructional improvement. For most significant changes to take place, the whole network of possible modifications in goals, structures, rules, physical facilities, and personnel must be explored and carefully pursued. Changes in only one of these domains can take many forms; for example, personnel changes can be effected through recruitment and selection, assignment or reallocation of duties, in-service, or termination of employment. The point is that while the recruitment and selection of personnel are extremely important processes that, if neglected, will negate most, if not all, other instructional improvement efforts, they should be viewed in the total educational context. The recruiting program, like all subsystems in human resources, derives its direction and impetus from the mission and goals established for the total organization.

Keys to Successful Recruiting

Obviously, only individuals who have been attracted to the organization and who actually become applicants are eligible for selection consideration and hiring. Therefore, the goal of the successful recruiting program is to build a large pool of highly qualified applicants by identifying and attracting them to the organization. If it is not possible to build a large pool of qualified applicants, then personnel selections must be made on the basis of the best available choice. When such choices are made, it is the immediate responsibility of the human resources system to intervene with training and growth opportunities for the individual selected. To do otherwise risks the future of students by exposing them to personnel who have less to offer than the students are entitled to receive. To avoid having to make selections on the basis of "best available" choices, schools must implement an aggressive, ongoing recruiting program to build a desirable applicant pool.

Prior to any attempt to recruit individuals, it is important to determine the type and caliber of applicants desired. It is essential to define tasks through job analysis and determine criteria and predictors of on-the-job success before making contact with potential applicants. The reward of these efforts is the selection of competent personnel who meet the expectations of the organization.

To meet the demands of an ever-changing school population and society, the recruiting program must have financial backing and creative leadership to locate and attract applicants who are not currently being attracted into the profession. Projecting an attitude to individuals, the community, or college placement officials that "we will be in touch when we need you" will surely doom the most aggressive efforts. Short-term efforts in recruiting generally reap short-term benefits. Successful recruitment is a long-term process built on years of effort and commitment. It is a year-round, ongoing process and the shared responsibility of everyone in the organization. Often, satisfied employees are the best recruiters. Remembering that "what is everyone's responsibility is no one's responsibility" reinforces the idea that the recruiting program must be a planned responsibility and must receive leadership.

The keys to successful recruitment include the following: (1) active and creative leadership, (2) financial and philosophical support, (3) implementation of the program in harmony with the overall goals and mission of the organization, (4) analysis of the job requirements and tasks, translated into written documents, prior to any other recruiting efforts, (5) predetermination of criteria and predictors of on-the-job success and use of these data in recruiting, (6) training of recruiters, and (7) an aggressive, ongoing recruiting program that operates throughout the year. Incorporating these into the recruiting program enhances the possibility that each person employed will truly be "selected" from a pool of highly competent and qualified applicants.

Assessing Needs

Prerequisite to any effort to recruit or select personnel should be a serious and deliberate assessment of needs. Unfortunately, in educational institutions this has often been limited to determining the number of people to be employed. This chapter suggests that assessing needs is a multifaceted process involving determination of organization goals and objectives, precise analyses and descriptions of jobs to be filled, and determination of the criteria for successful on-the-job performance. All of these steps are directed and carried out by leaders who have a sense of organizational mission and vision, who know where they want to go and what paths to take to achieve desired outcomes.

Equally important is a commitment to making the process a collaborative one, involving all who have a vested interest in the outcomes. It is appropriate—in fact, essential—that there be widespread involvement of people in the determination of the missions and goals of democratic educational enterprises. The best guarantee of humaneness and concern for people in a school system is the participation of students, parents, professional educators, and others in establishing and continuously monitoring the direction in which the system is going. This of is a responsibility of leadership:

> *The fact is that the people who work in an organization know more about the organization—its problems, concerns, and potential—than any number of planning consultants could possibly know. Beyond that, the local people are just as aware of global issues and circumstances, and are even more particularly sensitive to the impact of those factors on their unique situation. And, certainly, they alone understand all the complexities of local issues. In any school district, the best planning consultants available anywhere are quite often the existing staff. They together with the patrons, community leaders, and students already possess all the answers to the district's future. All they need are direction and impetus—in a word, leadership. (Cook 1988, 94)*

Needs assessment is a systematic way of determining the distance between what an organization is accomplishing and desired accomplishments, of comparing actual results with desired results, for students, educators, and community members. According to Cook (1988), needs assessment involves both internal and external analyses, and requires absolute honesty. Objectivity and forthrightness are essential, since these analyses serve as the prerequisites for developing objectives and strategies that are the heart of any planned improvement effort—the strategic plan. Internal analysis, as defined by Cook, "consists of a thorough, unbiased, tripartite examination of the organization: specifically strengths; weaknesses; and the organizational chart as it reflects function and information flow" (107). External analysis is futuristic in nature and involves the predicting of events and conditions that will occur during a three to five year period and the specific impacts on the organization of these events and circumstances (115).

In an ongoing school system, some identified needs will probably be adequately served without major changes in existing structures or practices; hence, the orderly and efficient maintenance of programs that require only occasional minor adjustments will not occupy much of the time and energy of personnel. One need not apologize for operating a smoothly functioning school or district; in fact, no organization can tolerate too much change, which is inherently disruptive. On the other hand, no organization can serve its clients well for an extended period of time with too little change; therefore, both organizational maintenance and change are recognized as desirable. Personnel may be recruited, selected, and deployed to serve both purposes, and although almost all positions require at least some ability to change as well as to maintain established practices, the emphasis will vary from position to position and from time to time.

Leadership for Change

A need for change, once identified, requires leadership and planning. Buffie (1989) describes the first step in introducing change as a visioning process. Leaders must know what to change and how to bring about that change:

> Visioning. *Both business and education leaders recognize the need for visioning when undertaking any improvement effort. Visioning is that capacity to conceptualize and communicate a desired situation or state of affairs, which induces commitment and enthusiasm. The vision provides the agenda, sets the expectations, and gives a sense of direction for achieving the desired outcomes. One of the most compelling examples of visioning was the Rev. Martin Luther King's "I Have a Dream" speech delivered from the steps of the Lincoln Memorial in 1963. (12)*

Colton (1985) describes vision as that "which establishes goals or objectives for individual and group action, which defines not what we are but rather what we seek to be or do" (33). After studying vision and the role of vision in the life of educational leaders, Sheive and Schoenheit (1987) define vision as "a blueprint of a desired state. It is an image of a preferred condition that we work to achieve in the future" (94). Vision has also been described as a "mental journey from the known to the unknown" (Hickman and Silva 1984, 151) and "the moral imagination that gives an individual the ability to see that the world can change for the better" (Blumberg and Greenfield 1986, 228).

Buffie (1989) describes visioning as a four-step process: (1) visualizing the desired situation, (2) identifying barriers to realizing the desired situation, (3) deciding how to overcome the barriers, and (4) implementing the changes needed to achieve the vision. (12). Sheive and Schoenheit (1987) identified five themes related to visioning that affect the work lives of educational leaders:

> *Valuing*—Each leader's vision is connected to strongly held values
>
> *Reflection*—With the leader's thought that "something is wrong" comes the thought that "I can do something about it"
>
> *Articulation*—The leader shares the vision with others
>
> *Planning*—A vision, by its nature, is a target and requires planning and securing of resources
>
> *Action*—The leader is a doer, since without action visions and plans are useless. (97–100)

In addition, Sheive and Schoenheit found that leaders who are change agents focus on possibilities and are concerned with outcomes (96). In a similar vein, it has been noted that effective leaders (principals) can describe their visions (Rutherford 1985).

Attempts at change are more successful when parents, teachers, and administrators work together. Professional collegiality breaks down barriers between departments and among teachers and administrators (Mace-Matluck 1987, 14). Community involvement and input breaks down barriers between school personnel and the community, which includes parents and others. The recent literature on schooling and education speaks to the value of effective schools, site-based management, teacher empowerment, collaboration, collegial coaching, adult cooperative learning, and community involvement. In a very global sense, all of these terms define efforts to enhance the cooperation between interested parties to bring about change for instructional improvement.

The key argument made here is that determining needs, settings goals and objectives, and creating change to promote instructional improvement cannot be the work of an individual—it must be the collective work of all interested parties. It is critical that the vision of what needs to be changed and the direction to go to accomplish change be a shared vision. Within an organization there are at least four areas that are impacted by every change: (1) the people, (2) the work (tasks), (3) the form of the organization (structure), and (4) how the work is to be done (technology). A determined need for teaching personnel with talents and skills different from those previously sought will inevitably impact on who is employed, how teaching is performed, formal or informal organizational patterns, and the methods with which teaching/learning is accomplished. The second argument made here is that successful recruitment and selection processes emanate from shared vision and the resulting goals established through needs assessment and collaborative planning.

To begin the work of recruiting and selecting personnel for improving and maintaining instructional excellence in schools, needs must be assessed first with respect to the mission and goals of the total organization and then with respect to the particular unit or job assignment, if it is known. The development of meaningful goals derived from the blending of vision, assessed need, collaboration, and leadership provides a solid foundation upon which to build a quality recruitment and selection program.

Job Analysis and Description

Once the system and subsystem organizational mission and goals are set, then jobs should be described in terms specific enough to provide meaningful guidance to recruiters and job holders. Job analysis is a descriptive process employed for the purpose of gathering critical information about a job. Gatewood and Feild (1990) define job analysis as a "purposeful, systematic process for collecting information on the important, work-related aspects of a job" (251). Belcher and Atchison (1987) suggest that organizations, including school districts, may use the information obtained by job analysis for such personnel programs as recruitment, selection, and placement; organizational planning and job design; training; grievance settlement; and job evaluation and other compensation programs (157). The job analysis may be conducted by interviewing incumbents of the job, observing an employee performing the job, administering questionnaires, and a variety of other information-gathering techniques. Information may be gathered from both employees and supervisors. The goal of the job analysis process is to determine the distinct tasks and responsibilities so that the job description may portray a clear picture for the recruiter, the potential employee, and the incumbent.

Two of the products of job analysis, job evaluation and job description, are helpful tools in human resource management. Job evaluation, discussed in Chapter 12, is the process by which wages are assigned. Job descriptions catalog the duties and responsibilities of the position. In education, job descriptions for positions with large numbers of employees—teachers—tend to be broad and vague and those for positions with a single or few employees tend to be more specific. A job description should contain all of the essential information that a prospective employee would need to "size up" the job, including title, qualifications, supervisor, supervision responsibilities, goal, performance responsibilities, terms of employment, and evaluation criteria. "A job description describes the job as it is being performed. In a sense a job description is a snapshot of the job as of the time it was analyzed. Ideally [it is] written so that any reader, whether familiar or not with the job, can 'see' what the worker does, how, and why" (Belcher and Atchison 1987, 175).

Frequently, there is a movement to make job descriptions for teachers very specific. It might be argued, however, that too much specificity in a job description sometimes works to the disadvantage of a school system trying to recruit people with outstanding abilities. In particular, when new positions or programs with unique goals are being staffed, it may be desirable to have new employees define their working relationships after being employed. Recruiting in such cases might better be conceived as seeking "talents" rather than "job applicants." For example, a new, ungraded, mainstreamed teaching approach to special education for handicapped students might best be defined in the planning stages in terms of service delivery goals. It might be advisable not to relate those goals to current positions because traditional patterns might not fit well. Furthermore, a combination of old and new staff competencies might lead to better team work if specific assignments and work relationships are decided after hiring, rather than beforehand.

In any case, it is important to determine the job specifications or essential qualifications the applicant must possess to be eligible for the job. Specifications for teaching and administrative positions usually include requirements such as education level, certification requirements, and experience requirements. In terms of fair employment practices, it is important that these job specifications be job-related and realistic. In the event of a discrimination complaint, the Equal Employment Opportunity Commission (EEOC) uses a test of "content validity" to determine whether discrimination in employment procedures has occurred. This requires demonstrating that the selection procedures represent important aspects of actual performance on the job. The evidence of this job-relatedness is determined by reviewing the job analysis, job specifications, and job description.

The National School Boards Association (NSBA) markets a comprehensive guide for school administrators working in the area of job description development. The *NSBA School Personnel Management System* includes models for nearly 200 different public school positions as part of a total system for developing and revising job descriptions. These model job descriptions were developed using the expertise of school board members, school administrators, personnel specialists and policy consultants. Tools such as this provide the administrator with a starting point for developing and keeping up-to-date the district's job descriptions. The use of such tools, however, should never replace the process of analyzing and studying the job to develop a quality job description. The effort involved in these tasks is worthwhile when the job description becomes "a written document—a blueprint—that profiles the design of the job, which makes the potential usefulness of such a description almost boundless. Every phase of human resources management, from job design through system design, staff, training, and performance control, can be aided with such a description" (Grant 1988, 53).

Predictors and Criteria

An important aspect of job analysis frequently overlooked, especially in educational institutions, is the use of job analysis data for the development of selection measures. As noted by Gatewood and Feild (1990), these data should be used to develop two types of measures: (1) predictors or measures of job applicants used to screen them and forecast who is likely to be a successful employee on a job, and (2) criteria or standards of performance that employees must meet in order to be considered successful on a job (252).

Deciding whom to hire requires the use of both criterion and predictor measures, a process that may be likened to the use of dependent and independent variables in behavioral research. In the research setting, the independent variable is typically used as the predictor and the behavior to be predicted is the dependent variable. For example, if through the job analysis process it is determined that skill in diagnosing student learning needs is an essential element of successful teaching performance, then this diagnostic skill is the behavior to be predicted—the criterion. A criterion, in this case, becomes a way of describing success. The method devised for identifying the level at which applicants possess or perform this skill may be thought of as the independent variable or predictor measure. Predictors are used as means of assessing the criterion. The level at which the applicant must perform this skill to be successful on the job must be predetermined through the job analysis process. The applicant's perceived performance level is then predicted in comparison with the standard required. Ultimately, through performance appraisal, the employed individual's actual performance in relation to the identified skill will be assessed and monitored.

To meet the challenge of selecting competent educators to improve education, a systematic approach should be used in personnel staffing. Recruitment and selection should be preceded by job analysis to develop a thorough understanding of the job and its requirements. The resulting data should be translated into written form: a job description (responsibilities and duties) and job specifications (needed qualifications). It is also necessary to identify criteria for successful on-the-job performance before recruiting and selecting personnel. These should, in turn, become a major portion of the criteria used to evaluate on-the-job performance. Performance evaluation data should feed back into the recruitment and selection activities and should be used in identifying training needs. Frequently, especially in education, a systematic approach has not been used, causing personnel to be recruited using one set of criteria, selected using another set of criteria, and evaluated using a third set of criteria. In such instances, the recruitment program operates in total isolation from the other components of the personnel staffing function, and this significantly weakens the possibility that the recruitment activity will contribute to planned instructional improvement. In the absence of coordinated planning and preparation, the recruiter becomes a hunter shooting randomly at any moving object, instead of a target shooter aiming with precision at the desired target.

Identification and Attraction of Potential Recruits

The next logical step after completing the job analysis and developing a job description and job specifications is to locate applicants to be considered for vacant or future positions. In an environment where the demographics of the workplace and clients served, the professional requirements for personnel, and the availability of personnel for employment is constantly changing, administrators charged with responsibilities for the recruitment and selection activities must learn to "work smart." This implies that the individual must understand the roles personnel play in moving the school system toward its objectives, know the type of personnel needed for each work situation, understand the marketplace, and operate within the context of a well-designed recruitment plan.

Supply and Demand

The supply of certified teachers and administrators follows historical trends reflecting a variety of factors, including birthrates and national emphases on education. Periods of increasing student enrollment heighten the demand for teachers and generally are marked by shortages of available certified personnel, and periods of increased national attention on education are generally marked by a shortage of teachers and administrators in critical areas. Periods of declining student enrollment are generally noted as periods of personnel surpluses. During the 1960s, 1970s, and 1980s, shortages changed to surpluses and changed back to shortages. Severe teacher shortages are anticipated during the 1990s and future decades.

   The potentially critical nature of future teacher shortages is illustrated by projections for the period 1987–1992 that call for the employment of

EXHIBIT 5.2   Teacher Supply—New Teacher Graduates Compared with Demand for Additional Teachers

Year	Estimated Supply of New Teacher Graduates	Estimated Demand for Additional Teachers	Supply as a Percentage of Demand
1970	284,000	208,000	137
1975	238,000	186,000	128
1980	144,000	127,000	113
1985	142,000	170,000	92
1990	139,000	183,000	76

Source: *Projections of Education Statistics to 1992–93.* Washington, DC: National Center for Education Statistics

approximately one and one-half million teachers in U.S. classrooms and, during the same period, training and certification of approximately 650,000 teachers. Obviously, this will create a shortage of considerable magnitude. The long-term continuation of this discrepancy between supply and demand would severely impact efforts to improve education. Exhibit 5.2 compares the estimated supply of new teacher graduates with the total demand for additional teachers for 1970–1990.

Projections related to the need for hiring new teachers are based on anticipated changes in student enrollment, turnover in staff, and changes in teacher/student ratios. As noted by Hawley (1986), developing precise estimates of supply and demand for teachers is problematic, since not enough is known about the magnitude and character of the teacher shortage that is anticipated (712). Critics believe the shortage estimates are exaggerated and alarmist in nature. In response, Hawley points out that for 1983 the National Center for Education Statistics (NCES) estimated there would be a need for 164,000 teachers, and 230,000 teachers were actually hired.

Exhibit 5.3 shows the projected annual demand for new hiring of teachers in elementary and secondary schools for 1990–2000, as projected by the National Center for Education Statistics (1990). The demand for new teachers is projected to exceed 200,000 each year, with the greatest demand at the elementary level. This exhibit also tracks the percentage of change in the projected new hiring of teachers from 1990 to 2000.

In this environment, one of the biggest mistakes that personnel administrators can make is to adopt a passive, hard-to-get, we-don't-really-need-you approach to recruitment. Even in periods marked by large surpluses of personnel, it must be remembered that each time a school district recruits and employs a new staff member, it has an opportunity to improve the quality of the instructional program and to benefit students. Bridges (1986) refers to this as a "window of opportunity" for district improvement. The recruitment and selection process is the vehicle through which windows of opportunity become cornerstones of reality.

EXHIBIT 5.3 Projected Annual Demand for New Hiring of Teachers in Elementary and Secondary Schools: Fall 1990–2000.

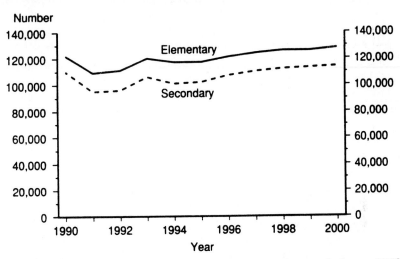

Percent change in the projected new hiring of teachers, relative to 1990

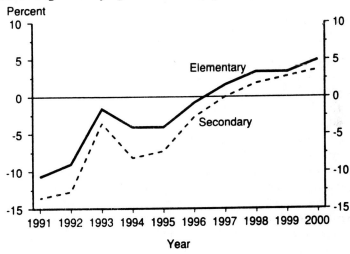

Jensen (1987), commenting on the increasingly competitive nature of the teacher marketplace, noted some reasons for the projected teacher shortage:

> *Districts that are able to offer employees higher salaries and pleasant working and living conditions may attract a large pool of qualified applicants. However, districts that are unable to offer these incentives—especially those in*

urban and isolated rural areas—already find it difficult to attract competent teachers. In most regions of the country, filling vacancies in math, science, foreign language, and special education has been particularly difficult.

The very reforms that are heralded as answers to education's problems ironically have also increased the demand for teachers. Reduced class sizes, stiffer graduation requirements, and new early education classes all require expanded teaching staffs. Increasing professional opportunities for women have also had an impact. Until fairly recently, teaching was one of the few careers pursued by women. Today, however, women have many more professional options and they may weigh opportunities in education against those in other fields. (6)

The Recruiting Plan

Nettles (1989), in a review of the literature on recruiting, selecting, and inducting personnel, delineates five common-sense guideposts for effective recruiting programs similar to those noted by Jensen (1987): (1) the district administration and school board must make a public statement through written policies, district goals, and budget about the recruiting commitment; (2) the recruiting program must be a year-round program; (3) recruiters must be selected and trained carefully; (4) recruiters must sell the community as well as the district; and (5) the district's intent to recruit and hire the *best* must be publicized with staff, patrons, and candidates (3–4).

With a district commitment to a quality recruiting program, the district recruiters, armed with estimates of the number and types of staff members needed, are ready to hit the road. The next question to answer is where to recruit. It makes sense to tap the usual sources, including university and college placement services. In addition, some university and college departments or divisions attempt to place their graduates, and individual professors may be excellent sources of candidates in their fields. Claughton and Eisel (1987) suggest that the following factors be considered in selecting specific college and universities for recruitment visits: projected number of graduates, number of experienced teacher candidates and alumni with active files in the placement office, quality of the teacher training program, special programs emphasized at the college or university, number of available candidates in "shortage fields," especially with dual certification, number of minority candidates available, past success in recruiting at the college or university, attitude toward out-of-state recruiters, efficient placement office procedures, opportunities for scheduled individual interviews, and job fairs and Career Days, which provide an opportunity to meet large numbers of candidates (5–6).

Government employment agencies, private employment services, and professional associations may be contacted. Professional journals provide a medium for wide dissemination of information about vacancies.

Competent ex-educators, people who were trained for but never entered the profession, even organizations and individuals not connected with education—such as community leaders or church ministers—may be fruitful sources of information. Qualified individuals who are not working as teachers may be identified through newspaper ads, contacts through churches and social clubs, and announcements in public places.

Minority Recruitment

The recruitment of minority group members and others who do not fit into the standard mold of teacher candidates is a problem of special significance and difficulty. Too few blacks, Mexican-Americans, Native Americans, and Asian Americans, and even upper- and lower-class Anglo-Americans enter the education profession, and many of those who do enter drop out or are underutilized. The recruitment of minorities into teacher training programs is essential to any long-range strategy for securing the best human resources for our schools.

Russell (1988) states that in all the rhetoric and debate about the school reform, the "one point on which there appears to be national consensus is that there will be a significant decline in the percent of minority teachers by the year 2000 unless there is a dramatic turnaround in the pool of available recruits." He goes on to predict that by 1990 only five percent of the national teaching force will be composed of minority teachers, while eighty percent of the public school student population will be comprised of minority students and concludes: "If this steady decline in minority teachers continues unabated at its present pace, there is a real possibility that by the mid-twenty-first century minority teachers could well become as extinct as the prehistoric dinosaur" (p. 1).

Graham (1987) states:

> . . . the problem is that as minority enrollments in the public schools are rising, the number of minority teachers, especially black teachers, is shrinking. This is the case because proportionately fewer blacks are going to college than a decade ago and, of those who do go to college, fewer are choosing to become teachers and, of those seeking to become teachers, too few are passing the new teacher tests, especially in the southern states, where about half of the nation's black teachers are prepared. (599–600)

Hopkins (1989) agrees that "the shortage of minorities attending college, choosing education as a career, passing competency tests, and staying in teaching as their chosen profession is becoming acute. It is a compound, multifaceted problem defying easy or quick solutions by even the best-intentioned school district" (p. 3).

Researchers studying this issue note that many efforts are underway to attract minorities into the profession. Scholarships, fellowships, and forgivable loans, along with proposals for special minority career ladders, the use of athletes as minority models for supporting minorities in teacher education, and restructuring teacher education are being suggested or implemented (Haberman 1989; Hopkins 1989). Graham (1987) suggests that elementary and secondary schools must be more effective with minority students, colleges must make greater efforts to recruit minority students, the private and public sectors must spend money to attract minorities into education, and midcareer professionals should be considered as a potential teaching candidates. A number of programs in school systems across the nation—in California, New Mexico, Pennsylvania, and Minnesota—are aimed at attracting minority youth to the teaching profession (Russell 1988). It appears that an awareness of the problem is developing and that long-term efforts are underway.

Immediate and short-term efforts to recruit available personnel from minority groups should focus on:

1. Identifying well-qualified personnel whose abilities are not being fully utilized.
2. Retraining or upgrading the training of personnel who lack certain qualifications but have high potential.
3. Attracting well-qualified personnel from other locations.

Nettles (1989) suggests that school districts must develop proactive, aggressive, ongoing programs of minority recruitment that include the following strategies: (1) involve minority staff members in the development of a minority recruiting plan; (2) train and use minorities as recruiters; (3) recognize minority staff members for their contributions to the district; (4) ask to serve on the teacher center board at minority colleges; (5) write to members of minority organizations about employment in the district; (6) attend minority conferences at the regional, state, and national level; and (7) employ a minority recruiter or consultant to help locate minority applicants both in the area and out of state (15–17).

Former participants in programs such as the Peace Corps, Teacher Corps, and VISTA are also viable candidates for educational assignments. These programs have demonstrated that a limited amount of retraining or new training can produce promising personnel for educational endeavors. Schools at local levels can hardly afford to ignore human resources of high quality wherever they can be recruited. Concepts pioneered by federal programs such as the Teacher Corps may be successful with minority groups that are already established in the community.

Since the early 1980s, another resource for attracting minorities to teaching has been state-mandated alternative teacher certification programs. Between 1984 and 1988 the number of state alternative certification programs increased from eight to twenty-three (Darling-Hammond 1988, 6). These programs require that an individual hold a bachelor's degree and meet specific requirements for earning teacher certification. About half are aimed at reducing the shortage of teachers in specific academic areas by encouraging individuals from other occupational fields to enter the teaching profession. Many of the programs allow currently certified teachers to earn additional certification in shortage areas. All of the programs actively encourage the involvement of minority participants. In general, these programs require fewer education courses for certification or provide alternatives to college coursework for meeting specific competencies. In addition to the alternative certification programs for teachers, several states provide alternative certification programs for administrators.

Summary

The successful recruiting program is a carefully planned staffing activity that devotes considerable attention to analysis and decision making and that is in tune with the mission and goals of the school system. The effective recruiter is armed with a thorough understanding of the school district's vision, the role of each job in accomplishing that vision, the criteria for successful job performance, and teacher supply and demand. The primary goal of the recruiting program is to develop a large pool of qualified and interested applicants; however, it must be recognized that often there will be only a few available applicants for a position despite aggressive recruiting efforts. The employment of competent, highly qualified individuals recruited for positions in educational institutions is the major outcome of a successful recruiting program. In addition, the recruiting program pays many dividends in terms of public relations and staff morale. From the human resources perspective, the recruiting program must be envisioned as an aggressive, ongoing effort dedicated to supplying the organization with applicants of the highest quality in order to meet the improvement goals established by the organization.

Suggested Study Sources

Buffie, Edward G. 1989. *The Principal and Leadership.* Bloomington, IN: Phi Delta Kappa.

In this book, the first in a six-volume set of monographs on topics related to the elementary principalship, the author lays out a set of expectations in terms of needed knowledge, skills, and beliefs for conceptualizing instructional leadership. Other volumes in the series address the topics of learning about the school and community, communication, supervision, discipline, and fiscal management.

Claughton, Stelle, and Jean Eisel. 1987. *A Practical Guide for Successful Teacher Recruitment*. Foster City, CA: American Association of School Personnel Administrators and Association for School, College and University Staffing.

This is a practitioner's guide to successful recruitment. The step-by-step format includes suggestions on conducting needs assessments, selecting recruiting sites, developing the recruitment schedule, advertising job openings, recruitment materials, making travel arrangements, selecting and training recruiters, the interview day, the interview, making the most of teacher job fairs, following up on campus visits, and making the most of in-district recruitment. The appendix includes recommended ethical standards for recruiting.

Cook, William J. 1988. *Bill Cook's Strategic Planning for America's Schools*. Arlington, VA: American Association of School Administrators.

The process, discipline, and implementation of strategic planning are explained in this book. Strategic planning concentrates a district's efforts and resources on goals that have been agreed upon by a planning team composed of community and district members. The planning team develops objectives, conducts internal and external analyses of the current situation, and develops strategies for achieving the objectives. The achievement of each strategy is accomplished through the use of action plans developed by smaller groups.

Jensen, Mary Cihak. 1987. *How to Recruit, Select, Induct and Retain the Very Best Teachers*. Eugene, OR: ERIC Clearinghouse on Educational Management.

This report examines issues related to the recruitment, selection, induction, and retention of competent teachers. In Part I, "Recruiting Teachers," the author addresses the competitive recruiting environment and reasons for teacher shortages and offers suggestions for improving the recruitment effort.

6

Selecting Competent Personnel

The selection and employment of highly qualified personnel for a school district or other educational institution is one of the most difficult of all administrative responsibilities. The ability to select the best candidate from a large or small pool of applicants is a skill that, without doubt, directly impacts the quality of the educational program and the success of the administrator responsible for selection. Gatewood and Feild (1990) define selection as "the process of collecting and evaluating information about an individual in order to extend an offer of employment. Such employment could be either a first position for a new employee or a different position for an existing employee. The selection process is performed under legal and environmental constraints to protect the future interests of the organization and the individual" (3).

This chapter deals with the topic of selection as one of the key activities of the personnel staffing function. Like all the staffing activities depicted in Exhibit 5.1 on page 89, selection should not be viewed as an isolated process but as one of the interdependent activities of the staffing cycle. This discussion of selection of competent personnel is based on an assumption that actual selection activities are preceded by other activities, including job analysis and recruitment, and will be monitored through the activities of placement, evaluation, and staff development. This discussion is also based on an assumption that selection activities are conducted in accordance with the requirements for fair and equal opportunity employment, as discussed in chapter 11. Finally, it is assumed, or at least desired, that the selection activities occur in an environment that is minimally impacted by political pressures.

The primary objective of the personnel selection process is to fill existing vacancies with personnel who meet established qualifications and who appear likely to succeed on the job. The selection process is essentially an information-gathering and prediction process. Confidence in the predictive aspect of the process is derived from empirical evidence that people tend to form behavior patterns and to act in the future as they acted in the past under similar circumstances (Owens 1976, 612). According to Hough (1984), the general suppositions supporting the critical review of background data and prior performance as predictors of future successful job performance include the following: "(a) past behavior is the best indicator of future behavior; (b) 'samples' of past behavior are preferable to 'signs'; and, (c) biodata are samples of past behavior and are the best indicators of future behaviors" (135). The task of those involved in the personnel selection process is to predict an applicant's future performance after a thorough review of gathered evidence related to his or her past performance and careful evaluation of observations made during personal interactions with him or her.

This responsibility can be overwhelming to the serious administrator who realizes that both personal and organizational success hinge on the collective competencies of the staff members selected for employment. Unfortunately, administrative training does not generally include in-depth preparation for this task; consequently, personnel selections are frequently made using a combination of intuition, hunches, and personal theory about how behavior is related to success in educational positions. Trying to determine how and why hiring decisions are made has been a goal of industrial and organizational psychologists for more than seventy years (Snyder et al. 1988, 973), but definitive answers to these questions still elude researchers (Arvey and Campion 1982; Snyder et al. 1988). Selection decisions made in school districts have inherent consequences for many—students, other professionals, parents, and community members—and must be considered carefully. According to Nicholson and McInerney (1988) each "decision in this case is based on human judgment and involves assessing and evaluating a variety of information that may be inaccurate, incomplete, or irrelevant. All this is filtered through a conceptual framework about which the decisionmaker may be largely unaware. Thus, mistakes made early, in how one conceptualizes and lays the ground rules for the process, will affect the entire decision making/selection sequence" (88).

Gross Screening

The intent of an effective recruiting program is to attract a large pool of highly qualified applicants to the district. Desirable applicants are those who possess the qualifications and competencies needed for successful performance as determined through job analysis and as described in the job description and job specifications. It is a fact that successful recruitment programs also attract a large number of less qualified or unqualified applicants, even undesirable applicants, particularly when the district or institution enjoys a reputation as a good place to work. When there are several candidates for a given job, some of the obviously less promising ones can usually be eliminated from the list of contenders by relatively gross screening devices. Granting that mistakes will be made occasionally, even in cases that appear to be beyond question, the need for economy and a relatively low element of risk often outweigh the disadvantages of narrowing the list to a manageable number early in the selection process, so that more time and resources can be devoted to a thorough examination of the remaining candidates.

The total personnel selection process has been envisioned as a process involving "a series of screens with progressively small holes" (Melohn 1987, 104). Obviously, the initial screens have the largest holes. The primary concerns in the initial screening process are that applicants who are screened out of the selection process feel that they have been treated with respect and consequently feel positive about the district and that the applicants' equal opportunity employment rights are not violated. Key to this process is finding a reasonable balance between the need for efficient use of time and the maintenance of fair relationships with applicants.

The gathering of information about applicants is central to any personnel selection process, and this information should serve as the basis for all decisions concerning the selection of an individual to fill a position. "A common procedure for the initial screening of a large pool of teacher candidates is to review resumes and paper credentials" (Bredeson 1985, 13). This generally includes a review of application forms, resumes, letters of recommendation, transcripts, certification, autobiographical data or biodata, and test results. These selection tools become predictive measures for forecasting employee performance and have a direct impact on the decision to accept or reject an applicant. The careful use of selection tools and the data derived from their use must be of paramount concern to the decision maker, since research points out that some selection tools are more useful for screening out the extreme "lows" than they are for selecting the best prospects. In fact, "the consensus of research findings is that in American schools administrators often fail to gather enough information about candidates. Decisions to hire teachers may be based on inadequate selection procedures" using selection tools lacking the reliability or validity necessary to provide sound data (Jensen 1987, 16).

Selection Tools and Processes

The one statement that can be made with complete and justified confidence about selection tools and processes is that no one device has enough predictive validity to warrant its exclusive use. As the following discussion will reveal, some familiar selection tools should be used with extreme caution, if at all, and others should be used in combination with as many relevant sources of information as can be feasibly used. The indiscriminate dependence on a small number of extremely questionable devices by employers who do not realize how questionable they are is at the bottom of many serious personnel problems.

Problems in personnel selection are compounded by a lack of precise description and measurement of the complex tasks required of educators. Through the years, the philosophical question of whether teaching is art or science has been debated frequently. In teaching, as well as in administration and other educational service roles, each specific situation requires the educator to respond through a blending of personality, skills, knowledge, and techniques to the specifics of that particular situation. There are no formulas or absolutes when dealing with individual human learning needs. The growing knowledge base related to effective schools and effective teaching reinforces the theory that teaching is a very complex act requiring a teacher to make thousands of decisions each instructional day. From the research base on teaching and learning also come data to support the position that if teachers consistently employ certain strategies and techniques with students, there will be greater student learning. The "art or science" question may never be answered. It is important to realize that working with only a partial definition and assessment of the skills and abilities that contribute to a teacher's capability to make appropriate and effective decisions impacts the selection process.

The literature on school reform demands that education be upgraded. It is reasoned that upgrading education is directly tied to improving the quality of educators and teaching/administration in education. Unfortunately, as stated by Hawley (1986), "we do not really know what qualities we want in the future labor force. For example, how smart does a teacher have to be to be effective?" (713). What *signs*—the predictors of potential or future performance—and *samples*—the measures of current competence— should be used in selecting educational personnel? Current practice in both business and education would appear to rely heavily on signs, as opposed to samples, of behavior. Researchers have concluded that academic criteria (Weaver 1983), superior cognitive skills (Browne and Rankin 1986), and measures of achievement (Jensen 1986) are not significantly correlated with success in the employment process. The inevitable conclusion is that there are large gaps between what is theoretically discussed and what is practiced in terms of teacher selection. Jensen (1987) suggests that school districts contribute to the educational crisis by preferring not to hire the most promising candidates or by failing to consider the most appropriate measures (13–14). The challenge, then, is to find the means and methods to translate theory into practical application.

In response to these selection problems, those charged with the responsibility are advised to use multiple criteria and predictors when selecting teachers. However, a definitive answer to the question of which criteria and predictors are the best to use remains elusive. Predictor variables may be thought of as the means through which the criteria are assessed. The predictors generally used to determine whether the applicant possesses the criteria needed for on-the-job success are background data collected from application forms, reference checks, and biographical inquiries and data compiled from interviews and testing. The Bureau of National Affairs (BNA), in two surveys (1983, 1988) of corporations, found that reference checks, interviews, and skill performance tests were the most commonly used predictor variables. Data from assessment centers, polygraph tests, and physical abilities tests were least likely to be used. Supervisory ratings for behaviors and characteristics were the most commonly used assessments of the applicant's ability in terms of criteria sought. In general, it would be assumed that surveys in educational settings would produce similar findings. According to Jensen (1987), investigators have examined the relationship between what they term successful teaching and a variety of measures—grade-point average, personality tests, National Teacher Examination scores, self-concept surveys, attitudinal inventories, vocational interest batteries, and academic tests—and the "researchers confirm what personnel directors sense; no one measure or test can assess a candidate's potential as a teacher. One variable cannot accurately predict all the skills and abilities required of teacher" (15). Further complicating the search for effective predictors is the fact "predictors used to select teachers in one school district may not be valid for selecting teachers in another school district because the actual and the desired teaching behaviors expected from teachers vary from district to district. A highly successful teacher in one school district may be only a mediocre teacher in another district" (Young and Ryerson 1986, 6).

A fairly common set of multiple predictors—resume information, application data, and placement folder information—have been used by school districts throughout the years to select teachers. Exhibit 6.1 on page 115 suggests a form for analyzing a variety of "papers" in search of useful information among the masses of data. However, legal requirements and legislated educational reform have changed the composition and content of these papers: "A request for photographs, once made of candidates by most school districts, is now illegal. On-site visits and observations, a common practice in the earlier part of this century, have been discontinued for practical reasons. The use of achievement measures . . . is receiving increased attention due to recent reports on teaching and teacher education" (Young and Ryerson 1986, 7).

Application Forms

"An application form typically consists of a series of questions designed to provide information on the general suitability of applicants for jobs for which they are applying" (Gatewood and Feild 1990, 379). The application form serves at least three useful purposes in the screening process: it establishes whether the applicant meets the minimum hiring requirements as designated by the job specifications; it serves as a source of biographical data and work history information for each applicant and as a means for comparing applicants in terms of categorical strengths and weaknesses; and it serves as a study document to be used by the interviewer in preparing and tailoring the interview so that impressions and perceptions gleaned from the written document may be confirmed or clarified. Serving as only one of the means for evaluating applicants, the job application, despite being taken for granted and appearing routine and innocuous, can be a very powerful screening tool. This is illustrated by the finding from a random survey of principals in the continental United States that more than ninety-eight percent used application information to screen and limit the pool of candidates (Young and McMurry 1986).

How to use the information on the application form in the selection process is a practical problem requiring study. Research, especially in education, is limited, but investigations have been undertaken to determine the effect of missing information or intentional disregard of items (Stone and Stone 1987), requests for illegal information (Bredeson and Caldwell 1988), the use of applications as prescreening devices (Bredeson 1988), and the effects of selected informational items (Young and McMurry 1986). Bredeson (1988) states that "as a selection tool, the application blank is efficient, robust, and highly valid as a predictor of a broad spectrum of very practical criteria. In addition, the standard application blank has a high degree of face validity for employees and employers" (69). The methods used to gather information from the application form constitute two broad categories: (1) biodata-gathering procedures and (2) application checklists and evaluations.

Biodata procedures are systematic methods for "assessing job applicants on the basis of personal biographical history factors (for example, past behavior, interests, attitudes, demographic background). The process involves giving information pertaining to an applicant's personal history a mathematical weight to produce a score for each individual" (Hammer and Kleiman 1988, 86). The weighted application blank (WAB) and the biographical information blank (BIB) are the two most common approaches used in biodata gathering. Generally, the WAB tends to focus on hard data—factual and verifiable information related to training, experience, and certification—and the BIB tends to focus on softer data that include interests, attitudes, and values. Shaffer et al. (1986) state that a general characteristic of biodata that is rarely challenged is their ability to predict a variety of criteria. Hard biodata items are considered superior to the soft biodata items in terms of predicting job performance criteria, but both types of items are useful (791–92).

Application checklists and evaluations are helpful tools for comparing applications against the job specifications developed through job analysis. The checklist is particularly helpful in the gross screening process to weed out applicants who do not have the essential skills and requirements sought. A preliminary checklist or evaluation form may be composed of critical, "make-or-break" items that immediately eliminate applicants not holding the necessary prerequisites (e.g., certification). The systematic evaluation of training and experience (T&E) information provided by applicants on resumes and applications is another form of checklist evaluation. In T&E evaluation, weights or points are assigned to an applicant's training and experience; the evaluations are "primarily used to rank order applicants following elimination of those who do not meet minimum required qualifications" (McDaniel et al. 1988, 284). A self-reporting form of measuring training and experience, the "accomplishment record," has the applicant describe accomplishments in highly relevant, behavioral job dimensions for selection and promotion purposes (Hough 1984).

Application forms are important sources of data in the personnel selection process. Unfortunately, the more sophisticated approaches to evaluating application data, which have been shown to be extremely useful in the selection process, are not frequently used in educational institutions. Perhaps this is because those prepared for administrative roles, especially in the public schools, are not provided the necessary knowledge base and methodological expertise to implement such processes. Also, there is a danger of violating an applicant's right to privacy if illegal or inappropriate information is sought. In addition, the use of these processes involves a considerable commitment of time and money to planning, development, and continuous updating of procedures. The preference in education for other approaches to evaluating application data is probably tied to a lack of resources.

However, as Bredeson (1988) indicates, application forms do "provide a low cost means of gathering biographical data, previous job experiences, and educational background, and a variety of personal information that would otherwise be impossible or impractical to collect on individuals. Application blanks can be used to ask candidates for personal and professional goals and philosophy, as well as to request self-assessments" (70). Since the format of the application is under the direct control of the school district, the application can be tailored to meet its needs. An example of an acceptable application form developed by members of the American Association of School Personnel Administrators (AASPA) is found in Appendix E.

Resumes

Resumes are written documents briefly describing an individual's previous experiences as they relate to a particular endeavor, such as career or vocational pursuits. It must be recognized that the purpose of a resume is to portray the individual in the best possible light, because the resume is often the first representation of the person seen by the prospective employer, and also that some people will do just about anything to get hired. Kevin Moore (1988) writes "if you worked in a library and were asked to put a stack of resumes on the shelf, you'd probably have a hard time deciding whether to put them under 'fiction' or 'nonfiction.' Let's face it. No one has ever written a resume in order to make himself (or herself) look bad" (2–4). Resumes are often skillfully tailored to appear to match the qualifications of a position even if the individual does not have the skills and training needed. The employer who accepts the information on a resume casually and at face value may be surprised to learn that it was distorted. The facts on resumes must be checked and verified.

It is important to compare the information found on resumes with the requirements of the job description and job specifications. Factors such as progression in job responsibility, unexplained gaps in employment, and evidence of professional accomplishment revealed in the resume may provide a basis for deciding whether additional consideration is to be given to the individual. Research shows that "ninety percent of all resumes are read in two minutes or less, and that negative information is weighted more heavily than positive. There is little recourse for the applicant whose resume is poorly received by the employer; a poor resume can serve as a 'knock-out' punch for the job seeker" (Holley et al. 1988, 51). Reviewers are influenced by the format of the resume and favorably regard those that are neat, attractive, informative, and concise.

Letters of Recommendation

Like resumes, letters of recommendation often accompany application forms. They serve both to introduce the candidate and as a source of reference information. As information supplied by the applicant without specification from the prospective employer, the letter of recommendation must be viewed with caution. By name alone, it may be inferred that the intent of such a letter is to portray the applicant in a positive light; like resumes, letters of recommendation may contain irrelevant or incorrect information and may have little validity in terms of identifying the individual's strengths and weaknesses. The literature on personnel selection abounds with suggestions that letters of recommendation are not reliable selection tools, but they continue to be valued by decision makers in personnel selection, making it imperative that information gleaned from them be integrated with other sources and not be the sole factor used in decision making (Bredeson 1985, 13).

In attempting to deal more systematically with the information found in letters of recommendation and reference letters, Vukovich (1987) developed techniques for objective and subjective analysis of statements in letters written by supervising teachers concerning the performance of student teachers. In these analyses, descriptive terms used to describe the student teacher's performance are examined and the presence of critical incidents is studied. Among his conclusions are: (1) teacher references and/or evaluations have certain identifiable characteristics that can be used as a guide in selection; (2) those that are innocuous, are short, and contain reserved statements are predictive of less successful teachers; and (3) those written by master teachers are generally consistent with the principal's rating (1). In a collaborative study, Trinka noted that references were the best single predictor and most efficient for second- and third-year teachers, and neither writing samples nor GPA are related to teacher effectiveness.

Due to the increased litigation that has impacted the personnel selection process, extremely critical written references and letters of recommendation are unusual. Those who review letters of recommendation are urged to "learn to read between the lines to find what the person would not or could not say directly" and to "listen with your eyes for the message being sent." If the letter states or hints at a problem, it should be followed up with telephone inquiries to the letter writer and others.

Rating Scales

Many school districts send rating scales to former employers or references to secure information about applicants. This is a time-consuming and expensive process when it is used for every applicant, and, unfortunately, most rating scales are little more helpful, if at all, than letters of recommendation (McIntyre 1974). The weaknesses of rating scales are numerous and complex. Most consist of a hodgepodge of undefined characteristics, many of which are largely irrelevant to job performance (Medley et al. 1984, 42). Most are judgmental, rather than descriptive, and give no indication of the nature of the characteristic or performance that is being judged. Typically, the categories have labels such as "outstanding," "adequate," "poor," and "needs improvement," but when an applicant's classroom management techniques, for example, are rated as "needs improvement," it is not clear how the teacher's performance fails to measure up in the rater's judgment.

Most raters tend to avoid using the lower part of the scale, even for individuals whose work is conspicuously inadequate. This leniency error not only contributes to the lack of discriminating power that is characteristic of rating scales, but it also unfairly handicaps the person being rated in those rare instances when a rater does not use the entire scale. For example, the middle category of many scales is labeled "average," but there is no definition of average. It would be quite logical for a rater to mark a teacher average and mean that performance is quite satisfactory and meets all job expectations, so that the rating would have no negative implications at all. Such a rating would very likely be interpreted as negative by a prospective employer, however, simply because ratings seldom go below the middle category.

Because of these weaknesses, rating forms are usually unreliable and, at best, should be used only for gross screening purposes.

Transcripts

In *A Nation at Risk* (1983), the members of the National Commission on Excellence in Education found that "too many teachers are being drawn from the bottom quarter of graduating high school and college students" (22). They recommended that "persons preparing to teach should be required to meet high educational standards, to demonstrate an aptitude for teaching, and to demonstrate competence in an academic discipline. Colleges and universities offering teacher preparation programs should be judged by how well their graduates meet these criteria" (30). According to Jensen (1987), "since the publication of *A Nation at Risk*, districts have increasingly sought transcripts as evidence of an applicant's academic achievement. Even districts that traditionally discounted the importance of grades now publicize their desire for good students whose achievement is reflected in GPA and test scores" (23).

Like other sources of selection information, transcripts should be read and interpreted cautiously and with consideration for the differences among individual professors, departments, and institutions. Most of the research involving undergraduate transcripts has dealt with the predictive validity of grade-point averages in relation to academic success in graduate or professional schools. Researchers studying the cognitive ability and academic achievement of prospective teachers have generally concluded that these factors, as reflected by grade-point averages and testing, do not have the same influence as other factors when hiring decisions are made (Browne and Rankin 1986; Jensen 1986; Perry 1981).

However, one might examine transcripts for more than the grade-point average. The expectations of the job will determine what to look for; for example, in appraising the transcript of an applicant for a position as an English teacher, one might not be unduly concerned about a few average grades in mathematics. In fact, the occasional deviation should not be of nearly as much interest as general patterns and trends, but one must always take into account that some departments and some institutions are notorious havens for the academically inept. Goldstein (1986) cautions against hiring a teacher whose transcript is studded with low grades, especially in the context of an environment of academic renaissance. Good transcripts mean good students in Goldstein's thinking, and they serve as one guarantee that candidates have an acceptable mastery of the subjects they are licensed to teach (15). Though one might not agree with Goldstein's faith in the grades on a transcript, it is advisable to follow his recommendations for careful scrutiny of the transcript to assess academic preparation. Attention should be paid to evidence of a solid general education

EXHIBIT 6.1   Evaluation of Candidate Papers

Candidate: _____
　　　　　　　　　　Last Name　　　　　　First　　　　　　Middle

Position Applied For: _____

This evaluation is based upon a review of the following documents:

_____   Application

_____   Resume

_____   Transcripts

_____   Placement File

_____   Other

EVALUATION QUESTIONS	YES	NO	COMMENTS
1. Do the papers indicate clarity of written expression and proper grammar usage?			
2. Are the papers neat and professionally presented?			
3. Is the candidate's educational background relevant to the position for which he is applying?			
4. Does the candidate have experience in the area for which he is applying?			
20. Do the papers indicate that the candidate has been awarded scholastic honors and/or other professional or community recognition?			

Additional comments pertaining to the candidate's papers: _____

_____

Do you recommend that this candidate be interviewed? _____ Yes _____ No

Evaluation completed by _____ Date _____

background, and poor grades in basic English, social studies, mathematics, and sciences should not be dismissed lightly. Additional information regarding grades may be sought in the interview to determine whether there are legitimate reasons for the grades earned during a particular period. As with most of the other selection tools, transcripts are more useful for screening out clearly inferior applicants than they are for selecting the best of several superior applicants.

Telephone Investigations

Although the value of using the telephone to discuss an applicant's past record with several knowledgeable people has not been the subject of many studies, it is reasonable to assume that two-way communication via telephone is more informative than one-way communication via letter or rating scale. It is also assumed that most people will make more complete and frank statements orally than they will in writing. Goldstein (1986) suggests that "as an antidote to the sterility and sameness of many letters of recommendation as well as to invigorate fact-finding, judicious use of the telephone is necessary. Calling a reference usually yields far more fruitful and precise information" (18). Of course, face-to-face conversations would be even better, but often this is not a practical alternative. Certainly the cost of making a few telephone calls is negligible in comparison with the enormous cost of making a mistake in selecting personnel.

Prior to conducting telephone investigations to discuss an applicant's past record or to check references, it is important to obtain written consent from the applicant. Failing to do so may create a problem for the district if the applicant believes that his or her privacy has been invaded. The most obvious method for obtaining written consent is through use of the application form. The model form in Appendix E includes a statement to meet this need.

Conducting background investigations should be the responsibility of someone who is trained to do so, and the information requested should be limited to what there is a genuine need to know. Individuals contacted for information need to be assured of confidentiality, and this confidentiality must be maintained throughout the entire process. The questions asked should be open-ended and job-related. The primary responsibilities of the person conducting the telephone check are to ask questions that will provide the type of information needed in the selection process and to listen carefully to the answers.

The information shared in a telephone investigation should be carefully considered. It may be necessary to learn more about the person who gave the reference in order to evaluate the information he or she gave. The results of a telephone investigation should be integrated into the total body of information about the applicant, not used as the only selection tool. In this regard, Young and Ryerson (1986) advise decision makers to remember that "telephone contacts are made on the premise that reference sources may be more frank about an applicant in personal conversations than in written communication. While this premise may be true, negative information acquired from telephone conversations can be difficult to substantiate in cases of litigation" (9).

Interviews

No selection device is so heavily depended upon as interviewing, and none may give more misleading results. "Industrial and organizational psychologists have been studying the employment interview for more than sixty years in a effort to determine the reliability and validity of judgments based on the assessment device, and also to discover the various psychological variables which influence these judgements" (Arvey and Campion 1982, 281). Despite its widespread use, the employment interview has a long history of low validity for selection, as determined by traditional research on interviewing. One reason interviewing is so carelessly practiced and so unquestioningly relied on is that usable records of impressions gained interviewing are seldom kept and validated against actual performance. In the absence of corrective feedback, the interviewer repeats the same mistakes interminably without being aware of it. Also, interviewing can be just as biased as other selection devices, if the usual stereotypes are present in the mind of the interviewer.

As to why almost all employers continue to use the employment interview when the research suggests that it does not accurately predict future job performance, Arvey and Campion (1982) offered four possible answers: (1) the interview is "really" valid and measures behaviors that cannot be assessed well or easily with current assessment tools; (2) the interview may not be valid, but certain practical considerations make it the popular choice because it allows employers to inform the applicant about the job and it may be less costly than other selection devices (tests); (3) the interview is not valid, but interviewers maintain great faith and confidence in their judgments despite the fact that in employment settings interviewers receive very little feedback concerning their judgments; and (4) the interview is not valid, but it does other things well, especially in the area of public relations (314–16).

The continued use of the interview despite its deficiencies has prompted continued examination of its usefulness (Campion et al. 1988; Gatewood et al. 1989; Loehr 1986; Maurer and Fay 1988). It has been suggested that problems attributed to the interview process may be the result of misperceptions about the use of the interview in the selection process. Questions have also been raised about the traditional research methods used in validating the employment interview (Arvey and Campion 1982; Dreher et al. 1988; McDaniel et al. 1988; Zedeck et al. 1983). Arvey and Campion note five themes emerging from more recent research on the employment interview: (1) there is increased research on bias in interviewing; (2) more interview variables are being researched; (3) research methodology is more sophisticated; (4) research tends to be microanalytic; and (5) interview research has neglected the related research in the person-perception literature (310–13).

Current research tends to support the position that interviewing can be useful, provided that the interviewer is extremely careful about the information collected and the inferences drawn from it. The preemployment interview provides at least one, and sometimes the only, opportunity for face-to-face communication between the prospective employer and the applicant. Interview formats should be painstakingly constructed to elicit responses that are describable and relevant to effective performance on the job. For example, if accurate use of the English language is an important consideration, then the interview can contribute evidence to add to the data compiled from other sources. Interviewing can also be used to build a good image of the school system, even with unsuccessful candidates.

The interviewing process can be significantly improved by training interviewers and by developing a systematic approach to the total selection process, as was described earlier in this chapter. Common interviewer mistakes that may be corrected through training include: failing to know about the job, failing to have a plan for the interview, asking questions "off the cuff," talking too much, overreacting to initial impressions, and failing to evaluate the interview. Problems related to interviewer bias and prejudice may need to be handled through other actions. According to Goldstein (1986), applicants are sometimes disappointed, even angered, by the cavalier behavior of an interviewer who:

Begins the interview late because he or she "got tied up";

Asks questions that are ephemeral, strictly procedural, and unchallenging;

Provides no opportunity for rebuttal or exchange when he or she has spent most of the interview lecturing on his or her philosophy;

Fails to read the application and credentials and then asks needless questions answered clearly in the paperwork submitted;

Shows how bored he or she is with the interview;

Fails to inform the applicant about employment procedures and when the position will be filled;

Ends the interview on an abrasive "Don't-call-us-we'll-call-you" note, poisoning the total experience (21–22).

Group interviews, involving several candidates in one setting, or panel interviews, involving several interviewers, are sometimes employed to refine and improve the interviewing process. Group interviews can save time, and they afford an opportunity to observe interactions and to compare candidates, but the temptation to read too much into such observations should be strongly resisted. Panel interviews may be time-consuming, but they do provide for a reliability check on the observers. Weston and Warmke (1988) suggest that "panel interviews have several significant advantages over traditional one-on-one interviews. These advantages include scientific ones (greater validity due to multiple inputs), political ones (greater acceptance of the decision due to broader participation in the selection process) and practical ones (faster decision time and turnaround time)" (111). Generally speaking, group and panel interviews are subject to the same abuses as one-to-one interviews, so they should be employed with care. In support of a team approach to selection and interviewing, Nicholson and McInerney (1988) state that "a team is less likely to miss key aspects of a candidate's personality or potential than is a single interviewer. The team approach also erases the problem of the dominant personality of a single interviewer being a factor in selection" (90).

An additional concern related to the use of interviews pertains to the avoidance of questions that are discriminatory with respect to race, ethnicity, national origin, religion, age, sex, sexual preference, or other factors. Anyone involved in the planning or execution of preemployment interviews should study the current federal regulations on acceptable and unacceptable inquiries. Following are some examples of unacceptable categories: inquiries concerning the birthplace of the applicant or the applicant's parents, spouse, or other relatives; questions about age; questions pertaining to religious affiliation; questions about marital status or dependents.

Logically the best way to avoid legal entanglements, while also improving the reliability and validity of the interview process, is to ensure that the questions asked in the interview are always job-related. The development of these questions is facilitated by knowledge of the job, necessary qualifications, standards of performance, and characteristics of successful performers. For example, if it has been decided that an important skill needed by classroom teachers is the ability to diagnose or identify the level of students' strengths and weaknesses, then questions should be developed to ascertain an applicant's skill in this area. Asking the applicant to describe formal and informal diagnostic techniques used in the classroom or to discuss different student learning styles would relate to the identification of this skill. The questions should also be open-ended, to allow the applicant to respond in some manner other than saying "yes" or "no." A general questioning strategy should include: (1) developing questions in advance of the interview; (2) asking the same basic questions of each applicant, to provide a basis for comparison of applicants; (3) using a variety of questions related to each key skill or characteristic sought; (4) asking, not answering questions; (5) being accepting of all answers; (6) asking open-ended questions and listening; and (7) avoiding stress-inducing techniques and cross-examining.

Interview questions should reflect the intent and purpose of the interview. Gatewood and Feild (1990) describe three types of interviewing strategies and the development of questions for each: the situational interview, the behavior description interview, and the job content interview (483–88). The intent of these interviewing strategies is to bring consistency and structure to the interview process by limiting questioning to job-related inquiries that may be analyzed or scored. The situational interview model is based on the identification of behaviors derived from a study of critical incidents related to a particular job. Applicants are asked to respond to a situation, and statements of intended action for dealing with the posed situation are scored on a behaviorally anchored rating scale (Latham et al. 1980). Maurer and Fay (1988) suggest that "situational interviews are more effective than conventional structured interviews in producing agreement about job applicants among raters" (339). The development of questions for the behavior description interview involves formulating initial questions and follow-up questions (probes) to determine how an applicant actually behaved in a particular situation (Janz et al. 1986). Answers to the questions are scored according to a rank-order scale. In the job content method, the interview is focused on personal relations, good citizenship, and job knowledge (Gatewood and Feild 1990, 487). Questions used in the interview are limited to the defined areas and are developed so that the applicant relies on personal experiences, decisions, and actions in formulating responses. The interview is scored first on the response to the question and then in terms of all responses to questions for a certain characteristic or skill sought.

To evaluate the applicant's responses, the interviewer obviously must know the types of responses that are being sought. The interview questions become part of a test, and the responses should be scored in some manner.

Master teachers, beginning teachers, administrators, counselors, and diagnosticians are valuable resources for developing questions—they may be asked to develop questions and responses they believe would be useful in the interview process. Potential questions may be posed to the same group, and the responses reviewed and summarized. The collaborative nature of such a process, combined with the use of the participants' broad base of knowledge and experience, enhances the selection process.

Tests

The use of standardized tests is undoubtedly the most controversial selection practice. In recent years, several pronouncements have been made by influential individuals and groups within and outside the education profession calling for the elimination of standardized tests from the personnel administration field. In contrast, the national reform movement in education has reemphasized the role of testing in the preparation and certification of educators. Madaus and Pullin noted in 1987 that by the late 1980s, seventeen states required prospective teachers to take the NTE (formerly called the National Teacher Examination) and another seventeen states administered examinations specifically created for them by external contractors. The adoption of precertification tests was being considered in other states, and at least three states (Arkansas, Texas, and Georgia) were considering the implementation of testing for recertification of experienced teachers (31). Particularly troublesome to Madaus and Pullin, "scores on teacher certification tests are currently being used to make career-determining inferences and decisions about preservice and inservice teachers—justified solely on the basis of content-related evidence" (32). As confirmation of this concern, it is noted that the Educational Testing Service (ETS) has refused to grant permission for the use of the NTE for determining retention, promotion, or salary adjustment for in-service teachers.

Before the advent of state teacher testing programs, the most widely used, critiqued, and litigated teacher tests were those comprising the NTE. The NTE tests are designed to measure academic preparation for teaching in three areas—general education, professional education, and teaching area specialization—to provide an independent assessment and to permit comparison of graduates from different colleges. Research on the use of these examinations as one of several selection tools reveals that the NTE can make a modest to moderate contribution to prediction accuracy. Ayers (1988), replicating the work of earlier researchers, found that correlations between principal ratings and NTE scores are generally low. However, he concluded that significant relationships exist between grade point averages and scores derived from the Communication Skill and Professional Knowledge tests of the Core Battery and the Elementary Specialty area test of the NTE. The best predictors were overall grade point averages (136). This is not to say that test scores have enough predictive value to be used without several other types of information, nor does it warrant the application of inflexible cutoff points. The position of the ETS, the developer of the NTE, is that NTE scores should be used as only one item in a multiple-criteria assessment process related to granting of teacher certification. It suggests that extremely low scores on tests like the NTE, as well as extremely poor transcripts or other evidence, should be regarded as red flags that should not be ignored. Extremely low scores can be used, along with other relevant information, for gross screening purposes to eliminate candidates unless there is convincing evidence to the contrary.

Cultural bias in tests has been a matter of increasing concern in recent years. It is evident that many tests contain biases that contribute to the low average scores attained by some minority groups. This suggests that rigid cutoff scores should be avoided, especially for minority applicants. Cascio et al. (1988), after critically analyzing the legal, psychometric, and professional literature on setting cutoff scores, offered the following guidelines for setting cutoff scores:

1. It is unrealistic to expect that there is a single "best" method of setting cutoff scores for all situations.
2. The process of setting a cutoff score (or a critical score) should begin with a job analysis that identifies levels of proficiency on critical knowledge, skills, abilities, or other characteristics.
3. The validity and job relatedness of the assessment procedure are crucial considerations.
4. How a test is used (criterion-referenced or norm-referenced) affects the selection and meaning of a cutoff score.
5. When possible, data on the actual relation of test scores to outcome measures of job performance should be considered carefully.
6. Cutoff scores or critical scores should be set high enough to ensure that minimum standards of job performance are met.
7. Cutoff scores should be consistent with normal expectations of acceptable proficiency within the work force. (21–22)

Confusion concerning the meaning and implications of court decisions and official guidelines contributes to the uncertainty that prevails at the school district level as to how tests can be used in the selection of personnel. Tests, of course, must be job-related to be used legally or ethically as selection tools. After the U.S. Supreme Court's 1971 decision in the case of *Griggs* v. *Duke Power Company*, several other cases seemed to make it clear that job-relatedness must be shown where any test is found to have a disparate racial impact. Furthermore, employer intent was not considered a sufficient defense if the impact was found to be racially discriminatory. However, the Court later departed somewhat from this position and also relaxed the requirement that tests be validated exclusively on job performance criteria; that is, the Court accepted the use of assessments within the training context as well as on the job in validating tests (*Washington* v. *Davis,* 1976). School districts using tests in the employment process should remain well informed concerning court decisions relating to the use of tests, because this field in under considerable legal scrutiny.

Despite the limitations of tests and the necessity of establishing job-relatedness, carefully selected tests of knowledge and verbal ability have a place in the selection of professional personnel. Obviously, care and caution should characterize the use of tests. As Goodison (1986) stated, it is critical that the strengths and weaknesses of paper and pencil instruments be kept in mind at all times. "The tests must not be made to carry a larger burden than they are capable of bearing; test results cannot solve all the problems of teachers selection, do not predict performance in the classroom and must not take the place of informed decision-making by experienced administrators" (3).

The use of inventories of interests, value, attitudes, or personality is not recommended. Such instruments may be useful for other purposes, in the hands of a skilled psychologist, but not for the selection of personnel.

Serious moral or emotional aberrations can usually be determined by other means, such as the telephone investigations discussed previously. The use of tests such as personality tests only increases the chance that errors will occur. For a personality test to predict an individual's future job performance, the following must be true: personality must be directly related to job performance; certain jobs must require certain personalities; and personality tests used for hiring decisions must accurately measure personality traits (Taylor and Zimmerer 1988, 64). When few or none of these statements is true, the level of risk in using such tests for personnel selection purposes is significantly increased.

Assessment Centers

"Since the 1950s, assessment center methods have been widely used in many countries. In the United States, some 30,000 persons each year are assessed by business, industry, and government" (Wendel and Sybouts 1988, 23). The purpose of these assessment centers is to gather a large amount of relevant information in a short time about candidates for management and executive positions. The results indicate that assessment centers can be effective (Gaugler et al. 1985; Hunter and Hunter 1984; Klimoski and Brickner 1987; Sackett 1987; Schmitt et al. 1984).

An assessment center is "a procedure (not a location) that uses multiple assessment techniques to evaluate employees for a variety of manpower purposes and decisions" (Thornton and Byham 1982, 3). The approach used in the assessment center involves the systematic observation of the candidates' behavior in individual and group situations by trained observers (assessors). At least one of the situations observed must be a simulation for the process to be considered an assessment center (Crawford and Halliwell 1986, 1). Evaluation techniques used in the assessment center typically include a variety of simulations and exercises: leaderless group activities, in-basket exercises, interviews, and paper-and-pencil tests. These techniques are designed to reveal behavioral strengths and weaknesses of those being assessed. Assessors combine their observations of each candidate into an overall evaluation report, which is shared with the candidate.

As defined by the Third International Congress on the Assessment Center Method in its "Standards for Ethical Considerations for Assessment Center Operations," the following kinds of activities do not constitute an assessment center:

Panel interviews or a series of sequential interviews as the sole technique

Reliance on a specific technique (regardless of whether it is a simulation) as the sole basis for evaluation

Using only a test battery composed of a number of pencil-and-paper measures, regardless of whether the judgments are made by a statistical or judgmental pooling of scores

Single-assessor measurement (often referred to as individual assessment)—measurement by one individual using a variety of techniques, such as pencil-and-paper tests, interviews, personality measures, and simulations

The use of several simulations with more than one assessor where there is no pooling of data—that is, each assessor prepares a report on performance in an exercise, and the individual reports (unintegrated) are used as the final product of the center

A physical location labeled as an "assessment center" that does not conform to the requirements noted above. (Moses and Byham 1977, 304–5).

DeMont and Hughes (1984) suggest that there are four fundamental conditions to be met in establishing and implementing an assessment center process. First, specific competencies related to successful performance in a specific role (the principal) must be identified and agreed upon. The assessment process then targets this specific role and the competencies needed. Second, the simulations and activities used during the assessment process must provide opportunities for those being assessed to demonstrate or display the competencies needed. Third, the levels of successful performance for each competency must have been identified prior to the beginning of the assessment process. Fourth, the assessors must have been trained and be thoroughly familiar with the competencies, the levels of successful performance, and the assessment activities (220). "One of the most vital elements in the success and validity of the assessment center is the training and subsequent performance of the assessors" (Milstein and Fielder 1988). A profile of successful assessors as developed by the National Association of Secondary School Principals (NASSP) project includes: eight to fifteen years of experience as a school-based administrator, commitment to the process, an energy level higher than average, and high regard by peers. Competence in skills related to performance observation and communication is also required of the assessors. Perhaps one of the greatest contributions of the assessment center process relates to the requirement that the competencies needed for a specific role must be identified and agreement must be reached on measurable outcomes related to that role.

In education, assessment centers have been developed primarily for use in selection, placement, and professional development of administrators. One of the first national efforts designed to improve the selection and development of entry-level school administrators using a validated assessment center approach was the NASSP Assessment Center Project (Hersey 1986, 16). Its first assessment center opened in Virginia in 1976. The assessment center as developed by the NASSP has been validated and court-tested, and operates in more than thirty states and three foreign countries (Richardson 1988, 4). In addition to the NASSP centers, school districts, colleges and universities, and intermediate agencies such as educational service centers operate assessment center projects.

Shulman (1987) and the research team working on the Teacher Assessment Project associated with the development of a national certification program by the National Board for Professional Teaching Standards have suggested the concept of a teaching assessment center:

> *A teaching assessment, for example, might ask candidates to examine several alternative textbooks in their special fields, critically analyzing their accuracy, the perspective they take on the material covered, the kind of pedagogy they represent, their contrast with other instructional materials in the field, their appropriateness for different groups of learners, and the goals to which they are directed. Candidates might then be asked to prepare for their departments or school boards reports on the suitability of the books.*
>
> *This exercise would provide evidence of each candidate's knowledge of curriculum understanding of alternative teaching methods and goals, and appreciation of differences among students. A candidate's writing and speaking abilities (if an oral report is required) and capability for critical reading and comprehension would also be evident. In addition, the context in which the basis skills of reading, writing, and speaking are assessed would be far more realistic and educationally relevant than in most current assessment. (40)*

Shulman goes on to state that "the use of an assessment center, though necessary to improve the state of teacher testing, will not by itself be sufficient. Some method must be found to document the performance of candidates in their classrooms" (40). In the assessment center process, as with all selection tools and procedures, the probably of success is enhanced when the selection decision is based on deliberate and reflective consideration of multiple job-related criteria and predictors.

Decision Making

Throughout this book the position is taken that all who will be affected by the person chosen for a given job should have considerable involvement in decisions concerning selection criteria and the procedures that will be followed. In teacher selection, for example, representatives of the teacher, parents, and students might well assist the school administration in determining the selection criteria and procedures. On the other hand, once the ground rules are set, actual selection decisions should be made by a small number of highly trained, competent, responsible people. The involvement of teachers in a team approach to selection is highly recommended. In a study of faculty participation in personnel selection, Gips and Bredeson (1984) found that "teachers do in fact want to be involved in the selection of fellow teachers and principals. However, there is a subtlety in terms of how teachers see themselves involved in the total process. Few teachers saw the selection of personnel as solely their responsibility. In fact, teachers saw themselves in supportive and consultative roles making recommendations on selection criteria, processes and candidates." (21) Too often, in the name of democracy, candidates are subjected to interviews with many people who are not trained interviewers and who are not aware of the severe limitations of interviews as predictors of performance. In short, policies and procedures should be determined by those who have a stake in the outcome, but the technical work should be done by the experts. An "expert" is anyone who has genuine skill and/or knowledge that is appropriate to the task at hand. Obviously, any staff member may have special expertise to contribute to recruitment and selection activities. Usually, specially trained administrators and supervisors are the ones with these competencies. If the experts (the school principals and the people in the central personnel office, for example) do not have the required expertise, then they should develop it or be replaced by those who do.

Drucker (1985) states that there is no magic involved in making good staffing decisions; rather, good decision making requires hard work, disciplined thought, and "careful understanding of the most important capabilities that a given job requires and of the strengths and weaknesses of each candidate. No mystery here, just good management" (22). Though he was writing about the business community, Drucker spoke indirectly to the needs and responsibilities of educational administrators as well by emphasizing the importance of personnel selection decision making:

> *Executives spend more time on managing people and making people decisions than on anything else—and they should. No other decisions are so long lasting in their consequences or so difficult to unmake. An yet, by and large, executives make poor promotion and staffing decisions. By all accounts, their batting average is no better than .333: at most one-third of such decisions turn out right; one-third are minimally effective; and one-third are outright failures.*
>
> *In no other area of management would we put up with such miserable performance. Indeed, we need not and should not. (22)*

As noted throughout this chapter, the selection of personnel is a complicated and complex decision-making process. Bredeson summarized (1985), that "even after years of rigorous empirical/analytical studies, we still cannot sum the findings of these studies to give us a meaningful total view of personnel selection" (9). In working to develop a decision-making model for school administrators, Bredeson suggested that a major problem with much of the research on selection stems from the fact that the relationship of the parts to the whole is lost when an attempt is made to reduce the selection process to only variables and subunits. Understanding the processes (components and relationships) of personnel selection may be an important first step in improving actual practice (14). In Bredeson's conceptual model, four theoretical strands—decision theory, impression formation, inference theory, and rating theory—are woven together to explain personnel selection processes and activities. "The four theoretical strands give support to the notion that the personnel selection process is made up of a series of selection activities which take place within an environment characterized by values and situations" (12).

Summary

Through effective staffing, a school district can make significant progress in accomplishing its mission of instructional improvement. The staffing activities of recruitment and selection are inherently linked and interdependent. The primary goal of recruitment is to locate and attract a large pool of applicants representative of the ethnic, racial, gender, and socioeconomic composition of the population to be served. The goal of the selection process is to identify and employ from the candidate pool the "best" applicant for each vacant position. Prior to any recruitment or selection activities, the criteria and standards for successful performance must be identified and studied. Then selection tools to be used as predictors of successful performance must be identified and those who will use the tools must be trained in their use. Predictors commonly used in education include: application forms, transcripts, resumes, letters of recommendation, telephone investigations, testing, and rating scales. The assessment center concept has been used primarily for selecting administrators but is being recommended as a selection process for teaching personnel as well.

Those charged with selection responsibilities are cautioned to proceed carefully in the use of selection tools and processes. No tool or process has enough merit to stand alone as a basis for decision making. The selection activity is enhanced by the use of multiple criteria, predictors, and decision makers. The input of those who will work with and support new employees is strongly encouraged as a means of giving credibility and strength to the activity. In schools, people are the most important assets and the greatest weaknesses. The careful selection of competent personnel enhances the probability of both personal and organization success.

Suggested Study Sources

Arvey, Richard D., and James E. Campion. 1982. "The Employment Interview: A Summary and Review of Recent Research," *Personnel Psychology* 35(2): 281–322.

This article summarizes approximately sixty years of research on the employment interview, including reliability and validity of the interview, methodological issues, decision making, interviewer training, minority characteristics, nonverbal behavior, interviewee characteristics, and interviewee training. The authors discuss the persistence of the interview as a selection tool and includes suggestions for further research.

Bredeson, Paul V. 1985. "The Teacher Screening and Selection Process: A Decision Making Model for School Administrators," *Journal of Research and Development in Education* 18 (3): 8–15.

The author's major assumption is that the employment of teachers and other personnel is one of the most important tasks of school administrators. The task is also a very complex one. Following a discussion of four theoretical strands—decision theory, impression formation, inference theory, and rating—for understanding, describing, and explaining personnel selection processes, a model for decision making is proposed.

Gatewood, Robert D., and Herbert Feild. 1990. *Human Resource Selection.* 2nd ed. Chicago: The Dryden Press.

This work presents an in-depth discussion of all aspects of the selection process. Chapters are devoted to topics on legal issues in selection, job analysis, application forms, reference checks, interviewing, and testing. The book is directed toward the selection of personnel in business and industry.

Vukovich, Eli. 1987. *Teacher Selection Process: Part I. How to Use References.* Foster City, CA: American Association of School Personnel Administrators.

This guide and its accompanying video tape offer instruction in how to use references in the teacher selection process. Subjective and objective analyses of the information found in references written by teachers and/or supervisors are studied and explained. The primary emphasis is on evaluation of reference material for beginning teachers.

Wendel, Frederick C., and Ward Sybouts. 1988. *Assessment Center Methods in Educational Administration: Past, Present, and Future.* Tempe, AZ: The University Council for Educational Administration.

This monograph describes past and current practices for recruiting and selecting school administrators and the potential use of the assessment center method in these staffing activities. The authors conclude that "the development of the assessment center method by government and industry has been adapted for educational purposes and has moved researchers to conclude that the assessment center process is far superior to the historically accepted approach that reflect the feelings, opinions and judgements of a hiring official base on data that were largely subjective" (42).

Young, I. Phillip, and Dean Ryerson. 1986. *Teacher Selection: Legal, Practical and Theoretical Aspects.* Tempe, AZ: The University Council for Educational Administration.

In this monograph the authors outline the legal, applied, and theoretical issues of teacher selection. A major portion of the work is directed toward the study of predictor refinement and validation. Models of teacher selection are discussed and analyzed. The need for cooperative research efforts involving school districts and universities is pointed out.

_7_

Assigning and Balancing Staff Groups

The staffing of schools should be carried out for the purpose of improving instruction as well as maintaining existing programs. This principle, if actively applied, will significantly affect the procedures for assigning individuals and balancing staff groups, which is one of the interdependent, ongoing activities of the personnel staffing function. Earlier chapters presented principles as bases for performing the tasks of personnel administration, among them the need for flexibility in assigning staff and the need for attention to influence and control factors affecting staff assignments. It has also been emphasized that two general characteristics desired of school personnel are functional competence and the ability to work effectively with students and adults. These principles and other factors related to assigning and balancing staff groups are interrelated in various ways.

Interrelated Factors

Assigning personnel and balancing staff groups involve personnel administration processes and decisions of many kinds. In the simplest sense, these tasks involve relating openings to requirements to needs. When improvement of instruction is the goal, however, such simple relationships become more complex. One of the tenets of this chapter is that personnel vacancies can be the stimuli for making need adjustments and structural and curriculum changes, rather than being treated merely as positions to be filled. Exhibit 7.1 on page 130 suggests three sets of factors to be considered: (1) categories of position openings, (2) positional requirements of personnel to fill such openings, and (3) assignment procedures flexibly applied to produce decisions that include both improvement and maintenance needs. If

EXHIBIT 7.1 Relationships Among Three Sets of Factors in Assigning and Balancing Staff

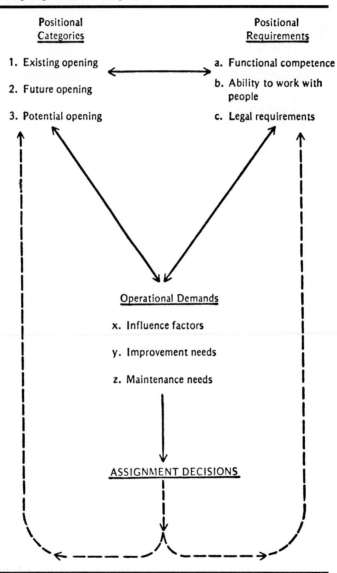

Positional Categories	Positional Requirements
1. Existing opening	a. Functional competence
2. Future opening	b. Ability to work with people
3. Potential opening	c. Legal requirements

Operational Demands

x. Influence factors

y. Improvement needs

z. Maintenance needs

ASSIGNMENT DECISIONS

instructional improvements are to be assured, the administrators responsible for filling an opening must be aware that innovations or program changes are pending. Effective communication and cooperation within the school organization are required, with supervisors and program designers given opportunities to review staffing recommendations before final decisions are made.

Positional Categories

Jobs can be specified in terms of any array of designated positions, but they can also be specified as existing, future, and potential. Obviously, existing openings often call for a direct response of some kind. It is tempting, of course, to expedite matters and simply seek the most readily available person who fulfills the positional requirements shown in Exhibit 7.1. However, future openings may influence decisions regarding the filling of existing vacancies in several ways. Present openings and future openings may suggest opportunities for reorganization or reassignment that might not be feasible with only one or another opening alone. If reorganization plans seem feasible because of the variety of openings being considered, then competence, too, may need to be redefined.

Potential openings are another category of positions that can become part of the assigning and balancing process. Positions may be *potential* in nature because of impending changes in legal, financial, or growth factors. Evaluation reports or project plans may generate potential positions where none actually exist. The process whereby these become specific estimates of need or desire as part of a plan for staffing in the future can make a genuine contribution to possible reassignment and balancing decisions.

Consider, for example, the situation in the foreign language program of a school system. Anticipated retirements, the promotion of one teacher of Russian to a vice-principalship, and a resignation may create five openings within a period of eighteen months to two years. However, in this case new legislation on bilingual education is pending, and new positions might be opened and demands for reassignment created. Instead of simply seeking five replacements of foreign language teachers, a careful reevaluation of needs may well be in order. The one and one-half positions devoted to Latin courses may not be high priorities any longer. Even the single series of courses in Russian may now be appropriately reviewed and a plan developed for using various positions, actual and potential, to restructure foreign language and bilingual programs.

Positional Requirements

Openings of all kinds need to be reevaluated in terms of the requirements guiding selection of persons for them. Exhibit 7.1 indicates at least three types of positional requirements that might be considered. Functional competence has repeatedly been stressed in previous chapters of this book. The ability to work with people is sometimes thought of as a competency, but it tends to be such a universal requirement of positions in schools that it deserves unique consideration. Finally, legal requirements (including quasilegal constraints, such as union contracts) inevitably influence the way positions are treated in assigning or balancing staff.

Functional competence is the subject of much of the discussion of a previous chapter as well as this one. The attention to competence, as personally held capabilities to perform, is directed by the nature of the position being considered for assignment or reassignment. Existing openings may need to be redefined in terms of desired competence based on prior experience with persons in the position and evaluations of outcomes produced. Future and potential openings, too, require redefinition in terms of functional competence, to ensure that past mistakes are not repeated, new demands are addressed, and changes are facilitated.

The ability to work with people is not easily determined, but it may be a crucial prerequisite for "sensitive" positions. The librarian, counselor, supervisor, team leader, home visitor, and principal are but a few positions where the ability to relate to many people, under stress, in constructive ways is essential to the proper exercise of technical competence. All teaching positions, of course, demand a large measure of this human relations capability. There are some positions in which such abilities are not crucial, even though highly desirable. Generally, however, the ability to get along with people is too important to ignore. Differences in this ability need to be assessed more in terms of coping with stressful situations, handling conflict, mediating opposing views, and adapting to changing relationships.

Legal requirements that influence assignment decisions are increasing in number and complexity. Union contracts, federal guidelines, state laws, court decisions, and local traditions imposed by local policy influence assignment and balancing decisions. These requirements can be viewed as constraints, and they often are. But too much emphasis on constraining effects tends to immobilize administrators and supervisors in personnel matters. In fact, legal requirements can be stimulators for change. The anticipated legal mandate of a bilingual program may be an opportunity for better compliance with EEOC guidelines, and it may also be an opportunity for a major programmatic effort to reduce dropout rates.

Operational Demands

The all-important vehicle for relating positional categories to personnel requirements to assignment decisions is a careful plan for operational change or maintenance, as demands require. Obviously, influencing factors may dictate either change or maintenance of programs; most frequently the influence of people both within and outside the school setting will be toward maintaining the status quo. However, if improvement needs have been clearly identified and prioritized along with maintenance needs, then staffing decisions can reflect both.

Influence factors often have little to do with instructional program maintenance or change. A staffing decision may involve personal ambitions, the path of least resistance, a way of saving money, or a way of extending a special favor to someone. Still other influences may be more clearly political or social in nature, as reflected in recent efforts to provide more adequately for handicapped students, for ethnic balance, or for bilingual needs of non-English-speaking minorities.

An array of influences nearly always reflects a great diversity of operational demands. Regardless of their legitimacy from an educational point of view, they are realities that must be accepted, changed, or manipulated in some way. The essence of good leadership may be found in the way the least relevant influence factors are dealt with in making assignment decisions.

Improvement needs may be associated with certain influences but require special attention to ensure fullest recognition and proper consideration when assignment decisions are being made. Improvement needs are often identified through public pressures or staff-expressed concerns. In both instances, they should be carefully defined in terms of personnel decisions that can be of assistance. Routine or special evaluation studies are valuable sources of information for use in determining improvement needs, but they often need interpretation as staff assignment alternatives. Still another source for the identification of improvement needs is in officially approved goals, priorities, and development programs. Where such commitments to change have been made, staff assignment decisions need to be made with such changes clearly in mind.

Maintenance Needs

It is rarely possible to ignore maintenance needs for long. The urgent requirements for maintaining operations are nearly always self-evident and clearly felt as persistent needs. Even so, unwise staff assignment decisions can be made under the pressures of influencing factors or improvement needs that ignore maintenance requirements. Such errors usually become evident quickly, but undesirable consequences then ensue. In Chapter 2 the tendency to ignore staff personnel requirements for the developmental function was discussed. This problem is often related to a neglect of maintenance needs that results from assigning new programs and project responsibilities to regular staff without relieving them of maintenance responsibilities. Under such conditions maintenance tasks may be temporarily neglected. Serious repercussions can follow, and the new program efforts may be abandoned or corrupted (Harris, 1985).

New Personnel Assignment

The employment contract rarely includes designation of the site to which an employee is assigned. The assignment process is generally carried out through administrative action, which may be reviewed or approved by the board of trustees, depending upon local policy. Most often the employment contract states that the employee may be assigned or reassigned by the superintendent of schools. The assigning or reassigning of personnel, therefore, generally is the result of executive action in a school district.

Policy and Regulation

School districts generally have a written school board policy on the assignment and reassignment of personnel. Development of such a policy helps to ensure that the district has an official position in the matter and also prevents problems that emerge when such actions are taken without guidelines. An illustration of a policy statement on assignment and reassignment follows:

> All personnel are subject to assignment or reassignment by the superintendent with the approval of the board of trustees.
>
> All personnel are subject to transfer within the district to ensure equal educational opportunity.
>
> Transfers by the superintendent that result from organizational changes shall be made so as to avoid reduction in pay grade and personal hardship whenever possible.

Such a policy statement makes clear the prerogative that the administration intends to retain. Union contracts may restrict such administrative authority with provisions for appeal, recognition of seniority, and just cause, but the constraints are more likely to apply to reassignment than to new personnel assignment.

Assignment of new personnel is not the sensitive matter that reassignment can become. Hence, policies and regulations covering the latter are more carefully considered later in this chapter. Guidelines to consider in formulating policies and regulations for new personnel assignment are as follows:

1. Assignment decisions are clearly differentiated from selection, employment, and salary decisions, even though they are inevitably interrelated.
2. Preliminary assignment decisions are always subject to change to accommodate the needs of the school program.
3. Systematic procedures for changing assignments are specified to ensure flexibility in staffing and also give due process consideration to the individuals involved.
4. Assignments are guided by clearly specified criteria and procedures.

5. Assignments are collaborative decisions involving those principally affected as well as those with competence in applying related criteria.
6. Competence to perform is always the overriding criterion in assignment decisions.

Selection-Assignment Relationships

Once the list of potential new staff members has been formulated, the task of the final selection and assignment of these persons to individual school campuses or other positions begins. To accomplish this task, it is imperative that consideration be given to the basis on which assignments are made.

The final selection of staff members must obviously be made with regard to the vacancies that exist or can be created by reassignment, the competencies needed in each position and specified by the job description, and other influencing factors. In essence, with the exception of those persons employed and placed in a pool for future assignment to known or projected vacancies, the final selection and employment of personnel and their assignments are accomplished simultaneously.

In most school districts, these initial assignments of new personnel generally are made in accordance with needs expressed in terms of an organizational vacancy (e.g., second grade or American history), the qualifications and certification of the new personnel, and federal, state, and local guidelines that affect the assignment process.

Alternative View of Needs

Traditionally, "needs" are expressed and responded to on a one-to-one, ad hoc basis. That is to say, a particular individual in a particular grade, subject, school, or assignment, with a particular positional title, *creates* a need by resigning, being dismissed, retiring, or being promoted or demoted. Such an isolated need is treated as a simple replacement problem, which calls for traditional selection and assignment procedures. Alternatives that might be considered in seeking to make a vacancy serve the improvement of instruction include a quite different approach, suggested by these alternative actions:

1. Fill the vacancy by reassignment so as to create a vacancy in another part of the organization where a change is desired.
2. Fill the vacancy by reassignment so as to create another vacancy in which an outstanding applicant, who could not otherwise be justifiably selected, can be selected to serve.
3. Decline to fill the vacancy, reorganizing the operating unit to make it more economical.

4. Reorganize the operating unit *prior* to filling the vacancy, thereby re-defining the position to be filled in order to improve the operation.
5. Combine any of the foregoing.

Traditionally, qualifications and certification of new personnel are considered in both selection and assignment decisions in rather superficial ways. The problem generated by this practice in securing well-qualified teachers and administrators was discussed in the previous chapter. New and serious problems emerge when new personnel assignments are not based on competence as well as basic selection criteria of more traditional kinds.

Various legal (and quasilegal) constraints exert enormous influence on the assignment of new personnel. Maintaining a close relationship between assignments and the recruitment and selection process so as to ensure improvements in staff quality requires skilled personnel management. Some of the constraints include (1) limits on funds (and positions) available; (2) limits on personnel imposed by physical facilities and kinds of instructional programs; (3) limits on class size imposed by traditions, teacher or parental expectations, local policy, accreditation standards, or space; and (4) limits imposed by the lack of available qualified personnel. Sources of these constraints are numerous and vary widely from state to state and within states because of local conditions. Some of the most common sources are state laws, state and local funding agencies, and local and state regulations. Less recognized sources of constraints include accreditation associations, federal program guidelines, professional association standards, organized teachers' associations, and lay pressure groups.

Involvement in Assignment

Another matter that should be considered in the process of determining the skills needed at the local level, as well as the eventual assignment of the new employee, is the involvement of other personnel in the decision-making process. There are members of the local campus staff and the supervisory staff who might justifiably be involved. The staff members in the local schools should be involved in the schools' instructional goal-setting process, as well as in the assessment of instructional competencies needed among the staff members to achieve these goals. Participating staff members not only are acquainted with and committed to the objectives of the local school instructional program, they are also aware of the competencies needed in new personnel. Hence, they may be very well qualified to assist in the selection and assignment processes.

Similarly, supervisory personnel—curriculum specialists, training specialists, coordinators and consultants of various programs—have specialized knowledge to bring to the selection-assignment process. They also have responsibilities for coordinating and developing instructional programs with superordinate goals in view. As such, they have a legitimate stake in the quality of the decisions reached.

It is not possible, of course, for every person with a conceivable interest to participate in assigning personnel. Nonetheless, the commonly employed decision rule—one man, one decision—is about as outmoded as the Texas fable—"one riot, one Ranger." Neither principals nor personnel directors or superintendents should be making critical instructional personnel selection or assignment decisions in monarchical fashion. A basically sound rule of involvement states: *All those people should be involved, as nearly as possible, who have the interest and are willing to participate, if they also have some responsibility for the consequences that follow, are directly affected by the consequences, or have special expertise that will enhance the process.*

In summary, the task of filling personnel vacancies can present opportunities to reanalyze and possibly revamp the instructional program for the purpose of improving its quality. In fact, this point of view not only is appropriate but also should be made operational by the personnel administrators in any district. For example, by the consistent use of a procedure whereby the personnel department formally requests that the school principal specify the major competencies and/or skills needed on the staff when any vacancy exists, a thrust toward improvement is made operational to some degree. Without such a dynamic orientation toward personnel assignment, only a few schools are likely to take advantage of the opportunity afforded by a personnel change.

Another suggested practice to use in assigning new personnel is to involve an array of staff members as well as the school principal in the various selection and review processes with prospective employees at the local campus and central staff levels. The involvement of these persons in the process will increase the likelihood of a quality appointment. Furthermore, feelings of responsibility for the appointment decisions and the manner in which the new employee will become an integrated team or faculty member will be enhanced. This procedure, of course, is time-consuming, but it generally will reap extensive benefits in the long run. The involvement of teachers in the selection and assignment of new colleagues may result in many rewards for the new employee, the staff, and the district (Gips and Bredeson 1984; Wise et al. 1987). An underlying belief is that such involvement "forces people to talk about good teaching—it's one of the ways in which people talk about what their shared knowledge base is and what their shared values are—and once you've selected somebody, you're much more inclined to support that person as a member of the faculty" (Meek 1988, 15).

Misassignment of Personnel

"A scandal in the making for the entire profession" is how Robinson characterizes the misassignment of teachers in the public schools (1985, 6). Assigning teachers to classes for which they are not trained and well prepared frequently occurs because of enrollment and program changes that result in either a need for new teachers who cannot be found or a need to release some teachers and make do with those remaining. Administrators in many states are permitted to make out-of-field assignments under specified conditions. Robinson found that "while three-quarters of the states possess an explicit policy or regulation acknowledging that out-of-field teaching is pedagogically unsound, few or none have reliable means for measuring its incidence within their own jurisdiction" (p. 6). In an attempt to deal with the growing concern over the misassignment of teachers and the teacher shortage, states have enacted several types of irregular certification—alternative certification, emergency certification, and out-of-field certification. Robinson continues:

> The effect of misassignment on teachers and the teaching profession is speculative. It can be assumed that teachers would rather teach a subject they know than one they do not, but there is some evidence that teachers do not always know what subjects they are officially authorized to teach, and are therefore reluctant to resist misassignments.
>
> On another level, it seems clear that most parents do not know that state laws or regulations permit assignment of teachers outside their fields of competence. In this case, inadequacy on the part of an out-of-field teacher will probably be ascribed to personal shortcomings or poor professional preparation; only the students may know that the teacher is improvising with unfamiliar material. (6)

McLaughlin et al. (1986) contend that administrative decisions to assign teachers outside their fields can actually contribute to incompetence: "Assigning teachers to courses outside their area of interest and competence is the administrative action most damaging to teachers' self-esteem and satisfaction" (423). They note that the consequences of misassignment are particularly harmful to new teachers: "Teachers whose initial assignments are frustrating or stressful seem more likely to experience decreased commitment, confidence, and satisfaction in later years than those whose initial assignments are supportive and satisfying" (426).

It is probably safe to say that many administrators are also misassigned due to the same factors involved in teacher misassignment. Administrators may also be misassigned because of failure on the part of superiors to take appropriate and needed action when an administrator's performance is unacceptable, thereby allowing an individual to pass through the administrative ranks to a position that has minimum impact on students and learning.

New Personnel Induction

Once the assignment decision has been made, new personnel must be inducted into the organization. While a school district can recruit, select, and even assign personnel, these individuals will not become highly productive until they are knowledgeable about the work to be performed and the environment in which it is to be performed. Castetter (1986) defines induction as a systematic organizational effort to minimize problems confronting new personnel, so that they can contribute maximally to the work of the school and at the same time realize personal and professional satisfaction. Harris (1985) defines orientation of new personnel in almost identical terms (11).

The importance of an effective induction or orientation program is becoming increasingly apparent to school administrators. Jensen (1987) notes that although state legislatures, teacher training institutions, and school districts are frequently accused of responding slowly to the suggestions of researchers, in recent years there has been an immediate response to the need for teacher induction programs. This has occurred for many reasons, but chief among them are the needs to retain individuals in the professional and to protect the investment of resources utilized in recruiting, selecting, and training competent teachers (36). Induction programs contribute significantly to personnel security and satisfaction. Perhaps at no time in a staff member's period of service is there a greater need for consideration, guidance, and understanding than during the first few months of employment. Nettles (1990) summarizes the problem of the new teacher as follows:

> *The teaching profession is probably the only profession where an entering professional is expected to be self-sufficient the first day he or she reports to work. It has been the practice of the education profession to place beginning employees in classrooms and expect them to perform at the same level as all other employees. New employees in most business and industrial settings are placed in extensive training programs once they report to work, and most professions have internships for those entering the profession. (1)*

Major problems confronting new teachers are associated with understanding and making adjustments to the community and the school district, the expectations of their position, and relationships with other school personnel. Some new teachers may also face problems of a personal nature, such as locating living accommodations, learning their way around the community, and securing transportation. If the sociocultural character of the community, staff, or student group is different from those the new teacher has known, there may be additional problems. Huling-Austin et al. (1989) note that new teachers find themselves on the spot personally and professionally: "Often they get the worst assignments and the heaviest loads. For many the first year is a sink-or-swim experience" (5). Clearly, induction programs are needed, and this should be a major concern of the school district personnel office as well as the local unit staff.

Personnel Reassignment

Some of the major problems confronting personnel departments in school systems are associated with reassigning personnel laterally. The authority to reassign teachers laterally in most school districts is vested in the super-intendent of schools, and this is usually specified in the teacher's contract. In some instances, the conditions and procedures for reassigning personnel are negotiated with teacher organizations, and the personnel office must adhere to those agreements when reassigning teaching personnel.

The need to reassign personnel in a school district may stem from several valid causes, such as: (1) achieving racial-ethnic-sex balance as required by law, (2) implementing special programs, (3) reducing job stag-nation, (4) improving team balance, (5) addressing student population changes, and, (6) reducing stress, burnout, or other symptoms of career disillusionment (Edelwich and Brodsky 1980). The transfer of personnel for reasons related to legal requirements, special programs, team balance, and the changing student population are addressed to some degree in other sections of this book, and reassignment to reduce job stagnation and stress is considered below.

Reduction of Job Stagnation

A problem quite often ignored is the need to consider reassignment as a means of reducing stagnation on the job. This is a difficult and touchy area for the school district, but it is critical to both individuals and the organiza-tion because of the inherent link between job stagnation and employee turnover and job satisfaction. The evidence is voluminous that many teach-ers become discouraged and abandon teaching: thirty percent of new teach-ers leave in the first two years of teaching and forty to fifty percent leave during the first seven years (Huling-Austin et al. 1989). Many leave because of a lack of assistance and support and many leave because their expecta-tions have not been fulfilled. Watts and White (1988) define job satisfaction as the degree to which the employee's expectations are met on four levels:

organizationwide factors, immediate work environment, job content, and personal factors. Lack of job satisfaction generally leads to stagnation and, eventually, turnover. The perceived lack of growth or promotion opportunities, dissatisfaction with co-workers and supervision, dissatisfaction with the work itself—repetitiveness, lack of autonomy, and stress—are common causes for dissatisfaction (81). The terms "teacher stress" and "teacher burnout" are frequently used to describe the stagnation-dissatisfaction syndrome, but regardless of the term used, the result is lower morale and productivity. Edelwich and Brodsky (1980) suggest that four predictable "stages of disillusionment" can be detected in burnout cases, permitting early intervention by individuals and institutions.

As noted by Elam (1989), the portrait of the profession painted by U.S. teachers is not pretty: they tend to regard themselves as martyrs and to believe they are unappreciated and underrewarded. Reporting on the second Gallup/Phi Delta Kappa survey of U.S. teachers' attitudes toward the public schools (1989), Elam concludes that the martyr syndrome is revealed through responses that indicate that teachers see their services as more valuable than medicine, the clergy, and the bench, and their prestige as lower than that of funeral directors, realtors, and advertising practitioners (785). They see themselves trapped by the system in which they work in unrewarding and stressful assignments. Holcomb (1983) suggests that few things are worse than feeling trapped, but that the trapped teacher is better off than the burned-out teacher: "The feeling of constriction can be relieved almost instantly through new challenges—challenges that provide opportunities for growth and personal testings. Whereas the burned-out teacher believes he must escape education to become whole again, the trapped teacher still is interested in himself and teaching" (39). Haskvitz (1987) identified six major traits of teacher dropouts: (1) average to above average in teaching ability; (2) a moonlighter who finds more satisfaction with the other job; (3) bored with no hope for advancement; (4) five to seven years of teaching experience; (5) experiences high levels of emotional exhaustion; and (6) between the ages of 25 and 34, usually more analytical, and frequently in nonelementary positions (24).

DiGeronimo (1985), considering the problem from a personnel administrator's perspective, concluded that boredom was the hidden factor behind many educators' decisions to leave the profession, and that potentially burned-out educators frequently were revitalized by transfer to another school, grade level, or assignment (178). Years of teaching the same subject in the same school at the same grade level takes a toll on many professionals. Many teachers learn what is needed to function effectively in an assignment within one to three years; job stagnation may occur as they remain on the job for a number of years after this learning period. Krupp (1987) notes that opportunities for growth and reversal of the disillusionment experienced by many mature teachers are inadvertently provided by situations involving the closing of schools and involuntary transfers:

"Teachers report that positive aspects of the transfer include higher levels of enthusiasm, more time spent reflecting, enlarged perceptions of student development and district needs, more dialogue and sharing with staff, and less likelihood that they will leave teaching" (26). She found that the teachers who felt most positive about reassignments were those who had been consulted about the change, whose reassignment requests were honored, or who had been consulted personally when requests could not be honored. Changes in staff assignment should be discussed regularly with staff, and administrators should take an active role in encouraging teachers to consider diversity of assignment (DiGeronimo 1985, 178).

If a school district seriously considers occasional lateral reassignments to reduce job stagnation, it should consider establishing a written policy. By doing so and positively recognizing this practice, it will reduce the stigma often associated with being transferred laterally. It should be noted that this practice may be appropriate for administrators, supervisors, and others, as well as for teachers. As Holcomb (1983) concluded, feeling trapped is not the exclusive province of the classroom teacher; it is experienced by counselors, administrators, and other educators, but perhaps in differing forms and to different degrees (39).

Stress Reduction

That teaching, administering, and supervising are high-stress jobs is widely recognized, and the serious and debilitating physical and emotional consequences of stress are widely recognized in the medical, educational, and business communities. It is also acknowledged that educators, like all workers, typically encounter a great deal of stress outside the workplace, such as interpersonal problems, family problems, and financial problems. The teacher or administrator who experiences personal stress outside the job must cope with it in the context of a demanding work situation, and this may create a difficult situation for everyone involved. Little attention is given to the fact that school organizations can help to reduce stressful conditions, for individuals if not for all personnel. The reassignment of personnel to assist them in resolving problems at home or to relieve them of job pressures can improve job satisfaction and performance. The temporary reassignment of a principal to a supervisory position in a central office may permit time for recuperation as well as offering new growth opportunities. A permanent reassignment from one school community to another, for a staff member who has been in conflict with influential parents, for example, can offer a chance to start over. A word of caution about this form of reassignment, however: it should not be used to evade responsibility when dismissal is in order.

Induction of Reassigned Personnel

The orientation and induction of reassigned personnel into their new situation is critical. This important task usually becomes the responsibility of individual principals or supervisors and consequently is performed with uneven quality. Attention is quite often given to orienting new teachers to a school district, but seldom is given to orienting and providing support services to personnel who have been in the district but have been reassigned or promoted. Often these individuals are expected to adjust to their new assignment or develop the skills necessary to function in their new role without help, and due to their prior experience in teaching and in the district, they may be reluctant to ask for the help they need. The personnel department can and should develop a procedure for routine orientation of this type.

Personnel Promotion

The promotion of personnel is a type of reassignment that requires a variety of administrative and supervisory arrangements to enhance the quality of the school's or district's program.

Personnel administrators must comply with legal constraints in considering promotions just as in selection decisions. Contractual agreements and court orders cannot be ignored in preference for competence. However, strong and continuing initiatives need to be directed by administrators to keep competence-based criteria as dominant as possible in all promotional decisions.

Preparation for Promotion

The essential aspect of a personnel-services program that manages promotions well is the early identification of promising promotees and provision for their professional growth. A program of personnel services should systematically project positions to which people can be promoted, identify potential applicants, and assist them in securing appropriate training and experience prior to the time when promotion decisions are to be made. Aside from legal and/or regulatory constraints that make such preservice training mandatory in many instances, there are advantages to the school system:

1. Prospective applicants demonstrate their motivation and interest in promotion.
2. The risk-taking character of the prospective applicant is tested.

3. Preparatory experiences may enhance the prospective applicant's performance even without a promotion.
4. A larger number of applicants from which to choose can be produced.
5. Preservice assessment data can be used for improving selection decisions.

From the point of view of the prospective applicant for promotion, the district that guides, plans, and facilitates professional growth activities makes a multifaceted contribution to the individual:

1. The individual gains a new appreciation for the openness of the organization.
2. The individual is often stimulated to explore and aspire.
3. The individual feels more a part of the larger organization.
4. The individual gets new options in his or her career within or outside the system.

Support and Development

Although it is not necessarily the personnel office in the school district that must assume the responsibility for providing staff-development support, such support should be there and these efforts should be coordinated with other personnel services. In cases in which there is no plan or set of procedures for this type of support and training, it is suggested that the personnel administrators assume responsibility for initiating such efforts.

Career-development information is one of the kinds of data that the personnel office can readily maintain and offer to in-service training specialists and others in the district who may be more directly involved in staff-development program planning. The concept of the personnel office staff serving as a part of the superintendency team is emphasized by the staff-development service problem. No need deserves more attention, for people are our best resource. But no task demands more sharing of responsibilities among all leadership personnel.

Balancing Staff

An ongoing concern that should be addressed by all personnel administrators within any school or district is the need to minimize imbalances that may exist or develop with regard to staff capabilities. Such imbalances may exist among staff groups from school to school, from level to level within schools, or from program to program. Balanced staff groups are essential to equality of educational opportunity. Balance must be maintained in all aspects of staff characteristics that can substantially affect the quality of instruction. Staff load, competence of personnel, race, ethnicity, sex, and even certain attitudes or orientations toward such important matters as maintenance versus change are worthy of careful consideration in balancing staff groups.

Quite often school districts formally address only those staff imbalances that are under the surveillance of outside authorities or are open public concerns. Staff imbalances in the areas of race, sex, ethnicity, and national origin as defined in the Civil Rights Act quite naturally receive attention.

Meeting nondiscrimination guidelines is extremely important. It is equally important, however, that personnel administrators and school boards give attention and time to rectifying imbalances that exist in many other areas. If severe imbalances exist in basic or specialized competence, in the size or workload of a staff group, or in their responsiveness to change, concerted action is indicated. If these imbalances are not corrected, the quality of the instructional program will surely be negatively affected. In the absence of continuing leadership, staff imbalances multiply, become accepted practices—even traditions—and cause severe and growing defects in programs. Imbalances tend to grow increasingly severe over time. Numerous forces at work in the school-community setting distort staff composition if they are ignored.

Individual principals or supervisors with authority have only limited power to correct imbalances once they have become well-established patterns of staffing. Even when a principal or program director can effect a change to alleviate an imbalance, the change affects only a single area of responsibility. In fact, interschool discrepancies in staff are often the direct outgrowth of the aggressive efforts of a principal, supervisor, or program director. The personnel office, on the other hand, can use a variety of staffing criteria to bring about change throughout an entire school district.

Principles of Staff Balance

Viewed positively, the task of developing and maintaining staff balance is guided by a set of rather fundamental assumptions regarding means/ends relationships in education. Some of these assumptions logically can be extended to provide operating principles:

1. Every student is entitled to equal educational opportunities within the system, however they may be defined.
2. Every neighborhood, community, and socioeconomic stratum in the community is entitled to equal educational opportunities for its children and youth.
3. Staff capabilities determine, to a large extent, the quality of the educational program provided.

EXHIBIT 7.2   Staff Characteristics and Operational Categories Related to Staff Balance

Operation Categories	Technical Competence	Conceptual Competence	Human Competence	Race or Ethnicity	Sex	Orientation to Change
Staff Charateristics						
By Programs						
Within						
Between						
By Operating Unit						
Within						
Between						
By Levels						
Within						
Between						

4. Personnel practices must ensure that the staffs are well balanced with respect to all significant variables in all instructional settings.
5. Personnel practices must ensure that every program and educational level is provided with equally well-balanced, equally high-quality staff.

Those five points, if accepted, permit the adoption of an analytical framework for viewing balance (and imbalance) in a comprehensive way. This framework is shown in Exhibit 7.2.

Monitoring for Balance

The number of staff characteristics and operational categories shown in Exhibit 7.2 makes clear the need for a systematic review process. A systematic survey to secure a variety of data is imperative. Without such systematic survey procedures, certain staff imbalances will very likely not be identified. The follow-up planning to alleviate problems will also require a well-developed data base.

Six different staff characteristics categories are suggested in Exhibit 7.2. Each could be subdivided further, of course. Three of these categories relate to technical, conceptual, and human competence generally applicable to all positions, even though the specific competencies vary from teacher to supervisor to aide to librarian. Racial and ethnic subgroups vary with local conditions. In the Southwest, Mexican-American, Native American, Asian-American, and Anglo-American categories may need to be included in data processing. However, some of these categories of ethnicity may be eliminated in other regions of the country. In a particular community in the Pittsburgh, Pennsylvania area, for instance, black, Polish-American, and Italian-American ethnic categories may be quite important. In Florida, Cuban ethnicity may be important.

The staff characteristics listed in Exhibit 7.2 are not intended as anything more than suggestions for consideration by personnel administrators. Obviously, local problems or concerns may dictate quite different categories of characteristics. Local resident versus nonresident commuter could be an important category in central cities. Long-time employees versus newcomers could be an important category for fast-changing suburban areas. What is important is the inclusion of categories that are really related to the quality of education that could be provided. Because it is not feasible to balance all conceivable variables within a staff, a limited number of "most important" categories needs to be selected.

Operational categories of three types are suggested in Exhibit 7.2. Programs or curricular offerings need to be balanced within and between each. Similarly, schools and other operating units must be balanced both within and between such units.

Programs, schools, and levels tend to be interrelated operational entities, not neatly separable. However, in a survey of staff balance, attention to each of these three operating categories will help to prevent overlooking staff-balancing problems.

Sources of Imbalance

A common staff imbalance in today's senior high schools is one that results from the effects of special programs. An example is the number of coaches required to administer the athletic program. When these individuals must also teach other classes, the situation can, and usually does, result in staff balancing problems; e.g., finding a person who is qualified to coach girls' volleyball and also teach mathematics can present problems. This situation tends to load a school with persons who place most of their energies and time on their coaching responsibilities rather than on teaching academic classes. However, the real character of this problem is best revealed by program analysis within schools and between programs. Only when the data on such situations are gathered and properly analyzed can decision makers act to alleviate the problem.

Another common source of staff imbalance stems from the presence of an aging, tradition-bound staff within a school or program. Personnel who were outstanding in earlier years may fail to keep abreast of new developments and skills and may become obsolescent in the absence of leadership and opportunities for renewal of competencies. This kind of problem demands in-service training. However, reassignments and reorganization to create better balanced staff groups can create more situational flux, call old practices into question, and provide a more stimulating environment within which all staff can grow and instruction can be improved.

Special Programs Imbalance

Special programs can create balance problems, too. They deserve special attention for this reason as well as for the contributions they make. Instructional programs or reforms implemented with "soft" money from the federal government or grant sources carry special liabilities for personnel staffing when the program is discontinued due to loss of funds or poor program performance. In these cases, two very real staff balancing problems exist. First, specialized staff personnel remain in assigned positions even after the priority commitment has been withdrawn. A more serious problem is the continued support of staff personnel whose competence and interests no longer fit the needs for staff balance. Rebalancing staffs after new programs have been abandoned is somewhat the reverse of the previously discussed process of using staffing decisions to help innovative programs succeed. The fact that programs tend to be abandoned in large numbers makes attention to staffing quite important.

It is evident that a pendulum effect operates in education. Slavin (1989) notes that "educational innovation is famous for its cycle of early enthusiasm, widespread dissemination, subsequent disappointment, and eventual decline—the classic swing of the pendulum (752). This educational faddism leads to the development and implementation of many programs that may be characterized as complex, difficult to administer, and personnel-intensive. Typically, these innovative programs start out in a shared funding mode, with the local district providing some portion of the funding. Eventually, however, the district must assume full funding or discontinue the program. A critical question that must be answered relates to the impact of the diversion of staff and funds on existing, continuing programs. Harris's review (1985) of the problem of high rates of "corruption" in innovative program adoptions emphasizes the importance of rigorous attention to special programs and projects in reviewing, reassigning, and balancing staffs (60).

Summary

The responsibilities for assigning, reassigning, and balancing staff personnel are numerous and important. Personnel administration can be the creative and dynamic orchestration of the staffing needs of the schools. The manner in which these tasks are accomplished can affect the instructional program offered to students in very direct ways. Over a period of time, the cumulative effect of not accomplishing these tasks or not doing them well can be serious. To ensure that these tasks are undertaken for the purpose of improving instruction, a proactive philosophy with many dynamic approaches is suggested. By approaching these tasks in imaginative, dynamic ways, many crises can be avoided and the quality of the program can remain a superordinate concern. Personnel administration then not only becomes more widely shared as a leadership function, but those who assume major responsibilities—personnel directors, supervisors, principals, teachers, superintendent, and others—will be working collaboratively toward the goal of instructional improvement.

Suggested Study Sources

Castetter, William B. 1986. *The Personnel Function in Educational Administration*. New York: Macmillan.

The first edition (1962) of this text is considered a classic treatment of school personnel administration. Chapter 11 explores the means by which the personnel induction process can be designed to enhance the development of performance.

Elam, Stanley. 1989. "The Second Gallup/Phi Delta Kappa Poll of Teachers' Attitudes Toward the Public Schools," *Phi Delta Kappan* 70 June (10): 785–98.

This survey, along with previous and past surveys of teacher attitudes, reveals some of the deep concerns of educators. A review of the trends and major issues in such surveys is helpful to the practitioner and student.

Harris, Ben M. 1985. *Supervisory Behavior in Education*. 3d ed. Englewood Cliffs, NJ: Prentice-Hall.

As a comprehensive treatment of instructional supervisory practice, much of this volume has implications for personnel practice that is directed toward the improvement of instruction. The topic of teacher orientation is addressed in Chapter 1, "The Instructional Supervision Function."

Hodgkinson, Harold L. 1989. *The Same Client: The Demographics of Education and Service Delivery Systems*. Washington, DC: Institute for Educational Leadership. ED 312-757.

This report draws on numerous data to explore the complex relationships among family demography, housing, transportation, health, crime, and education. The bewildering array of agencies and services serving, or not serving, the same client is addressed. It is noted that after almost a decade the reform movement has flunked the demographics agenda.

Huling-Austin, Leslie, et al. 1989. *Assisting the Beginning Teacher*. Reston, VA: Association of Teacher Educators.

In the foreword, it is noted that "this volume is published by the association to communicate some of the best thinking on assisting the beginning teacher to those who will make decisions about and carry out the complex tasks of helping the novice" (vii). The appendix includes descriptions of seventeen beginning teacher programs.

Robinson, Virginia. 1985. *Making Do in the Classroom: A Report on the Misassignment of Teachers*. Washington, DC: American Federation of Teachers and the Council for Basic Education. ED 163-108.

This report outlines the problems of teacher misassignment or out-of-field teaching in all fifty states. The discussion addresses the efforts to regulate teacher assignment at various levels, the results of such assignments, and reasons why teachers may be misassigned.

8

Personnel Evaluation

The process of using criterion measurement for the purpose of describing the strengths and weaknesses within and among employees is generally referred to as personnel performance appraisal or personnel performance evaluation. Its role in educational improvement, although long recognized as important, has been identified as a critical issue in recent studies of school reform and restructuring (Holmes Group 1986). "The need for sound evaluation of educational personnel is clear. In order to educate students effectively and to achieve other related goals, educational institutions must use evaluation to select, retain, and develop qualified personnel and to manage and facilitate their work" (Joint Committee on Standards for Educational Evaluation 1988, 5).

Despite their recognized importance and the attention focused upon them, performance appraisals are not well liked. Supervisors are not happy being involved, subordinates dislike being on the receiving end, and the personnel officer shudders at the thought of warehousing all the forms (Zemke 1985, 24). Performance appraisals are frequently characterized as "a lot of work that nobody really wants to do" or as "meaningless exercises that waste time and build bad feelings." Harris characterized them as "games" principals play with teachers (1986, 8–11).

Such expressions arise in part from the apprehension felt by both parties when one is called on to judge the performance of the other. Concern and apprehension escalate to anxiety and hostility when such judgments are tied to employment status in serious doubt. The fact that these judgments are mandated by an empowered authority does not ameliorate the concerns and often contributes to the negativism surrounding evaluation. These negative feelings are especially strong when the personnel being evaluated feel that they have not had input into the evaluation processes implemented and that they are being told that there is only one way to perform—the evaluator's way. A major challenge in personnel evaluation is to reduce the inherent conflicts and negative associations so that meaningful improvement can occur. Sensitivity to both the tasks and the attitudes of evaluation are cornerstones of such an undertaking.

Hoyle et al. (1990) describe the current state of personnel evaluation in the following manner:

> *Staff evaluation systems stand at the crossroads. One road leads to a system created by legislators and special interest groups. The other road leads to a system created by educational researchers and practitioners working with legislators and state department personnel to improve administrators, teachers, and student performance by designing evaluation systems based on best practice. . . . A staff evaluation model must be based on the belief that school personnel will work cooperatively to improve district and individual performance and deserve to be viewed as competent professionals. No single evaluation is adequate to cover all elements of personnel performance. (149)*

This position makes good sense, but it fails to recognize that a substantial part of the problem is the crude and indefensible methods and procedures widely utilized, even when mandates have not been imposed. In short, leaders in personnel administration must get serious about performance appraisal and sharpen their own performance.

In a very practical sense, evaluation of anything is essentially a matter of deciding what we want, describing what we have, and then making judgments and/or decisions about the latter in relation to the former. Personnel evaluation, specifically, is a three-phase process involving (1) determination of the competencies desired, (2) description of performance in terms of the desired competencies, and (3) making of judgments or decisions based on the closeness of fit between the desired and described competencies. This chapter deals with evaluation as one of the multidimensional, ongoing activities of the personnel staffing function cycle that was introduced in Chapter 5. The topics discussed in Chapters 3–5 as they relate to research on teaching, specification of competencies, and job analysis are quite pertinent here.

Purposes of Evaluation

The potential purposes of teacher evaluation have not changed significantly since serious study of the topic began in the early 1900s. In 1939, Cooke suggested that the purposes of teacher evaluation included: (1) the selection of teachers to be prepared and appointed, (2) determination of salaries and promotions, (3) guidance and in-service education, and (4) dismissal, retention, and retirement (185–87). A 1988 Education Research Service report stated that teacher evaluation systems in public education in the context of school reform must serve three major purposes: (1) to ensure that all teachers are at least minimally competent; (2) to improve further the performance of competent teachers; and (3) to identify and recognize the performance of outstanding teachers (1). These statements illustrate that the primary purposes for the evaluation of educational personnel, especially teaching personnel, have remained remarkably constant, but they have also remained very general and readily open to misconception. As a general rule, all purposes of evaluation may be placed within the context of one or more of the following: (1) formative evaluation—to assist in making a process more effective as it continues; (2) summative evaluation—to provide a basis for making decisions with greater, more final consequences; and (3) validation of the selection process—to test the predictive validity of whatever clues and procedures were influential at the time of selection.

Other ways of viewing personnel evaluation are sometimes useful. Stufflebeam and Brethower (1987) have long advocated viewing evaluation in terms of context, input, process, and product evaluation. This has been interpreted for personnel evaluation purposes as preoperational, immediate process, intermediate process, and product evaluation. In still another variation, Harris emphasizes the "diagnostic" characteristics of certain evaluation purposes and instruments (1986, 20, 164).

Regardless of somewhat differing conceptions, there is strong agreement that formative evaluation processes encompass purposes which speak to the identification of strengths and weaknesses or needs for improvement in teaching. In contrast, summative evaluation processes encompass purposes related to selection, retention, promotion, and reward and recognition. These tend to be purposes that relate to career patterns. The information utilized and the data collected in formative and summative evaluation efforts can and should be used to validate the selection process. To the individual being evaluated, the formative purposes are most useful and the summative most crucial, and validation is of little concern. These two major purposes are compared and analyzed in Exhibit 8.1

The relationship of personnel evaluation to *program* evaluation continues to be one of the most neglected in educational affairs. Obviously, neither can be adequately served without relating to the other. The literature remains silent on this issue, so it is not pursued here either.

The Ultimate Goal of Evaluation

The ultimate goal of all performance evaluation in education should be to improve the delivery of instructional services to students. The evaluation process should be focused on the improvement of educators' skills through professional development, and, in a few necessary cases, it should contribute to the removal of incompetent individuals from the profession. Performance appraisal that is positively focused on the improvement of professional competencies has a greater potential for motivating and challenging the individual to strive for improved performance. This is best

EXHIBIT 8.1   Two Major Purposes of Evaluation of Personnel Performance

	Instruments	*Processes*

FORMATIVE
 	
To help the individual to improve performance
	Focused
	Diagnostic
	Descriptive
	Objective
	Process
		Quasiformal
		Evaluatee highly involved in:
		    goal setting
		    data analysis
		    planning
		    evaluating
		Continuous
		Many resources
		Multitargeted focus:
		    evaluatee
		    evaluator
		    organization

SUMMATIVE: To make decisions about personnel	Broad view (e.g., not just classroom teaching) Judgmental Process and product	Formal Evaluatee informed of decision Contractual, legal concerns Infrequent Single-target focus: evaluatee

Adapted from model suggested by David Krathwohl at Educational Testing Service, Princeton, NJ, at a meeting on October 25, 1972.

achieved when the individuals being appraised perceive that they are being evaluated fairly in terms of criteria over which they have some sense of control. Motivated and challenged individuals view the evaluation process in a more positive light and have more confidence in the outcomes of the process. Those who feel threatened or powerless in the evaluation process become defensive and generally resist change: "If personnel evaluation policies and procedures are understandable, cooperatively developed, acceptable to all interested parties, and officially adopted, they are likely to ensure continued cooperation within the personnel evaluation program. Such cooperation fosters support for the program, commitment to its purposes, acceptance of its methods, effective implementation, confidence in the reports, and trust in evaluation outcomes" (Joint Committee on Standards for Educational Evaluation 1988, 75).

Formative Evaluation

Formative evaluation concentrates on pinpointing teachers' strengths and weaknesses to assist them in becoming better teachers: "Most formative models are 'feedback models,' with multiple evaluations spread over an extended period. Coaching may be provided for teachers and formative models can be connected with staff development activities" (Weber 1987, 5). It has been suggested that these activities and processes would be better defined as formative supervision or instructional supervision, as a means of distinguishing them from formal summative evaluation (Streifer 1987, 3). The distinction between components of the summative and formative processes to enhance performance is a critical one that must be reflected in the institution's official evaluation policies (Harris 1986, 213). This is an absolute necessity to avoid raising anxiety levels needlessly and generating confusion regarding expectations, risks involved, and the professional rights and responsibilities of teachers. These feelings can threaten morale and the effectiveness of the processes.

Formative evaluation processes in some districts or schools may be defined using terms that stress informal procedures, personal growth, and collaboration. But when teaching is scrutinized, criteria are employed, and information, points of view, or data are analyzed, then evaluation is in process, and the reality should not be disguised.

Formative evaluation can and should use observations, student reports, and other formal data-gathering processes similar to those involved in summative evaluation. Fortunately, formative evaluation permits the use of a much wider array of types of data. Teacher self-reports can be provided, using forced-choice instruments such as the one illustrated in Appendix D (see also Harris and Hill 1982). These reports do not have the faults of rating scales, and in a formative context produce reliable and reasonably valid information. Because of the lower levels of concern and focus on improvement purposes, formative evaluation can make systematic use of student achievement test data, lesson plans, and other "portfolio" materials (McGreal 1983). Tests of teacher knowledge that are of dubious value for selection or other summative decision-making purposes can be useful in a formative context when the level of knowledge adequacy may be important in diagnosing a problem or suggesting new learning.

Valid data sources for formative evaluation purposes are limited to three *primary* sources—observations, self-reports, and student reports. All of these are useful, and all have special advantages and limitations. Observations are most widely regarded as independent, objective, and essential for an "outsider"—principal, supervisor, or peer—to gain the insights needed to assist in analysis. However, observations are limited in that they are time-consuming and hence costly, they require the participation of highly skilled and experienced professionals, and they are rarely valid beyond the specific lesson, class, period, or subject.

Self-reports, when properly instrumented as described above, are reasonably valid and reliable, not time-consuming, and require no special expertise. They are limited, however, in that they have a very broad time frame of reference and they do not give an "outsider" a real sense of know-ing about the teacher. Student reports are much like teacher self-reports in that they can report with considerable accuracy what does and does not happen in the classroom. Of course, students cannot report on those aspects of teaching that they haven't seen or cannot understand, and very young children have more difficulty with valid reporting than do older children.

When peer teams, parents, or individual faculty members have been observing and working in close proximity to the teacher, their opinions may be useful. However, this is generally not the case, and these reports are therefore not recommended for use in formative evaluation. Useful data could be provided by peer coaching teams trained as classroom observers or parents who work as teacher's aides. Team teaching arrangements would greatly expand the number of informed individuals who could provide information for formative evaluation.

The use of peer supervision in contrast to evaluation is encouraged in the professional literature: "Periodic reviews of individual teachers' perfor-mances should be conducted by expert peers and administrators using a wide range of indicators that deal with both the substance and process of teaching. The results of these reviews and of self-evaluation should guide professional development" (Darling-Hammond 1986, 544). Teachers may accept informal peer review and assistance more readily than they accept the notion of formal peer evaluation. Weber (1987) finds that teachers do react positively to peer *supervision*—the formative observation of teachers by their peers—and that such activities are often described as "colleague consultation" or "peer consultation." Team teaching also includes an ele-ment of this activity when teachers share objectives, materials, students, and space (49).

Discussion of formative evaluation processes generally includes refer-ences to clinical supervision. Clinical supervision is one example of a pro-fessional development model employing formative techniques for the primary purpose of improving instructional practices. Generically, the steps of clinical supervision are planning, observation, and analysis of teaching episodes by the teacher and supervisor. Essential to as well as a limiting factor in successful implementation of clinical supervision is the development of a trusting, collegial relationship between the parties. The concepts of collegiality, collaboration, skilled service, and ethical conduct are imperatives that, when put into action, form the essence and domain of clinical supervision (Garman 1982, 35). Unfortunately, "much of what must be present for true clinical supervision to occur seem to be significantly prohibited by the nature of real-life teacher evaluation . . . and it may be that some of the techniques inherent in clinical supervision are especially useful as part of an effective teacher evaluation system, but it is not appro-priate to view clinical supervision as an evaluation model" in the summa-tive sense (McGreal 1983, 29).

The DeTEK system of teacher evaluation (Harris and Hill 1982) is another formative evaluation system that incorporates many of the features distinguishing the formative process from the summative. Appendix A includes the detailed performance criteria utilized in this system. In contrast with summative use of criteria, DeTEK employs a ten-step sequence starting with a teacher self-report, a preliminary classroom observation, and a conference for collaborative decision making in order to select a focus for further diagnosis. The diagnostic process utilizes another teacher self-report, a diagnostic observation, and a student report. These three sets of data are analyzed collaboratively to generate agreements on accomplishments and needs for improvement. The last steps involve preparing a growth plan, implementing the plan, and reviewing the outcomes. No quantitative scores are generated, and no summative decisions are made.

Formative evaluation processes focused on the development of professional skills and knowledge allow educators to increase their decision-making and problem-solving capabilities by promoting the development of the "habit of professional inquiry" (Conley and Bacharach 1990, 312). Educators who can analyze, question, and reflect on their own personal practices generally become stronger practitioners. Individuals with a strong "habit of inquiry" constantly ask themselves and others "why" and "what if" questions about their professional practice: Why did this particular technique work with this group and not with others? What would happen if I did this? Why can't this be done? The habit of professional inquiry must be developed and nurtured, and this occurs best in an environment where activities related to induction into the profession, continuous professional growth, and formative evaluation are emphasized.

Misconceptions about formative evaluation abound. Some that are common include:

It is always very informal.

It requires no systematic data gathering.

No value judgments are involved.

Only peers can be effective as formative evaluators.

Summative and formative go hand in hand.

Summative Evaluation

It has been suggested that summative evaluation addresses the needs of the few by providing school districts with the necessary documentation required by statutes, the courts, and collective bargaining agreements for dismissing teachers. Perhaps a broader view of summative evaluation encompasses acknowledgment of the professional responsibility of those charged with supervision responsibilities for ensuring that students are taught by competent individuals. Clearly, this level of professional accountability has not always been met by those charged with such responsibilities. It is also frequently suggested that formative evaluation and summative evaluation are incompatible and cannot be equal components in a single evaluation system: they are viewed as competing, mutually exclusive processes. In fact, a total evaluation system cannot be based only on formative evaluation or only on summative evaluation (McGreal 1983, 2; Weber 1987, 13). The total evaluation process must address the needs of the individual and of the group through determination of professional growth areas (formative evaluation) and the safeguarding of professional rights and competence (summative evaluation). Wise and Darling-Hammond (1985), in a study of effective teacher evaluation practices, found that districts were able to utilize evaluation for teacher improvement and for personnel decisions. The districts were able to monitor general teaching quality and improvement of specific teaching performances by dividing evaluation responsibilities between administrators and expert teachers (32). In essence, then, two distinct subsystems were created.

If formative evaluation is well done, most summative evaluation decisions should be routine (e.g., continuation on the job for the great majority of the teachers) or nonthreatening (e.g., transfer, change of function, or elevation to tenure status). Recommendations for termination of contract or other unpleasant eventualities are and should be relatively rare. If initial selection of personnel is carefully done and if formative evaluation and follow-up growth activities are carried out as recommended, such decisions should be extremely rare. However, when summative evaluation decisions are needed they should be based on a process that is legally and contractually defensible. If the stated teacher attributes are really related to the desired products of teaching, and if the teacher's performance is adequately described, then decisions concerning the teacher should be relatively easy to defend.

One of the distinguishing characteristics of summative evaluation is that it requires a much greater array of behavioral categories than formative evaluation. Furthermore, summative evaluation requires standardized procedures, high levels of reliability and validity of measures, and thoughtful valuing and judgment making with detailed documentation and procedures (Medley et al. 1984). None of this is essential to formative evaluation because decisions based on formative evaluation are not momentous and collaboration offers the protection of shared responsibility. If the decision not to renew a contract is in error, a grave injustice has been committed against the teacher, the children, and the school. If the joint decision to try a cooperative teaching approach in place of excessive lecturing is in error, time and energy is lost, experience is gained, and no injustice results.

The recommended strategy, then, is for administrators to concentrate on formative evaluation with teachers in a continuous, supportive, nonthreatening manner. This strategy implies a serious commitment to the improvement of instruction. If teachers are selected carefully and receive adequate support and assistance on the job, there should be little need to dismiss them. Consequently, every effort should be made to reassure teachers through processes that are assistance-oriented and instruments that are objective, descriptive, and diagnostic. In those few instances in which a teacher's performance is unacceptable, and all efforts to improve it are unsuccessful, then the difficult summative evaluation process should not be avoided. By that time, the administrators should feel confident that all feasible remedies have failed, and summative processes can follow in good conscience. Models for linking formative to summative efforts have been given little attention and require further testing. Harris (1986) has elaborated a "linking mechanism" model with only limited field testing (see Chapter 10).

Due process is very significant in the summative evaluation process. The general requirements for due process are discussed in Chapter 11; they also apply to any adverse action taken against an employee as the result of the evaluation process. Macy (1988) outlines six protections that should be afforded the teacher being evaluated: (1) the right to be fully aware of the evaluation process; (2) the right to be fully aware of the observation criteria; (3) the right to have a postobservation conference; (4) the opportunity for follow-up observation visits; (5) enough time for remediation; and (6) follow-up reports (51–56). Documentation is an essential ingredient of due process, especially when termination of employment is likely. Written memoranda, based on facts—not vague generalities or hunches—should be built into the system and used conscientiously.

Validation of Selection Processes

Ideally, each person selected for employment in a school district or educational institution should match the criteria established for successful performance on the job. Realistically, it must be acknowledged that all selection processes are less than perfect, and perfect matches between the individual and the criteria will not always occur. There will always be occasions when, despite the best recruiting efforts and selection processes, there will be an individual who does not meet all the established criteria available for employment. When it is necessary to select an individual who does not possess all the attributes and competencies necessary to perform the job successfully, it is incumbent upon the organization to initiate and carry out a program of support and training for the individual. The immediate goal of such a training program is to improve the individual's skills. The ultimate goal is to ensure that students will not suffer instructional losses because the employee hired did not fully meet the established criteria. Induction and staff development activities become a critical part of the resource system used to support the teacher or administrator hired under such circumstances. In cases where the individuals selected were perceived to have met all the criteria, performance evaluation outcomes should feed back into the selection process for validation and modification purposes.

The focus here is on the evaluation of teaching performance, since one of the primary responsibilities of administrators is to assist teachers in improving their performance. The general principles that are discussed also apply to the appraisal of other educational personnel. Due to the abstract nature of many administrative activities and responsibilities, the development of measures and standards of performance may be even more difficult than the exceedingly complex task of defining measures and standards for teaching personnel. Particularly for administrators, the job description is a key element in development of the performance appraisal system. The job description defines the essential qualifications and responsibilities of a job that may have only one incumbent in an educational institution. The uniqueness and small number of incumbents in many administrative positions tend to make goal setting a basic activity in administrative evaluation systems. Alternatively, there are emerging sets of performance criteria for principals (Castleberry, 1983), supervisors (Bailey 1985; Harris 1980), and superintendents of schools (Carter et al. 1991; Hord 1990). These, and others as they are carefully validated, can be utilized to guide both the formative and summative evaluation of personnel in these positions. (See Appendices B and C.)

Approaches to Personnel Evaluation

Basically, there are three approaches to the evaluation of personnel: (1) the characteristics of the individual, sometimes called "presage criteria," (2) the products attributed to the individual, and (3) the processes used by the individual. Each approach has limitations, so we must guard against the common tendency to look for the easy way out. There are no easy ways, as we shall see when we examine the complexities of each approach.

Characteristics of the Individual

When we refer to the characteristics of the individual, we have in mind such relatively easy-to-measure qualities as knowledge of the subject or accepted professional practices, grade point averages, college hours or degrees held, and years of professional experience. Some of these items, such as grade point averages and knowledge, are legitimate considerations at the time of initial employment but not in evaluating a person on the job.

When we evaluate performance in terms of characteristics of the performer, we are making an assumption that there is a reasonably high correlation between those characteristics and effectiveness, however we define effectiveness. The trouble with this assumption is that it has never been supported by research. We must grant that correlations with "success" in doing anything are reduced significantly if the success criteria are shaky or unreliable—and they are in education and most other professions. However, if we cannot show that what we call success is associated with characteristics such as college degrees or years of experience—and we cannot—then our evaluations cannot rest on very solid ground. Most salary schedules are based on these factors, and although one might build a defense for such schedules upon other considerations, it would be futile to attempt it on a basis of correlations with currently known effectiveness criteria.

We cannot, then, recommend that personnel evaluation be geared to characteristics of the evaluatee, especially evaluation for instructional improvement purposes.

Products Attributed to the Individual

Evaluation of personnel on a product basis has a lot of appeal. In fact, it is the only direct way to evaluate an individual's performance because the other methods are based on the assumption of a reasonably high correlation with products. In the long run, products are what schooling is all about, so we must validate whatever we do by showing relationships with outcomes. Having made that statement, however, we must face up to the problems that product evaluation entails.

First, products in education are hard to measure, and the more important and complex the product, the harder it tends to be to measure. For example, it is not difficult to measure students' knowledge of information, but how well can we measure their *thirst* for knowledge that endures beyond schooling?

Second, even if we had valid measures of important learnings, we would then have to find ways of ascribing outcomes to individual teachers—not to mention the problem of evaluating the contributions of individual administrators, supervisors, and others to those outcomes. Who would say that the measured learnings of third-graders were not influenced by teachers in previous years? Who would say that measured learnings of students in a high school course are not affected by concurrent as well as previous learnings in other high school courses?

Finally, and perhaps most troublesome, we must deal with the problem of influences that are external to the school. It would be foolhardy to ignore the fact that students' present capacities for learning are extremely variable from group to group, due to a complex combination of such factors as native ability, home environment, peer relationships, and past and current advantages or disadvantages.

If individual teachers and other professionals are to be judged by student learning products, we must be sure that we are limiting the scope of our evaluation purposes. Furthermore, we must gather information over a period of several years, assembling enough comparative data to justify tentative conclusions. For example, we might study the results that teacher X gets with a certain level of economically disadvantaged children year after year and compare them with the performance of other teachers with matched groups. Only then can we begin to draw conclusions about the effectiveness of teacher X. If we are thinking of formative evaluation, if we have data for only a short period of time, or if we have no comparable data from matched groups, then we had better avoid product evaluation of individual persons.

The preceding discussion has dealt with student-learning products only. To complicate the picture further, there are other types of "product"— as manifested in a person's effects on colleagues, on the school district, or on the community. Such products are probably even more difficult to measure and hazardous to ascribe to individuals than is the case with student learning.

Processes Used by the Individual

Although the processes used by the individual must ultimately be validated against products, when we evaluate for the purpose of improving performance, the only handle that we have is process, as far as the evaluatee's performance is concerned. As indicated earlier, over a period of time, product data might be helpful in identifying strengths or weaknesses in individual performance, but there is no way to do anything about those strengths or weaknesses by working directly on the products.

Bolton (1974) makes an interesting point in showing that products at one level of the school district hierarchy become processes at the next lower level. This conceptualization is helpful in planning instructional improvement innovations. Consider, for example, the case of a school district in which there is a perceived need for improving individualization of instruction. The Bolton model would portray one type of system-wide effort to meet the need, as shown in Exhibit 8.2 on page 162. This model shows the role of employees at various levels in the school system organization in generating the final product, students' learning. It also suggests the importance of recognizing the complexity of well-designed programs for instructional improvement and the way in which processes and products tend to interact.

EXHIBIT 8.2   Roles of Employees in Generating Products

Level	Process	Product
Assistant Superintendent for Instruction	Train school principals in the use of instruments	Principals' skill in using the instruments
Principals	Principals' using the acquired skill to gather data to assist teachers	Teachers' skill in using newly acquired methods
Teachers	Teachers' using the acquired skill in teaching	Students' learning

Other Approaches to Personnel Evaluation

Approaches to teacher evaluation other than the three just discussed have been sought for a number of years. This search has led to experimentation with innovative practices. Goal setting as a basic evaluation activity in school systems has been practiced through the use of the Management by Objectives Approach (MBO), the Performance Objectives Approach (POA), and the Practical Goal-Setting Approach (PGSA) (McGreal 1983, 44). The major differences in these three approaches relate to the flexibility given to individuals in setting goals and to defining how the goals and outcomes are to be measured. In 1987, The National Board for Professional Teaching Standards began work on development of certification standards, assessment methods and processes, and education policy that would culminate in the Board's offering of a voluntary, nationwide certification for teachers. "The Board's work in assessment methods and processes focuses on methods that will be used to assess teachers' abilities in a fair and trustworthy manner. The evaluation system will include assessments of what teachers know as well as what they are able to do. Assessment techniques to be considered include interactive video, simulations of classroom situations, observations of teachers in a school setting, interviews, essays, multiple choice tests, teaching portfolios and various combination of these technologies" (National Board for Professional Teaching Standards 1988, 7).

Yarbrough (1989) suggests that a revolution in assessment techniques is needed because of "the shift from conceiving of education as a primarily behavioral activity to conceiving of it as a primarily cognitive activity" (226). His emphasis on the need for a cognitive-psychological perspective in teacher evaluation is supported by researchers who describe the numerous dimensions involved in expert teaching—the contexts in which teaching occurs, the characteristics of the learners, the pedagogical knowledge, the subject-matter content knowledge, and skills in pedagogy, group dynamics and communications (Berliner 1986; Shulman 1987). But we must also be cautious about the work of the National Board. Its efforts are extremely preliminary, and many tough problems have not been resolved. If a working system of "certification" as a "expert" teacher becomes available, its feasibility, utility, and validity will still need consideration.

Provision of the Data Base

Once the desired competencies have been determined—teachers themselves having been involved in the process—the second stage of the evaluation process can be undertaken. All three of the previously stated purposes for evaluating personnel (formative, summative, and validation of the selection process) depend ultimately on a strong data base, the Achilles' heel of most evaluation efforts, which is far too dependent on hunches and not dependent enough on appropriate, systematically collected, objective information. Observation and numerous other data-gathering tools, properly used, can provide a wealth of information for personnel evaluation. The description of teacher performance should have certain characteristics:

1. It should be discriminating—related to the competencies.
2. It should be comprehensive and varied enough to include all relevant data.
3. It should be objective and verifiable.
4. It should begin with broad-scope, comprehensive observation with teachers who are new to the school or whose patterns of behavior are unknown but become focused as diagnosed needs are identified.

Some of the information collected to serve formative evaluation purposes can be used for other purposes as well; however, the instruments and processes that are appropriate for various purposes tend to be quite different. For example, relatively formal and infrequent summative evaluations are quite appropriate for the purpose of determining whether to renew the contracts of most teachers, assuming that continuous formative evaluation has occurred in the meantime; on the other hand, to complete a rating scale on a teacher once a year on the assumption that it will help the teacher to improve is an exercise in futility. The point is that school administrators setting out to examine their personnel evaluation systems should approach the task one purpose at a time and avoid the usual inclination to seek one simple, easy, all-purpose solution. This type of oversimplification has contributed much to the bad reputation that the whole evaluation process now has; supposedly aimed mostly at the improvement of performance, in practice the process tends to be negative and punitive, feared and rejected by evaluatees, and not helpful to anybody.

Data sources and their uses were discussed in relation to formative evaluation. When summative evaluation purposes are involved, still more careful consideration of alternatives and their validity is required. Routine summative "monitoring" can also be distinguished from those summative evaluation instances when critical decisions are to be made. A general principle to consider is that a variety of reasonably valid data sources produces better judgments than any one source. Hence, a further review of available and promising sources is provided here.

Classroom Observation

It is generally conceded that the evaluation of teaching performance requires classroom observation. Current practice confirms that this is the mainstay of teacher evaluation systems, even though the process, by its very nature, intervenes in the classroom (Educational Research Service 1988, 3). Classroom observations provide the opportunity for the observer to witness firsthand the teacher in action and, more important, the impact instruction has on student behavior and success. However, a single classroom observation provides no guarantee that the teacher exhibits the same level of performance consistently or when the observer is not present. Assurances related to the accuracy of appraisal and the consistent quality of teaching are gained by the use of multiple appraisers, multiple observations, and numerous sources of information. The primary responsibility of the observer is to record in an objective manner the events and behaviors as they occur during the teaching episode or lesson. In a classroom observation, "the focus is the teacher in action and the classroom story that unfolds as a result of this action. It is what the teacher says and does, how students react, and what actually occurs during a specific teaching episode that forms the basis for the data collected" (McGreal 1983, 28). Weber (1987) states that "the cardinal rule of observing is to focus on whatever behaviors and events might aid the teacher to teach more effectively" (45). How useful the data collected during the classroom observation are in improving instruction depends on the quality of the data collected, the analysis of the data, and the ability to communicate the information gained to the teacher. McGreal (1983), after reviewing sources on classroom observation, suggested that there are four tenets of classroom observation:

1. The reliability and usefulness of classroom observation is directly related to the amount and kind of information the supervisor obtains beforehand.
2. The accuracy of the classroom observation is directly related to the supervisor's use of a narrow focus of observation.

3. The way data are recorded directly affects the supervisor-teacher relationship and the teacher's willingness to participate in instructional improvement.
4. The way feedback is presented to the teacher directly affects the supervisor-teacher relationship and the teacher's willingness to participate in instructional improvement. (98–123)

For more details on observation procedures, see Harris (1985, 146–82) and Appendix G for an outstanding example of a complete set of observation forms.

Peer Review

Teachers' reactions to peer review were discussed in the section on formative evaluation. Although peer review is widely discussed in the literature on teacher evaluation, many teachers appear reluctant to have peer-dominated teacher evaluation systems. Weber states: "Summative peer evaluations—that is, judgments of teachers' performances by other teachers—have also not proven beneficial. In fact, most research and followup studies indicate that summative peer evaluations are destructive. They harm teacher morale and create lasting grudges among the faculty. Teachers often become testy about peer evaluations. 'That's what the administrators get paid for. I'm not going to do their job. I refuse to get involved in evaluating people I have to work and interact with every day' " (1987, 48–49).

In 1985, seventy percent of the teachers responding to an Educational Research Service (ERS) teacher opinion survey indicated that they did not want their peers to evaluate them. Secondary teachers (35 percent) were more willing to involve peers in their evaluation than were elementary teachers (17.8 percent). In a 1987 ERS opinion survey, fifty-two percent of the respondents indicated that they approved of using lead teachers to evaluate new teachers, but only thirty percent approved of using lead teachers to evaluate experienced teachers (Educational Research Service 1988, 6).

The organizational structure of the typical school and the normal working pattern—teachers working in self-contained classrooms isolated from their peers—are not conducive to the concept of peer review. In most schools, there are limited opportunities for teachers to interact with each other, and even fewer opportunities for teachers to engage in extended and meaningful discussions about teaching and learning. Peer review requires a great deal of open-mindedness and trust among colleagues—commodities often lacking in schools (McGreal 1983, 128).

Student (Subordinate) Sources

In discussions on who should evaluate educators, it is often suggested that subordinates and clients of the educator's services should be involved in the evaluation process. A frequently raised question concerns the participation of subordinates in performance evaluation—students in the evaluation of teaching, teachers in the evaluation of administrators, and the like. Certain advantages of such data are obvious, particularly if the data are descriptive rather than judgmental; for example, there are usually many subordinates to provide the data, which tends to average out individual errors, and the observers are in a position to see the evaluatee in action much of the time. Most of the research on student evaluation of teaching has been done at the college level, and although the results tend to be supportive of the process, some of the studies raise questions about extraneous influences on students' views of their teachers and undesirable effects of students' ratings on teacher behavior. The use of client review for teachers is discussed more than it is practiced. The notion of having parents and individuals external to the school environment giving input into the evaluation of teachers or administrators produces resistance from professionals who are concerned about the political aspects of such a process. Parents can legitimately provide feedback about personal interactions with the individual being evaluated, but they can give little input into other aspects of teaching or administrative performance. When student or client reviews are used in the evaluation process, they should be objective, descriptive, and nonjudgmental. Evaluation is a professional endeavor, not to be delegated to amateurs. Input and involvement do not equate with abdication.

Student Achievement

If teaching is acknowledged to be an intentional act that has as its outcome student growth and learning, then it seems, at least to some, that a logical basis for evaluating teachers is student achievement. Medley et al. (1984) stated: "Advocates of this approach to teacher evaluation argue that if a factory worker's productivity is measured by the number of items he turns out, and that of a salesman by the dollar amount of the sales he closes, why not evaluate a teacher's productivity by the scores her pupils earn on systemwide tests administered at the end of the school year? The idea is both simple and appealing to the layman. It is an excellent example of what the late H. L. Mencken meant when he noted that every complex problem has a simple, obvious solution which is wrong" (33). Nonetheless, "results-oriented" and "outcome-based" evaluations were the fads of the 1980s and still have advocates.

The appeal of using student achievement as a tool for evaluating teachers has gained considerable attention in recent years and has prompted considerable discussion among educators and laypersons. McGreal (1983) comments: "There is no question that data about student learning are an important source of information about the effect of teaching. But, like so many other issues concerned with teaching and learning, the logic of the idea is often overwhelmed by the practical and political implications" (129). Teachers fear being held accountable for factors over which they exercise no control, such as wide variances in students and demographics, and the public fears that teachers are not held accountable.

In contrast to outcome-based proposals for personnel evaluation, state-mandated assessment systems usually are *not* effective for either summative or formative purposes, for various reasons. However, they usually do have some desirable features, as noted by Ellett (1987). Some of the fairly common characteristics of these new systems are: (1) state-of-the-art observation instruments that measure specific teacher behaviors known to be related to important student and school outcomes; (2) well-defined observer training programs; (3) standardized assessment/data collection procedures; (4) continuous research, development, and refinement of observation instruments and procedures; and (5) training in the use of observation data for supervision and development of teachers. Deciding to incorporate measures of student achievement in these statewide appraisal systems would compound already serious problems for local design and development of a new generation of efficient personnel evaluation programs.

Conley and Bacharach (1990), exploring what should be evaluated in teaching, concluded that the use of outcome measures such as student achievement scores are, at best, the most indirect measures of teacher effectiveness (310). They suggest that the greatest emphasis in teacher evaluation should be on teachers' skills and knowledge. In a similar vein, Soar et al. (1983) suggested that teachers be evaluated as professionals and not as technicians—technicians being evaluated on the results they produce and professionals on how well they follow what is considered to be "best practice" in a given circumstance. Stiggins (1989), in examining the recurrent interest in the use of student achievement data for the summative evaluation of teachers, states that other researchers have shown the use of such data to be indefensible because of the insensitivity of the assessment instruments to the effects of particular teachers as well as the long list of factors beyond the control of the teachers that influence test scores (Berk 1988; Haertel 1986). However, to conclude that student achievement data have no place in teacher evaluation or that the interest in such measures will eventually go away would be a serious mistake. "Best practice" demands that teachers continuously use data about student performance and success to improve teaching. Whether to continue using student achievement data as one of various formative measures in teacher evaluation, and not as a summative measure, may ultimately be decided on the basis of the alternate measures developed by the profession to report to the public how well students are learning and achieving.

Self-Evaluation

The critical examination of one's own strengths and weaknesses as a professional practitioner is a powerful tool for improving performance, when such a task is approached with objectivity. However, in summative decision-making situations involving such matters as selection, promotion, termination, nonrenewal, and salary benefits, self-assessments are not likely to be of great value (Redfern 1980, 53). Their use might still be legitimate as a way of formally documenting a teacher's perceptions of his or her teaching practices, for the record and appropriate review. Such documentation may have value as part of the due process required in some instances. (See chapter 11 for details.)

Who Is "the" Evaluator?

A much overlooked aspect of planning effective formative and summative evaluation systems involves more careful consideration of the individual responsibilities for various processes when purposes vary. In formative evaluation, there is much emphasis in the literature on peer involvement (Darling-Hammond 1986b) and the role of the principal (National Association of Elementary School Principals 1990). Harris and Hill (1982) used the term "collaborators" to refer to a number of individuals—teacher, principal, local supervisor, personnel director, visiting consultant, and so on—who could be productively involved in the developmental teacher evaluation process.

In summative evaluation situations, it is widely assumed that the principal is "the" evaluator of teachers in his or her building. In practice, this is true to a substantial degree. However, continuing to assume that what *is,* is what is *best* may be one of the problems facing the restructuring of effective teacher evaluation systems. Obviously, principals can and should be involved in both formative and summative evaluation processes in some ways. The question that requires more attention from both scholars and practitioners is: What should be the responsibilities of principals and other personnel in the summative evaluation process?

This question is not difficult to answer with regard to routine monitoring of classroom practices. When critical, career-determining, legally compelling, summative decisions are to be made, no one individual is likely to be fully capable, and it seems cruel to expect full responsibility to rest on the principal. An equally compelling argument against placing such awesome decision-making responsibilities in the hands of the principal derives from the long years of experience suggesting that principals understand the ramifications of the problem and simply avoid it as much as possible.

Harris's (1986) model for linking formative and summative evaluation systems using a "linking system" proposes a sequence of duties that can clearly be assumed by the principal. A separate summative system is proposed that might well be the responsibility of a special evaluation team.

The Trouble with Ratings

The use of a data base upon which to make evaluation decisions does not refer to the usual judgmental ratings found in personnel evaluation. Although as most often practiced, personnel evaluation is heavily dependent on such ratings, there is overwhelming evidence to indicate that they are ineffective, at best. The use and limitations of such ratings for selection purposes were discussed in Chapter 6. Unfortunately, school officials not only depend far too much on ratings at the time of personnel selection, they also compound the error by dissipating their scarce resources of time and energy by depending on judgmental ratings to assist teachers and others in improving instruction and other aspects of the school program.

One of the many problems associated with the use of judgmental rating scales for formative evaluation purposes is that there is usually no requirement or even suggestion that the judgments be based on organized data. In evaluation, as in recruitment and selection, description must precede judgment making. Once a desirable type of teacher behavior has been decided, the next task is to determine the extent to which the individual teacher demonstrates this behavior. This task requires observation of and interaction with the teacher by a highly trained appraiser or supervisor. Following the data-gathering process, the decision maker must analyze and reflect upon these data to determine the level of actual performance in comparison to the level of desired performance. The decision-making process requires the use of factual, observable data and subjective professional judgment. The possibility of rating error looms even with the best data and the most conscientious use of subjective professional judgment, but such error can be controlled by a properly trained appraiser.

All appraisal is jeopardized to some degree by the presence of rating error. Rating errors may be broadly categorized as leniency errors, central tendency errors, halo errors, constancy errors, and recency errors. Leniency errors are generally the result of the evaluator's reluctance to describe the individual's performance accurately if the individual is likely to disagree or confront the evaluator about the rating. They may also be the result of the evaluator's fear that low ratings will reflect poorly on the evaluator as the individual's supervisor. In both cases, the evaluator applies a set of personal standards to the individual's performance. The rating of nearly all individuals in a group at approximately the same level is generally the result of central tendency error. The evaluator avoids the use of the extreme ends of the rating scale, rating most individuals as satisfactory or average. Halo errors are generally the result of the evaluator's attention to a single factor in the evaluation process. The evaluator forms an impression of the individual and then rates him or her based on that impression. This impression may be negative as well as positive, and the effect caused by a negative impression is sometimes called "pitchfork error." Recency error is similar to the halo error in that a single factor often influences the entire evaluation. This type of error occurs when the evaluator focuses only on recent events, rather than considering performance across time. Constancy errors are generally a reflection of the evaluator's adjustment of individual scores to create an artificial rank-order. Individuals are not given credit for individual performance but are assigned a performance level in a hierarchy designed by the appraiser.

Rating error is a factor in all evaluation. The most grievous rating errors occur when the evaluator consciously manipulates the rating system to produce results that favor the evaluator. In addition to the problems caused for the individuals in these cases, the organization loses when blatant rating errors are permitted, since all possible uses of evaluation results for validation of selection processes are negated. To reduce rating error and to provide for reliable measurement, the Joint Committee on Standards for Educational Evaluation (1988) recommends the following:

> (1) Acquire evidence for all types of reliability that are relevant to the intended uses of the instrument; (2) check for inconsistency in interpretations of measurement results; (3) estimate and report reliability of instruments; (4) train observers to apply the rating criteria consistently and objectively; (5) train the evaluators to use procedures and instruments correctly; (6) take into account research that has identified internally consistent dimensions of pertinent behavior; and (7) employ multiple measures, multiple observers, and multiple occasions for data collection as appropriate, to minimize inconsistency and discern consistent patterns and trends. (104–5)

Without cautious and careful use of data and judgment, the evaluation process becomes simply another process that contributes nothing to the effort of instructional improvement.

The Personnel Evaluation Standards

In 1985, in response to the widespread dissatisfaction with personnel evaluation in education as expressed by teachers, administrators, and numerous national reports, the Joint Committee on Standards for Educational Evaluation undertook the development of standards for the evaluation of educational personnel. The Committee found that dominant criticisms of education personnel evaluation practices were that they failed to: screen out unqualified persons from certification and selection processes; provide constructive feedback to individual educators; recognize and help reinforce outstanding service; provide direction for staff development programs; provide evidence that will withstand professional and judicial scrutiny; provide evidence efficiently and at reasonable cost; aid institutions in terminating incompetent or unproductive personnel; and unify, rather than divide, teachers and administrators in their collective efforts to educate students (6–7). The development of *The Personnel Evaluation Standards* (1988) represents a concerted effort on the part of representatives from educational constituencies to define principles for guiding and assessing personnel evaluation in education in order to correct the deficiencies in current practice. Defining personnel evaluation as "the systematic assessment of a person's performance and/or qualifications in relation to a professional role and some specified and defensible institutional purpose" (7–8), the Committee developed twenty-one standards divided into four categories: propriety, utility, feasibility, and accuracy. The standards are listed in Appendix E. The five propriety standards reflect the fact that personnel evaluations may violate or fail to address certain ethical and legal principles. The five utility standards are intended to guide evaluations so that they will be informative, timely, and influential. The three feasibility standards promote evaluations that are efficient, easy to use, viable in the face of social, political, and governmental forces and constraints and that will be adequately funded. The eight accuracy standards aim at determining whether an evaluation has produced sound information about an educator's qualifications or performance (12–13). The standards permit educators to answer questions about the design, implementation, and effectiveness of the personnel evaluation systems employed. "The degree to which the standards will contribute to the improvement of personnel evaluations in education and, in doing so, will help to achieve the most fundamental goal of the Joint Committee—the enhancement of the quality of services provided to students and society—will only be determined by careful observation in the future" (Linn et al. 1989, 212).

Summary

The evaluation of personnel performance is an important but exceedingly difficult responsibility of school administrators. Formative evaluation, for the purpose of improving performance, requires different instruments and processes than summative evaluation, which is done to make decisions about personnel. For both of these purposes and others, desired attributes must be clearly stated, and then performance related to the desired attributes must be fully and accurately described. The difference between the desired behavior as stated in the attributes and the actual behavior becomes the focus for judgments, plans for change, and decisions. Many instruments are available for describing behavior, especially teacher behavior, and they can be of great value if they are selected with discrimination and if the users are skilled. However, instrumentation is a secondary issue in evaluation, because at the heart of the evaluation process is the interaction and communication between the person being appraised and the person performing the appraisal. Descriptive data can be gathered from various sources—superordinates, subordinates, and the evaluatees themselves. If the initial selection of personnel was done well and if the formative evaluation process is carried out effectively, there should be relatively little need for unpleasant summative decisions.

Suggested Study Sources

Darling-Hammond, Linda. 1986. "A Proposal for Evaluation in the Teaching Profession," *The Elementary School Journal* 86(4): 531–51.

This article examines the role of teacher evaluation in school organizations and in the teaching profession. The author argues for a more professional approach to the evaluation of teaching and offers suggestions on how this might be achieved.

Duke, D.L., and R.J. Stiggins. 1986. *Teacher Evaluation: Five Keys to Growth*. A joint publication of the American Association of School Administrators and the National Education Association. Washington, DC: National Education Association.

This brief pamphlet clearly identifies major arguments and values in formative teacher evaluation. In addition, it represents a statement of agreement between two professional groups.

Educational Research Service. 1988. *Teacher Evaluation: Practices and Procedures*. Arlington, VA: Educational Research Service.

This report presents and analyzes the results of an extensive survey of school districts across the United States concerning teacher evaluation practices. The topics addressed include appraiser training, bargaining clauses for teacher evaluation, rewards for excellent teachers, and sources of data for teacher evaluation. The emphasis is on summative evaluation.

Harris, Ben M. 1986. *Developmental Teacher Evaluation*. Boston, MA: Allyn and Bacon.

The concept of using teacher evaluation processes for purely formative, growth, and development purposes is carefully developed. Developmental evaluation emphasizes both formative and diagnostic aspects of teacher evaluation. Concepts and procedures for such evaluation are rigorously detailed and there is a unique chapter on linking formative and summative evaluation.

Harris, Ben M. 1987. "Resolving Old Dilemmas in Diagnostic Evaluation," *Educational Leadership* 44(7): 46–49.

This detailed description of diagnostic uses of the evaluation process also distinguishes it from traditional practices.

Joint Committee on Standards for Educational Evaluation. 1988. *The Personnel Evaluation Standards: How to Assess Systems for Evaluating Educators*. Newbury Park, CA: Sage.

This book contains the complete standards, with descriptions and examples. How to apply the standards, the history of the standards development, and information on the research are included.

McGreal, Thomas L. 1983. *Successful Teacher Evaluation*. Alexandria, VA: Association for Supervision and Curriculum Development.

This is a comprehensive treatment of teacher evaluation concepts, issues, and problems, with special emphasis on the formative modes of teacher evaluation. Models of formative evaluation are discussed along with sources of data.

Medley, Donald M., Homer Coker, and Robert S. Soar. 1984. *Measurement-based Evaluation of Teacher Performance: An Empirical Approach*. New York: Longman.

This is the most comprehensive and technically rigorous of all publications on this topic to date. The authors bring long years of experience as researchers and practitioners to the complex task of synthesizing the state of knowledge in the field. Despite their emphasis on measurement as the basis for evaluating performance, they err on the side of cautious optimism. As a resource for those designing instruments and systems and testing them, this work is invaluable.

9

Staff Training and Development

The development and maintenance of the best possible staff for the total educational enterprise is what personnel administration is all about. Hence, recruitment, selection, assignment, evaluation, and so on are ideally directly related to the development of a superior staff at all levels. The term "staff development" is intended, however, to place special emphasis on the development of individuals and groups, ensuring continuous growth and increasing productivity over time. The overreliance on technology to improve organizational productivity is a serious mistake in many Western industrial nations; in the field of education it can only lead to catastrophe.

Staff development as defined here is more than staffing; it is also a logical extension of the traditional tasks, embracing in-service education and training as well as advanced professional preparation. The concept of continuous staff development can and should permeate the entire operation of the school system, because the investment in "human capital" must be enhanced and protected against loss, abuse, misuse, neglect, and obsolescence. The staff member who is not growing and developing is obsolescing. Human resources are the essential capital on which we rely for quality education.

Differentiating Staff Development

Various meanings of the term "staff development" are in common use. Throughout this book, staffing and personnel administration have referred to recruitment, selection, assignment, and other tasks directed toward ensuring the best person in the right assignment, with optimum conditions for effective functioning. Staffing is, in one sense, staff development. However, in-service education and training and the preparation of personnel for advancement and for changing responsibilities are also essential for quality staff development. Whether or not such training and development programs are under the direction of the personnel office, they must be consistent with and related to other personnel administration endeavors.

A Variety of Terms

The variety of basic terms currently used to refer to in-service education is bewildering: professional development, training, skills development, professional growth, continuing education, adult development, clinical supervision, consultation, organization development, coaching, mentoring, networking, and others. Some of these terms are so general in meaning or so broad in scope that they may not be useful. Others are specialized techniques or approaches with substantial, though limited, utility. "Renewal" is one of those curious euphemisms used by some in an effort to avoid connotations. Unfortunately, such terms often result in confusion.

Many writers distinguish between three widely used terms: preservice, in-service, and continuing education. When the focus is the roles of colleges and universities in professional development of personnel, some of these distinctions may be quite useful. However, schools that must relate to the training needs of clearly designated individuals and groups in specific positions cannot be so concerned with sequence; instead, position-person-purpose relationships must be primary.

Staff Development in Perspective

The focus on school operations is important in giving perspective to staff development as both *staffing* and *training*. Exhibit 9.1 emphasizes the relationship of the change function in contrast with the maintenance function in school operations (Harris 1985, 142). In addressing the needs of the schools to *maintain* their current levels of operations, fairly standard operating procedures are employed. The traditional tasks of staffing are of these kinds. However, when the *change function* is invoked, goals, tools, conditions, resources, and practices are subject to change. Changes of any of these kinds call for staff development, especially training with distinct purposes; and the more numerous and dramatic the changes desired, the more crucial are the staff development concomitants (Kochan and Chalykoff 1987). In-service education and advanced preparation are shown in Exhibit 9.1 as distinct kinds of training related to implementing change.

In-Service Education

Education and training activities related to job performance expectations after assignment are widely recognized as in-service education. While terms vary, the underlying concepts are fairly widely supported in both theory and practice. Harris's definition is generally well accepted: "any planned program of learning opportunities afforded staff members . . . for purposes of improving the performance of individuals in already assigned positions" (1989, 18). Definitions in business and government circles are very similar, even though the terms used are on-the-job or staff development training: "any attempt to improve . . . employee performance by increasing . . . the ability to perform through learning" (Schuler and Youngblood 1986, 388).

Such definitions eliminate unplanned programs and emphasize the institutional frame of reference. The emphasis on improving performance *in position* helps to distinguish between in-service training and advanced preparation for promotion or reassignment. The emphasis on learning helps to distinguish training efforts from assignment, dismissal, replacement, or work organization changes.

Despite the general acceptance of these limitations regarding the place of in-service education, strategies, philosophies, and methodologies advocated and in operation are quite diverse. Numerous scholars argue for relating in-service plans to stages of development in one way or another (Burke and Heideman 1985; Levine 1989; Steffy 1989). Many programs, on the other hand, give heavy emphasis to the needs of the institution for overcoming deficiencies found in individuals (Schuler and Youngblood 1986). Such programs address concerns about training design (Cavender 1986; Mouton and Blake 1984; Showers et al. 1987). Other programs that emphasize institutional needs are less concerned with deficiencies than with increasing productivity (McAfee and Champagne 1988) or implementing innovations (Hall and Hord 1987; Harris 1989; Joyce and Showers 1983).

On the international level, in-service training has gained prominence in both developing (Asia and Pacific Program of Education 1985; Commonwealth Secretariat 1982) and highly industrialized countries (Teshner et al. 1983).

Perhaps most common in the reports of both scholars and practitioners are programs and practices, regardless of their purpose or strategy, that emphasize specific techniques or activities. Needs assessment (McAfee and Champagne 1988), assessment centers (Carter and Harris 1990; Rea et al. 1990), new technologies (Ulmer 1986), and coaching and clinical practices (Crehan and Grimmett 1989; Glatthorn 1990; Showers 1985) are a few examples.

Advanced Preparation

The use of training for purposes of developing staff to assume responsibilities in *new positions* has some distinctly different features from those

EXHIBIT 9.1   Implementing Educational Change via Staff Development

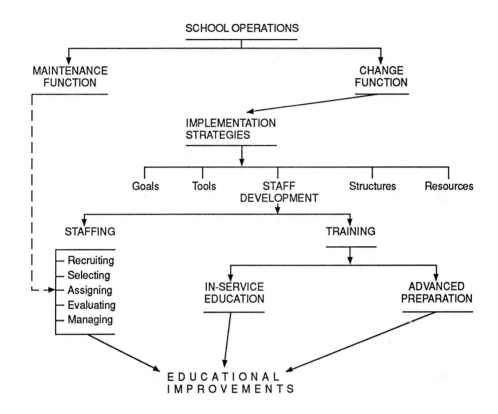

identified as in-service education. The term "advanced preparation" is used in Exhibit 9.1 to suggest programs of training for staff who are being prepared to assume new, different, unfamiliar positions. These may be promotions, but they may also be reassignments dictated by curricular restructuring, changes in organizational structures, or technological or demographic innovations.

Advanced preparation differs from in-service education in deriving its goals and objectives from projected or anticipated future needs rather than current expectations. This tends to create a whole array of relationships between institution, staff members, and training requirements that are distinctly different from those normally involved with in-service education. Work force projections, selective admission to training, transfers, promotions, and reassignments are some of the differing realities that call for advanced preparation programs.

Programs of induction for new personnel—teachers and others—are a somewhat unique example of specialized efforts to utilize advanced preparation training. With teachers entirely new to teaching, administration, or counseling, preservice preparation of various kinds has already been provided. Certain competences are already possessed and ready to be demonstrated. However, the school to which the individual is assigned may have special expectations, and there may be considerable uncertainty regarding which competencies can be demonstrated. The new person in the new assignment may also be very unsure about both expectations and competences he or she can demonstrate. Under these circumstances, induction programs must be individualized, just as most in-service programs should be, but they must also deal with more uncertainties. They also can be temporary in the sense that they are soon converted into continuing in-service professional development plans.

Innovations of various kinds call for highly specialized training that targets competencies that may be strange and confusing to nearly all who implement them. Many of the usual approaches involving intervisitation, clinical supervision, and collaborative decision making and planning may have less utility. Support systems that deal with some of these realities are clearly important for assisting teachers as the bewildering new expectations are recognized.

Changes that are more routine and less innovative may be implemented with fairly standard in-service education designs. Once the implementation of an innovation is well underway and the new expectations are made clear and can be demonstrated, the training needs can be shifted from the special advanced forms to those utilized in a variety of other in-service programs.

Training requirements for *promotions and reassignments* are not well understood. In education, as in most professional fields of endeavor, excessive faith is placed in prior preparation or an advanced degree program. A masters degree in counseling and guidance or a doctorate in educational administration are surely useful in preparing staff members for positions as counselor, principal, or superintendent. However, much is missing and still more is left to chance if such formal graduate preparation is all that is provided. Internships, field surveys, mentoring and coaching arrangements, and diagnostic assessment center programs are some of the promising possibilities for more effective advanced preparation (Carter and Harris 1990).

Purposes Served

Identifying staff development as staffing, in-service training, and advanced preparation and then focusing on the two forms of training as most crucial to the processes of educational change begins to suggest a variety of somewhat distinct purposes to be served. *Advanced preparation* purposes have been distinguished as promotions, reassignment, and induction into new positions. Similarly, in-service education purposes vary considerably, depending on person-situation relationships. When individuals or groups lack basic competences, again the purpose is clearly to develop those new capabilities. When inappropriate behaviors or patterns are to be eliminated and replaced, a different purpose with different circumstances is involved. Similarly, *specialized* competency development and *innovations* competency development can be differentiated as purposes.

Basic competency development involves in-service training that often relates to preservice education. The development of a common core of generally accepted and widely employed competences can be a purpose with high priority for large numbers of staff members. Such training is provided in recognition of the limited character of preservice programs for most professional positions. Hence, it seeks to ensure more than minimum levels of performance and to promote high levels of quality.

Remediation of inappropriate performances involves retraining of special kinds. This purpose recognizes the need not only to eliminate certain practices but also to substitute new practices. Since inappropriate behaviors may have become habitual over years of practice, resistance to even trying to change may be a difficult problem.

Specialized competency development refers to in-service training purposes of importance to only a limited number of staff members because of a unique position, role, or problem. Hence, such training sometimes involves advanced levels of generic competencies or specialized applications.

Innovations competency development is perhaps most clearly seen as distinct and is still widely ignored. Any systematic effort to introduce a significant change in the operation that demands substantial changes in people as well as structures requires special training. In-service activities supporting systematic adoption of innovations involves awareness training, systematic trials, and specialized skill development (Harris 1985, 57–60).

The distinctive features of the training programs that respond to these four purposes are widely recognized: the clients served; the timing and locale for training; content; and incentives for participation, involvement, and decision making. When basic competencies are to be the focus of training, the assessment data utilized for selection and/or formative evaluation are often the basis for making decisions regarding individual and group goals. However, for specialized competency development other data are needed, only certain individuals will be involved, and the locale may be remote from the worksite to accommodate several schools (Harris 1989:35–36).

Needs Assessments

Selecting goals and objectives for training regardless of purpose presumes that some needs assessment has been undertaken. Assessing needs is part of the goal-setting process (McAfee and Champagne 1988). As commonly used, this term refers to individual or group needs, but needs can and perhaps should be defined in a variety of ways. Individual performance deficits, individual aspirations, and individual interests and group deficiencies, group aspirations, and group interests represent different ways of thinking about needs. How we define needs also affects the assessment process that is most appropriate.

Individual and Group Needs

Needs defined as "performance discrepancies" are based on some systematic assessment of actual performance compared with expectations. But individuals have needs that reflect interests and aspirations, too. Surely these should not be neglected, for they are the growing edge of educational practice. On the other hand, individual needs that are essentially whim, self-interest, or rationalization and evasion do not deserve the same respect as those defined in more responsible ways.

Group needs are hardly the same as individual needs. Even when a survey of opinions has been conducted and "needs" have been identified as objectives or topics different from those most frequently chosen, individual needs are inevitably neglected. There are fundamental differences between a needs assessment process that attends to diagnosing and prioritizing needs for an individual (Harris and Hill 1982) based on objective data gathering and those procedures utilizing public opinion-polling techniques. The former deals with estimates of behavior and the latter with off-the-cuff impressions. Even carefully reviewed data derived from portfolios, testing programs, and routine observation reports can provide promising needs assessments.

Institutional Needs

The needs of schools, programs, students, and communities can and should be surveyed and critically analyzed as a basis for making in-service training decisions in many instances. A school with a high dropout rate may have an associated need for training of teachers and administrators, who often contribute to such problems. When library skill deficiencies are detected in test scores or accreditation reports, needs may extend beyond improving the library collection or schedule to training for librarians and teachers as well. An inappropriate science program reflected in low student enrollments and high failure rates may be both a curricular and an in-service training problem. A program that has not been adequately developed or is nonexistent across a district or state may suggest needs for in-service education at odds with or in addition to the needs individuals may identify.

Demographic changes in student populations or community structures may be reflected in unemployment, housing shortages, homelessness, ethnic conflicts, and welfare problems. These changes may have implications for in-service education, and these needs may not be identical to those perceived by teachers or other staff members.

Needs of institutions or of the larger community should be recognized along with those of individuals and groups that have high priority. It is not usually necessary to ignore one set of needs while addressing another. Priorities can be established carefully to respond to an array of needs if long-range strategic planning is employed. Furthermore, the design of high-quality training programs often permits simultaneous outcomes of several kinds. Collaborative planning should be fully utilized, striving to find common bases for giving priority to selected goals without neglecting individual or school needs. In all of this, mandates about training objectives should be resisted as much as possible (Cavender 1986).

Useful Objectives

Training objectives, like all instructional objectives, must communicate intended outcomes. It is generally agreed that these objectives should describe the behaviors or performances that the training experiences are expected to produce. Objectives are most useful when they are explicit and clearly related to the job situation itself, as well as clearly related to larger, longer-range goals.

The usefulness of objectives is greatly enhanced when they are explicated in detail. Grandiose statements such as "Our objective is to improve your power of communication" are useful for commercial interests, such as attracting customers, but are not very useful in planning and designing effective training.

Operational objectives are very different from instructional objectives. They, too, can be very useful in planning, but they should not be confused with objectives that specify learning outcomes. Both instructional and operational objectives should be clearly stated to make explicit the *operations*

Exhibit 9.2 Examples of Operational and Instructional Objectives

Revised as Operational Objective	Confused, Unclear Statement	Revised as Instructional Objective
To verbalize personal experiences connected with readiness problems	"To analyze a personal experience as a basis for discussing readiness."	Given a set of readiness principles or concepts, will analyze anecdotes to match principles and concepts to events described, to concur with peers 85 percent of the time.
To write a set of anecdotes, briefly reporting experiences		
To use a list of readiness principles and concepts as the basis for discussing anecdotes		
To meet with a specialist following a lesson that is tape-recorded to apply guidelines and check agreements	"To evaluate own performance during a lesson applying guidelines."	To analyze a tape-recorded lesson applying performance guidelines so as to agree with a specialist on 80 percent of the items.

Source: Ben M. Harris, 1989. *In-Service Education for Staff Development.* Boston: Allyn and Bacon, p.59.

planned and the *outcomes anticipated.* Exhibit 9.2 illustrates both kinds of objectives and their relationship to each other. The exhibit also emphasizes confused or unclear statements that serve neither purpose well. Harris provides detailed suggestions and illustrations for making objectives useful in planning for in-service training (1989, 48–63).

Selecting Important Objectives

When objectives have been identified, clearly stated, and shown to be usefully related to larger goals and needs, they may still not be very important. The process of selecting from among those that have been carefully specified can lead to choosing the simplest, rather than the most important, objectives. Rarely can all objectives be given the required attention; therefore, careful decisions as to their importance must be made. A simple technique for testing the importance of selected objectives is to allow a few days to pass before finalizing decisions. Another approach involves comparing and contrasting selected objectives with those cast aside. The more elaborate process of peer review, in which staff members with different perspectives reach consensus on the most important objectives, is likely to produce the highest-quality decisions.

Organizing, Planning, and Staffing

Maintaining and developing an array of training opportunities for school personnel is a complex responsibility. The best organizational and staffing arrangements for the "delivery" of continuous professional development opportunities is not really known. Proposals and current practices range from the ridiculous to the sublime. Resorting to more of the same—meetings, lectures, courses—clearly will not suffice. The development of entirely new and specialized training institutions, such as those now in operation for leadership training in Australia and Malaysia, have exciting possibilities. The recent proposals of the Holmes Group (1990) for the organization of "professional development schools" seem to have potential beyond traditional modes of delivery. Countywide or regional education service centers (intermediate units) such as those now operating in many states, have demonstrated their capacity for delivering quality training to many schools.

Assuming that in-service education and training will remain a responsibility of the local school district to a large extent, organizational arrangements and staffing patterns at this level should be considered, while recognizing the need to utilize training available from colleges, professional associations, state agencies, and others.

Delivery Systems

The delivery of a diverse array of training opportunities for large numbers of staff members with diverse needs on a continuing basis calls for a very complex organizational unit. Both developmental, change-oriented systems and standard operating systems are required. Furthermore, every training effort requires close coordination with the teaching, supervision, management, and special student service functions of the school operations. Harris proposed a systems diagram for planning and operating a delivery system for in-service education within a local school district (see Exhibit 9.3 on page 184). Advanced training programs were not considered in this proposal.

Four operating subsystems for producing in-service training outputs are shown schematically in Exhibit 9.3. The key subsystems relate to administration, planning, and design, and these are coordinated via a program operations subsystem. Each subsystem is organized, staffed, and funded to undertake specific tasks. The sequence of delivery is administration to planning to design, leading to a coordinated operation of training

EXHIBIT 9.3 In-Service Education as a Delivery System

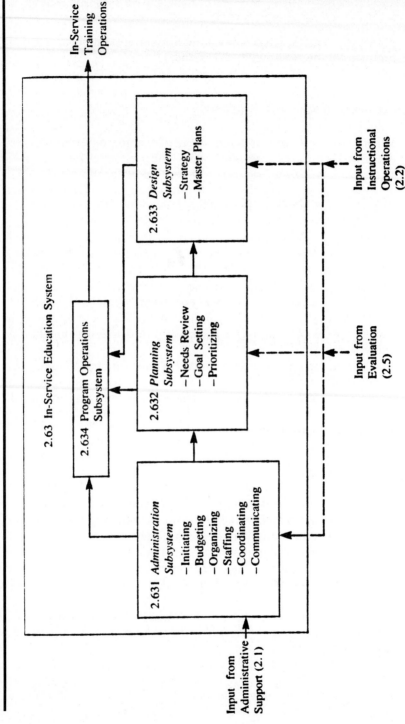

Source: Adapted from Ben M. Harris. 1989. *In-service Education for Staff Development*. Boston: Allyn and Bacon, p. 223

opportunities. Inputs from outside the delivery system are especially important in shaping the kind of training activities that emerge.

The importance of a delivery system approach to training as distinguished from other approaches (special projects or school-based, or integrated) is the potential for the institution's training needs to become high priorities. An organized system with its own staff, budget, and linkages to instructional, supervisory, and administrative systems can help to make training the important operation that it must be for quality education to be maintained.

Organizing Programs

Clearly distinguishable programs of training will emerge from the collaborative efforts of delivery system staff members and those of schools and other divisions and agencies. Programs should be structured to avoid taking on a life of their own. A proper time frame for accomplishing goals should be clearly specified and resources allocated accordingly. When a program is long-term in the sense that many related goals are being addressed in systematic sequence, then periodic review of both processes and products are especially important. Training resources are too scarce and needs too numerous to allow any program to continue year after year on the basis of faith or tradition.

Discontinuous operations characterize many training programs, even when carefully structured and enduring over long time frames. Training programs are discontinuous in that participants, for the most part, have other assignments as much of their responsibility. Furthermore, these "other" assignments are very likely to have higher priority than training. The difficulties posed by these realities are numerous. To overcome some of these problems it is especially important that training programs be responsive to real needs, that participants be actively involved as much as possible, that activities be stimulating and realistic, and that school officials clearly give training all of the status it deserves.

Collaborative Planning

The highly individual nature of training creates a demand for collaboration in all facets of program operations. Collaboration should be more than advisory or representative. Those directly affected by the training and those who have a contribution to make to its quality should be involved in as many ways as possible. An advisory council, planning committees, evaluation teams, and special design groups are utilized increasingly in local school districts in preference to "packaged" commercial or prefabricated offerings. Such groups of local collaborators can include classroom teachers in substantial numbers as those often most affected.

Collaborative decision making involving a variety of groups and individuals at different levels of the organization creates problems unless responsibilities are rather carefully delineated. Each decision-making group needs a charter clearly indicating its rights, responsibilities, and restrictions. A comprehensive master plan for staff development serves to guide various groups. Systematic routines for reviewing plans, allocating funds, and seeking board-approved priorities help ensure optimum involvement without waste or chaos.

School-based training offers still greater opportunity for faculty collaboration in selecting, planning, implementing, and evaluating specific programs. Hence, collaboration should be greatest at school levels.

Planned Variations

Thoughtful use of the many ways to organize for the delivery of training program activities requires careful planning. The search for the most effective approach or the best possible model is fruitless. For instance, the school-based approach to in-service education may have strengths in the proximity of staff to decision makers and funding sources. Small schools can plan and implement with less bureaucratic control. However, decentralized training programs can also be very inflexible. School staffs can be unresponsive to needs defined through other eyes. Isolation of staff groups within self-contained schools can be just as stultifying as isolation of the individual teacher in self-contained classrooms has been.

Currently embraced training approaches such as coaching and mentoring (Showers et al. 1987) and interactive video training (Ulmer 1986) should be neither ignored nor overvalued. The diversity of needs and contexts makes variations in organization and program designs the only wise course to follow.

Planned variation with respect to training programs offers much promise as an alternative to experimental and mandated efforts and argues for more variation, using pilot programs with thoughtful design and rigorous evaluation. Planned variation is not to be confused with hit-or-miss. There is a substantial body of scholarly research and theory on adult learning (Levine 1989; McLogan 1989) and principles of design (Harris 1989, 313–15; Tracey 1984) to guide practitioners in piloting a host of promising alternative organizations and programs.

Staffing Requirements

The diversity of alternatives complicates the problems associated with adequately staffing for training. Every kind of program is likely to require specific competencies in planning, organizing, designing, implementing, presenting, and evaluating. Fortunately, many classroom teachers, administrators, and, especially, supervisors of instruction have basic skills related to planning for and designing instructional activities. The special competencies needed are not, however, always so readily available. Planning collaboratively with a diverse group of concerned individuals is more complex than solitary lesson planning. Designing for experienced, sophisticated practitioners so as to stimulate, challenge, and avoid boredom is demanding. Evaluation competencies are almost always lacking or too unsophisticated to be effective.

Borrowing staff competences is both necessary and feasible in most school settings. Regardless of who is given official responsibility for planning, designing, implementing, and evaluating, their competences are likely to be insufficient. The school is generally a gold mine of technical resources, and the range of resources is even more varied when the community and local colleges are involved. But the problem of mounting high-quality training programs is rarely one of limited technical resources; rather, the problems tend to be lack of involvement and coordination.

The availability of human resources in the delivery of quality in-service education or advanced preparation sometimes leads to the false assumption that no designated person need be assigned the responsibility for giving leadership to staff development and training. The complex kinds of operations described require a leader who is competent in administering such operations as well as a technically competent individual or group. Finally, ample staff time must be allocated.

Funding Training

Much of the emphasis on using available human resources leads to another misconception—that little or no budget is required to meet training requirements. In fact, it is true that many of the personnel costs for implementing training programs are already included in the school's or district's salary budget. But there is a widely held misconception that other costs are so minor that "we'll find the money some place."

Every staff development program should have its own budget, and fairly detailed program budgets should be prepared and approved for every major training effort. Materials, consultants, travel, release time for planning, substitute salary funds, overtime pay for participants, equipment, and facilities rental are but a few of the numerous expenditures often required for quality training programs.

Leadership Training

Advanced preparation and in-service training for leadership personnel has a unique place in the school's staff development efforts. In-service teacher development deserves special attention because of the critical role teachers play in making instructional programs effective and because teachers comprise such a large portion of the total instructional staff. In-service leadership development deserves special attention also, because a small corps of administrators and supervisors has an enormous potential for influencing the work of teachers and promoting overall quality education.

The official leadership of U.S. schools includes more than 16,000 superintendents of local districts, plus an estimated 40,000 supervisors, consultants, directors, and assistant or associate superintendents. Principals and their assistants number about 100,000; hence, some 160,000 administrative and supervisory personnel are directly responsible for the instructional leadership provided in our schools and communities. Obviously, a much larger number of individuals provides important kinds of leadership that influences the quality of education. These leaders include classroom teachers, counselors, school board members, parents, and community leaders. Furthermore, state, regional, county, and national organizations employ thousands of professional educators who work to influence the quality of education in our schools.

Instructional leaders at the local level are the primary focus of leadership training. Large as the numbers seem, official leadership personnel represent only five percent to seven percent of the total professional staff of public schools in the United States.

Demographics and Dilemmas

Numbers and routine needs for training tell only a small part of the story of the urgent need for unprecedented leadership training in the next few decades. Our nation is approaching a population of 250 million people who are rapidly growing older and more ethnically and linguistically diverse in an economic environment simultaneously increasing in both severe poverty and unbridled wealth (Scribner 1990a). A new baby boom has been in progress for over ten years, crowding our elementary classrooms with over four million students per grade level. Teachers are reaching middle age and administrators are growing elderly. Retirement rates of both groups are at record highs and increasing steadily.

These are but a few of the present and emerging realities being reported by demographers and futurists (Hodgkinson 1987; Naisbitt and Aburdene 1990; Toffler 1990). Important implications for education, and especially for staffing and leadership training, derive from many of these societal changes. Recruitment, selection, and assignment of new principals to replace those retiring and being promoted and to fill new positions is a massive undertaking. Experienced principals and supervisors who are moving into superintendency (Burnham 1989) will produce additional openings and also add to the training requirements in all leadership positions. Shortages in all of these positions are increasing and being aggravated by growing pressures, conflicting demands, and social unrest (American Association of School Administrators 1990; National Association of Elementary School Principals 1990).

Training requirements for leadership personnel become more numerous and more demanding as the number of experienced individuals decreases. The continuing reluctance to utilize women fully in many administrative positions adds to the problem of retraining secondary teachers to become elementary administrators and supervisors. Additional requirements for continuing professional development result from the ferment in the nation demanding steadily improving education for all students. To this is added the need to provide training in many aspects of site-based management, educational technology, and community involvement.

Advanced preparation for teachers, assistant principals, and others already on staff will need to be greatly expanded and made more intensive to fill vacancies from within. Training for "insiders" will need to involve collaborative efforts with universities in providing carefully structured internships and field study activities. Special precautions will be required to avoid excessive "inbreeding" and to avoid promoting marginally competent individuals as a "marriage of convenience."

Continuing education and training of the "old guard" could easily be neglected in the coming years. The most experienced administrators who have not been promoted will likely be very busy mentoring their new assistants and peers. As those who have been passed over for promotions, their own needs for professional development may be more urgent than would be true in a more stabile environment.

The Current Scene

There is much happening in the public schools related to in-service training and advanced preparation of leadership personnel. As pressures continue to mount for reforms and restructuring of our schools, leadership behavior comes under even closer scrutiny than teaching practices. The strengthening of the movement toward school-based management places new attention on the capabilities of principals as instructional leaders, but also as managers, negotiators, and community leaders (Johnson and Snyder 1990; National Association of Elementary School Principals 1990).

Preservice preparation of leadership personnel continues to be a crucial aspect of leadership training throughout the nation. Graduate education for administrator development is in ferment, much as it was in the 1950s (Clark 1989). State departments of education are increasingly focusing their attention on improving both graduate preparation programs and providing for continuing education, especially as new statewide programs—testing, early childhood, dropout prevention, and so on—are mandated. Local school districts, professional associations, and private interest groups are all in the act of improving education through leadership training.

Graduate preparation of leadership personnel continues to be mistakenly regarded as a responsibility of university degree programs. It has not been possible, of course, for such programs fully to serve the leadership training needs of the vast enterprise known as elementary and secondary education. Even the best of preservice programs for administrators and supervisors are widely acknowledged to be only preparatory. Criticisms of graduate preparation by practitioners are commonly reported. Doud (1989) reports that only about one-third of the elementary principals are positive about the value of their graduate preparation. This may be more a criticism of expectations than of the character of the programs. However, there is wide and growing agreement emerging under the influence of the University Council for Educational Administration, several professional associations, and the National Policy Board for Educational Administration that graduate preparation must be upgraded and collaborative relationships established and improved (Scribner 1990b).

The National Association of Elementary School Principals (1990) contends: "Graduate schools of education must join with local school districts . . . and . . . professional organizations to assure that graduates in . . . school administration have been trained in a manner as to effectively cope with the demands and challenges of the 21st century" (16).

Such programs do exist, of course, but they tend to be few in number. Many graduate programs are primarily degree-oriented, staffed by small faculty groups, and poorly funded. Selective admissions criteria tend to be low and related to academic criteria, to the exclusion of other professionally relevant concerns. Part-time study programs allow few opportunities for field study and intern experiences.

Beyond the need for overcoming these long recognized defects in graduate preparation in most universities is the urgent problem of dramatically restructuring programs. The urgent need is not to prepare "coping" administrators and supervisors, but to prepare a new breed that can lead the nation's schools into the future.

Professional associations are increasing their involvement in leadership training. A wide variety of training activities are being made available to members and others on a fee basis. Much of this is in traditional forms—conference speakers, short courses, workshops, seminars, and the like. Limited though these kinds of training activities are in promoting professional competency development, they do provide awareness of concepts, new technology, and emerging issues and practices. These activities have value in readying the practitioner for more meaningful training. The same activities could also be useful as resources for more structured programs of leadership training.

The Leadership for Educational Administrator Development (LEAD) Center grants in the late 1980s provided federal funding to help in establishing training organizations especially addressing in-service training needs of administrators and supervisors. Some of these centers were associated with universities, and others were organized in association with professional associations or state departments of education.

The National Academy of School Executives, organized by the American Association of School Administrators, has regularly provided numerous workshops and seminars focused on the interests of school superintendents. While these training activities tend to be brief and discontinuous, they do address an extensive variety of topics of current interest. A similar program of workshops is made available by the Association for Supervision and Curriculum Development. Referred to as the National Curriculum Study Institutes, this program is planned to respond to the current interests of school principals and instructional supervisors.

The production of training materials for use in leadership training has become a booming industry for private vendors but is also an active endeavor of various professional associations. The publication of tapes, study guides, video cassettes, and computer disks that augment the traditional publications of some professional associations have potential use in training programs. As a result of this growing number and variety of media in publication, media centers and professional collections in large districts, association headquarters, and college libraries now hold a vast potential for more and better leadership training. Unfortunately, most of this media tends to be used sparingly and superficially.

The current scene in leadership training in U.S. schools cannot be accurately depicted. However, a persistent observer gains the strange impression of massive quantities of resources—personnel, organizations, and media—having only casual and incidental engagement with a ready, willing, and needy corps of educational leaders. The problems are both strategic and logistical.

Basic Model Types

On-the-job leadership training, one of the most promising practices, continues to suffer from very limited use. The obstacles facing busy administrators and supervisors are not unlike those that teachers face. Demanding jobs leave little time and energy for professional development activities, release time is generally too limited for meaningful, intense training, and the traditions surrounding the practitioner support ad hoc knowledge acquisition without concern for or expectation of behavior changes.

Peterson (1985) analyzed problems associated with the use of an experiential learning model as applied to the work of school principals. He shows that "task brevity," a nonsequential variety of demands on time, and fragmentation of the work flow are such that there is little opportunity for reflection, analysis, dialogue, or generalizing about one's own practices. These characteristics of work in schools extend to some degree to all leadership personnel, and are exacerbated by organizational patterns as well (195–96). These realities explain, in part, the limited place of in-service education and advanced preparation in the lives of most administrators (Burnham, 1989). They also suggest the need for models that have greater power of engagement under such difficult circumstances.

There are four identifiable basic models for the on-the-job leadership training, each with its own variations. Combinations of two or more models are sometimes utilized. These models are:

1. Independent study
2. Diagnostic-prescriptive analysis
3. Study groups
4. Mentoring/coaching/networking

Independent study for professional development of leadership competencies is widely utilized informally. Individuals elect to read, attend professional meetings, and even try an occasional new technique or procedure. More formal use of independent study involves the selection of a goal or objective with more systematic allocation of time and a planned program of readings and other activities to produce intended outcomes.

This type of on-the-job training has its strengths in focusing on personal needs, providing for flexible use of time, and allowing the individual to control the learning process. These strengths also tend to be serious limitations of independent study, especially when informally utilized without carefully structured action plans.

Diagnostic-prescriptive models rely on some formal program of testing or assessment to provide feedback to the leader regarding strengths, weaknesses, and suggestions for remediation. The use of diagnostic procedures in this type of training takes many forms, ranging from the very elaborate assessment center operations of the NASSP Assessment Centers (Hersey 1986) and the DECAS Executive Diagnostic Workshop (Carter et al. 1991; Loredo et al. 1990) to simple self-assessment inventories, such as the Educational Administrator Profile (Human Synergistics 1984) and the Principals' Behavior Profile (Appendix B; Castleberry 1983) or the Task Analysis Inventory for executives (Hord 1990).

Regardless of instrumentation or process, diagnostic analysis that provides feedback on strengths or weaknesses can be informative and motivational. However, realistic prescriptions are not readily provided by many assessment instruments. Furthermore, the strength of models of using prestructured instrumentation and analytical processes also represents a weakness: the "client" is dependent on the assumptions, rationale, and philosophy of those who designed the diagnostic material. Hence, the motivation for initiating action for growth and improvement tends to be limited.

Study group models avoid the isolation of independent study and diagnostic-prescriptive models. The emphasis on group activity takes many forms, and the groups themselves vary in size, task, length of time they meet, kind of leadership, activities employed, and locale (Harris 1989, 154–87). The strengths inherent in study groups include socialization, shared knowledge, and an enormous variety of activities that can be utilized. In practice often too much reliance is placed on talk—lectures and discussions—study groups are excellent vehicles for quality circles, demonstrations, role-playing, buzz sessions, brainstorming, simulations, and laboratory training activities. Cooperative learning arrangements can also be used, resulting in a uniquely powerful effect on participants (Mouton and Blake 1984).

The weaknesses of study groups include the loss of personal identity and diversion from explicitly defined individual needs. Furthermore, groups can develop knowledge, skill, and attitudes, but the transfer of this training to individual job realities is not clearly provided for.

Coaching/mentoring/networking models are still somewhat ill-defined in practice as well as in the training literature. In general, these terms are used to suggest training arrangements in which two or more individuals team up to observe, discuss, share, and provide support and assistance to each other on some kind of a reciprocal basis. The term "peer coaching" was popularized following proposals by Joyce and Showers (1983) for a modified form of clinical supervision as the last phase of a training program sequence. The term mentoring has come to be used to refer to dyadic relationships between professionals where classroom observation is not necessarily involved as it is in coaching. Mentor relationships are almost always voluntary, are usually, but not always, peer relationships, and may or may not be reciprocal. The purposes and activities of mentoring are not very well reported but seem to embrace a wide variety of alternatives including "shadowing", interning, consulting, and intervisitation.

Networking has many of the same characteristics as coaching and mentoring, with a wider array of individuals involved. It also involves the use of telephone and other distance communications devices, whereas mentoring relies heavily on face-to-face communications.

If these very small group interaction-support models are effective in promoting training outcomes, their contributions may be in the area of facilitating transfer. Such effects are not yet clearly understood; however, given the weakness of most models in producing transfer, it seems that coaching and the like should be encouraged in designing training programs.

A Continuous Professional Development System

In an effort to design a prototype operating model for executive training, the Meadows Project at the University of Texas has been testing various combinations of all of the models discussed above. Each model type has strengths and weaknesses; the Texas Project has endeavored to combine models into a system with a wide variety of alternatives while avoiding the weaknesses. Such a system is being tested under the guidance of AASA's National Executive Development Center Advisory Committee (1989), with some encouraging results.

The focus of this system is provided by a set of performance criteria illustrated in Appendix C. Exhibit 9.4 illustrates the major components of the system and indicates the rational sequence of events from left to right. Performance descriptors, volunteer leaders, and professional commitments from individuals and organizations are all prerequisites for the system's functioning. The Lead Resource Bank is designated in this exhibit as an example of an organization in existence that can supply training materials and other resources to individuals and groups.

The large bold rectangle represents an operating system composed of four subsystems, and the arrows emanating from the subsystems indicate a sequence of events for any given participant leader. Diagnostic assessment is followed by planning for improvement. The experiential delivery system represents any of a variety of training programs based on the models described above. The delivery systems discussed earlier in this chapter would all be potentially useful in this subsystem. The last of the four subsystems, outcome review, provides for formal or informal review of training experiences in relation to plans for improvements; this review would be used as a basis for making decisions as to further diagnostic assessment.

The networking-mentoring-coaching subsystem in Exhibit 9.4 represents an organized effort to relate such processes to the operating system, to facilitate improvement planning, training experiences, and outcome reviews.

The continuous nature of this professional development system is the result of the recycling capability of the diagnostic assessment subsystem. Normally, any identified individual or group need is responded to in an ad hoc fashion, using any of the model types discussed above. In this system, which is currently being tested, the diagnostic assessment subsystem is designed to respond to a broad array of potential needs. Under such circumstances, of course, the experiential delivery subsystem must also be responsive, with the individual improvement plan providing the linkage between diagnosis and training. Such a system keeps the control of action planning and prioritization in the hands of individual leaders. However, both group and individual training models can be utilized.

Summary

Staff development and training must be closely related to personnel administration regardless of how these task areas are organized in the school

EXHIBIT 9.4 Professional Development as a System

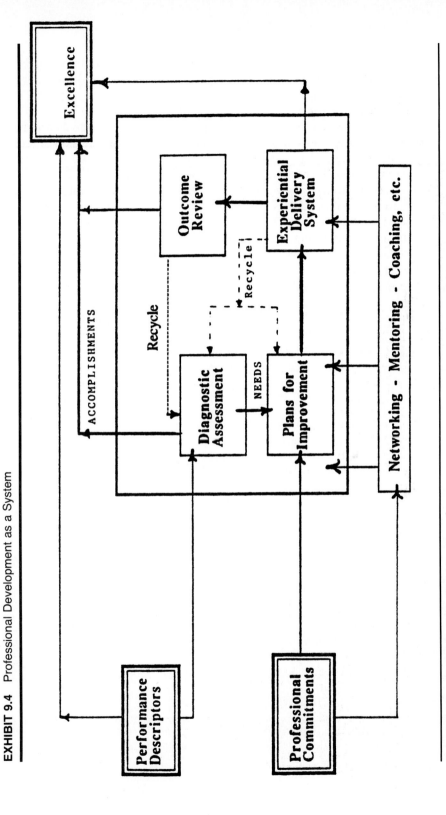

195

system. This chapter differentiates staff development into staffing, in-service education, and advanced preparation. The emphasis here is on on-the-job training because it is the element essential to a quality educational program under pressure for change.

Needs assessments should be performed for individuals and institutions for continuing competency development. The sections on organizing, planning, and staffing for training address these complex endeavors. Collaboration and systematic procedures are essential.

There are four basic models of leadership training that have special promise for more intensive on-the-job leadership training efforts. This may be done in collaboration with various organizations, but most of the sustained effort must come from the local district. Finally, a continuing professional development system is a practical, economical vehicle for accomplishing these ends.

Suggested Study Sources

Burke, Peter J., and R.G. Heideman, eds. 1985. *Career-Long Teacher Education.* Springfield, IL: Charles C. Thomas.

This comprehensive volume presents many points of view on adult education, directed toward the needs of teachers. Chapter 8, "Adult Learning and Teacher Career Stage Development," reviews various theories, including maturational, life-age, life-cycle, and stages of development. Andragogy and pedagogy are contrasted in a very useful way.

Commonwealth Secretariat. 1982. *In-Service Education of Teachers in the Commonwealth.* London: The Commonwealth Secretariat, Marlborough House, Pall Mall.

This document on in-service education programs and activities in widely differing countries of the Commonwealth reports, for each region, on the results of a survey that focused on purposes, priorities, costs, coordination, and the like. A most interesting facet is the description of innovations adopted.

Harris, Ben M. 1989. *In-Service Education for Staff Development.* Boston: Allyn and Bacon.

This is a basic reference, source book, and text addressing a wide range of practical problems related to leading in-service education programs in elementary and secondary schools. Operating policy and principles, strategies, goal setting, and designing and evaluating training programs are emphasized. Specific chapters address personalized training, simulations, and group approaches. The appendices include illustrations of plans, documents, and instruments.

Harris, Ben M. 1985. *Supervisory Behavior in Education.* 3d ed. Englewood Cliffs, NJ: Prentice-Hall.

This general reference on instructional supervision includes chapters and sections on designing training programs and reports of cases of training programs in operation (Chapter 11). Appendix B details competencies for directors of in-service education.

Hewton, Eric. 1989. *School Focused Staff Development: Guidelines for Policy Makers.* London: The Falmer Press.

This volume is one of many recent works providing a British perspective on in-service education and/or staff development. A pilot project, described in detail in the two initial chapters, depicts diverse in-school staff development in seven East Sussex County schools. Other chapters focus on assessment and policy to support school-focused staff development. In the final chapter, training, coordination, support, evaluation, and financial provisions are discussed as essential elements in the success of such programs.

Levine, Sarah L. 1989. *Promoting Adult Growth in Schools: The Promise of Professional Development.* Boston: Allyn and Bacon.

This book has its greatest strength, perhaps, in using a developmental "perspective" for guiding in-service activities in schools. It also emphasizes both personal and professional development more than most sources. The section "Theory into Practice" includes interesting segments on the role of the principal and the school environment and includes illustrative cases. The section "Promising Practices" is a bit disappointing in that it is rather brief and deals with only a limited array of known alternatives that are not very new.

May, Leslie S., et al., eds. 1987. *Evaluating Business and Industry Training.* Boston: Klower Academic Publishers.

An array of authors report on specific approaches to the evaluation of training. The ideas are very diverse, offering useful approaches for many situations. The chapters focus on product evaluation, content validity, cost/benefit analysis, and personnel decisions.

Orlich, Donald C. 1989. *Staff Development: Enhancing Human Potential.* Boston: Allyn and Bacon.

This work is a fairly comprehensive guide to staff development, program planning, and evaluation. Some chapters focus on activities, funding, incentives, and evaluation. Chapters of special uniqueness include those on administering staff development, the reform "climate," and various theoretical models or paradigms. Chapter 2, on needs assessment, is especially interesting in that it suggests program evaluation techniques above and beyond traditional opinion surveys.

Rea, Peter, et al. 1990. "Training: Use of Assessment Centers in Skill Development," *Personnel Journal* 69(April): 126–30.

The authors review the use of assessment centers in AT&T and GTE and other business hiring and promotion efforts. The assessment feedback provided is criticized as being too limited. Examples of incorporating participant feedback within the center activities are described and discussed as a form of valuable training.

Showers, Beverly, et al. 1987. "Synthesis of Research on Staff Development: A Framework for Future Study and a State-of-the-Art Analysis," *Educational Leadership* 45(November): 77–87.

This is a review of a substantial array of studies, presented in a nontechnical form. Studies done prior to 1980 are neglected; however, the conclusions are for the most part supported by earlier works. Together they dispel many myths about enthusiam, participation, and training locale as overriding requirements for effective training.

Teschner, W.P., et al., eds. 1983. *In-Service Teacher Training Models, Methods, and Criteria of Its Evaluation.* Strasbourg: The Council of Europe and Swets and Zeitlinger, Lisse.

This is a collection of reports on various aspects of forward-looking teacher training plans. Experimental plans, a German case study, and reports from Denmark, Finland, Norway, and Sweden make this an eye-opening volume for American educators.

Tracey, William R. 1984. *Designing Training and Development Systems* Rev. ed. New York: American Management Association.

This is a comprehensive sourcebook for nearly all aspects of planning and designing training from a business management perspective. Much emphasis is given to measuring and evaluating training outcomes. Selecting and sequencing content, using various training strategies, and the use of media are addressed in useful ways.

Ulmer, Dale. 1986. "Inter-Active Video for the Electronic Age," *Workplace Education* 4 (March–April): 6–7.

This article describes a training system using interactive videodisc technology for vocational-technical education purposes. Various examples of such simulated training are discussed.

10

Managing Personnel Services

It has been said that in education there are three kinds of problems and three solutions to those problems: (1) people, (2) people, and (3) people (Black and English, 1986). Due to the labor-intensive nature of education, every administrator deals daily with personnel issues and personnel-related functions, but the magnitude of these responsibilities can be overwhelming to the site-based or central office administrator charged with multiple responsibilities for instructional improvement. In recognition of the importance and intricacies of personnel administration, this has become a specialized leadership role in many school systems. The size and complexity of the personnel office operation are such that a separate division or department with staff and a chief personnel officer may be required.

The point at which oversight of the personnel function should become the responsibility of a separate department or division within the organization has not been clearly established. Castetter (1986), after studying available data on the number of personnel specialists in relation to the number of employees, notes that school systems tend to have systemwide personnel positions after the system has 200 or more employees (55). Even in smaller school systems in which the superintendent of schools or an assistant superintendent is the designated personnel officer, an office with specialized staff positions may be needed to offer a full array of support and developmental services.

The collaborative, cooperative relationships advocated throughout this book for recruiting, selecting, assigning, and evaluating school personnel are not inconsistent with a well-organized, adequately staffed personnel office. On the contrary, managing personnel office operations in ways that ensure full professional participation by many staff members in these crucial service activities demands top-quality leadership. A personnel administration operation that is highly centralized—that is, one in which decisions are made in routine, perfunctory ways—demands little leadership and a simple organization. Similarly, a highly decentralized personnel operation that allows each unit administrator to make independent, uncoordinated personnel decisions demands only clerical services at a system level. The thrust of this book is to show how personnel administration can be a form of leadership for the improvement of instruction; while that leadership must be drawn from many staff groups throughout the school system, the personnel office itself must be staffed for initiating, coordinating, directing, and monitoring personnel services of the highest quality.

This chapter focuses on the personnel administrator, the historical development of personnel administration, guiding principles that have come to be recognized as standards for personnel administration, and the specific character of the services for which a personnel office must assume responsibility. The two chapters that follow address significant legal and financial issues that impact personnel administration. It is within the framework of humane, societal, legal, and financial expectations that the personnel administrator has the opportunity to make valuable leadership contributions.

Historical Perspective

As is all true too often in our society, personnel administration in the public schools was more slowly accepted in school systems than in industry. Until 1988, the historical development of personnel administration as a field of specialization within school administration was recorded primarily in the remembrances of early pioneers in the field. In 1988, in celebration of its fiftieth year as an organization, the American Association of School Personnel Administrators (AASPA) published a commemorative document recalling the development of both the field and the association. Due to the loss of historical records, the document relied heavily on the memories of past officers and a doctoral thesis, "The Public School Personnel Administrator," by Eleanor Donald (1962). Early leaders in the field of public school personnel administration recalled the early years—the 1940s and 1950s—as follows:

> Personnel administration developed rapidly as a specialized function in business and industry, beginning as early as the late 1800's. School districts were much slower to identify the personnel function and assign it to one administrator.
>
> The first public school personnel administrator was appointed in Dallas, Texas in 1919, but only eight districts had such a position by 1939. By 1950 there were 35 positions, and 130 districts had established a personnel administrator position by 1960.

Primary responsibilities tended to be the recruitment of teachers and the maintenance of personnel records. In many districts the personnel duties were assigned to a person charged specifically with this function only after the baby boom of the 50's caused a need for many more new teachers.

Titles varied widely (assistant superintendent, director of, administrative assistant for, coordinator of, etc.). Positions were almost always assigned to the staff function and, though salary level varied substantially, usually were part of the superintendent's cabinet. Personnel administrators were usually relatively young (30–50), male and white. In 1960 they earned a median salary of $12,300 for a 12-month year! Typically, they were trained and certificated as teachers, often had educational administrative experience, but seldom had any personnel training or experience.

Talks with personnel administrators about their early experience often revolved around tales of recruiting, sometimes for several months a year and on a nationwide basis. Most recruiters interviewed by day, traveled by night and carried a sheaf of contracts in their breast pockets for the superior candidate.

Recruitment, selection techniques, consolidation of the personnel function, development of personnel policies, record keeping—these were the staples of school personnel administration. (6)

As noted, the number of personnel administration positions began to grow rapidly after World War II, with the most rapid growth coming in the late 1960s and early 1970s. That growth involved expansion of existing personnel organizations and a great increase in the number of new operations as teacher shortages created serious personnel problems in school districts of all sizes.

Emerging even as public education was evolving and changing, school personnel administration underwent significant changes during the decades following the 1950s. This period of change and evolution was also recalled by early practitioners in the AASPA's commemorative document.

While no specific dates can be given for the beginning of major changes in the content of personnel administration, 1963 is not a bad dividing line. Although the seeds of change had been plainly visible earlier, many events occurred during the 60's which assured that major changes must take place in the personnel administration area. Some have characterized these changes as constituting a revolution, and certainly personnel work hasn't been the same since.

Some of the changes include:

1. *The loss of cohesiveness in employee relations and the impact of hardnosed collective bargaining.*
2. *The effect of federal level financial support, laws, and judicial decisions regarding affirmative action and integration.*
3. *The computerization of record processing.*

4. *The propensity of individuals and groups to resort to legal means to settle problems.*
5. *The expansion and management of benefit programs.*
6. *Refinements in employee selection process.*
7. *Emphasis on techniques for setting equitable salaries, classification—comparable worth.*
8. *The administration of layoffs.*
9. *New services to employees such as employee assistance programs.*
10. *The increasing public demand for quality education.*

School personnel administration has become much more complex and its role has become much more critical to the districts. The ability of schools to carry out their mission successfully depends heavily on the quality of the personnel function.

There have been many other changes. Personnel departments are found in many smaller districts. Great progress has been made in staffing personnel departments. Many women and minorities now have major leadership roles in personnel departments. (8–9)

The American Association of School Personnel Administrators

The evolution of the AASPA paralleled the development of school personnel administration as a specialized function of school administration. The fledgling organization had sixteen members in 1940, and early meetings focused almost exclusively on teacher selection issues. The history of the AASPA reflects a search for clear identity and purpose, which was achieved during the early 1960s as personnel administration emerged as a vital force in school administration. The history of the association, included in the AASPA document, began in 1938 with informal discussions held by members of the New York City Board of Examiners and faculty of Teacher's College, Columbia University regarding teacher selection processes. With a growing membership, the AASPA is now a full partner with other major educational organizations, and its representatives serve on joint committees studying national education problems. Through affiliation with state school personnel associations and the Association for School, College and University Staffing (ASCUS), AASPA is recognized as an important resource and support organization for personnel administrators.

Principles and Standards

In 1960, the AASPA (1988a) first produced a "statement of the principles and functions of personnel administration and evaluative criteria for testing a school system's personnel program in terms of accepted principles" (i).

The fourth edition, now in use, includes 27 standards and 217 associated practices and policies (AASPA, 1988b). The book begins with a "Statement of Ethics for School Administrators" that was approved by the AASPA Executive Committee in 1976; this statement is found in Appendix H.

The authors proceed to describe the policies and practices they propose for an effective personnel operation. and present twenty-seven standards, divided into five major groups: (1) organizational structure, (2) staff procurement, (3) staff selection, (4) staff development, and (5) conditions of service. Appendix A includes a complete list of the standards. The authors emphasize that they are not presenting a standardized appraisal instrument; rather, they take the position that "school districts vary from one another in highly important ways and each personnel program will have its own unique characteristics. In this context, it is believed that these *Standards for School Personnel Administration* will provide valuable guidance to school districts as they continue their efforts to meet the educational needs of these times" (4).

Listed by standard are 217 associated statements of policies and practices, which the AASPA believes may be used in the following ways: (1) as guidelines for identifying personnel functions in school districts, (2) as an instrument for personnel department self-evaluation or evaluation by outside consultants, (3) as a guide for new or aspiring personnel administrators, or (4) as a study document for boards of education or classes in educational administration.

The Personnel Administrator

Perhaps one of the driving forces behind the establishment of a centralized personnel operation in many districts is related to the adage "that which is the responsibility of everyone is often the responsibility of no one." The same wisdom applies to the personnel operation itself. In a typical organizational pattern with a specialized personnel unit, the major share of personnel responsibilities is delegated by the superintendent of schools to a chief personnel administrator (e.g., assistant superintendent for personnel, personnel director, or director of human resources). Depending on the organizational pattern, the chief personnel administrator's position may be a line position or a staff position. Castetter (1986, 55) and Rebore (1982, 13) note that usually the position is a staff position providing service to other line administrators, but this depends on the organization. The chief personnel administrator generally reports directly to the superintendent, but different organizational arrangements may have the position reporting to a superior in general administrative services or business services.

The *Standards for School Personnel Administration* speak specifically to the role of the chief personnel administrator. Included in the fifteen practices and policies outlining the role of this administrator are the following:

The personnel administrator has a clear understanding of the goals, objectives and processes of the school system and the role which the personnel administration function has in accomplishing those ends.

The position guide for the chief personnel administrator reflects the needs of the professional position and its importance in the administrative hierarchy of the school district as a key member of the management team.

The personnel administrator is a resource person for other administrators, groups and committees within the school system in personnel matters.

The chief personnel administrator has major responsibility for interpretation and administration of negotiated agreements and a voice in establishing negotiation guidelines, parameters, and goals. (8–9)

A Service Orientation

The provision and management of personnel services, whether the services are handled by the superintendent of schools or a specialized division in the district, must occur in a service-oriented environment. Personnel services are, and must be perceived as, services for the employees of the district. This is emphasized in the AASPA *Standards.* Teachers, administrators, paraprofessional and auxiliary staff members, members of the board of education, and applicants are the primary clients of the district's personnel services unit. Indirectly, the list of clients also includes students, parents, and the community since the ultimate goal of personnel services is to improve quality instruction for the students of the district.

As described by Castetter (1986), the keys to clarifying and understanding the role of the personnel function are found in the terms "advice" and "service." *Advice* includes functions related to advising others concerning personnel policy development, personnel policy implementation, control of personnel services, and improvement of personnel services. *Service* includes the processes that actually bring about the delivery of personnel services to both individuals and the institution (57).

Fundamental to the development of strong, effective advisement and service roles are basic administrative functions related to decision making, planning, and communication. In providing leadership to improve instructional services for students, the personnel administrator has to understand the role and place of personnel services in accomplishing the district's mission, goals, and objectives. In the face of numerous reform and restructuring reports, taxpayer revolts, research findings, financial crises, and legislative mandates, school districts have recognized the need for strategic planning to accomplish the district's tasks effectively. Personnel services divisions have also come to recognize the need for strategic planning for the personnel operation. Planning for the acquisition and utilization of human resources within an educational institution must be a priority. This planning effort is a primary responsibility of all who are involved in the delivery of personnel services to the district.

Exhibit 10.1 illustrates several aspects of a strategic plan for a school district's personnel services division. The plan begins with a statement of beliefs developed by the personnel staff to communicate their vision of the division as a service-oriented enterprise committed to the success of students and the district. From the statement of beliefs, the personnel services staff develops a mission statement that summarizes what the personnel services division is all about and why the staff does what it does. In setting parameters for themselves, the staff commits to certain actions as guiding principles to be used in conducting the business of personnel services. Finally, the strategic objectives for the division are specifically stated. Not illustrated in Exhibit 10.1 on page 206, but a necessary part of such a plan, would be short-term objectives to be attained in six months or less and long-term objectives to be achieved in six months to a year. Additionally, such a plan would define the strategies to be used in achieving the strategic objectives set. For example, to work toward achievement of the strategic objective related to reduction of selection error, two strategies might be a training program for principals and supervisors to develop selection processes and a thorough examination of the statements on the "reasons for termination" section of the employee exit report. A number of other strategies would need to be implemented to deal with the reduction of selection error.

Effective management of each service provided by the personnel function begins with the collaboratively developed vision of how that service is to be provided within the district. With the development of the vision of the service, specific targets are set to reach the goals in terms of short-term and long-term objectives. Barriers to be overcome are identified and strategies to remove or reduce the obstacles to obtaining the desired outcomes are identified. With the attainment or achievement of the objectives and goals, the outcome is analyzed and new targets for growth are set for that service or new services. As noted by Webb et al. (1987), the purpose of strategic planning in personnel services is the effective use of personnel resources to move the organization toward its mission and achievement of the district's strategic objectives (61).

Both philosophically and operationally, administrators charged with responsibilities related to the provision and management of personnel services are called upon to be service-oriented. The establishment of goals and objectives for improvement of personnel services cannot replace the necessity of being in a service mode, even as plans are formulated for the future. Looking to the future in order to become service-oriented implies that current actions are not as important as those of the future. To the contrary, the results and implications of current decisions impact the immediate and long-term success of students, employees, the district, and the personnel administrator.

EXHIBIT 10.1   Division of Personnel Services Strategic Plan

Statement of Beliefs

WE BELIEVE

In order for employees to be effective they must be treated in a humane, personal, and professional manner with an assurance of confidentiality.

It is imperative we meet the needs of our customers in a timely, efficient, and effective manner.

Our staff relationships are built on a strong level of trust and sharing.

The operational excellence of the Division is directly related to communication and the key to effective communication is time, consistency, regularity, and follow-up.

It is absolutely essential to hire the most qualified applicant for every position.

What we do is critically important to the effectiveness of District 6 and the success

of students.

Mission Statement

Our mission is to enable the District to be eminent by ensuring the highest possible standards are used to recruit, select, and develop staffs as they impact each other and the education of students in a dramatic, positive manner, creating an environment of caring and growth for everyone every day.

Parameters

WE WILL

Never recommend an unqualified applicant who does not meet certification or job description criteria.

Treat every request for information or an application as significant.

Be proactive in working cooperatively with other departments to meet concerns or resolve conflicts.

Be proactive in our career counseling, implementation of the transfer procedures, and in staff development in encouraging employees to grow personally and professionally.

Have an adequate applicant pool so that positions can be filled with a quality applicant at any time of the year.

Never give people information without checking the policy and procedures where appropriate.

Strategic Objectives

By December 1992, selection error for classified and certified employees will be no more than one percent of those employed during the 1992 calendar year.

By January 1994, we will find no evidence of operational errors and breakdowns in basic services as we evaluate the 1993 service effort.

By August 1995, we will be operating in a paperless work environment with all personnel transactions conducted electronically.

Source: Personnel Services Division, Weld County School District 6, Greeley, Colorado, 1990.

Provision of Personnel Services

Over the years, the scope of the staff personnel administration program has broadened as its processes have grown more complex. The original task of employing certified personnel is today only part of a larger array of services commonly recognized as responsibilities of the personnel office. A current trend in personnel administration is to have the centralized personnel unit serve as an umbrella organization responsible for administering personnel services for all categories of personnel—professional, paraprofessional, and auxiliary. Not every personnel administration unit is given full responsibility for all of these services for all categories of personnel, but most units perform the majority of them.

Four activities of personnel staffing—recruitment, selection, assignment, and evaluation—are clearly the core responsibilities of personnel administration. As discussed in preceding chapters, the activities related to job analysis, induction, and staff development are also key activities in effective personnel administration. Chapters 1 and 2 gave indications of the numerous services that are necessarily related to these tasks. Still other tasks are suggested in the AASPA standards. However defined, the responsibilities of the personnel office demand that the unit provide a broad array of services.

A Variety of Services

Several services appear frequently in the literature on personnel administration. Recruitment and employment of personnel would, of course, appear on every list. Increasingly, school districts have initiated formal programs of induction, orientation, and communication. An important service that is often taken for granted is the placement and assignment of employees. In fact, the literature has limited coverage of this service. Personnel office operations, development of policies and procedures, and administration of rules and regulations are services that have little glamour but are essential to efficient and effective utilization of personnel resources. Evaluation of personnel has taken on greater importance as a service because of the accountability movement and the increased demands for a full catalog of teacher rights. Employee relations is one of the newer services provided by the personnel office, due to the changing relationships between employer and employees. The provision of substitute personnel is certainly not new but is a critical service. The variety of services provided by the personnel office increases, and will continue to do so, as superintendents and school boards recognize the importance of personnel resources in developing a high-quality instructional program and an efficiently run operation.

Projection of Needs

From the standpoint of the personnel office, there are certain requirements essential for accomplishing the task of employment. One of the first steps is to determine the projected personnel needs. Generally this determination is made using information related to student enrollment and instructional program changes. After determining each school's projected needs, the personnel office builds a master list detailing human resources needed for the school year. Because the requirements vary from year to year and because personnel costs are the major portion of a school's budget, guessing can be a very expensive game. Whether formally or informally, scientifically or unscientifically, every institution must project personnel needs. The *Standards for School Personnel Administration* address this staffing issue with the following statement: "A well-developed system of personnel accounting and research helps predict staff needs and enables the administration to make sound projections for current and future employment needs" (American Association of School Personnel Administrators 1988b, 13).

Due to the indisputable relationship between the number of students to be served and the number of employees to be hired, the projection of student enrollment is the key factor in determining personnel needs. In recent years, districts, especially those undergoing dramatic changes in growth and demographic patterns, have made serious attempts to devise and refine methods of projecting student enrollment. Staff specialists, external consultants, and computer software are employed in this process. Districts depend heavily on demographic information about the community and the school-age population, including current school enrollment; live births in the county or community area; housing starts and new construction in the area; types of housing in the community (number of single family residences, apartments); average household size per type of housing; income levels in the community; median age of the community; and a variety of work force statistics.

Evaluation of the size and composition of the staff is an ongoing process. When "population trends and shifts, age distribution, housing starts, etc., are not considered, decisions on where to staff, what type of staff, and number of staff may be made erroneously" (Pennsylvania School Board Association 1989). Decisions made on the basis of all available information stand the best chance of being accurate and have more integrity than those made based on only political, special interest, tradition, or judgmental considerations.

Recruitment and Selection

The recruitment and selection process is the oldest personnel service; it was also the origin of the personnel division in the public school administrative structure. Historically, recruitment and selection have received the greatest share of the personnel budget. Much of the personnel staff's time and energy has been devoted to the development of recruitment materials and activities. Administrators, supervisors, and teachers have also been involved in the personnel selection process. The realities of supply and demand, especially as they relate to the availability of candidates for positions, tend to influence the allocation of time spent by the personnel office in these services. The *Standards* address these activities as follows: "the recruitment process provides present as well as potential employees with information on available positions and provides them the opportunity to compete for vacancies" (14) and "decisions involving staff selection are based upon a carefully planned program of investigation, screening, appointment and follow-up support" (17). Recruitment and selection of competent personnel as activities of the staffing function are discussed in chapters 7 and 8.

Placement and Assignment

Placement and assignment are sometimes viewed separately, but they naturally combine to form a major activity of the personnel staffing function. Proper placement must be based on two sets of needs: those of the educational institution and those of the individual. The AASPA (1988b) states: "Placement, assignment, and transfer of personnel is a basic administrative responsibility through which attempts are made to meet the needs of the educational program, implement affirmative action plans, provide balanced staffing and meet the desires of individual employees" (18). The responsibility for placement and assignment should be shared by the personnel office, other appropriate central office staff members, and the building principal. A principal should not be expected to be responsible for the recruitment and employment of teachers, although his or her skills can be used; however, he or she should have a major voice in the selection of the school staff. The personnel office should screen candidates' credentials and interview them to provide a candidate pool and then present several candidates to the principal for interviewing and recommendation for employment. Usually individuals besides the principal need to be involved in both screening and selection. Supervisors, program directors, team leaders, and department chairpersons all may have a legitimate interest in the final selection. Participation in the selection process motivates all those involved to help the selected teacher be successful and also neutralizes the tendency to place the burden for a teacher's poor performance on the central office.

Assignment on campus should be made by the principal, but some guidelines for placement should be developed by the personnel administrator. The personnel department has two other responsibilities to the principal in helping to place personnel: consultation and provision of complete personnel data. As noted in the AASPA *Standards* (1988b), every effort should be made to give teachers assignments within their fields of preparation, and makeshift assignments should be for as brief a period as possible (19). The principal's effectiveness in assigning teaching duties is contingent upon the availability of current information about the teacher's preparation and certification. The personnel administrator, as the holder of the employee's personnel file, is a major resource to the campus administrator in this area. Practices related to the hiring and utilization of unqualified or minimally qualified personnel are pervasive throughout the educational system and impact student success significantly (Robinson 1985).

Reassignment of personnel is a component of the placement and assignment process that can be used for both long-term and short-term improvement of the district's instructional program. The *Standards* indicate that the students' welfare, the school system's program, and the employees' interests are the prime factors to consider in reassigning personnel. Transfer policies—governing both voluntary and involuntary transfers—should facilitate instructional improvement by providing opportunities for teachers to request new teaching situations and for administrators to assign teachers to new teaching situations.

Orientation

A new employee's success is greatly influenced by the orientation he or she is given to the new position. Unless the total orientation program is a good one, the complexities associated with a new position can quickly generate frustration and produce a morale problem. An orientation program should be comprised of several activities that are carefully planned and then well executed by the district's staff: (1) a warm, personal welcome to the work site, district, and community; (2) a review of the institution's history, goals, and organizational structure; (3) a description of the community to be served; (4) presentation of role expectations for the organization and the individual employee; (5) an explanation of employee benefits and services; (6) an introduction to supervising administrators; (7) a description of and guided visit to the physical environment of the school and district facilities; and (8) follow-up contacts to reinforce the initial orientation experiences, answer questions that may arise, check the employee's adjustment to the job, and make assignment decisions.

Except in very small organizations, these orientation activities should occur on more than one level. New employees should be taken through the actual employment processes by the personnel staff in what might be termed "an employment orientation." The focus of this orientation is to assist the new employee in completing all the paperwork related to employment. The new employee's perspective on district-level activities should be built through a "district orientation" process conducted by key administrators. Frequently this orientation program includes a welcome by the board president, superintendent, and top-ranking officials in the district. Many districts incorporate into the district-level orientation program a luncheon or dinner for new employees that is sponsored by community groups, simultaneously welcoming the new employee into the district and into the community. The most important orientation sessions occur at the work site level, where the building administrator and key teachers introduce the new member to the culture, procedures, and faculty of the campus. At this "work site orientation" the new employee is frequently teamed with an experienced staff member who serves as both an immediate and a long-term resource person. Regardless of the level or number of orientation activities, the personnel services division of the district is responsible for ensuring that orientation activities are provided for new employees. The provision of an induction program for teachers new to the profession should be provided during the first year of employment.

Communication

Personnel services are essential for good employee morale. However, the mere existence of services is not enough. Employees must perceive the quality of the services to be high and also believe that the institution values its employees. Personnel staff members become key communicators for the organization, conveying impressions of the total organization and its leaders to all who have contact with the personnel office. As a service-oriented division of the district, and because its staff members deal with both external and internal publics, the personnel office staff has a special responsibility in the area of human relations and communications. The personnel staff must be sensitive to the needs of the people it serves and make a special effort to develop credibility with employees through consistent, fair, honest, and empathetic treatment of all employees, who need to feel that they will find a cordial reception and hearing in the personnel office. As noted in the *Standards* (AASPA 1988b), personnel operations should be "conducted in a manner that provides for effective and friendly employee relationships and contribute to individual motivation and morale" (12).

Many practices have been developed to cultivate communication between an organization and its employees. The possibilities for communication are numerous and generally limited only by the ingenuity of the administrators. Kindred et al. (1990) suggest that there are three reasons why a good internal communication program is important: (1) a good external communication program cannot survive without it; (2) constructive ideas will be suggested by employees because someone is listening and informing them; and (3) human needs, such as recognition and a sense of belong, will be met, thus making employees more productive (100).

An Ombudsman

The practice of appointing a nonpartisan government official to hear and investigate the complaints of citizens against their government was introduced in Scandinavia early in the nineteenth century. In recent years, many governments have begun using an ombudsman to improve their relations with the people they serve. A number of school districts have found this practice effective in providing employees a special medium to air complaints as well as efficient in finding solutions to employee concerns and problems. Obviously, the ombudsman must be chosen with care. The position requires a person who is a combination of investigator, judge, and diplomat. The responsibilities of the position should be meticulously described and communicated to all affected parties.

A Hot Line

Especially in larger organizations, employees often feel they cannot get information to or from their employer. Unanswered questions often lead to employee frustration. Some school districts and governmental agencies have set up an information center with a hot line to facilitate responses to employee inquiries. This system of immediate response to most questions and rapid follow-up for more difficult ones provides the employee with accurate information, rather than making the employee dependent on gossip or unreliable sources for data on the school district. The anonymity of a telephone conversation appeals to many employees who would not seek information if they had to ask a superordinate. A variation on this tool uses tapes that discuss a particular topic of general interest to employees, such as sick leave. The employee may call and ask to hear this tape on a twenty-four-hour basis.

Adjustment Counseling

At any time, an employee may need special help in coping with his or her role. In smaller organizations, administrators often have the time for adjustment counseling. They may also have a relationship with subordinates that is conducive to adjustment counseling. In other organizations, large or small, this service to employees is often not available. To provide such counseling, or any type of employee assistance program, the district may employ special personnel or use the services of consulting firms. Confidentiality is a prime concern in this type of communication.

Internal Publications

Throughout the United States, school districts of every size and description have developed ways to report to their staff members. Internal publications may be short reports prepared by the superintendent or sophisticated journals prepared by highly trained public relations staffs. Regardless of the degree of sophistication, the reports are an attempt to tell about the organization and its activities. Properly prepared and edited, such publications can convey most important information to employees and, at the same time, be popular with employees. The administrator interested in developing or improving school district publications, internal or external, can receive assistance from the National School Public Relations Association, which is dedicated to improving communication services in the public schools.

Dissemination of School District Rules, Policies, and Practices

The necessity for rapid changes in rules, policies, procedures, and practices in today's educational organizations makes it important that a special effort be made to keep employees informed about such changes. Such changes should be publicized through every appropriate medium. Notices should be posted in designated places on every campus, and up-to-date information should be given to teachers and administrators in a usable form. In-house video systems and cable television also provide efficient means of disseminating information.

Recordkeeping and Reporting

Routine functioning of the personnel office in an efficient and effective manner is an essential element in the successful management of personnel resources. The staff should be so organized and trained that each contact with an employee or prospective employee is a supportive encounter. Records and documents should be maintained in a manner that provides for security and, at the same time, affords accessibility. Data for decision making are often difficult to develop, file, and retrieve, and the requirements for data collection have increased with the reports mandated by state and federal court orders and legislation.

The imperative need to improve data collection, storage, and retrieval has been widely recognized among educational administrators. As noted in the AASPA *Standards* (1988b), whenever feasible the computerization of personnel records and procedures is considered the best practice for providing effective and efficient processing and integration of records (11). The need for computerizing personnel services is directly tied to the magnitude of information that must be maintained and retrieved. There is a wide array of software and hardware available. Some districts have in-house computer services, employing microcomputers, minicomputers, and mainframe computers, and some use computer services provided by external agencies such as educational service centers.

The maintenance of personnel records and files involves considerable effort and physical space. Computerization lessens the amount of time required to gather and maintain personnel information. The use of microfilming and optical disk systems may reduce physical space requirements. The objective of using technology in the personnel operation is to facilitate the flow of information from the location in which it is stored to the user. Technology becomes an important tool in enhancing the service-oriented image of the personnel function. The degree to which technology is used to support the personnel function will be determined by the priority the function is given by the institution's top management, and management's understanding of technology's potential to facilitate the personnel office operations.

Policies and Procedures Development

Each administrator has an obligation to the school board to develop a set of policies and procedures that will stand against an administrative or judicial challenge. No service in education generates more serious challenges to policy and procedures than does personnel—selection, assignment, contracts, evaluation, and other difficult aspects of the job. Even student problems are second to personnel problems as a source of court cases. The AASPA *Standards* (1988b) note that "responsibility for recommending personnel policies and procedures is a function of the chief personnel administrator and his/her staff" (8). Initiating, editing, and advising on matters of policy do not encompass the personnel administrator's total responsibility for policy. Policies and procedures, to be properly understood and interpreted, must be communicated to the staff regularly and explicitly.

Because policy is not static, the personnel staff must continuously review and update yesterday's policies to meet today's needs. No policy at all is often better than an erroneous one. Keeping policies and procedures current is a never-ending task that should have priority for effective personnel administration.

Personnel Evaluation

Evaluation of personnel is a collateral responsibility shared with other departments. Ordinarily, personnel departments assume the following duties: (1) developing guidelines for evaluation, (2) devising forms and materials, (3) training supervisory and appraisal personnel in evaluation techniques, (4) keeping a repository of records, and (5) hearing appeals on evaluation results. According to the AASPA *Standards* (1988b): "The personnel evaluation and supervision system, while directed toward helping employees improve the quality of their performance, provides information which enables evaluators to make objective and fair decisions concerning termination, retention, or discipline when the employee's performance or conduct is marginal or clearly unsatisfactory, and rewards excellent performance" (22). Chapter 8 discusses personnel evaluation in detail.

Employee Relations

With the advent of mandatory collective bargaining, the personnel function has had to expand its operations to augment the institution's efforts to manage a new relationship between the institution and the organizations representing employees. Given the adversarial nature of collective bargaining, personnel administrators have had to work diligently to prevent the negativism associated with this process from affecting the total personnel function.

During negotiations, the personnel administrator is generally involved in representing management's positions on the issues under discussion. Following negotiations and the necessary processes leading to the signing of a formal contract, the personnel administrator is responsible for carrying out a series of functions, including the handling of grievances. Throughout the entire process, the personnel administrator remains responsible for the delivery of services to the district's clients. The personnel administrator continuously acts as advocate for both the district and the employees.

As noted in the section on communications, it is extremely important that employees have access to information about the district that is timely and accurate. To respond to employee inquiries and concerns, many districts establish an ombudsman position and/or hot lines that allow employees to ask questions concerning what may they may perceive as sensitive matters. Some districts use vehicles such as brown bag lunches in the schools or town hall-type meetings to provide communication channels for employees. The district or personnel office makes a commitment to securing answers and information related to the inquiries or concerns expressed through these channels. A primary objective for this type of effort is to curb the feeling that district employees need a third party to represent them in their relations with the district.

Substitute Services

The importance of substitute services can be quickly ascertained by a look at this item in a school's budget. It is a costly item in terms of dollars, and it can also be a costly item from the standpoint of morale and the quality of services delivered to students. Absences, tardiness, and turnover in personnel are often indicators of employee attitudes toward an institution. Absenteeism is a critical problem that continues to grow: "As the teacher shortage continues to grow, so the substitute teacher shortage will follow, causing the picture of teacher absenteeism to become even more bleak" (American Association of School Personnel Administrators 1987, i).

In the public schools in the United States, substitutes are employed for millions of teacher days each year; in fact, a student in the public schools will spend an average of six days per year with a substitute. Providing substitute services is not an emergency program but a long-term operation that deserves the attention of the chief personnel administrator. A quality program of substitute services can take several forms, but it requires well-planned and organized recruitment, employment, placement, orientation, and evaluation of substitute personnel. Otherwise, instruction can be seriously impeded or even cease when the regular teacher is absent. Substitute services require timely recordkeeping because the turnover in substitute personnel may be high, an institution's need for substitutes may change from day to day, employee supervisors may change regularly, the investment in in-service training is usually limited when dealing with transitory personnel, and a changing geographical location of the work station adds to the normal assignment problem. To handle this recordkeeping, districts have installed central call-in substitute services and computerized substitute services. In these programs, the personnel office staff is aided by telephone or computer technology for the requesting, assignment, and paying of substitutes. Teachers may notify their supervisor early concerning the need for a substitute, and supervisors may request a substitute on a twenty-four-hour basis.

Substitute teaching does provide the district with a unique opportunity to conduct an on-the-job observation of a candidate's performance for employment purposes. The amount and kind of data that can accrue contrast with the short personnel interview and other inadequate evidence that are normally part of the selection process.

Management Team Responsibilities

Meyer (1976) states: "The personnel department has been represented on many a corporation organization chart as an orphaned box—one that came from nowhere and did not seem to fit anywhere" (84). This description may have fit in past years, but today the personnel function has been recognized widely as an indispensable element of the management process. The role of the personnel administrator, regardless of the title held, is rapidly gaining stature in both business and education. Instead of being a dead end for the executive or administrator who has not performed up to the organization's norms, an assignment to personnel is viewed by more and more as a step toward the top.

The chief personnel administrator has the opportunity to sit in on the highest-level administrative discussion and to participate in the decision-making process at the highest echelons. The amount of power and prestige accorded today's personnel directors in business and education bears little resemblance to that which their predecessors received. As noted by Higginbotham (1988b), the personnel office "has become, over the years, one of major importance in the management of a school district" (2). Today, in most school systems the personnel administrator is an important member of the management team. Personnel services and human resource management are viewed as an integral part of the functions of top management. The personnel administrator is looked to for advice and assistance by other administrators as they carry out their responsibilities.

The rise in status and power of the personnel administrator paralleled a similar ascent in business and industry. How well the personnel office serves at its new place in the hierarchy will depend greatly on the instructional focus of the activities of the office and the willingness of the personnel administrator to work collaboratively with other administrators in a team effort. The successful personnel administrator must have demonstrated skills in interpersonal relationships, instructional leadership, communication, and decision making. Andrews (1987) states: "Proactive human resources managers must work constantly to build positive relationships with other managers and employees. Doing so ensures the human resources manager knows what is going on in the organization, can identify opportunities to contribute, and has chances to market the function appropriately. The best time to plant new ideas is when they apply to current discussions and their benefit can be immediately perceived. These opportunities are nonexistent if the human resources manager does not communicate frequently with peers" (89). Given a new awareness in business, governmental, and educational organizations of the potential benefits of effective and efficient management of human resources, what is the future of personnel management in educational systems?

The Future of Personnel Administration

Likert (1967) begins *The Human Organization: Its Management and Value* with a rather impressive statement on personnel management: "All activities of any enterprise are initiated and determined by the persons who make up that institution. Plants, office, computers, automated equipment, and all else that a modern firm uses are unproductive except for human effort and direction. . . . Of all the tasks of management, managing the human component is the central and most important task, because all else depends on how well it is done" (1).

If school administrators recognize that personnel is the essential component in the operation of schools, then appropriate emphasis on the task of personnel administration will follow. Increased emphasis will bring changes. Three leaders in the field of school personnel administration—George Redfern, E. Edmund Reutter, and Carroll Sawin—were asked in 1988 to predict what might occur in the field of school personnel administration during future decades. This request was made by the AASPA, and each respondent's thoughts were recorded in their commemorative document (1988a).

Redfern looked ahead to the year 2038 and suggested five challenges of the future that school administrators would face: (1) demographic imperatives (changing clientele and environments), (2) technological resources (the only way to prevent a gridlock in personnel office activities), (3) proactive management (anticipating the personnel operations changes), (4) strategic planning (long-range planning to move forward), and (5) personnel advancement (the development and testing of new personnel techniques) (13).

Reutter noted that to try to assay the future is at once exciting, perplexing, and awesome, and that to attempt to do so requires a careful assessment of long-term trends:

> *The evolution of the specialization into a truly professional one will accelerate. The setbacks and diversions to this trend brought about by the advent of the highly adversarial collective bargaining of the last two decades will be overcome . . . personnel administrators will concentrate more on the substance of policies designed to solve problems and enhance education, rather than on strategies and tactics for handling "demands" of employees and gaining acceptance of school district proposals within the fixed time frame for a "contract" . . . The position of human resources administrator increasingly will be recognized as an explicit specialization within education administration, neither a steppingstone to the superintendency nor a career entered late in one's professional life. (15)*

Sawin noted that the importance of the human resources function in assisting corporations, businesses, or schools to reach their objectives and to meet the challenges of a rapidly changing world was well documented. The challenge of the future is to continue to do all that was done in the past while dealing with old and new priorities in a productive and cost-effective manner. Sawin examines areas that touch the special relationship of personnel and the site-level administrator in his forecast of the future: (1) data processing (on-line systems linking principals and the personnel office), (2) selection and assignment (innovative programs will be developed), (3) principal development (shared decision making in all operations), and (4) personnel administrators certification (a means of attaining credibility among peers in business, industry, and schools).

The future will see personnel administration in education change and keep pace with the developing needs of society, or it will lose its credibility, face changes imposed from outside the educational organization, and then lament the lack of control over the educational system it once had power to administer.

Summary

Personnel operations in school systems are becoming larger, more specialized, and more complex. If the personnel administration function is viewed as a key element in the improvement of instruction, as it is in this book, then the personnel office must exemplify high-level leadership in the provision of services.

Personnel administrators have come onto the educational scene relatively recently—within the past seventy years. Since World War II there has been rapid growth in the number of persons serving as personnel administrators. The American Association of School Personnel Administrators, organized in 1939, has expanded rapidly and is now influential throughout the United States and Canada. Its publication, *Standards for School Personnel Administration* (1988b) is a useful guide for the development of standards, practices, and policies for school personnel administration.

The role and position of the personnel officer have grown in importance and prestige. Current trends indicate that in the future the personnel function will become an even more crucial element in the successful administration of schools. The challenge of the personnel administrator is to stay close to the system's human resources by providing efficient and effective personnel services. It is anticipated that improving services to personnel will improve services to students. This is the ultimate goal of personnel administration.

Suggested Study Sources

American Association for School Personnel Administration. 1988. *Standards for School Personnel Administration.* Foster City, CA: American Association of School Personnel Administrators

These standards may be used for a variety of purposes, as noted in this chapter. They are excellent sources for studying personnel administration or for use in the evaluation and improvement of current personnel operations. The full text provides a working document for evaluating personnel services.

Castetter, William B. 1986. *The Personnel Function in Educational.* 4th ed. New York: Macmillan.

In Part 1, "The Personnel Function Foundations," the author of this, the fourth edition of a classic treatment of school personnel administration, addresses the nature and scope of the personnel function, social change and the personnel function, organizing the personnel function, and fundamental of human resource planning. The author notes that this edition concentrates on a long-term agenda that is designed to improve American education.

Rebore, Ronald W. 1982. *Personnel Administration in Education: A Management Approach.* Englewood Cliffs, NJ: Prentice-Hall.

Chapter 1 discusses the rationale and organizational structure that support effective personnel administration. Other sections deal with a variety of topics related to personnel

acquisition and retention. There is a special emphasis on the factors that have led to the development of personnel administration as a specialized function in school administration.

Webb, L. Dean, John Greer, Paul Montello, and M. Scott Norton. 1987. *Personnel Administration in Education: New Issues and New Needs in Human Resource Management.* Columbus, OH: Merrill.

The first three chapters describe the development of personnel administration and explore its place in the modern school system. Strategic planning for human resources administration is emphasized. The authors state that the text is based on a broad research base.

11

The Legal Environment of Personnel Administration

Schools, like all other institutions in modern society, operate within a framework of laws and regulations. Other chapters in this book address the limitations and considerations imposed by the legal requirements to which schools in general and administrators working with personnel functions in particular must attend. This legal framework, frequently referred to as *school law*, is not a unique body of law developed only for educational institutions, but an integrated body of federal, state, and municipal statutes and regulations governing a variety of enterprises and relationships. School law is primarily composed of many layers of civil law—all law that is differentiated from criminal law and designed to protect the rights that exist between individuals and entities and between individuals and employers. Of concern to all educators is that portion of school law, especially state law, that defines how educational institutions are to be governed and operated. Of particular concern for personnel administrators are the statutes passed by the U.S. Congress and state legislatures and the judicial decisions interpreting these statutes, which form the special segment of civil law known as civil rights. The local policies that translate school law into operational procedures for each educational institution provide the most specific layer of legal requirements and guide the day-to-day work of all administrators. Within this highly legalistic environment, the school personnel administrator plays a significant role—quasilawyer who knows when to consult the school attorney, when to apply personal knowledge, and how to help others avoid legal problems.

It is unrealistic to expect a school administrator to be an expert in all aspects of federal, state, and municipal law. What is reasonable to expect is that the administrator will be thoroughly familiar with the policies and administrative regulations of the district and the state statutes and rules upon which the local policies are based. This chapter provides an overview of (1) major federal laws and judicial decisions that impact personnel functions related to the recruitment, selection, and retention of qualified, competent educators, and (2) legal considerations that have a major effect on the decision-making processes involved in personnel administration. It must be recognized that the major legal forces in education are state law and local policy—laws that differ from state to state and policies that vary from district to district. In practice, it is these state laws and local policies that provide the basis for most personnel decision making and for litigation against the district. Specific personnel problems and issues, therefore, must always be addressed within the context of applicable law and local policy.

Throughout the myriad of daily actions and interactions related to the personnel decision-making process, the astute administrator consciously practices "preventive law." This requires staying current on legal requirements; securing the best legal documents, journals, and materials as resources; and seeking professional legal assistance when the issues involve serious legal consequences. The expense involved in practicing prevention is minuscule when compared to that incurred as the result of a complex and lengthy legal action brought against the school district because of administrative error. The importance of preventive action in school administration was evident as far back as 1939, when Dennis Cooke spoke to the need for being well informed in legal matters: "It is highly essential that school executives become familiar with the court interpretations of school law. To know the statutes is important, but this in itself is not sufficient. Many of the wrongs that are committed against the law of schools are caused by lack of information and not by intentional wrongdoing" (120).

With regard to the legal aspects of personnel administration, the administrator is expected to be a thoroughly knowledgeable expert who can function as an interpreter, implementer, and mediator of the law. This is an awesome responsibility. Perhaps even more awesome is the manner in which the administrator is expected to carry out this function. The ability to present the legal requirements in a manner that causes others to want to implement them is a special skill that blends dedication to task and awareness of human processes. Remembering that students are our focus and first priority is an anchor that gets many school administrators through the tough and difficult decisions involved in adverse legal actions against other people. The willingness to go the extra step and to "stop, look, and listen" to the concerns of others, even when such action is not statutorily mandated, generally produces the desired results. In a sense, the administrator working with personnel functions needs to approach every issue from a perspective of due process. This perspective emanates partially from a sense of concern and regard for others and partially from a sense of almost overwhelming responsibility for ensuring the protection of the students and the district.

In addition to having a thorough knowledge of the law and a genuine concern for others, the administrator must be committed to ethical behavior in carrying out legal requirements. This is exemplified in the "Statement of Ethics for School Administrators," which has been adopted by the American Association of School Personnel Administrators (AASPA) and many school administrator organizations. This statement is found in Appendix I.

Fair Employment Practices

Public schools derive their existence from state legislatures and are recognized as agencies of the state government. The actual governance and operation of schools occurs within a tangled, complex web of federal and state statutes; rules and regulations created by federal, state, and local government agencies; and judicial decisions interpreting the statutes, rules, regulations, and their application. Virtually every aspect of personnel administration is governed by some application of these laws and regulations. The number of statutes and rules governing all of the educational process, but especially administration of the employment process, seems to increase annually at an exponential rate: "Voluminous quantities of labor laws were enacted during the past 100 years or so. Although most promoted and provided rights for workers, a few modified those decisions, some set rules and regulations, and collectively they set the stage that governs and determines the day-to-day actions, reactions and interactions between employer, employee, unions, and government" (Lawrence 1987, 75).

One of the assumptions of this text is that personnel practices are especially influential in determining the character and quality of the instructional programs because of the essentially humane character of schools. As social institutions, schools reflect the virtues and faults of the larger society and are frequently viewed as the means through which to cure society's ills, since "about one of every four Americans is involved as student, teacher, administrator, counselor, aide or service worker in some aspect of education" (Burrup et al. 1988, 41). Nowhere has the demand for change been more evident than in the area of equal protection and nondiscriminatory employment practices. Halcrow (1987), in interviewing attorneys and human resource managers, found a commonly held opinion that the U.S. Congress sought to eliminate social inequities and create a color-blind, nonsexist society by making employers bear most of the responsibility for eliminating racial and other forms of discrimination (61). School districts as employers have the same responsibilities related to fair employment as their counterparts in the business community. As the nation's largest employer of approximately one-seventh of America's work force, school districts have become the focus of attention to employment practices, and monitoring of these practices has been an ongoing effort of the federal government.

The prohibition against employment discrimination, especially in recruitment and hiring, is found in the language of federal, state, and municipal statutes and regulations that speak to many issues other than the employment process. This section highlights major federal statutes and regulations that together form the basis for prohibiting employment discrimination on the basis of race, color, national origin, religion, sex, pregnancy, and handicap: Title VII of the Civil Rights Act of 1964, the Age Discrimination in Employment Act of 1967, the Equal Pay Act of 1963, the Rehabilitation Act of 1973, and Title IX of the Education Amendments of 1972. These laws form the legal umbrella protecting the civil rights of individual employees and groups of employees. The review of these selected federal mandates that follows should serve to raise the awareness of the reader, who may undertake further investigation of their provisions and impact.

The chapter highlights the actions of the national government in addressing and attempting to solve social and economic problems of society through regulation. Unlike earlier models of regulation, the current national trend is toward a regulatory model that is not applied specifically to a single industry but, rather, to many industries including education. Administrators working with personnel functions need to understand the thrust and intent of these mandates to operate effectively in the current environment and to anticipate future regulations. Administrators must also be aware of state laws that pertain to fair employment practices, because they are generally more restrictive and prescriptive than the federal statutes.

Federal Constitution and Statutes

Through its silence on the subject of education, the U.S. Constitution delegates development and creation of educational systems for the nation's citizenry to the various states. Each state, as creator of the educational system within its boundaries, becomes the employer of thousands of individuals. The Constitution is not silent on how citizens employed by the state are to be treated by their employer. The Equal Protection Clause of the Fourteenth Amendment to the U.S. Constitution prohibits employment discrimination through the guarantee that the state shall not "deny to any person within its jurisdiction the equal protection of the laws." The coverage provided by this amendment is limited to government bodies and to the intentional act of discrimination. The protection of the Fourteenth Amendment extends to school employees because of their status as employees of subdivisions of state government. Applicants and school employees are also guaranteed certain protections under federal and state civil rights statutes. Whereas the Fourteenth Amendment addresses intentional discrimination, these laws address and give consideration to claims of *perceived* discrimination, based on the concept that it is not the intent but the consequences of a practice that determine whether the practice is discriminatory.

Title VII of the Civil Rights Act of 1964

The objective of Congress in enacting Title VII of the Civil Rights Act of 1964 (Public Law 88-352) was to achieve equality of employment opportunity and to remove artificial, arbitrary, and unnecessary barriers that had previously operated invidiously to favor some groups of employees over others (U.S. Equal Employment Opportunity Commission 1979, v). Title VII prohibits discrimination in employment on the basis of race, color, religion, national origin, sex, and pregnancy. The coverage of Title VII was expanded by the Equal Employment Opportunity Act of 1972 to all institutions with fifteen or more employees, including state and local governments, school systems, and labor organizations.

Under the provisions of the act, it is unlawful practice for an employer "to fail or refuse to hire or to discharge any individual, or otherwise to discriminate against any individual with respect to his compensation, terms, condition, or privileges of employment, because of such individual's race, color, religion, sex, or national origin." It is also illegal to limit, segregate, or classify employees or applicants for employment in "any way which would deprive or tend to deprive any individual of employment opportunities or otherwise adversely affect his status as an employee."

Amendments to Title VII provide protection from discrimination based on pregnancy and sexual harassment. The Pregnancy Discrimination Act of 1978 prohibits discrimination on the basis of pregnancy, childbirth, or related conditions. Pregnant women are to be treated in the same manner as other temporarily disabled employees. Districts may specify the amount of time allowed for leave related to childbirth and may require the employee to secure a clearance to return to duty. Women on leave for childbirth are to be treated as other employees on medical leave and are not entitled to additional special protections. Title VII also specifically prohibits sexual harassment of any employee or applicant. School districts and institutions are responsible for acts of sexual harassment on the part of their agents or supervisors, whether or not the district or institution knew or should have known of their occurrence. An institution has a responsibility on receipt of a sexual harassment complaint to investigate the complaint, and on discovering sexual harassment has an obligation to take immediate and corrective action.

To enforce the provisions of Title VII, Congress established the Equal Employment Opportunity Commission (EEOC), a federal agency with litigation authority that can investigate and act in cooperation with state and other federal agencies and/or bring suit on its own. In addition to administering Title VII, the EEOC administers the Age Discrimination in Employment Act and the Equal Pay Act. Under Title VII, complaints may be filed by individuals or organizations on behalf of an aggrieved employee or applicant. Even members of the EEOC may file charges. It should be noted that no investigations can be made unless complaints and charges have been filed, and administrative remedies with the EEOC must be pursued before an individual is allowed to file a complaint against the employer. When discrimination in employment is proven, the plaintiff may not be awarded punitive damages but may be eligible for benefits including, but not limited to, back pay, accumulated seniority, and legal counsel fees.

Discrimination claims under Title VII are divided into *disparate treatment* and *disparate impact* claims. Under the claim of disparate treatment, the plaintiff charges that the adverse action taken was the result of the individual's race, color, sex, religion, national origin, or pregnancy. Under the claim of disparate impact, the plaintiff charges that a policy of the employer has an adverse impact on a minority or protected group. Although it can be fairly stated that the burden of proof in discrimination claims under Title VII shifts back and forth between the plaintiff and the defendant, in reality the greatest burden always resides with the employer to defend actions by showing cause and necessity for the actions.

The *Uniform Guidelines on Employment Selection Procedures* are used by EEOC to enforce Title VII and the Equal Pay Act of 1963. These guidelines are designed to eliminate the adverse impact of selection procedures on minorities and women by regulating the selection procedures used to make employment decisions. The guidelines are not law, but they represent the articulated viewpoints of the agencies charged with enforcement of the law, and they are frequently consulted by the judiciary in deciding court cases involving claims of employment discrimination. Selection procedures are defined by the EEOC in Section 1690.107(Q) of Procedures on Inter-Agency Coordination of Equal Employment Opportunity Issuance as "any measure, combination of measures, or procedure used as a basis for any employment decision. Selection procedures include the full range of assessment techniques from traditional paper and pencil tests, performance tests, training programs, or probationary periods and physical, educational and work experience requirements through informal or casual interviews and unscored application forms." The *Uniform Guidelines* clearly define discrimination in selection as the use of any procedure that has adverse impact and extend the concept of selection to any employment decision. The guidelines require the maintenance of records to support the selection procedures and the demographic characteristics of applicants and employees.

Age Discrimination in Employment Act of 1967

The Age Discrimination in Employment Act of 1967, amended in 1978, 1984, 1986, and 1987, prohibits discrimination against persons aged forty and older by making it illegal to use age as a criterion for employment unless age can be shown to be a bona fide occupational qualification. The stated congressional purpose for the act is "to promote the employment of older persons based on their ability rather than age; to prohibit arbitrary age discrimination in employment; to help employers and workers find ways of meeting problems arising from the impact of age on employment." The act is intended to address individual differences in workers of all ages and to acknowledge that age is not a valid indicator of ability to perform. The provisions of the act apply to all private employers with twenty or more employees, labor unions with twenty-five or more members, local and state governments, and employment agencies that serve covered organizations. Part of the Fair Labor Standards Act (FLSA), the act is administered by the EEOC. The act abolishes all mandatory retirement due to age but does permit dismissal at any age for good cause or when the position held is eliminated. Until the end of 1993, tenured faculty and certain other government employees could be forced to retire at age seventy.

Equal Pay Act of 1963

The Equal Pay Act of 1963 requires all employers subject to the Fair Labor Standards Act to provide equal pay for men and women performing similar work. In their declaration of purpose, Congress stated that "the existence . . . of wage differential based on sex (1) depresses wages and living standards for employees necessary for their health and efficiency; (2) prevents the maximum utilization of the available labor resources; (3) tends to cause labor disputes . . . ; (4) burdens commerce and the free flow of goods in commerce; and (5) constitutes an unfair method of competition." In 1972, coverage of this act was extended beyond employees covered by the Fair Labor Standards Act to an estimated 15 million additional executive, administrative, and professional employees who had been exempted under the original provisions of the act. In 1974, additional amendments to the Fair Labor Standards Act brought state and local government employees, including academic and administrative personnel and teachers in elementary and secondary schools, under the provisions of the act. Specifically, the act provides that a man and a woman working for the same institution under similar conditions in jobs requiring substantially equivalent skill, effort, and responsibility must be paid equally. Job titles and assignment do not have to be identical. Bona fide merit and seniority systems that result in pay differentials are allowed, provided that the systems themselves do not discriminate on the basis of race or sex. The EEOC enforces the act and has the authority to investigate and examine all records related to the wage system used by the employer.

Rehabilitation Act of 1973

Under the provisions of Section 504 of the Rehabilitation Act of 1973, an "otherwise qualified handicapped individual" may not be denied employment opportunity, fringe benefits, promotional opportunities, or special training solely on the basis of handicap. The otherwise qualified handicapped individual is one who can perform the "essential functions" of the job "with reasonable accommodation." A handicapped person is defined as one who has a record of, or is regarded as having, physical or mental impairments that limit major life functions, which include activities such as communication, ambulation, and transportation. The employer is required to make reasonable accommodations for the handicapped person unless doing so would create an undue hardship for the employer. Exact definitions of "reasonable accommodation" and "undue hardship" are not provided. Reasonable accommodation may include the need to restructure facilities, jobs, and work schedules and to provide special equipment or resources. The burden of proving an undue hardship in providing these accommodations rests with the employer. The U.S. Supreme Court has ruled that tuberculosis and other contagious diseases are considered handicaps under Section 504. In *School Board of Nassau County* v. *Arline* (1987), the Court declared that the purpose of Section 504 is to ensure that handicapped persons are not denied jobs because of prejudice or ignorance. The Office of Federal Contract Compliance Programs (OFCCP) of the U.S. Department of Labor has primary responsibility for enforcing the act with government contractors. The Department of Education and the Department of Health and Human Services enforce Section 504 of the act.

Title IX of Education Amendments of 1972

Title IX of Education Amendments of 1972 (Higher Education Act) states that "no person . . . shall, on the basis of sex, be excluded from participation in, be denied the benefits of, or be subject to discrimination under any education program or activity receiving federal assistance." The provisions of the act cover employment concerns and practices of elementary and secondary schools. Religious institutions are exempt if application of the Title IX provision is not consistent with their religious tenets.

In filing claims of sex discrimination, the plaintiff must decide whether to file under Title VII or Title IX. Generally, if the remedy sought relates to changing an institutional policy the claim is filed under Title IX and if it relates to the individual the claim is filed under Title VII.

Affirmative Action

Since the early 1960s, two prevalent and persistent themes have influenced the work of administrators working with personnel functions: *affirmative action* and *due process* emerged as concepts associated with, and within, the areas of civil rights legislation and litigation. The definitions of these terms remain ambiguous, since the judicial decisions describing what is appropriate and inappropriate action related to affirmative action and/or due process are primarily made on a case-by-case, circumstance-by-circumstance basis. The emerging nature of these themes requires constant attention on the part of the administrator.

As its name suggests, affirmative action involves making a deliberate effort to correct imbalances in minority employment by ensuring that applicants and employees have an equal opportunity for employment, benefits, promotion, and training. Affirmative action plans may be developed as a requirement of federal law, as part of a reconciliation agreement with federal and state agencies, by court order, or as a voluntary action. The elements of an affirmative action plan include a written policy, self-evaluation to identify deficiencies, steps required and a timeline to correct the deficiencies, and procedures for monitoring, evaluating, and reporting on the plan. The Office of Federal Contract Compliance and the EEOC monitor affirmative action programs and plans.

A criticism of affirmative action is its characterization as *reverse discrimination*. In interpretive guidelines on affirmative action, the EEOC in 1979 addressed this as follows:

> *Many decisions taken pursuant to affirmative action plans or programs have been race, sex, or national origin conscious in order to achieve the Congressional purpose of providing equal opportunity. Occasionally, these actions have been challenged as inconsistent with Title VII, because they took into account race, sex, or national origin. This is the so-called "reverse discrimination" claim. In such a situation, both the affirmative action undertaken to improve the conditions of minorities and women, and the objection to that action, are based upon the principles of Title VII. Any uncertainty as to the meaning and application of Title VII in such situations threatens the accomplishment of the clear Congressional intent to encourage voluntary affirmative action (1979, II: 69).*

Following judicial decisions in two cases, *Regents, University of California* v. *Bakke* (1978) and *United Steelworkers* v. *Weber* (1979), and the reorganization of the EEOC in 1984, the Commission took a different position and approved a statement that "racial preferences merely constitute another form of discrimination."

As a general rule, voluntary affirmative action plans adopted by school districts will not be considered reverse discrimination if the plan is a temporary measure designed to expire when balance has been achieved. In addition, the plan should be the result of obvious disparity between the races or sexes or prior discrimination and should not stigmatize or impinge unnecessarily on the rights of nonminority employees (*Johnson* v. *Transportation Agency* 1987; *Wygant* v. *Jackson Board of Education* 1986; *Britton* v. *South Bend Community School Corp.* 1987; *United States* v. *Paradise* 1987). Court decisions in recent years have tended to support the concept of affirmative action "targets," not quotas. These decisions leave open some difficult questions: "How can an employer reliably determine whether its work force is plagued by the 'manifest' racial or sexual imbalance necessary under Title VII to adopt a voluntary affirmative action plan? Under what circumstances can an employer use quotas in such a plan? And are such plans adopted by public agencies proper under the Equal Protection Clause?" (Sendor 1987, 40).

Despite the uncertainties resulting from less direction from the courts, affirmative action should not be viewed as something to practice only when the organization is in trouble; it should be a conscious part of all personnel decision making and practiced on a daily basis. A deliberate and aggressive effort should be made to attract and recruit qualified minorities and women into the applicant and promotion pools. When this is successfully accomplished, then the selection process should ensure that the best person is selected or promoted. When a formalized voluntary affirmative action plan is desired, the criteria and processes used in the plan should be developed with the assistance of legal advice.

Due Process

The second theme that has evolved from the legislation and judicial decisions related to the civil rights of school employees is that of due process. The concept of due process is complicated by the use of a number of terms—procedural due process, substantive due process, property interests, and liberty interests. In the simplest of terms, the protection of individual rights known as due process may be defined as fair play. *Procedural due process* relates to the provision of certain steps that allow the employee recourse when adverse actions against him or her are considered by the district. *Substantive due process* relates to the issue of fairness of the actions. Property interests relate to the right or expectation of continued employment, and liberty interests relate to the reputation of the employee. Due to the adverse impact on the employee, due process concerns are generally raised when termination of employment is considered, but they may also be raised when changes in status or condition of employment occur.

The two definitive legal cases with regard to procedural due process rights for teachers are *Board of Regents* v. *Roth* (1970) and *Perry* v. *Sinderman* (1972) According to the *1989 Deskbook Encyclopedia of American School Law* (1989):

Roth and Sindermann *emphasize, first, that there must be an independent source for a liberty or property interest to exist. Such interests are not created by the Constitution, but arise by employment contract or by operation of state tenure law. Second, if a liberty or property interest is not established, no requirement of due process exists under the 14th Amendment. Third, if a teacher possesses a liberty or property interest in employment, then due process is required and the teacher may not be dismissed without a hearing. (292)*

Procedural due process procedures require that the employee be given fair notice of impending actions and an opportunity to be heard by those considering the actions. The notice must adequately define the reasons for the proposed actions so the employee will have the chance to improve performance or time to prepare a defense. The U.S. Supreme Court spoke to the need for this requirement in *Mathews* v. *Eldridge* (1976), declaring that by providing reasons the district ensures a fairer and more open process through which the local board may make a determination. Ultimately the fact that the board's decision was made on the basis of written reasons may prevent the courts in subsequent litigation, if such action is pursued, from substituting the court's judgment for the decision of the board. The Supreme Court implied that providing reasons for actions requiring due process was good for employees and good for the district. The notice must be in the form prescribed by state law or district policy, must be delivered in accordance with the prescribed procedures, and must be presented within timelines defined for the process. Failure to adhere to the statutory provisions will almost automatically ensure that the district will lose when the board's actions are reviewed.

As with the notice, hearings must be conducted in strict compliance with state law and district policy or the district may face reversal due to procedural violations. The hearing is the essence of the due process procedure, since it provides the employee with the opportunity to refute charges and to be heard by those making the final decision. Hearings must be held at a reasonable time, in a reasonable location and be conducted before an impartial decision maker. The question of impartiality becomes an important issue when the school board must by law act as both the initiator of charges and the hearing panel. In *Rouse* v. *Scottsdale Unified School District* (1987), the court expressed confidence in the impartiality of elected school boards. The Supreme Court has indicated that school boards are to be presumed impartial unless proven otherwise. Since the hearing is an administrative hearing and not a criminal proceeding, the school board must adopt basic procedural rules to serve as guidelines for the hearing process. The district and the employee should have equal opportunities to present witnesses and evidence. Both should have the right to cross-examine witnesses and to make oral argument. All testimony offered at the hearing should be sworn to before an officer, such as a notary public, who is qualified to take oaths. The board members should not be subject to questioning by counsel or witnesses and should be given time to ask questions of witnesses and counsel. The board must make a record of the proceedings and must make a finding of fact.

Due process, when viewed from the perspective of fair play and the interest of students, should be part of every personnel decision. Substantive due process requires that there be fairness in decision making; procedural due process requires that the procedures used in decision making be known and available. Due process calls for decisions to be made on the basis of fact, not supposition, and in consultation with those affected by the decision. Throughout the personnel decision-making process as it relates to the recruitment, selection, and retention of competent staff for the ultimate purpose of improving instruction, the school administrator's perspective is shaped and molded by the concept of due process. Every aspect of personnel administration is influenced by this concept that the interests of students and society are paramount and yet compatible with the rights of individuals.

Employment Conditions

The boards of trustees for school districts derive their authority to employ personnel from the broad discretionary powers granted the board by the constitution and statutes of the state. The exclusive right to enter into contracts belongs to the school board and cannot be delegated to an individual board member or administrator. The contractual employment relationship is an agreement between the individual employee and the school board, entered into at a legally convened meeting of the board.

Employment Contract

The general requirements of contract law apply to school employment contracts. The standard elements of an employment contract include: (1) parties who are authorized to enter into the employment relationship, (2) subject matter not prohibited by law, (3) an offer and acceptance, and (4) the exchange of something of value (money) for services rendered. The parties authorized to enter into the contract relationship are the school board and an individual who meets state and local eligibility standards. The contract must not violate the law and must be within the power of the board to execute. The school board has the authority to adopt rules and regulations governing employment, and in signing the contract the employee agrees to abide by the specified rules. The employee also agrees to carry out assigned duties reasonably related to the position offered. In exchange for the performance of the duties, the board offers consideration in the form of money and benefits. The relationship between the employee and the school board is created and fixed by the terms of the employee's contract when the contract is legally construed and meets statutory requirements.

Certification

To be eligible for a teaching position and most administrative positions, individuals must meet state certification requirements prior to employment by a school district. Certification or licensure is a state process through which an individual earns the eligibility to perform specified duties in the public schools. Certification affects placement and assignment as well as access to teacher employment, but it provides no guarantee of employment or tenure (Valente 1987, 180). School boards may not expend funds for the employment of an uncertified teacher when certification is a prerequisite for employment. Failure to meet certification standards constitutes grounds for denying initial employment or for terminating employment.

In addition to the requirement for certification, many states require employees to file their certificates prior to the beginning of employment with the district. Section 13.045 of the Texas Education Code exemplifies this: "(a) Any person who desires to teach in a public school shall present his certificate for filing with the employing district before his contract with the board of trustees shall be binding, and (b) A teacher or superintendent who does not hold a valid certificate or emergency permit shall not be paid for teaching or work done before the effective date of issuance of a valid certificate or permit." In relationship to requirements for certification and the filing of the certificate prior to beginning the employment period, an exception to the general rule of "paying for services received" is considered legal when the employee fails to meet such standards.

Given that the state has full plenary power to grant certification and to make certification a prerequisite for employment, then the state also has the authority to deny, revoke, cancel, or suspend certificates and thus deny eligibility for employment. Under the statutory provisions established by the state, procedures for carrying out these actions of denying or revoking certification require careful deliberation and justification to ensure compliance with nondiscriminatory employment and to avoid the denial of property right. In general, the denial or revocation of certification results from conviction of certain crimes or a violation of the law that makes the individual unworthy to work with youth. The nature of the violation and the period during which it occurred are considered in such actions. Initial certification procedures generally include provisions for a criminal history check and appeal processes when an adverse decision is considered or made. The abandonment of an employment contract is usually justification for revoking certification and dismissal.

Citizenship, Loyalty, and Residency

Whether the state or a school district can require school personnel to be citizens of the United States, to sign a loyalty oath, and to be residents of the state or district have been addressed by the courts. On the question of citizenship, the courts have held that since educators have a state-mandated responsibility for teaching and developing the attitudes of young people about the country and its government, then it is reasonable to require that educators be citizens (*Ambach* v. *Norwick* 1979). The test used by the courts is that of a rational relationship between the requirement and a legitimate state interest. The provisions of the Immigration Reform and Control Act of 1986 require school districts to verify eligibility for employment for U.S. citizens and aliens authorized to work in the country without regard to position. U.S. citizens and aliens authorized work in the United States must possess and present to the employer documents establishing both identity and employment eligibility. In the *Handbook for Employers*, the U.S. Department of Justice, Immigration and Naturalization Service advises that "seeking identity and employment eligibility documents only from individuals of a particular national origin or from those who appear or sound foreign violates the new immigration law and may also be a violation of Title VII of the Civil Rights Acts of 1964" (1987, 9).

On the questions of loyalty oaths and residency, the courts use tests similar to rational relationship. The government has the right to exclude dangerous subversives from public positions, but the means used to ensure such exclusion must not be vague or excessively broad so as to suppress individual rights (Valente 1987, 184). When such requirements do not violate state law, they have generally been upheld and remain as part of the employment process. Simple pledges to defend and uphold the laws of the country and the state will not be viewed as violations of freedom. The following pledge, reviewed by the courts in *Knight* v. *Board of Regents, University of State of New York* (1967), is acceptable:

> *I do solemnly swear (or affirm) that I will support the constitution of the United States of America and the constitution of the State of New York, and that I will faithfully discharge, according to the best of my ability, the duties of the position of _____ to which I am now assigned.*

The advantages of living in the employing district have been accepted and acknowledged by the courts. These perceived advantages include more involvement in the community, less absenteeism and tardiness, a higher stake in the outcomes of education in the community, and an increased interest in what happens in the district where taxes are paid (*Pittsburgh Federation of Teachers* v. *Aaron* 1976; *Federation of Teachers* v. *Board of Education* 1975; *Wardwell* v. *Board of Education of Cincinnati* 1976). The test of residency requirements is the strength of the perceived advantage in terms of job-related benefit to the individual and the institution.

Fitness for Duty

As part of the employment procedures, new employees are generally required to furnish proof prior to assuming the position that they are in good health, free of infectious diseases, and physically able to handle the responsibilities of the position. These conditions of employment have been upheld by the courts, provided they do not unreasonably violate the individual's privacy. During the course of employment, an individual may be required to furnish proof of continued good mental and physical health. The public's interest in the institution's provision of a safe environment for students has been accepted as a justifiable reason for requiring such information (*Daury* v. *Smith* 1988; *McNamara* v. *Commissioner of Education* 1981; *Hoffman* v. *Jannarone* 1975).

In the area of fitness for duty, there are two issues of extreme concern: the use of drugs and infectious diseases. The nebulous and evolutionary nature of both legislation and judicial opinion related to these topics causes many administrators to do nothing, or to do only what is minimally acceptable when dealing with employees in this area. Lee I. Dogoloff, a former White House Advisor on Drug Abuse and official with the American Council for Drug Education, argues against the "do-nothing" approach. His comments, as recorded in *Drugs in the Workplace: Solutions for Business and Industry* (1987), speak to his belief that doing nothing is sinful: " one drug abuser in a work setting . . . can contaminate a number of nonusers" (8).

In actions against individuals accused of alcohol and drug abuse, the courts have looked at the seriousness and the continuation of the usage. As a general rule, incidents that occur on a teacher's own time and away from the school are difficult to use for dismissal. However, viewing educators as role models who have unique opportunities to influence students and their thinking, the courts uphold cases where educators use drugs around students, encourage students to use drugs, or use drugs on duty time (*Blaine* v. *Moffet County School District* 1988; *Board of Education* v. *Wood* 1986; *Nolte* v. *Port Huron Area School District Board of Education* 1986). The prevailing opinion related to drug testing, specifically urine testing, appears to be that there must be probable cause for suspecting that the individual has engaged in drug use (*Patchogue-Medford Congress of Teachers* v. *Board of Education* 1986).

As discussed in the section on Section 504 of the Rehabilitation Act of 1973, the courts have declared tuberculosis and other contagious diseases as handicaps. AIDS (acquired immune deficiency syndrome) also falls into this category. In *School Board of Nassau County* v. *Arline* (1987), the court developed a test that has been used in other cases involving infectious diseases, specifically AIDS. The test provides that if a person poses a significant risk of transmitting the infectious disease to others in the workplace, and reasonable accommodations will not remove the risk of infection, then the person is not qualified for the job under Section 504. Viewing the possibility of transmitting AIDS as very limited in the classroom or administrative setting, the courts have generally upheld appeals by educators to be returned to work (*Chalk* v. *U.S. District Court* 1988).

When dealing with problems related to fitness for duty, the administrator is advised to practice preventive law and to secure legal assistance. Under no circumstance should an administrator diagnose a drug or infectious disease problem unless personally licensed as a physician. Confidentiality, in both written records and conversation, concerning a suspected problem is absolutely essential. Breach of the right to know, even for confirmed cases, may result in prosecution under state statutes that protect privacy.

Compensation

As a topic of discussion, compensation is like the weather—a topic that is talked about continuously but about which little can be done. Despite the fact that money is often considered a dissatisfier, constant demands are made to improve the compensation systems in educational institutions: "Pay, like a coin, has two sides: it represents income to employees, costs to the employer" (Belcher and Atchison 1987, 4).

As the employer, the school board has the power to set salaries for district employees. This power, once considered plenary, has been limited by increasing legislation related to teachers' salaries. Virtually every school district has a local salary schedule plan that outlines minimum and maximum salaries for employees and gives attention to state regulations. Generally there are few legal concerns about salary schedules or plans if they provide uniformity of treatment for those performing similar services and having like training and experience. Once a salary schedule is set, the district has an obligation to use the schedule (*Vilelle* v. *Reorganized School District No R-1* 1985). When not operating in contradiction to statutory mandates, the school board may set rules for determining how individuals may receive credit on the salary schedule (*Wygant* v. *Victory Valley Joint Union High School District* 1985; *Kramer* v. *Board of Education* 1977; *Sullivan* v. *Hannon* 1978).

The provision of fringe benefits varies from state to state and from district to district. Benefits such as teacher retirement plans, workers' compensation, unemployment insurance, and sick leave provisions are required by federal and state law. Workers' compensation is paid by the institution as provided by state law, for the intended purpose of providing benefits to employees injured on the job. Unemployment insurance provides protection against loss of income related to loss of employment and is paid for by the institution under federal and state statutes. Other benefits, such as medical insurance, dental insurance, and liability insurance, result from the action of the local school board, either of its own initiative or as part of a collective bargaining agreement.

Employment Status

A fundamental goal of effective personnel administration is to ensure, to the greatest degree possible, the success of each district employee. This makes the primary goal of the personnel staffing process the recruitment, employment, and retention of personnel who are successful on the job. When the employment decision-making process is viewed as one of the interrelated components of the total personnel staffing process, then the probability of assuring success on the job is enhanced. Specifically, the administrator's responsibility is to work toward the use of common criteria for the selection and evaluation of employees. These criteria should be viewed as methods of describing success—in the selection process as well as on the job. The use of these common criteria also provides input for the staff development or training process. The EEOC (1978) defines employment decisions as including but not limited to "hiring, promotion, demotion, membership (for example, in a labor organization), referral, retention, and licensing and certification, to the extent that licensing and certification may be covered by federal equal employment opportunity law. Other selection decisions, such as selection for training or transfer, may also be considered employment decisions if they lead to any of the decisions listed above." Federal agencies examine these criteria closely to determine whether the policies and practices of the institution promote fair employment or if they have an adverse impact on individuals or members of protected groups. When the criteria are job-related, fair, and used consistently throughout the employment process, then institutional practices generally are considered valid.

Employment status relates to each employee's standing in terms of continuation or termination of employment. Continuation of employment may be conditional, requiring the satisfaction of certain requirements to become unconditional and for the employee to be in good standing with the district. Employment status is determined primarily by the district through performance evaluation, although factors such as economic cutbacks, loss of student enrollment, or an individual's failure to meet mandated training requirements can also affect the employment situation.

Probationary Employment

Probationary employment implies that the individual is employed for a designated period of time and must meet specified conditions to be reemployed. Most state statutes that provide for probationary periods and probationary contracts do so in recognition that a trial period is needed during which new employees of an institution can be closely observed and not rehired if they do not meet standards set by the institution. Probationary periods tend to be one to three years, three years being most common. The significant aspect of probationary status is that, unless otherwise provided for by specific statute, it exempts the teacher from the provisions of due process that are automatically accorded to a teacher in another employment status. As a general rule, unless the district violates a constitutional liberty right of the probationary employee, it is not required to give cause or to provide a hearing when releasing the employee (*Central Education Agency* v. *George West School District* 1988; *Meyer* v. *Board of Education* 1981). The probationary period demands careful attention and should be implemented within statutory guidelines. Probationary status provides school officials with a unique opportunity to observe and scrutinize the employee's performance carefully without the constraints of due process. It is during this probationary period that tough decisions about continued employment should be made. A review of the complexity of terminating a teacher with due process rights should be sufficient reminder of the importance of the probationary period.

Employment for a Specified Period

Under the provisions of what are generally called *term contracts*, teachers and administrators are employed for specified periods of time—one year, two years, or more. During the term of the contract, the employee develops a property interest in continued employment. As described in the section on due process, the Fourteenth Amendment guarantees that the state shall not "deprive any person of life, liberty, or property, without due process of law." The individual whose contract has not expired is entitled to full due process, including notice and a hearing, when an adverse action related to employment status is considered. If the individual's contract has expired and he or she is not rehired due to circumstances involving violation of a constitutional right or for reasons that threaten the individual's future employment, again, the individual is also entitled to due process. Term contract employees, unlike tenured teachers, are not guaranteed due process in all cases. State statutory requirements that direct the process of nonrenewal of employment for teachers who are not tenured or are on probation must be thoroughly and carefully addressed (*Niedbalski* v. *Platte Center Board of Education* 1988; *Nordlund* v. *School District No. 14* 1987).

Tenure

A special employment status created by statute in at least forty states is tenure. Tenure was originally created as a form of protection for teachers against the political whims of unethical school boards. Intended to provide security of employment for competent teachers, tenure has frequently been characterized as the protector of incompetent teachers. This characterization has developed out of the stringent due process procedures required to dismiss tenured teachers. "It's more trouble than it's worth to try to dismiss a tenured teacher" expresses the sentiments of many administrators. In most cases, the acquisition of tenure is preceded by a probationary period during which the district has the option to terminate or continue employment. Once granted, tenure becomes a property right, and the tenured teacher's rights are protected by the property rights provision of the Fourteenth Amendment and state law. The dismissal of a tenured teacher must be for good cause as defined by the state tenure law and local board policy. States with continuing contract laws have a form of quasi-tenure that provides for certain guaranteed procedures related to dismissal. The frustrations growing out of attempts to dismiss tenured personnel reinforce the view that the time for close observation and decision making is during the probationary period.

Grounds for Termination and Dismissal

The process of ending the employment relationship under any condition is confused by the use of a number of terms—dismissal, discharge, termination, nonrenewal—interchangeably, the meanings of which are often confusing to both administrator and teacher. Discharge and termination are the broadest of the terms, referring primarily to the general separation process. Nonrenewal is the term most frequently associated with the board's decision not to rehire a probationary employee, although under some state statutes this term also applies to the decision not to rehire a term contract employee. Dismissal is the term generally associated with ending the employment relationship during the course of the contract period or the termination of a tenured teacher. Correct use of the terminology and understanding the process required under state law is of critical importance, especially when dealing with teachers who are not tenured and not probationary.

As described in the section on employment conditions, the state has a need to ensure that students are in a safe educational environment that provides protection from those not suited to teaching and influencing students. When it is evident that an educator cannot meet the test of fitness for duty, then it is the responsibility of the district to remove that individual from the schools. As Valente (1987) explains, the concept of fitness has a double focus:

the first looking to capability to teach or administer and the second looking to personal conduct and character, in or out of school, that may harm the school, its students, and personnel. State statutes implement these goals by specifying broad grounds for discharge, such as incompetency, incapacity, insubordination, unprofessional conduct, immorality, intemperance, sufficient cause, *and so on. These grounds often overlap in coverage, so that the same conduct may be subject to multiple charges, or may be prosecuted under different labels in different states. (209)*

Incompetency

One of the major problems associated with attempting to discharge a teacher on the grounds of incompetency is that he or she has been certified by the state as competent to teach. In judicial decisions related to incompetency, the courts have maintained a broad definition of incompetency and have reached decisions on a case-by-case basis. Challenges to the courts to provide a more precise definition before an employee is dismissed for incompetency have caused the courts to respond that it is not necessary (*Benke* v. *Neenan* 1983). Chester Nolte is credited with describing the incompetent teacher as one the courts find to be performing at a subacceptable level after having been warned, helped, counseled, cajoled, threatened, and/or urged to resign (Neill and Custis 1978, 11). When considering cases involving incompetency, the courts have tended to look for a pattern of behavior on the part of the employee and documented effort by the district to assist in remediating the behavior (*Saunders* v. *Anderson* 1987; *Stamper* v. *Board of Education* 1986; *School Committee* v. *Needham Education Association* 1986; *Hamburg* v. *North Penn School District* 1984; *Parmeter* v. *Feinbert* 1984).

Insubordination

Dismissing a teacher for insubordination—willful disregard for school policies and/or administrative directives—is a frequently cited cause for discharge. It is often perceived as easier to prove than incompetency. The reasonableness and job-relatedness of the policy or rule violated is used as a factor by the courts in deciding insubordination cases; for example, the district may not cause the individual to participate in illegal or unethical conduct. As with incompetency, the courts tend to look for a pattern of behavior, as opposed to a single incident (*Ware* v. *Morgan County School District* 1988; *Simmons* v. *Vancouver School District No. 37* 1985; *Russell* v. *Special School District No. 6* 1985).

Immorality

As models for students, teachers are expected to conduct themselves in a moral and ethical manner. The emphasis in court decisions is on teachers' conduct around and with students, as opposed to in the privacy of their homes. What is moral and ethical is open to debate, and the proof of immorality rests with the test of how the conduct impacts or affects the ability of the teacher to carry out assigned responsibilities. Sexual misconduct is a general reason for seeking dismissal based on immorality. When students are involved, directly or indirectly, the courts tend to uphold dismissals on these grounds (*Schmidt* v. *Board of Education* 1986; *Keating* v. *Riverside Board of Directors* 1986; *Lile* v. *Hancock Place School District* 1985; *Shipley* v. *Salem School District 24J* 1983). The failure of the teacher to supervise students or sponsors involved in sexual misconduct adequately has also been upheld as grounds for dismissal (*Ross* v. *Robb* 1983). Cases that fail to show the impact of the teacher's conduct on his or her effectiveness in the classroom are generally not sustained by the courts.

Other Good Cause

Criminal conviction, use of alcohol and drugs, unprofessional conduct, lying to the school board, unwed motherhood, and classroom language are included in what is described as good cause for discharge. "Good cause" is the catchall reason for termination when the specific reason is not included in the list of termination reasons set by statute or policy. Unprofessional conduct may include questionable business dealings or inappropriate actions in the community or school (*Weaver* v. *Board of Education* 1987; *Gleason* v. *Board of Education* 1986; *McBroom* v. *Board of Education* 1986). When questioned about specific activities, the employee who lies to the board may be terminated for failure to tell the truth (*Board of Education* v. *McCollum* 1987; *Welch* v. *Board of Education* 1983). Personal sexual preferences and relationships outside traditional marriage are extremely complex and difficult issues to use in termination procedures, and cases based on these reasons are frequently overturned by the courts (*National Gay Task Force* v. *Board of Education* 1984; *Avery* v. *Homewood City Board of Education* 1982). The use of inappropriate language in the classroom and around students is examined by the courts in terms of the context and impact (*Fiscus* v. *Board of School Trustees* 1987; *Pryse* v. *Yakima School District* 1981). Excessive absenteeism and tardiness can be grounds for termination when a pattern or direct insubordination is shown (*Philadelphia School District* v. *Friedman* 1986; *Willis* v. *School District of Kansas City* 1980). Cases upheld under "good cause" are upheld because of substantial documentation of both the conduct and the impact of the conduct on students and the school, as well as an indication that the behavior was not accidental or incidental.

Voluntary Departure

Employment status may be altered by the employee through voluntary departure, resignation, or retirement. The legal implications in this area revolve around the "voluntary" nature of resignations and retirements. A resignation or retirement must be of the employee's free will and not be the result of coercion or illegal promises (*Findeisen* v. *North East Independent School District* 1984; *Bellefonte Area School District* v. *Lipner* 1984). When employees change their employment status by resignation or retirement, the school board is not bound to reconsider the action once submitted. The role assigned to the superintendent for acceptance or rejection of resignations is a key factor when employees attempt to withdraw resignations. In *Braught* v. *Board of Education* (1985) and *Warren* v. *Buncombe County Board of Education* (1986), the courts held that the superintendent is a legitimate agent of the board and can accept resignations, and the action becomes binding when the resignation is accepted. When an employee attempts to resign only certain duties and retain other duties, the nature of the employment contract demands careful consideration. For coaching duties that are performed under a supplemental contract, the courts have held that the teacher can terminate the coaching duties and retain the teaching contract (*Swager* v. *Board of Education* 1984). When the contract is a dual teaching/coaching contract, the issue is more complex; many district policies state that the termination of one duty is termination of the entire contract.

Voluntary departures create the need for replacement of personnel; this is referred to as employee turnover. While a certain amount of turnover is expected in any organization, a high turnover rate is generally of concern to school officials, due to the difficulty of replacing competent teachers and administrators. Although not every voluntary departure is undesirable, each departure may increase the costs of selection and training, decrease productivity, and disrupt relationships (Watts and White 1988, 80). The administrator is frequently presented with the challenge of assessing the cause of turnover and setting objectives to reduce it. Watts and White continue: "Often the assumption is that any turnover is undesirable and should therefore be reduced. While the intent in reducing turnover is to retain superior employees, the more common result is the retention of marginal employees. On the other hand, turnover may actually benefit the organization and the individual employees" (81). Turnover, then, may be viewed from two perspectives. One perspective relates to the loss of competent personnel. Turnover requires close examination when it is suspected that it results from arbitrary actions on the part of administrators or poor working conditions. Unfair labor practices can result in legal action against the district (*Equi* v. *Board of Education of School District of Philadelphia* 1987). The use of exit interviews and close review of termination paperwork can provide clues to inappropriate administrative actions or work situations. The other perspective relates to the opportunity to improve the instructional program through the infusion of new personnel into the system.

Employment Rights and Responsibilities

Of course, educators enjoy the rights and privileges of citizenship, but because of teachers' ability to influence their students the courts have been inclined to scrutinize and examine their behavior carefully. A recurring theme in judicial decisions related to teacher behavior is that teacher rights must be balanced carefully against student rights and the rights of tax-payers in the community. A second theme is that teachers may not exert their rights to the point of disrupting the operation of the school.

Constitutional Rights

The First, Fourth, Fifth, and Fourteenth Amendments to the Constitution all provide protections for teachers. Teachers have a right under the First Amendment to criticize their school boards (*Wichert* v. *Walter* 1985), to speak out on public issues (*Piver* v. *Pender County Board of Education* 1987), and to form and join associations. Teachers may not proselytize students (*Breen* v. *Runkel* 1985), use school property for religious activities (*May* v. *Evansville Vanderburgh School Corp.* 1986), or dress in religious dress at school (*Cooper* v. *Eugene School District No 4J* 1986). The courts have generally upheld reasonable district regulations regarding the dress and appearance of teachers, based on a test of whether there is disruption of school opera-tion caused by what the district considers inappropriate. The burden is on the district to prove how dress, appearance, and grooming disrupt school operations. The question of academic freedom is generally associated with higher education, but it has received some attention at the elementary and secondary levels. The state's right to dictate the curriculum is an important factor, considered along with the teacher's right to use controversial mate-rial and to inject personal opinion into discussions (*Fisher* v. *Fairbanks North Star Borough School* 1985; *Nicholson* v. *Board of Education* 1982; *Palmer* v. *Board of Education of City of Chicago* 1979).

Collective Bargaining

Prior to the 1960s, decisions related to the terms and conditions of employ-ment in school districts were made by school boards acting primarily on the recommendations of administrators. Teacher groups were often invited to meet informally with administrators and boards to discuss salaries and other matters related to employment. In the best situations, these discus-sions were collaborative and collegial in nature, with the administration, particularly the superintendent or personnel administrator, acting as the spokesperson for teachers. In the worst situations, teachers and staff mem-bers were ignored and totally excluded from the discussions related to employment terms and conditions. With the help of external agents, teach-ers began to view administrators as being only on the side of the board and as representatives of only the management point of view. Teachers were labor and administrators were management. Teacher demands for the right to participate in the process resulted in the formalization of the process through collective negotiation or bargaining.

From 1959 to 1983, thirty-four states passed collective bargaining laws, with eighteen of the states authorizing the collection of forced dues from nonunion members (Staub, 1989). Twenty states attempted to restrict collective bargaining by passing right-to-work laws. The right to strike has been granted or prohibited on a state-by-state basis. Where state law permits or mandates collective bargaining, the courts have clarified and upheld the rights of teachers to engage in the process. When a union becomes the exclusive bargaining agent for its members, it has a legal responsibility to represent its members fairly (*Schneider* v. *Ambach* 1988; *Baker* v. *Board of Education* 1987). Where the law does not prohibit or mandate collective bargaining, the judicial interpretations indicate that the courts are divided in their opinions on the topic.

Right to Strike

As an ultimate weapon for attaining desired working conditions, teacher organizations use an organized work stoppage strategy for withdrawal of services—the strike. Teacher strikes are illegal in the majority of states, with at least twenty states having specific statutory prohibitions against strikes (*Labor Relations Commission* v. *Chelsea Teachers Union* 1987). The interpretation of the courts has generally been that public employees do not have the right to strike, and school districts have been able to convince the courts to intervene and halt strikes through injunction. Teachers who strike illegally may be discharged (*Ash* v. *Board of Education* 1983; *Board of Education* v. *Ambach* 1983; *Barni* v. *Board of Education* 1978). Whether teachers may picket is tested by examination of the purpose and consequence of the action. Where strikes are illegal, many public sector employees, including teachers, have turned to picketing as a means of attracting attention to their cause. In *Collective Bargaining: How It Works and Why* (1986), Colosi and Berkeley explain that picketing has a dual nature:

> *Nowhere is this dichotomy between striking and picketing, between purposeful economic activity and communication, more clear than in the public sector, where strikes are generally unlawful. Many public sector unions have sought to utilize the picket line to influence public opinion, especially concerning political figures. Thus, before or after the school day, public school teachers will, for example, picket the school superintendent's office or the men's haberdashery store owned by the chairman of the school board. Such picketing is usually upheld as an exercise of free speech and is legal unless it runs afoul of laws governing boycotts. (39)*

Assignment, Transfer, and Demotion

As long as a school board acts legally under the provisions of applicable state law and its own policies, it has the right to assign teachers in the best interest of the district and the students of the district. Teachers and staff members do not have a vested interest in a single assignment or in assignment in a single location unless that interest has been granted by statute, policy, or the terms of the contract. In the absence of regulations providing otherwise, teachers are not entitled to a hearing when being transferred or reassigned involuntarily. Teachers who refuse to accept assignments may be dismissed for abandonment of the contract or for insubordination (*Franklin* v. *Alabama State Tenure Commission* 1985; *McLaughlin* v. *Board of Education* 1983).

The concept of demotion is often viewed as one of perspective. Generally, if a teacher or employee is reassigned and there is not a loss of salary or rank, then it is not considered a demotion. However, in the eyes of the employee, the assignment change may be viewed as a demotion because of perceived loss of prestige or standing (*Ellis-Adams* v. *Whitfield County Board of Education* 1987). It is not unusual for a person facing reassignment to claim that the reassignment is a demotion. Sorting out what is reassignment and what is demotion is not a simple task. As a general rule, the individual facing a demotion is entitled to notice and a hearing. However, the provisions of state law and local policy govern the procedures to be followed (*Snipes* v. *McAndrew* 1984; *Mroczek* v. *Board of Education of Beachwood City School District* 1979).

Individuals reassigned due to failure to perform satisfactorily in the previous assignment have not generally found a sympathetic ear in the courts. Similarly, the courts have recognized the need for institutions to conduct education in an efficient manner with regard to economic necessity related to personnel and salary costs. Reassignments or demotions resulting from reduction in force or for disciplinary reasons are upheld when the proper procedures are followed by the district (*Board of Education for Garden City* v. *Brisbois* 1987; *Laird* v. *Independent School District No. 317* 1984). The impact of tenure and collective bargaining agreements cannot be ignored in relation to the procedural requirements of demotion.

Grievances

Recognizing that employees may from time to time believe that they are being treated unfairly by their employer, state constitutional provisions, state statutes, and local board policies provide for procedures through which complaints may be presented. When these complaint procedures are formalized under statute or a collective bargaining agreement, the procedures are typically referred to as grievance procedures. Grievance procedures are designed to deal with wages, hours of work, and terms and conditions of employment. The procedures generally consist of a set of sequential steps designed to hear and resolve the complaint at the lowest level. A typical pattern would begin with informal discussions with the immediate supervisor and move through formalized steps to central administration and finally to the superintendent. The school board acts as the final decision maker when appropriate.

Prior to collective bargaining agreements, most complaints were settled through an informal process involving the concerned parties. With the advent of collective bargaining and the emphasis on teachers' rights, the number of grievances filed each year has increased significantly in most districts, for a variety of reasons. In some instances, the nature of grievances has changed from concerns of an individual to concerns of an organization. What was originally conceived as a simple process to assist employees in presenting concerns has evolved into a very complex procedure utilized to maintain the power of an organization. It has been estimated that this issue alone consumes a major portion of the personnel administrator's time. The *Standards for School Personnel Administration* (American Association of School Personnel Administrators 1988b) explain the difference in grievances and complaints as follows:

> *A differentiation in procedures is made between grievances and complaints. A grievance is defined as an alleged violation, misrepresentation or misapplication of any of the specific provisions of the negotiated agreement which may end in binding arbitration; while a complaint is described as an alleged violation, misrepresentation or misapplication of any rule, order, regulation or policy of the board outside the negotiated contract which should not be subject to binding arbitration. (27)*

The real clarification in the difference between grievances and complaints in a particular situation or environment is determined by applicable state law and negotiated agreements.

Personnel Records

The maintenance and retention of records related to personnel administration are responsibilities of the school administrator, governed by applicable federal and state statutes and agency regulations. These records must be available on an approved need-to-know basis as directed by statutory limitations when requested by an authorized individual or agency. Educational institutions, like all institutions, are required to make annual reports related to personnel activities to both federal and state agencies. The personnel department is generally responsible for the collection and maintenance of the statistical information used in these reports. Due to the voluminous nature of some of the information, the question of how long to retain data is a real and pressing issue. Under federal requirements, the length of time records should be retained varies from three months to three years. It is therefore generally advised that personnel records be retained for at least three years (current year, immediate past year, and preceding year) as a minimum precaution.

EXHIBIT 11.1 Typical Personnel Office Records

Type of Record	Contents	Retention
Individual Employee Personnel File	All records related to employment: application, transcripts, certificates, service verification, medical records, termination forms, disciplinary forms, and related material	Permanent
Eligibility Lists	Lists or rosters, if maintained, of eligible candidates for positions	2 years
Test Records	Applicant and employee test records, including answer sheets, interview data, ranking sheets, and similar material	2 years
Personnel Policy Files	Memoranda, reports, announcements, and similar records related to the policies, rules, and regulations	Permanent
Job Announcements	Announcements of job openings	2 years
Employment Applicants (Not Hired)	Applications for employment, preemployment reports, and application materials	2 years
Performance Appraisals	Official copies of signed personnel performance appraisals and supporting documentation	Permanent—last four appraisals in current file
Position Descriptions and Analysis File	Records documenting the development, modification or redefinition of each job or position; job descriptions for each job	3 years after position becomes obsolete
Worker's Compensation Claims Files	Accident reports; claims forms, hospital, physician, and emergency medical service bills and reports; correspondence; legal papers; other documentation relating to claims	5 years after final settlement
EEOC/Affirmative Action Case Files	Legal and investigative documents and correspondence involving grievances, complaints, or charges of discrimination brought in relation to EEOC/Affirmative Action programs	Permanent—copy of formal judgment Case papers—5 years after final disposition
Disciplinary Files	Files related to the dismissal, suspension, progressive discipline steps taken, and other action against employees	5 years after termination
Collective Bargaining Agreements	The contracts and agreements and supporting documentation	Permanent

Exhibit 11.1 lists typical records that are to be maintained in municipal or government personnel offices. School districts, as subdivisions of state government, have a responsibility for maintaining similar records. It is important to note that the maintenance of school district personnel records should conform to applicable state and federal law. The list of records in

Exhibit 11.1 is not exhaustive; it merely illustrates the volume of records to be maintained on both an immediate and long-term basis. Other files to be kept would include travel requests, personnel action notices, training records, leave records, attendance reports, salary schedules and records, accident reports, award records, and retirement records.

Within the context of all records management, the question of what is public and what is personal information looms as an important issue. Public information acts usually apply to the access to and release of various records, including some personnel records. For example, it is common for state open-records acts to exempt certain personnel information if its disclosure would constitute an unwarranted invasion of personal privacy. On the other hand, the name, sex, ethnicity, salary, title, and date of employment of all employees and officers of school districts are generally considered public information. Open-records acts usually specify the manner in which a request can be made to the school district and the procedures by which the district may release information. The confidentiality of the contents of employee files has been questioned in recent years. In addressing this question, the courts have given varying opinions. In a recent decision, the court found that certain information (e.g., transcripts) may not be withheld from public disclosure (*Klein Independent School District* v. *Mattox* 1987). In other decisions, in the absence of specific statutory provision to the contrary, it was held that all employee file information may be considered public information (*Hovet* v. *Hebron Public School District* 1988; *Mills* v. *Doyle* 1981).

Due to the open-records acts and a trend in judicial decisions to make public employee information public, the key to personnel record keeping is, as it always has been, objectivity. All personnel records should be free of unwarranted subjective opinion and personal bias. Careless words are difficult to defend once they have become part of a legal record or a court proceeding (*Goralski* v. *Pizzimenti* 1988; *Vinson* v. *Linn-Mar Community Unit School District* 1984).

Summary

Nothing in personnel administration is exempt from some form of legal scrutiny. The key to effective personnel administration is the development of a working attitude that permits the administrator to deal with both legal and human needs simultaneously. The legal considerations do not serve as an excuse for not meeting human needs and human needs do not provide a defense for disobeying the law.

The fundamental question regarding education in a pluralistic, democratic society is how best to serve the instructional needs of a diverse population in an ever-changing social and economic environment. The fundamental challenge for the administrator working with personnel functions is how to provide staffing that will ensure fair representation of all groups within the society, to maintain high expectations for employee competence and performance, and not to violate the rights of individual employees simultaneously. In meeting this challenge, the administrator has the opportunity to model standards of fairness and equity that are emulated throughout the organization and to provide leadership for other professionals dealing with instructional and human issues. Careful attention to the legal environment of personnel administration contributes to the development of a quality program by permitting the system to move forward, concentrating its resources on instructional improvement rather than litigation.

Suggested Study Sources

Colosi, Thomas R., and Arthur Eliot Berkeley. 1986. *Collective Bargaining: How It Works and Why*. New York: American Arbitration Association.

This book examines how collective bargaining actually works. The authors serve as arbitrators and trainers of arbitrators and are considered "neutrals" in the collective bargaining process.

Data Research, Inc. 1989. *1989 Deskbook Encyclopedia of American School Law*. Rosemount, MN: Data Research, Inc.

This encyclopedic compilation of state and federal appellate court decisions affecting education, updated annually, is a valuable resource for the practitioner and student of school law. Chapters are devoted to employment practices; employment discrimination; termination, resignation, and retirement; employee notice and hearings; employee reassignments, suspensions and demotions; and professional associations and collective bargaining agreements.

U.S. Equal Employment Opportunity Commission. 1979. *Job Discrimination: Laws and Rules You Should Know*. Washington, DC: U.S. Government Printing Office.

This document contains the text of Title VII of the Civil Rights Act of 1964 as amended and the rules and regulations pertaining to the administration of this law. In addition to pertinent sections of several acts, executive orders and regulations governing employment discrimination and unfair employment practices are included. The publication is intended for use by the public and the EEOC personnel.

Valente, William D. 1987. *Law in the Schools*. 2d ed. Columbus, OH: Merrill.

This comprehensive volume on school law addresses a broad spectrum of legal issues— student rights and privileges, employee rights and privileges, and the legal foundation for schools. The section on employee rights covers a broad range of topics related to those discussed in this chapter.

12

The Economic Environment and Personnel Administration

The administration of personnel functions occurs not in a vacuum, but within the context of philosophical, economic, social, legal, union, and organizational environments that, collectively and individually, influence the overall performance of the educational institution. This chapter examines personnel issues specifically related to the economic environment (school financing, state staffing plans, and compensation) and the union environment (the balance of power). The philosophical, social, legal, and organizational environments considered in other chapters are recognized as important influences on the issues discussed here.

In personnel administration, the keys to successful leadership are planning, decision making, and communication. These processes impact virtually every aspect of personnel responsibility, from staffing and salary administration to staff development and appraisal. The outcomes of careful planning, decision making, and communication, or the consequences of ineffective planning, decision making, and communication, affect the success of the administrator and the effectiveness of the school program. Nowhere is this more evident than in the area of resource planning and decision making. On an annual basis, school administrators, along with other advisors, participate in the process of preparing and recommending to the district's governing board the district's budgetary requirements for the next school year. Burrup et al. (1988) state: "Since the function of the school is to provide those who attend with human services in the form of high-quality academic instruction, the biggest cost of public education is salaries to instructional personnel. Thus, the problems of school finance are directly related to the problems encountered in personnel administration" (436).

As an enterprise, education may be classified as an institution with an exceedingly high demand in the area of human capital. Schools and educational institutions are recognized, by virtue of their nature and structure, as high labor-cost organizations. The producers of educational services, particularly instructional services, are viewed in terms of the economic environment as a quality labor force. This designation of quality is determined by required levels of formal education, on-the-job training, and experience for instructional and professional personnel. As employees providing services, workers in education expect to be paid and to receive reasonable employment benefits. When compensation levels have not met their expectations, educators have not been reluctant to use organized bargaining tactics to achieve their goals. Costs for employee compensation represent the largest expenditure of funds for school districts, with seventy-five to eighty-five percent of the annual operating budget dedicated to these costs. The impact of personnel expenditures in terms of payroll costs is reflected in the example of a school district budget shown in Exhibit 12.1 on page 252, where the payroll costs are approximately eighty-two percent of the total budget. It is, therefore, inevitable and necessary that the relationship between financial resources and personnel administration be considered.

Reforming Education and School Finance

The area of school financing has generated national attention and discussion in recent years. As the questions of how to improve American education have been debated, the fundamental issue related to financing the costs of a quality education system remain largely unanswered. Despite the desire expressed by President George Bush to be remembered as the first "education President," the financing of public education remains the joint responsibility of state government and local school districts. With the federal government providing less than ten percent of the funding for American education, school improvement is viewed as a national concern; school financing is viewed as a state and local problem. Walker (1987) states:

> The public schools are a major institution in society for the development and maintenance of public virtue and republican democracy. As such, the institution of public education is frequently the center of philosophical struggles arising from political, social, and economic values and beliefs. One of the

EXHIBIT 12.1 Annual School District Budget: General Fund Budget Expenditures

Function	Payroll Costs	Purchased Services	Supplies Materials	Other Expenses*	Debt Service	Capital Outlay	Total
Instruction	32,214,979	184,775	799,764	153,771	0	120,017	33,473,306
Instructional computing	774,414	28,500	16,844	200	0	31,242	851,200
Instructional administration	1,272,382	112,671	84,002	59,503	0	329,060	1,857,618
Media services	1,279,606	29,517	59,626	850	0	171,175	1,540,774
School administration	3,606,073	93,070	98,018	31,300	0	21,228	3,849,689
Instructional research and development	2,532	60	18,700	0	0	0	21,292
Curriculum and personnel development	219,576	15,000	4,750	65,558	0	3,050	298,934
Communications	307	25,900	0	0	0	0	26,207
Guidance and counseling	2,559,372	78,635	89,427	2,000	0	575	2,730,009
Attendance and social work	224,379	35,476	946	4,500	0	0	265,301
Health services	453,742	3,145	18,305	2,882	0	0	478,074
Transportation—regular	777,669	18,525	148,000	50,706	0	197,000	1,191,900
Transportation—exceptional	326,702	12,000	30,000	6,050	0	5,200	379,952
Cocurricular activities	495,775	106,440	204,450	144,564	14,592	12,000	977,821
Food service	1,633,174	74,800	1,527,600	7,600	0	21,500	3,264,674
General administration	2,000,963	1,012,145	155,100	353,134	0	46,850	3,568,192
Plant maintenance	4,146,128	2,854,911	746,100	74,250	0	183,550	3,004,939
Facilities acquisition and construction	0	200,000	0	0	0	0	200,000
TOTAL	51,978,773	4,885,570	4,001,632	956,868	14,592	1,142,447	62,979,882

*Operating expenses

common areas of concern is the funding of public education. Public school finance issues represent a microcosm in which we can view the larger principles of American society at work. (1)

According to Burrup et al. (1988), "Education has been and continues to be primarily a function of state government. This responsibility is . . . documented by state constitutional provisions acknowledging and accepting this power, plus numerous court decisions supporting it" (158). School districts, as creatures of the state legislatures, are frequently affected by the political, social, and economic struggles of their creators. Under changing economic and demographic conditions, the trend has been for state legislatures, by means of their statutory mandates, to assert their control over school districts through what has been described as "micromanagement." Broad policy statements and flexibility have been replaced, in instance after instance, with narrow and prescriptive mandates: "There is a trend toward greater state responsibility for financing public education in all states, resulting in greater state controls and an erosion of the power and authority of local school boards" (182). The tendency toward more state control and micromanagement is particularly evident in personnel issues related to class size, compensation, and employee performance evaluation.

Reforming the school finance system, a never-ending quest for achieving equity and adequacy, has been going on since the early years of the twentieth century (Augenblick 1985, 5). The great American experiment in education calls for universal, relatively free schooling, with each student having the opportunity for a quality education financed by means of an equitable taxation program that does not adversely affect any single group of taxpayers. During recent years, the costs of providing a quality educational program have risen dramatically, due in part to increasing general enrollments, reduced class size, increasing numbers of students with special learning needs, social problems, and personnel salary costs. The economic picture during this same time period for the most of the nation as a whole, many individual states, and most local communities has been characterized as depressed. In frustration, taxpayers have voiced greater and greater concern over the need for annual increases in school taxes. By public referendum and legislative action, limits have been placed on the taxing authority of local school boards. Thus, the educational goal of a quality education with minimal imposition on the taxpayer has been a topic of considerable debate and a generator of controversy. Referring to the 1980s as a time of ferment, the Task Force on Teaching as a Profession (1986) stated that these years "will be remembered for two developments: the beginning of a sweeping reassessment of the basis of the nation's economic strength and an outpouring of concern for the quality of American education. The connection between these two streams of thought is strong and growing" (11).

The declared primary objective of the school finance reform movement has been to equalize the resources available for schooling in each of the school districts in a state. A more subtle but equally strong objective has been taxpayer equity. The inherent conflicts resulting from demands for equity in educational funding and declining financial resources have been addressed through legal action (*Serrano* v. *Priest* 1971; *San Antonio Independent School District* v. *Rodriquez* 1973; *Edgewood* v. *Kirby* 1989), legislative action, and considerable rhetoric. Educational funding in the 1960s and 1970s was impacted by a series of judicial decisions declaring the reviewed state school funding plans unconstitutional in the worst cases and highly questionable in other cases. Following the court decisions of these decades, educational funding remained a topic of major consideration during the 1980s, as a series of national reports called for general educational reform, including school finance reform. Following the publication of *A Nation at Risk* (1983), 17 states developed major pieces of reform legislation within a three-year period and more than 150 educational reform studies were undertaken (Burrup et al. 1988, 309). To date, solutions to the dilemmas of educational reform and funding have been attempted through a variety of judicial, legislative, and combined judicial-legislative actions without apparent success.

Due to their tremendous drain on the financial resources of an educational institution, personnel staffing and compensation issues have received considerable attention in the myriad of reports addressing education reform. Beginning in the early 1980s, critics of schooling and commentators on the education scene have questioned every aspect of the staffing process—who teaches, where they teach, and what they teach. It is interesting that the blame for the poor use of staff has been placed on both school administrators and teacher unions. Reformers have suggested that the entire system of education should be overhauled by redesigning teacher education, realigning pay scales, restructuring career models, and reviewing tenure guarantees (Johnson and Nelson 1987, 591). To those who have suggested that more funding was needed to improve education, critics have responded in a manner similar to Bennett (1988), who stated that "in truth, we are spending enough on education to do the job well. The trouble is not our level of investment; rather, it is the low rate of return we get for it" (45). The challenge of attracting and retaining competent personnel to meet the needs of an increasingly diverse and difficult-to-educate student population has cast personnel administration into the limelight.

State Plans for Financing and Allocating Personnel

Rebore (1982) states: "If a school district is to achieve its objectives, it needs financial resources, physical resources, and people. Too often the people are taken for granted, and yet they are the force that directly effects the main objective of a school district—to educate children. Manpower planning thus translates the organization's objectives into human resource terms" (26). For many districts, this planning is influenced heavily by direction from the state, because in the face of taxpayer revolts, judicial intervention, and legislative mandates, the burden of financing education has shifted onto the states.

State Staffing Alternatives

The state constitution and statutes provide the basis for funding education in each state. Typically, funding is a shared responsibility between the state and the local district. The state makes certain decisions about the cost of educating students in the state and then prorates state funding, using complex funding formulas that include factors such as district wealth and types of student population. State allotments for professional personnel are often one of many factors used in these funding formulas. Although there are many variations in education staffing patterns among the states, there are basically five alternative approaches. The degree of flexibility permitted at the local level varies among these alternatives. Exhibit 12.2 compares the five alternatives in terms of the factors used in staff allocation formulas and the flexibility provided by each formula.

Alternative 1
A commonly employed approach to determining a school district's staff allocation involves the application of ratios that relate each specific type of employee (teacher, counselor, administrator, and so on) to a variable, such as the number of pupils in average daily attendance or classroom teacher units. For example, state law may specify that each school district of a certain enrollment be allotted one teacher for every twenty-five students in average daily attendance; statutes might further require that one counselor be assigned for every forty classroom teacher units provided to the district.

Of the staffing alternatives presented, this option affords the least flexibility to local school districts. Through the application of uniform staff-student ratios for each employee category, the exact number and type of staff to be funded through the state's basic education program is predetermined for a district. The school district has no opportunity (assuming no local enrichment) to select the mix of staff that best meets the unique needs of its student population.

Alternative 2
Another method of allocating staff to school districts involves, in its simplest form, the application of ratios relating a general category of staff (direct instructional personnel, professional support personnel, and the like) to a variable such as number of pupils in average daily attendance.

EXHIBIT 12.2   Flexibility of Factors Used in State Plans for Allocating Personnel

Alternative	Staff Allocation Factors	Flexibility
1: Specific employee type system	Ratio of specific employee type to ADA or teacher units—e.g., 1 teacher per 25 students	Minimal flexibility without local enrichment; district has no option for mixing staff according to local needs due to use of specific personnel types
2: Personnel category system	Ratio of general category of staff to variable like ADA—e.g., 10 professional support personnel per 1,000 students	Increased flexibility over alternative 1 due to the use of a range of personnel categories instead of single personnel type
3: Weighted personnel unit system (WPU)	Each specific type of employee assigned a weight —e.g., teacher is 1 WPU	More flexible than alternative 1 and 2 since district can select and mix staff types based on local needs
4: Weighted pupil system	Funds to use in purchase of employee services are allocated on the basis of weights assigned to pupils based on type of service required by student	Flexibility limited only by statutory requirements related to factors such as class size and minimum teacher salary
5: Adjusted instruction unit system	Employees are allocated on basis of number of students in basic instructional unit and weights assigned to pupils based on type of service required by students	Flexibility limited only by statutory requirements related to factors of staffing formula and salary requirements

ADA=average daily attendance

Unlike the first option, this alternative associates a staffing ratio with a range of personnel categories instead of a single employee type. For example, a plan of this nature could specify that ten professional support personnel be allocated to a school district for each one thousand pupils in average daily attendance. These professional support personnel could be a mix of counselors, diagnosticians, or librarians. This approach to staff allocation offers more flexibility to local districts, but it still limits local options.

Alternative 3
A third method for allocating staff to school districts is to apply a ratio that relates weighted personnel units (WPUs) to a variable such as a district's average daily attendance (ADA). In this scheme each specific type of employee is assigned a weight and the complement of weighted personnel permitted each school district is limited (generally, the number is based on

ADA). For example, assume that state law allocates a total of fifty weighted personnel per one thousand ADA and establishes the teacher weight as one WPU and the superintendent weight as three WPUs. The district of one thousand ADA can expend its limit of fifty WPUs in any staffing pattern based on the WPU cost of each personnel unit. This staffing alternative is the most flexible of the first three alternatives. However, any weighted structure contains an implicit assumption concerning the makeup of an *appropriate* staff. This limits the mix of personnel that can be feasibly employed in a district and, as a result, tends to impede local discretion in the selection of types and number of school personnel.

Alternative 4

During recent years, many leaders in education and government have advocated the allocation of total state program funds on a basis of pupil units weighted according to the type of educational service preferred by the educational unit. This approach is most flexible, even though it is often limited by certain general restrictions, such as a provision that a certain minimum percentage of funds be devoted to teacher salaries. Frequently referred to as the weighted pupil method, this plan is based on the assumption that populations of students with special needs require differentiated educational services. Researchers have shown that the provision of these differentiated services involves lower teacher-pupil ratios and higher operating costs, as compared to regular educational services. Costs for these differentiated services are generally computed against a base or weight of one, which is the weight assigned a regular education services student. Special needs populations include special education students, vocational students, bilingual students and those who speak limited English, migrant students, and socioeconomically disadvantaged students. The district generates state funding based on the number of students assigned to each educational program. For example, if a kindergarten student is assigned a weight of 1.30 and there are 700 kindergarten students in average daily attendance in the district and the basic unit value in dollars is 1,000, then the kindergarten population generates 910,000 dollars in revenue for the district (1.30 × 700 × 1,000). Each state using this plan must determine its own cost differentials so that the assigned weights meet the needs of students in that state.

Alternative 5

The last method presented as an alternative for determining state support is commonly known as the adjusted instruction unit technique. The regular elementary program frequently serves as the basic unit in this plan. The elementary program is assigned a pupils-per-instructional-unit (25 students per class in elementary grades one through four). Teaching staff is allocated on the basis of the mandated class size ratio (125 students in grade three would require 6 teachers). Other instructional units are assigned pupils-per-instructional-unit sizes based on differentiated instructional needs. For example, a physically handicapped class might have a 7.69 pupils-per-instructional-unit limitation.

Restraints

The restraints imposed on local districts by states are evident in areas other than numbers of personnel and instructional units. Collective bargaining alone, when mandated by state law, acts as a considerable restraint on school districts' staffing practices. The union becomes another party to be considered in all decision making related to staffing. Other restraints include state salary schedules and mandatory state retirement systems. Work load limitations set at the state level restrain local utilization of personnel. A new statute guaranteeing a duty-free lunch period of thirty or forty-five minutes for each teacher gives local administrators new personnel problems to address. Another example is a legislated requirement for a planning period during the instructional day. Coupled with limitations against lengthening the school day, this restraint could make it necessary for a district to provide approximately one-sixth more personnel resources. Without arguing the merits of the instructional effectiveness of such requirements, one can readily recognize the implications for personnel utilization and finances.

New Program Influences

When the state instigates a new program or major changes in existing programs, the consequences for school district can be significant. In the late 1950s and early 1960s, following the Sputnik scare, the national government and state governments intervened in traditional education programs and placed great emphasis on mathematics and science. More recently, special education, bilingual education, and compensatory education have been given high priorities at both the national and state levels. Such major efforts to expand educational services rapidly to target populations necessitate a large number of additional personnel who are specially trained to staff the new programs. The local district is affected not only by new program requirements but also by the state's personnel planning. The district in these evolving situations is dependent on the state to: (1) determine personnel needs, (2) support staff development activities for personnel currently employed, and (3) allocate human and material resources to support teacher preparation programs. New programs can be mandated at the state and even the federal levels, but most local districts cannot cope with rapid program implementation and the concomitant staffing problems without state-level planning and assistance. The impact of new state programs and legislative mandates on the financial resources of local school districts have led school boards and administrators at the local level to plead for no new mandates or programs without new funding and assistance.

Reward Systems

In 1983, in *A Nation at Risk,* the National Commission on Excellence in Education made recommendations related to the recruitment, training, and compensation of teachers: "Salaries for the teaching profession should be increased and should be professionally competitive, market-sensitive, and performance-based" (30). Related recommendations called for extended contracts and career ladders that differentiated between categories of teachers for purposes of setting salaries. In the section on leadership and fiscal support, the Commission recommended that "state and local officials, including school board members, governors, and legislators, have *the primary responsibility* for financing and governing the schools" and were encouraged to incorporate the proposed reforms through educational policy and fiscal planning (32). Since the publication of this report, it appears that many have viewed increasing teacher compensation as a cure-all for the problems in education. This view seems to be based on the assumption that a teacher's only motivation to teach comes from a concern for financial rewards and that pay alone will attract, retain, and motivate teachers (Frase and Conley 1990).

To the contrary, teachers in a 1985 survey cited "a chance to use your mind and abilities" (63%), a "chance to work with young people" (62%), and "appreciation of a job well done" (54%) as more important on the job than "a good salary" (51%). In a similar survey, employed adults chose "a good salary" (63%) and "job security" (53%) as being important on the job (Feistritzer 1988, 42). Teachers would appear to be motivated equally or perhaps more than other employed adults by intrinsic and nonfinancial rewards. However, the need for equitable salaries cannot be overlooked, since fifty-one percent of the teachers in the same survey reported being dissatisfied with their salaries.

The reward system for employees includes both extrinsic and intrinsic rewards. Cash payments and fringe benefits, referred to collectively as compensation, together comprise the extrinsic, or monetary, rewards. Intrinsic rewards are related to the satisfaction an individual finds in performing the job. The elements of compensation and the needs being addressed are outlined in Exhibit 12.3 on page 260. Overall job satisfaction is influenced by both intrinsic and extrinsic rewards and, in turn, influences how the employee performs. In terms of Abraham Maslow's hierarchy of needs, it would seem that by sufficiently satisfying an employee's basic needs (the ability to purchase adequate food and shelter), a district lays the foundation

EXHIBIT 12.3 The Total Compensation Program: Employee Needs, District Objectives, and Costs

Form of Compensation	Employee Need	District Objective	Type of Cost
Direct compensation: salary	Reward for services provided that sets standard of living	Attract, retain, and reward competent employees	Fixed cost, base for other forms of compensation
Direct compensation: merit pay, career ladder pay	Extra income and recognition for achievement of certain goals	Motivational incentive used to attract, retain, and reward personnel	Variable cost that may be open-ended or or limited, based on set factors
Direct compensation: supplemental pay	Extra pay for additional work assignments; provides extra income for employee in setting	Permits district to offer special programs or services without cost of full-time staff for positions	Variable costs based on the number and types of services or programs provided
Indirect compensation: benefit programs required by state or federal government	Protection against loss of income due to injury or dismissal	Good faith, social responsibility; good employee-employer relations; meet legal requirements	Fixed costs that are part of the general costs of being an employer
Indirect compensation: benefit programs provided by district option	Security against economic loss or risks related to death, illness, or disability; time off without income loss	Increase morale and satisfaction; attract, motivate, and maintain employees; reduce turnover	Variable costs that fluctuate according to industry costs
Indirect compensation: employee services	Programs or services that enhance the lifestyle of the employee with limited cost to the employee	Build favorable attitudes; provide assistance to employes in non-work-related area	Variable costs based on the types of services provided and relationship with provider of services

for promoting the attainment of job-related, higher-level needs (morale, satisfaction, and motivation).

Management of the compensation program is an extremely important personnel function, due to the inherent importance of compensation to the employee and the potential for using compensation as an effective management tool. The district's compensation plan must be developed within a philosophical and fiscal framework established by the school board. Through the development and administration of the compensation program, the system reflects its philosophy and intent regarding the worth of its employees. These goals communicate the school board's commitment to the recruitment, rewarding, and retention of competent employees.

The objectives for an effective compensation plan that carries out the goals established by the school board generally include the following: (1) internal and external equity, (2) salary levels based on the skill, effort, and responsibility required for each job, (3) controllable costs within the financial ability of the district, (4) employee understanding of the system, (5) adherence to all legal requirements, and (6) minimal system administration costs. To be competitive in attracting and retaining quality personnel, the system's compensation plan must provide salaries that are comparable to those offered by other organizations and benefits that are at least as attractive as those offered by others. The potential or current employee must also perceive that there is a possibility that compensation will improve over time.

Salary Administration

The largest single expenditure in education is for the payment of salaries. Typically, salary administration in school districts involves the development of annual salary schedules outlining minimum and maximum salaries for different categories of personnel. The two factors generally used to determine advancement on district salary schedules are professional development, through either additional degrees or training hours, and accrued years of experience in the teaching profession. These salary schedules have portrayed advancement as a series of steps based on year-to-year increases determined by longevity (that is, reward for experience). In utilizing these salary schedules, the local school board frequently finds the district locked into either real or perceived promises of annual salary increases. Employees often anticipate an annual increase based on the previous year's salary schedule and are extremely angry when the anticipated salary increase does not materialize. These promises or guarantees become increasingly difficult to manage as financial resources become more limited. Critics of school district salary administration practices have challenged the concept of reward for experience and pushed for reward for performance.

It is estimated that after adjustment for inflation, average teacher salaries rose twenty percent from 1981 to 1987 (Bennett 1988, 41). Unfortunately, in many districts the increases in average teacher salaries were the result of "backloading"—the largest increases were added to the top end of the salary schedules, giving the largest increases to the most experienced teachers; little attention was given to entry-level salaries, causing the gap between beginning salaries and experience-based salaries to widen (Monk and Jacobson, 1985). Without competitive entry-level salaries, school districts found it increasingly difficult to attract individuals to the profession. The challenge of retaining an aging work force within growing financial constraints posed another set of financial problems because of the increased salary and benefits costs associated with maintenance of older, highly experienced professional personnel.

During the 1980s, the pattern of salary administration began to change significantly in many local school districts. In some cases, the changes resulted from professional and public cries for improving the rewards for teachers who were performing effectively. In other cases, they resulted from financial setbacks that prohibited the continuation of across-the-board annual salary increases. The disadvantages of using salary schedules that result in automatic salary increases with little attention to entry-level salaries also became increasingly apparent as school districts faced significant workforce problems. General increases in student enrollment in the public schools and massive increases in the number of students identified as needing special services coincided with a decrease in the number of students in teacher preparation programs and a significant number of retirements from the profession. By 1985, after years of teacher surplus, jobs and job seekers were roughly in balance. Predictions of a looming teacher shortage suggested that 1.3 million new teachers would have to be hired between 1986 and 1992 (Task Force on Teaching as a Profession 1986, 31).

Kirst (1986) noted that across the nation all kinds of intervention, including career ladders, higher-based salaries, improved working conditions, and forgivable loans, were attempted in response to the expectations of both the public and the profession. By the late 1980s, more than twenty-nine states had implemented career ladder or merit pay plans for educators. Cornett (1987) noted that most of the attempts to alter teacher compensation linked compensation to different career roles for teachers.

In response to these challenges, many school districts turned for assistance to external experts in the field of compensation. Guided by principles from the field of compensation, school districts have begun to focus on developing new compensation and employee pay systems. Salary administration in educational institutions, particularly public school districts, is evolving from a *salary schedule* system, in which each employee is treated as an exact duplicate of other employees with similar credentials and experience, to locally determined *pay structure* systems, in which pay is differentiated on the basis of skill, effort, responsibility, and performance. Salary administration is becoming a critical administrative function involving the matching of identified needs and careful stewardship of financial resources.

Differentiation of Salary and Job Classification

A topic of considerable interest to both teachers and administrators involves the determination of appropriate differences in levels of pay. Often, an individual—a teacher or administrator—perceives that his or her role is undercompensated and that those in other roles are overcompensated. Although these differences may never be totally reconciled, pay systems that are designed in a rational and impartial manner stand a better chance of being understood and accepted by all employees. An important consideration in the development of a pay system is the process of job classification. This begins with an evaluation process through which all jobs are grouped based on the requirements of the work itself. The relative worth of each job to other jobs in the organization is then determined, based on the skill, effort, and responsibility needed for each, and a continuum of all jobs in the organization is established. The continuum is broken into classes of jobs, which eventually become pay grades. The emphasis in job evaluation and classification is on the objective nature of the process: it examines jobs, not the personal characteristics of the people holding the jobs.

After the job classifications are determined, a salary range is set for each pay grade, using both internal and external comparisons to determine equity. An eight percent difference between pay grades is generally considered an equitable pay difference. Salary ranges are set in terms of a minimum, midpoint, and maximum daily rate of pay, and annual pay is determined using the number of days worked and the daily salary rate.

Incentive Programs

In what has been called the largest education experiment in the United States, hundreds of millions of dollars have been spent in recent years as part of state and local incentive programs to reward teachers and administrators for doing a better job or for taking on additional responsibilities in schools (Cornett 1987, 1). By 1988, there were more than twenty-four state-developed or state-supported teacher incentive plans in operation. These incentive plans were designed to reward teachers for better performance, extended contract periods, and additional responsibilities. Incentive plans and career ladder plans replaced unpopular merit pay plans.

Merit pay as a system designed to pay for performance has been tried in education and has failed to generate the desired results. Recent attempts to resurrect merit pay have resulted in similar disappointments. Proponents of merit pay claim that such a system would attract a higher caliber of individual to teaching, would help retain good teachers, and would motivate teachers to improve their instructional abilities. Critics point out that such pay systems have failed historically and in recent times, because of controversies that arise related to funding and performance evaluation.

Merit pay and education have never seemed to mix well, despite repeated efforts to make such a system work. The question of why this system does not seem to work in education has been addressed in several ways. Bacharach and Conley (1986) suggest that merit pay has been effective in occupational settings where cooperation among workers is not necessary and where the contribution of each worker can be differentiated from that of other workers. Merit pay also may be effective in settings where the workers directly contribute to the earnings of the organization. Education is obviously not such an occupational setting. Rosenholtz (1986) identified four major problem areas that were among those investigated by researchers studying merit pay plans in thirty large school systems: evaluation standards, quota systems, teacher morale, and teacher isolation from administrators. Schuster and Zingheim (1987) suggest that pay for performance (merit pay) may be hopeless in the public sector because of the following barriers, which are widely practiced in the public sector: (1) increases are considered an entitlement, and even poor performers receive increases; (2) no one likes to be classified as average in performance level; (3) managers are reluctant to rate employees accurately; and (4) the pay systems are open systems, in which everyone knows how much someone else makes (83–84). For these and other reasons, merit pay based primarily on the single factor of performance has been replaced by systems that provide increased pay based on the teacher's willingness to work longer days and to assume more responsibility.

Career ladder plans have been designed around the concept that a teacher should have the opportunity over time to advance through career stages where there are additional rewards in terms of status and money. Proponents of these plans suggest that this type of incentive plan addresses the teacher's need for personal challenge and self-fulfillment. The goal of many career ladder plans is to keep good teachers in classrooms. Critics of the plans contend that career ladders are nothing more than differentiated teaching duties. Unlike merit pay plans, which use annual lump sum bonuses as the financial reward, career ladder compensation is generally considered a permanent financial reward inherent in the career step attained.

Career ladder systems are typically begin with an entry-level step and culminate in a "master" teacher step. Advancement up the career ladder generally requires the attainment of designated performance levels, specific training, and years of service at each step. The problems with merit pay—evaluation, quotas, morale, isolation—are also problems with most career ladder plans (Rosenholtz 1986, 520). It is interesting to note that given the option of making more money for teaching nine or ten months and doing other professional activities for two or three months, seventy-nine percent of the responding public school teachers in a 1986 National Center for Education Information survey responded that they would still prefer a nine- or ten-month contract to a twelve-month contract.

Cornett (1987) states:

> *Are career ladder programs working? Where is the "best" incentive program for teachers? The answers to these questions vary depending on whether you*

ask a legislator in a state with funding problems, a teacher who is earning an additional $7,000 because of a career ladder program, the president of a teachers' organization opposing a particular incentive program, or an enthusiastic school principal who supports a district or state plan.

Incentive plans—merit pay or career ladder—require the investment of considerable sums of money to keep the plan operational and attractive. In prior years, incentive plans were perceived as novelties and controversial innovations and were generally prime targets when budgets were cut. Recently, incentive plans have been initiated in response to criticisms of the pay practices of school districts, and as such they have survived even when budgetary reductions have been made in other areas. It should be noted that despite their survival, most incentive plans are still considered controversial and fail to receive the blessing of teacher unions. The unions favor the single salary schedule system largely because of the general guarantee that all teachers will receive an annual salary increase.

Benefits

Benefits are a component of the extrinsic reward system referred to as indirect compensation. These rewards have historically been viewed as "membership" rewards, since they are provided as incentives for employment in the particular school district or organization. As noted in Exhibit 12.3, the district's objectives in providing employee benefits center on the idea of being a good employer, providing forms of protection for the employee against adverse conditions that may affect the employee's quality of life.

As a general rule, employee benefits are not highly appreciated by employees, and the perceived value varies greatly from employee to employee. This lack of appreciation may stem from poor communication about benefits or from the fact that benefits are appreciated most when they are needed most. The lack of appreciation may also emanate in part from the terms used to describe these indirect forms of compensation. Terms such as "fringe benefits," "indirect compensation," "wage supplements," "nonwage benefits," "social wages," "supplementary employee remuneration," "supplementary compensation," and "indirect payments" all suggest that the rewards are ancillary and not a significant part of total compensation (Belcher and Atchison 1987, 311). The perception that benefits are not valuable compensation is both false and unfortunate, given the costs of providing them. It is generally felt that benefit programs fail to get a good return for the dollars expended. Whether providing benefits is truly a reward for membership in the particular organization may also be debated, since employees have come to expect certain types of benefits in all work situations, and there are legal provisions for mandated benefits.

Under the provisions of federal and state laws, school districts as employers are required to provide benefits related to social security, unemployment compensation, worker's compensation, and retirement. These mandated benefits are provided to employees as protection against temporary financial loss due to adverse conditions related to sickness, injury, loss of employment, and permanent financial security when the person is no longer able to work. The management of these programs is frequently referred to as "risk management," since abuse of the programs by an unethical person can have devastating effects on a school district's financial resources. As employers, school districts either pay the full cost of the benefits provided or share the costs with another entity or the individual. Recent federal legislation provides protection for employees related to the continuation of group insurance coverage as they move from organization to organization. There is no federal law requiring employees to provide health care insurance for employees. However, when an employer does provide health care insurance, the Consolidated Omnibus Budget Reconciliation Act (COBRA) grants the employee the right to continuation of the coverage after he or she leaves the group. The employee assumes payment of the cost of the plan and has the option of converting it to an individual plan. The COBRA regulations have impacted what traditionally has been considered optional benefits.

In school districts, optional benefits often include health insurance, life insurance, dental insurance, and liability or legal insurance. There is no set of requirements that applies to all districts, unless such requirements are generated at the state level. Typically, the same benefits are available to all employees at the same level in the district. Historically, however, many districts have differentiated between benefits for different levels of employees. Recent federal requirements related to the removal of tax exemptions for benefits that are not available to all employees have caused districts to reexamine their practices in this regard. Employers who provide uniform benefits to all employees have few problems with the law. Employees who fail to comply with the law may have to pay taxes on the value of the benefits. Although school districts have frequently differentiated between levels of employees in terms of benefits, they have not provided a choice in the selection of benefits to meet individual needs. This type of program, referred to as "cafeteria-type" benefits, provides the employee with a lump sum amount to use in purchasing benefits. Some programs allow the employee to take the lump sum designated for benefits as a cash payment.

As in all areas of compensation, union demands directly affect the provision of benefit programs and services. Attempts to "cap" the rising costs of employee benefit plans are strongly opposed by bargaining groups. Attempts to provide cost-containment measures in employee benefits programs are sometimes met with resistance at the bargaining table. Often, no matter what is done with respect to benefits, it is less than what the union wants. Securing benefits for their membership enhances a union's status. The importance of benefits to unions, even when the benefits are not clearly understood by employees, has sometimes caused them to seek benefit increases even when salary increases were not feasible.

Collective Bargaining

When asked to identify the most dramatic and traumatic change in education during the twentieth century, many administrators quickly respond: "collective bargaining." Due to the unprecedented number of changes in education during recent decades, it might be assumed that selecting a single change in answer to this question would be difficult. However, the economic and political implications of collective bargaining have so altered the function and roles of educational leaders that this is an easy choice for many administrators.

The economic factors associated with collective bargaining are obvious. Approximately eighty percent of a school district's operating budget is consumed directly or indirectly by labor costs—salary, insurance, sick leave, class size ratios, preparation periods, duty-free periods, number of days worked, and staff development days. The union's primary goal in the negotiations process is to obtain better wages, better hours, and better working conditions for the union members. To fund these increases, the board of trustees must use money that potentially could be targeted for support of the instructional program—better facilities, instructional materials, library and media resources, technology, and support services to students. The economic realities of school funding require that all needs—student, employee, and public—be addressed with the limited dollars available for financing the total operation of the district. This economic reality leads to competition among the forces in the school system. In the collective bargaining situation, a union serving as the agent for a group of employees must compete against other forces (even other unions) in the district for dominance of the district budget. Adversarial relationships among the competing forces frequently develop.

The political implications of the collective bargaining process have affected school board members, administrators, and teachers. In the adversarial environment created by collective bargaining, school board members often find it difficult to represent the public's interest and to maintain a focus on what is best for students. This may be especially true when a school board member finds that the union and its membership are working to unseat him or her for failure to support union positions. Superintendents and other school administrators must deal with the political realities associated with not supporting the union's demands and must maintain a focus on students, difficult as this may be in the face of political controversy and threat. Teachers also must deal with the political fallout associated with collective bargaining. Strikes and other political actions by teachers that impact the educational process often generate public hostility toward teachers. The professionalization of teaching has been questioned because of collective bargaining. Collective bargaining has been viewed, practically and conceptually, as the final nail in the coffin of professional ethics in education (Lieberman 1988, 160). The political factors associated with collective bargaining have left a lasting mark on education and represent one of the most significant changes in education during the twentieth century.

The emerging role of employee unions and collective bargaining has paralleled the role of the state in circumscribing the local board's decisions on personnel matters. Education administrators have found their functions and roles being influenced by laws, state board of education policies, and state agency directives, many of which relate directly to personnel administration. While learning to cope with ever-changing regulations, the administrator working with personnel functions has also learned to cope with collective bargaining. Webb et al. (1987) believe that collective bargaining has impacted personnel administration in at least two distinct ways: "The process of collective negotiations has had an impact upon virtually every process and activity within the personnel function; and the personnel unit generally has assumed a major role in the administration of the collective negotiations process itself" (92).

Collective Bargaining Defined

Collective bargaining may be defined as the process in which the two parties, management and labor, meet together in good faith to negotiate with respect to wages, hours, and other terms and conditions of employment that are permitted within the scope of bargaining subjects. By statute, labor and management are equal parties in the bargaining process, and bargaining subjects are defined as mandatory, prohibited, or permissive. The parties do not have to reach an agreement on mandatory subjects, but the subjects must be negotiated. Permissible subjects are bargained by mutual agreement. The purpose of the process is to reach an agreement that may be set forth in a written contract that is ratified by both parties.

In some states, in the absence of mandatory or permissible collective bargaining legislation, a "meet-and-confer" process is created by statute. This process is similar to collective bargaining in that it establishes a formal labor-management relationship, giving employees the right to organize and make recommendations to management through a representative. Unlike collective bargaining, this process does not mandate the reaching of an agreement on issues. In many instances, meet-and-confer statutes have been enacted as a first step toward collective bargaining.

As subdivisions of state government, school districts are public sector institutions. The organizations representing employees of public school districts are considered public sector unions. In recent years, it has become increasingly difficult to distinguish public sector and private sector unions; they are differentiated primarily based on the limitations imposed by legal guidelines. The private sector bargains under the provisions of the National Labor Relations Act, while the public sector bargains under various federal, state, or local laws. Exhibit 12.4 on page 270 summarizes the sources for legal guidelines governing the collective bargaining process in the private and public sectors.

Collective Bargaining in Education

Many have wondered why the unions were interested in organizing teachers in the first place. Stated simply, education is big business. By the end of the 1980s, there were 15,700 school districts, 83,000 schools, 2,700,000 teachers, and 45,600,000 elementary and secondary students in the United States. Education is the nation's largest employer. Total expenditures on education in the 1990s were projected to exceed $353 trillion, with an average per-pupil expenditure of approximately $5,200 (Staub 1989).

Unions exist where there is an adversary and when they have dues-paying membership. During the first half of the twentieth century, when employees' unions in the private sector were scoring victory after victory for employee welfare through an adversarial relationship in the bargaining process, teachers were spectators. The rather spectacular economic gains made through militant union activity in industry spurred an interest among at least some teachers. The sheer size of many school districts and the accompanying bureaucracy created in many teachers a feeling that the individual was helpless and that unity of employees was essential for them to control their own destiny. Compounding these fears was a lurking concern that managerial power was being exercised arbitrarily. Thus, to the unions, teachers were ripe for confrontation with their employers and a fertile field of untapped dues.

In this fertile field of teacher unrest, two existing organizations—the National Education Association (NEA) and the American Federation of Teachers (AFT)—began flexing their muscles. These groups were sleeping political giants who throughout their early histories differed in philosophy and operational procedures. Until the mid-1960s, the NEA billed itself as a professional organization for educators and proclaimed its concern with the quality of American education. The AFT was influenced from its formation in the early 1900s by its close ties to private sector unions and central labor councils. When the AFT became a formidable power in American education in the 1960s by scoring victories in representation elections in several large cities, the NEA began to adopt its militant philosophy and tactics.

By 1986, eighty percent of public school teachers in the United States belonged to a union—seventy percent to NEA and ten percent to AFT. In

EXHIBIT 12.4 Summary of Legal Guideline Sources for Collective Bargaining

Guideline	Major Concept	Sector
Norris-LaGuardia Act, 1932	Workers have right to organize into unions	Private
Wagner Act, 1935	Guaranteed workers' rights to organize and join labor unions for purpose of collective bargaining; prevent unfair labor practices by employers; established National Labor Relations Board (NLRB) to administer act	Private
Taft-Hartley Act, 1947	Amended Wagner Act to prevent unfair labor practices by unions	Private
Norwalk Teachers Association versus Norwalk Board of Education of City of Norwalk, 1951	Boards of education allowed to bargain with teachers so long as boards do not abrogate their right to have the last word in the bargaining process; teachers may not strike	Public school teachers
Landrum-Griffin Act, 1959	Sought to correct corruption in labor unions; amended Taft-Hartley Act	Private
Executive Order 10988, 1962	Affirmed right of federal employees to join labor unions and participate in collective bargaining	Federal
Executive Order 11491, 1969	Brought federal labor relations procedures into line with those of private sector; established Federal Labor Relations Council	Federal
National League of Cities versus Usery, 1976	Revised certain basic principles regarding the the power of the federal government to regulate relationships between public employer—employees	Public
Garcia versus San Antonio Metropolitan Transit Authority, et al., 1985	Cleared the way for federal legislation governing organization and bargaining for state and local employees	Public

comparison, only twenty percent of adult workers in other industries in the United States belonged to a union (Feistritzer 1988, 44). It was estimated that by 1988, seventy-five percent of the teachers in the United States were covered by some type of collective bargaining agreement: "In America, just three unions, the National Education Association, The American Federation of Teachers and the American Federation of State, County and Municipal Employees account for over half of total public sector membership" (Troy 1988, 5). Typical of public sector union membership, the members of NEA and AFT are primarily women and live in all areas of the country.

Labor-Management Relations

Prior to 1950, few educational administrators had studied or worked in environments with a heavy emphasis on labor-management relations. The introduction of organized labor into the educational workplace changed the situation dramatically. Since the 1950s, collective bargaining has become, and will continue to be, a major concern for all educational administrators, particularly for the personnel administrator.

In many states, dealing with collective bargaining has become such an integral part of the administrator's responsibilities that it might appear to a novice that it has always been part of the management process and perhaps even an outcome of the educational process. To the contrary, labor-management relations as practiced within the collective bargaining arena in education is almost totally a replication of the collective bargaining process used in the private sector or industrial setting. Shedd (1988) states:

> *Except for restrictions on strikes and the substitution of various third-party impasse procedures, most of the features of collective bargaining in public education were borrowed from the private sector: districtwide bargaining units, the periodic negotiation of comprehensive agreements that last for fixed periods of time, legal restrictions that limit bargaining to so-called "bread-and-butter" issues and that require the parties to negotiate "in good faith," multistep grievance procedures for the resolution of disagreements that may arise during the life of an agreement, and the use of binding arbitration to resolve such disputes if the parties are unable to resolve them on their own. (407–8)*

How the industrial model of collective bargaining came to be used in educational labor-management relations is not difficult to understand when two factors are taken into account. The first is the bureaucratic model of educational management that was prevalent during the period collective bargaining was being instituted in education. In this bureaucratic environment, early union organizers were effective in dividing teachers and administrators along the traditional labor-management lines used in private sector bargaining. The second factor is the geographical locations where early bargaining rights in education were won. Collective bargaining in education began in the areas of the country where there was an established pattern of successful bargaining in private business and industry.

In Michigan, the passage of Public Act 379 required the NEA state affiliate, the Michigan Education Association, to declare itself a union. Michigan, a strong union state, thus became a battleground for the two powerful employee welfare organizations. The AFT's position on the use of strikes in the public schools had long been criticized by the NEA, but it was soon adopted by the Michigan Education Association as a survival technique in its battle for teacher votes. The rivalry was bitter, but Michigan was an ideal political climate for the development of new labor-management relations in education. The effectiveness of union-type activism in Michigan had a strong influence on the behavior of other state and local teacher welfare groups.

The Wisconsin Legislature, in 1959, passed the first statewide statute granting collective bargaining rights to government employees. Other states soon followed Wisconsin, and today the majority of states have such legislation. Every state legislature has been under pressure to give serious consideration to initiating or improving collective bargaining laws.

The 1960s and 1970s saw rapidly changing practices in employee-administration relations. The processes that developed slowly in the private sector after the passage of the Wagner Act of 1935 were adopted quickly by public school employees. Collective bargaining for teachers evolved into a common practice for a majority of school employees. Although it came late in comparison with labor bargaining in the private sector, the school board-teacher bargaining process has grown in such an astonishing manner that it would be difficult to think of a more drastic change in the entire field of educational administration.

The Bargaining Process

To the inexperienced, the collective bargaining process may appear to be a series of difficult meetings in which labor representatives and management representatives argue face-to-face the issues to be resolved in the ratified agreement. In reality, the bargaining process is an ongoing process that impacts virtually every administrative or policy decision. As depicted in Exhibit 12.5, the bargaining process is a cyclical process that includes negotiations preparation, face-to-face bargaining, impasse procedures settlement, and contract administration. Each of the activities in the cycle leads to another and determines how successful the process will be ultimately.

Lifton (1990) stated: "The critical element of the bargaining process—the building of credibility and trust—dictates the success of most negotiations insofar as the climate of the relationship is concerned, as well as getting to an agreement quickly and expeditiously while generating the least amount of discord" (2). The development of mutual respect and trust, along with credibility earned through consistency of representation, facilitates the carrying out of each bargaining activity. When individuals believe they can talk with each other, disagree without reprisals, and believe what the other party is saying, the chances are increased that fewer grievances will be filed, fewer unfair practices charges will be made, and fewer disruptions to the educational process will occur.

Bargaining Items and Subjects

The subjects that may or must be bargained have been determined through legislative, judicial, and regulatory agency mandates. "In all but the federal sector, wages and all forms of employee compensation are topics of mandatory bargaining" (Colosi and Berkeley 1986, 31). Wherever collective

EXHIBIT 12.5   Cyclical Activities of the Bargaining Process

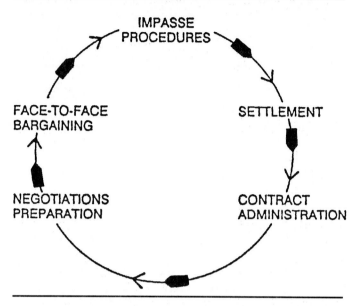

IMPASSE
PROCEDURES

FACE-TO-FACE
BARGAINING

SETTLEMENT

NEGOTIATIONS
PREPARATION

CONTRACT
ADMINISTRATION

Source* Board Members' Guide to the Negotiations Process. 1988. A
Publication of the Michigan Association of School Boards Labor Relations Service.

bargaining occurs in education, whether through statutorily mandated provisions or local board permission, organized labor has moved from being
concerned primarily with salaries and working conditions to a concern for
all aspects of the educational enterprise; virtually no area of educational
policy or programming is exempt from bargaining consideration. According to Hoyle et al. (1990), typical of the items to be negotiated are:

> *salaries, schedules, wage increases; work hours; work loads, scheduling;
> assignment of personnel; promotion, transfer, layoff provisions; length of
> school day and year; observations and evaluations of teachers; preparation
> periods and extra duty assignments; class size; changes in curriculum, pro-
> grams, innovations; personnel files, charges against teachers, parental com-
> plaints; after school meetings, extra work assignments; relief from
> clerical/non-teaching duties. (193)*

There is every reason to believe that new issues and bargaining subjects will continue to arise for inclusion in bargaining agreements. It has
been suggested that "collective bargaining will become more closely linked
with student achievement during the coming decades" and that "because
of the risks involved, innovative site-based experimentation cannot occur

in districts that deny teachers the security and structure provided by a strong collective bargaining agreement" (Tuthill 1990, 780). The subjects of future bargaining may be focused on areas such as school renewal, site-based management, and educational restructuring. Watts and McClure (1990) found in their review of the expanded bargaining issues that there are a number of lessons to be learned related to future education undertakings and collective bargaining. One is that union/management collaboration on school-based restructuring does not consign the collective bargaining contract to the dustbin of history. There will always be different perspectives and divergent self-interests to protect. That the collective bargaining process and the contracts that result are likely to be decidedly different and far broader in scope than they have been in the past is the second lesson. The third lesson is that teachers and administrators (as well as school boards, parents, communities, and students) will work more cooperatively and collaboratively in the future. This, however, does not signal an end to union/management conflict and discord (772–74). The items brought to the bargaining table and issues to be resolved through negotiations appear to be limited only by the willingness of the parties to consider them. Future trends are apparent in the following excerpt from the Addendum to the Contract between the Dade County Public School and the United Teachers of Dade (July 1, 1988, through June 30, 1991): "Beginning with the 1988–89 school year, the parties agree that a new model for expanded joint decision-making must be established in order to accommodate the ever-increasing range of educational topics requiring joint deliberations and the development of joint recommendations" (130).

The Agreement

The term "agreement" is used most often to describe the binding contract between a board of education and an employees' union. Often referred to as the contract, the master agreement, or the comprehensive agreement, it serves as the legal guide for the relationships between the school district's management and employees. The agreement is in force for a specified period of time, most frequently one or two years. After negotiations have been completed and the contract signed by all parties, the agreement is published and disseminated to all of the constituents. Some contracts cover many subjects in great detail, while other contracts are concise. A savings clause is included in nearly all contracts. Typically, this clause reads: "If any provision or any portion of this agreement is ultimately ruled invalid for any reason by an authority of established and competent legal jurisdiction, the balance and the remainder of the agreement shall remain in full force and effect. The parties will renegotiate the provision in question." Mutually agreed-upon changes to original provisions of the contract made during the period the contract is in force are handled through addenda or memoranda of understanding signed by both parties to the contract.

Weapons of Conflict

"When most people consider the topic of weapons of conflict . . . they think first of the strike. To be sure, the strike (and the threat of a strike) is very powerful, but the union has two other principal weapons: . . . the boycott and the picket line" (Colosi and Berkeley 1986, 35). A strike involves the withholding of services by union members. A boycott involves an organized effort to coerce or punish an entity or individual through refusal to do business with the entity or individual. The picket line tactic involves the use of individuals and media to express dissatisfaction with an entity or individual. For public sector employees such as teachers, the distinction between these weapons of conflict is important. In most states, teachers are prohibited from striking and to participate in a strike is illegal. Participation in picketing or boycotting when these activities do not violate any laws is protected as a freedom of speech right.

Despite the fact that the strike is legal in few states, teacher unions have used it with relative impunity. In 1988, 72 strikes were called in 13 states, affecting 19,000 teachers and 312,000 students. In 1989, there were 34 strikes in 9 states, affecting 12,300 teachers and 213,000 students (Staub 1989). Statistics compiled over a fifteen-year period by the Public Service Research Council indicate that strikes increased sevenfold following the advent of collective bargaining in education. An interesting variation of the strike in education is the short-term work stoppages known as "sick-outs" or "chalkboard flue," where teachers fail to report for duty for one or two days.

If a strike occurs, the school district is called upon to continue the delivery of services to students, and how to do this should be part of a contingency plan agreed upon by the administrative team. This involves answering questions such as: Will substitute teachers be used to provide these services or will striking teachers be replaced? What other groups are supporting the strike? Are auxiliary employees—food service workers, custodians, bus drivers, maintenance personnel—supporting the strike? Can schools be kept open without the services of auxiliary personnel? What programs will be curtailed or temporarily discontinued?

The complexities of keeping schools open during a strike or closing them, computing the costs of a contract, administering a negotiated contract, maintaining employee morale before and after a confrontation, and similar problems require a special set of skills for the educational administrator. Above all else, in the event of a strike, line communications with the striking employees must be kept open. The Michigan Association of School Boards Labor Relations Service (1988) cautions that "a strike is not 'the end,' it is simply a union means to an end which can be incredibly destructive in terms of its impact on staff, students, the community and the board" (20). Eventually, the parties involved in the bargaining process must get back together and reach an agreement. Following the strike, a time of healing and rebuilding must occur, and this period can be shortened by effective

communication between the parties. The first uneasy moves toward reconciliation may surface at the building level, since teachers and principals
share a common interest in educational quality, and curriculum issues
provide a common ground for mutual decision making and action. The
education of the district children is the *raison d'être* of all groups (American
Association of School Personnel Administrators 1982, 21). All steps
directed toward healing must be encouraged and nourished by the management team.

The Future of Collective Bargaining

The rising tide of collective bargaining since the 1960s cannot be denied.
However, some analysts of the current educational scene are not con-
vinced that the continuation of industrial-type labor-management relations is an inevitability in education. Administrators may be victims of
their own worst fears and prophecies in relation to the future of collective bargaining. Those who convince themselves and others that something
worse is going to happen tend to act in ways that are consistent with that
occurrence and, in doing so, tend to set in motion those very events.
The rise of teacher unions, formal bargaining, confrontations, lobbying,
slowdowns, and strikes during recent years must be studied to avoid
repeating the mistakes of the past. It may be helpful to view the events
that began in the 1960s as a transitional period in the course of educational progress. The process of change and evolution for education
in general, and for collective bargaining specifically, will continue into
the future.

Shedd (1988), in a study of collective bargaining in public education,
suggests that the pressures that prompted reform in education will also
prompt an adjustment in the collective bargaining system in education. He
believes changes will occur in the present scope of bargaining, the forms
and forums for bargaining, the nature of resulting agreements, rules governing the application of districtwide agreements to individual schools, the
principle of management's "retained rights," and the structure of the teaching profession:

> *Teachers, we expect, will always be more sensitive to the need for flexibility*
> *and individual discretion, while system managers will continue to be more*
> *sensitive to the need for coordination of programs and to the flow of students*
> *through the system. The parties will continue, in other words, to have differ-*
> *ent perspectives on what their clients need as well as different interests and*
> *priorities in their dealings with each other. Those perspectives, interests, and*
> *priorities are not (we trust) mutually exclusive, but they do require constant*
> *reconciliation. The fact that collective bargaining is well-suited to just such a*
> *task is one reason it is likely to assume more prominence in the overall*
> *management of school systems in coming years. (414)*

Rauth (1990) notes that the negotiations in education up to 1981 reflected the mentality of industrial labor/management relations and dealt primarily with wages, hours, and terms and conditions of employment. By 1981, however, it was obvious to most union officials that this type of collective bargaining had gone about as far as it could (782). In a RAND Corporation report, McDonnell and Pascal (1988) confirm that by the mid-1980s collective bargaining in education based on the industrial model had peaked in usefulness:

> By 1980, a majority of bargaining units had included in their contracts provisions regulating the length of the school day, allowing teachers to respond formally to administrators' evaluations, permitting teachers to exclude disruptive students from their classrooms, and outlining clear procedures for districts to follow if they must reduce the size of their teacher force. However, less than a third of the teacher unions in our contract sample had attained strong limits on class size, curbs on requirements for teachers to teach out of their field, or the establishment of an instructional policy committee at each school. Furthermore, teacher unions have made little progress in obtaining new contractual provisions since 1975. With relatively few exceptions, the improvements in working conditions teacher unions had attained by 1975 were not enhanced in the 1980 and 1985 contracts. (v–vi)

Faced with truths about their ability to secure additional concessions related to wages, hours, and conditions of work as they related to the funding of public education, labor leaders in the mid-1980s began to reconsider the role of collective bargaining in education. Particularly in situations where the union and management had been at each other's throats for years, union leaders began to talk of "win-win" or mutual gains bargaining (MGB) as a way of beginning to reconcile the bitterness of former relationships. Since one of the most unfortunate aspects of collective bargaining has been the attempt on the part of both parties to cast the other party in the role of villain, union officials and school administrators—following discussions related to win-win, MGB, or similar attempts to cease unnecessary confrontation—began to approach bargaining activities with the attitude that both parties represent legitimate interests. Spurred on by the realization of their own limitations in the face of declining educational resources and public demands for change, union officials and educational managers have embarked on a number of projects promoting the professionalization of teaching and school restructuring. Noteworthy for their efforts to address the problems of professionalization and educational reform collaboratively are projects mutually undertaken by the union and management in Florida (Dade County), New York (Rochester and Greece), Ohio (Toledo), California (Petaluma and San Diego), Indiana (Hammond), Kentucky (Jefferson County), Washington (Bellevue), and Pennsylvania (Easton and Pittsburgh). These efforts were supported by the union and management through the development of the terms of the bargaining agreement.

To those who hope that collective bargaining in education will go away and who take recent events as evidence that the unions have gone soft, Rauth (1990) responds:

> *Although the progress of change, especially in a bureaucracy, sometimes seems glacial, the steady advance of collective bargaining is a hopeful sign. Some still wait for the demise of collective bargaining. But it is stronger than ever, and evidence of its benefits to quality education are mounting. As long as the schools, the unions, the profession, and collective bargaining continue to evolve together, restructuring retains the potential to become reality. (790)*

As the Task Force on Teaching as a Profession pointed out in *A Nation Prepared* (1986), "all sides have to work hard to overcome a legacy of conflict and confrontation. Unions, boards, and school administrators need to work out a new accommodation based on exchanging professional level salaries and a professional environment, on the one hand, for the acceptance of professional standards of excellence, and the willingness to be held fully accountable for the results of one's work, on the other" (95).

Summary

There is an inevitable link between the human resources and financial resources of an educational enterprise. In public education, seventy-five to eighty-five percent of a district's annual operating budget is consumed by the compensation costs involved in purchasing human services for the delivery of instructional services to students. Personnel issues related to staffing and compensation have traditionally been sources of conflict between the organized labor forces and school management. To be successful, administrators dealing with personnel functions must understand the complexities of the human resource environment and the economic environment.

Educational reform issues and school finance reform issues have significantly impacted education in recent decades, and this trend is not likely to change. Progress in the development of new and improved labor/management relationships is to be found in educational settings across the country. These new relationships do not promise an end to differences of perspective between the parties, but they do foster the restructuring and rebuilding of education, which the public has demanded. The professionalization of teaching and the development of these collaborative relationships have the potential to improve and enhance learning for students, which is the only legitimate reason for the existence of public schools. Educational reform and school reform are ongoing processes. The future course of events will be determined by numerous social, economic, and political forces, and administrators working with personnel services should play a significant role in determining the innovations and changes that will enhance the quality of personnel serving students.

Suggested Study Sources

Belcher, David W., and Thomas J. Atchison. 1987. *Compensation Administration.* 2d ed. Englewood Cliffs, NJ: Prentice-Hall.

> *This book addresses the major decision areas that must be dealt with in compensating employees: wage level, wage structure, wage system, wage form, wage treatment, and wage administration. Part I includes a chapter on the environment of compensation.*

Burrup, Percy E., Vern Brimley, Jr., and Rulon R. Garfield. 1988. *Financing Education in a Climate of Change.* 4th ed. Boston: Allyn and Bacon.

> *The philosophical position of the authors is that education is an investment in human capital. Chapters in the book trace the history of school finance, theoretical finance concepts, the legal issues that have changed school financing, and the reform movement in school finance.*

Hoyle, John R., Fenwick W. English, and Betty E. Steffy. 1990. *Skills for Successful School Leaders.* 2d ed. Arlington, VA: American Association of School Administrators.

> *The purpose of this publication is to delineate the essential skills school administrators need to carry out critical functions in school management and improvement. Chapter 8 addresses budgeting, facilities planning, personnel administration, collective bargaining, and other topics in a very concise manner. Collective bargaining is addressed in a chapter on building support for schools.*

Feistritzer, C. Emily. 1986. *Profile of Teachers in the U.S.* Washington, DC: National Center for Education Information.

> *This report analyzes the results of a questionnaire survey of public and private school teachers conducted in 1986, the intent of which was to portray teachers as they see themselves. The survey questionnaire and methodology are covered in the appendices.*

Holdway, Cindy. 1985. *Designing Employee Pay Systems.* Austin, TX: Personnel Services of Texas Association of School Boards and Texas Association of School Administrators.

> *This guide for school administrators was prepared to introduce practitioners to the subject of compensation administration. Job analysis, job evaluation, job pricing, and the development of salary structures are covered. Special attention is given to communication of the compensation plan. The step-by-step approach provides a valuable tool for learning about or designing plans.*

▪ APPENDICES ━━━━━━━━━━

DeTEK Criteria List

Performance Area	Behaviors and Indicators

1. BUSINESSLIKE
The teacher is organized, systematic, goal oriented, and prepared.
 	
The teacher performs in a variety of ways that clearly reflect planning, goal orientation, prioritization, and detailed consideration of relationships between purpose, activity, sequence, materials, delegation, time constraints, and space utilization. In essence, the teacher clearly knows what is intended and facilitates its realization.
	1a. *Organizes classroom activities to produce a smooth flow of events with a minimum of confusion or waste of time.*
	    1a (1)—Gives clear, simple directions for shifting from one activity to another.
	    1a (2)—Initiates changes in activity for individuals who are ready while others are still busy with prior assignments.
	    1a (3)—Arranges all materials for easy distribution as needed during activity.
	    1a (4)—Makes prompt use of supplemental activities or plan modifications to assure full use of all available time.
	    1a (5)—Organizes and directs clerical and housekeeping chores to prevent waste by time by teacher and students.
	
	1b. *Informs students of objectives, sequence of events, the rationale, and responsibilities well in advance of lesson or activity.*
	    1b (1)—Displays and/or verbalizes the planned sequence of events for the lesson or period.
	    1b (2)—Specifies objectives in clear, explicit terms before students are given directions, and refers to such objectives as needed for clarification and evaluation purposes.
	    1b (3)—Discusses the rationale for assignments in terms of objectives, course goals, and the realities of student life.
	    1b (4)—Defines student responsibilities, emphasizing expectations, growth, progress, excellence, and effort.
	
	1c. *Delegates responsibilities to students, aides, and others in ways that keep them involved and conserve teacher time and energy for the most demanding responsibilities.*
	    1c (1)—Assigns routine clerical and housekeeping chores to students (and aides) on a scheduled basis, dispersing the workload and conserving time.
	    1c (2)—Arranges for students to work individually or in small groups, defining the responsibilities of all students.
	    1c (3)—Leads students in evaluating their own assignments, providing all necessary materials and directions to assure objectivity.
	    1c (4)—Stimulates students to seek assistance from other school personnel, parents, and others in conjunction with regular course assignments.
	
	1d. *Paces activities to assure task accomplishment, arranging for assistance for those who need it to make progress and reach goals.*
	    1d (1)—Surveys the progress of students toward task accomplishment, and reminds students of time allocations, urging greater speed as needed.
	    1d (2)—Adjusts time frames to fit needs of students, allowing time, shifting to new activities more quickly, or rescheduling target dates.
	    1d (3)—Provides tutorial assistance or guides small groups to assist with task accomplishment on schedule.
	    1d (4)—Encourages and directs students in assisting each other to assure task completion.

2. FRIENDLY
The teacher is warm, empathetic, outgoing, positive, and personal.
 	
The teacher displays warm, friendly, personal relationships with all pupils by emphasizing the positive, avoiding negativism, being accessible to students, considering their feelings and problems, recognizing differences in interests, abilities, and experiences. In essence, the teacher clearly regards every individual and the student group as persons who are likeable, worthy, interesting, and capable.
	2a. *Speaks to students in positive, praising, encouraging ways.*
	    2a (1)—Acknowledges student comments or responses verbally without interrupting or reducing focus on the student.
	    2a (2)—Praises student efforts, using phrases, sentences, and tonal inflections which are meaningful to the student(s) involved.
	    2a (3)—Frees students from embarrassment by using reassuring and supportive statements.
	    2a (4)—Avoids giving negative reactions, criticisms, threats, sarcasm, etc.
	    2a (5)—Interacts personally with all students, balancing the attention given the more aggressive and the less aggressive students.
	
	2b. *Expresses interest in individuals as persons over and above being students.*
	    2b (1)—Seeks out individual students and groups of students for informal personal contacts.
	    2b (2)—Encourages students to share thoughts and feelings, reflecting and clarifying in ways that help students assess the effectiveness of their behavior patterns.

Performance Area	Behaviors and Indicators

2c (3)—Inquires about students' personal accomplishments or interests.

2b (4)—Assists students in defining realistic self-development goals.

2c. *Reflects empathy, concern, and warm liking of students as related to both school and other aspects of life.*

2c (1)—Comments sympathetically on feelings of students.

2c (2)—Asks about and comments with acceptance on family and personal affairs.

2c (3)—Shares personal experiences.

2c (4)—Encourages students to recognize peer accomplishments.

2c (5)—Tells and listens to jokes, puns, or amusing incidents.

2d. *Demonstrates interest and concern for students nonverbally in a variety of ways.*

2d (1)—Maintains eye contact with students when interacting verbally with them.

2d (2)—Listens attentively when students are talking or presenting.

2d (3)—Smiles openly, broadly, and frequently; and laughs freely when appropriate.

2d (4)—Moves close to students when assisting them, leaning, stooping, sitting, etc., as needed.

2d (5)—Uses with, and accepts from, students such physical contacts as handshakes, pats on the back, or embraces.

3. VERBALLY INTERACTIVE
The teacher listens, accepts, probes, questions, and encourages.

The teacher utilizes a variety of verbal interaction techniques to enhance clarity of communication, stimulate verbalizations by students, and provoke higher-level thought processes; and encourages students to relate talk, listening, and thinking to their various classroom learning experiences.

3a. *Communicates clearly and concisely.*

3a (1)—Gives directions or comments as needed to assure progress.

3a (2)—Avoids directions or comments which disrupt students and waste their time.

3a (3)—Uses a level of language students can understand.

3b. *Encourages and guides student responses and teacher-student interactions.*

3b (1)—Gives and asks for information and suggestions.

3b (2)—Encourages alternative answers, rephrasing to suggest responses from different students.

3b (3)—Prompts, reflects, accepts disagreements, and waits extended periods of time for students' thoughts to emerge.

3b (4)—Listens thoughtfully to students' ideas, incorporating them into the lesson and recognizing their worth.

3b (5)—Utilizes activities which allow for a high degree of student interaction—discussion, simulation, experiments, problem solving, games, inquiries.

3c. *Utilizes a variety of questioning techniques which provoke different levels of thinking on the part of all students.*

3c (1)—Uses open-ended questions to stimulate discussion, probing in ways that keep the question open-ended and enhance student thinking.

3c (2)—Adjusts pace of questioning to allow periods of silence so all students may engage in higher-level thinking.

3c (3)—Uses an array of question types, ranging from simple recognition and recall to analysis, synthesis, and evaluation.

4. STIMULATING
The teacher is imaginative, stimulating, exciting, provocative, interesting, avoiding dull routine.

The teacher expresses interest in the subject matter and activities of the class. The teacher avoids dull routines in favor of many variations in procedures, materials, and activities. The teacher utilizes student interests.

4a. *Expresses interest, enthusiasm, and curiosity about subject matter and other events.*

4a (1)—Decorates or arranges the classroom in ways which reinforce the theme of the lesson or the subject.

4a (2)—Shares personal books, artifacts, experiences, reading, or other materials with the students.

4a (3)—Uses self-invented written materials, models, drawings, or processes.

4a (4)—Improvises furniture, objects, costumes, or sets to meet unique or spontaneous needs.

4a (5)—Raises questions about others' thoughts, opinions, or ideas in ways which reinforce the theme of the lesson or event.

4a (6)—Communicates excitement, surprise, wonder about lesson or event by inflection and by varying speaking rate, gestures, and body movement.

4a (7)—Elaborates on subject matter by drawing from a personal knowledge base which is accurate, up-to-date, and of significant depth.

Performance Area	Behaviors and Indicators

4b. *Uses a variety of styles, techniques, and approaches to present subject matter.*

4b (1)—Organizes subject matter presentations to show relationships between disciplines and connections of subject matter to the real world.

4b (2)—Uses shifts in sensory modes, levels of thinking, interaction styles, or in location of teacher/learners to keep the lesson flowing and student interest and attention high.

4b (3)—Models, and guides students in using, a wide array of higher cognitive operations, e.g., classifying, comparing, evaluating, inferring, generalizing, hypothesizing.

4b (4)—Plans and executes presentations which are surprising, out of the ordinary, and memorable, increasing active response of the students and motivating them toward further participation.

4b (5)—Sets up and provides resources for a wide variety of challenging learning activities, e.g., inquiries, experiments, simulations, case studies, interviews, brainstorming.

4c. *Draws upon students' interests and current events for content, illustrations, and applications within the classroom.*

4c (1)—Substitutes current problems, issues, or happenings of interest to students for those offered in commercial materials or texts, when doing so makes for lively and efficient learning.

4c (2)—Refers to up-to-date bulletin boards, exhibits, interest centers, newspapers, periodicals, books, or other selected sources of information.

4c (3)—Provides students with choices in topics for study, in activities, or in coworkers.

4c (4)—Encourages students to reveal their interests by facilitating such student-centered activities within the classroom as sharing books of particular interest, displaying artifacts, or talking about experiences or current issues.

4c (5)—Invites students to initiate projects, experiments, or other learning activities, assisting them directly when called upon.

4d. *Responds spontaneously to unplanned events, using them as reinforcers or illustrations.*

4d (1)—Maintains a planned but flexible learning environment in which unplanned events *can* emerge.

4d (2)—Cues students that the event is important by recognizing the event and calling attention to it.

4d (3)—Guides students in relating the event to past, present, or future learning, tying the event to specific learnings, materials, or processes.

4d (4)—Introduces extension activities as a followup to the event when doing so aids significantly in accomplishing the learning objectives set up prior to the event's occurrence.

5. INDIVIDUAL ORIENTED
The teacher treats each individual as a unique learner.

The teacher makes learning different for individuals in many ways. Intraclass groupings are utilized routinely, as well as for special occasions, along with total group instruction. Assignments are routinely differentiated to provide for individual needs with respect to objectives, time allocations, and mode of learning. Materials assigned for use are varied. Individual students are provided freedom to pursue learning tasks differently, to progress more rapidly, and to go beyond basic requirements. Teachers and students are both tutors in formal one-to-one relationships.

5a. *Collects, organizes, and analyzes diagnostic data about individual students' current learning needs.*

5a (1)—Develops and administers tests and other evaluative procedures which are diagnostically scored to indicate what individuals *have* learned and what they *need* to learn.

5a (2)—Observes students' learning styles, recording individuals' rates of learning and use of time and their preferred study skills, sensory modes, and working relationships.

5a (3)—Maintains cumulative profiles of individuals' learning behaviors, highlighting those needs which *can* and *will* be met through the school program.

5b. *Plans an instructional program which meets the unique needs and learning styles of individual students.*

5b (1)—Uses diagnostic information about individuals' current needs in lesson planning.

5b (2)—Departs from standard curricular expectations to respond more directly to urgent individual needs.

5b (3)—Differentiates experiences by providing objectives, varied assignments, materials, activities, working relationships, time on task, and teacher assistance tailored to the needs of individual students.

5b (4)—Organizes materials and resources for student use so that individual learners have what they need when they need it.

Performance Area	Behaviors and Indicators

5c. *Directs instruction in response to the unique needs and learning styles of individual students.*

    5c (1)—Guides the work of student groups whose membership, tasks, location, and size change periodically in response to individual learning needs.

    5c (2)—Provides for and processes feedback to and from individuals about class activities and homework assignments, adjusting instructional modes, materials, or time on task if needed.

    5c (3)—Encourages individual initiative in pursuing learning, reinforcing such actions as seeking help from other students, bringing materials from home, moving about the room to get resources, going to the library independently, or suggesting alternatives.

5d. *Responds to individuals in ways that assist them in accomplishing their objectives.*

    5d (1)—Encourages and guides students in finding their own "best" way of learning.

    5d (2)—Makes self available to individual students and groups, conferring during independent study time, arranging for peer tutoring, reteaching, checking to see work is done correctly, or clarifying.

    5d (3)—Recognizes and responds positively to efforts and approximate performance of learning objectives.

    5d (4)—Grades papers and projects with diagnostic notations clearly indicating strengths and needs of students.

    5d (5)—Leads students in checking and correcting their own work diagnostically.

    5d (6)—Discusses graded work with individual students and small groups, assuring their recognition of ways of improving performance or overcoming difficulties.

    5d (7)—Shares diagnostic profile data with individual students, helping them to set specific, realistic learning objectives.

6. MULTI-MEDIA INTEGRATIVE
The teacher provides, through diverse media, for visualization, dramatization, demonstration, manipulation, reading, and listening.

6a. *Uses a variety of audio-visual and manipulative aids regularly as integral parts of lessons and assignments.*

    6a (1)—Utilizes print materials which are illustrated and colorful.

    6a (2)—Uses chalkboards, charts, bulletin boards, displays, photographs, posters, slides, and transparencies to portray content visually.

    6a (3)—Makes audio materials such as records and tapes a regular part of lessons.

    6a (4)—Incorporates audio-visual materials such as television, videotape, sound film, etc., regularly in lessons.

    6a (5)—Provides manipulative experiences through games, puzzles, clay, painting, drawing, construction, etc.

6b. *Involves students actively and regularly in such multi-sensory experiences as dramatizations, verbal interactions, games, drawings, and field studies.*

    6b (1)—Directs students in using role-plays or socio-dramas in connection with their assignments.

    6b (2)—Structures discussion groups to provide extended opportunities for students to verbalize and share knowledge with each other.

    6b (3)—Encourages students to illustrate learning in graphic or artistic forms.

    6b (4)—Utilizes games in ways which stimulate interest and participation without excessive competition.

    6b (5)—Provides for out-of-classroom learning in school and community settings.

    6b (6)—Arranges for laboratory experiments, special projects, or action research studies as a part of regular assignments.

6c. *Participates with students in multi-media, multi-sensory activities—demonstrating, helping, and extending learning.*

    6c (1)—Utilizes teacher-made as well as commercial and student-made materials in the classroom.

    6c (2)—Serves as participant as well as leader or observer in role-playing, discussion, or game activities.

    6c (3)—Demonstrates and helps students understand ways of using multi-media.

    6c (4)—Introduces multi-media carefully to assure student awareness of their purpose in the lessons.

    6c (5)—Follows use of multi-media/sensory activities with discussion, testing, or other planned activity.

PRINCIPAL'S BEHAVIOR PROFILE
INTERPRETIVE GUIDE

This Guide is intended for use in the development of a professional growth plan based on the Principal's Behavior Profile. For each of the eight areas included in the Profile, the Guide defines behaviors which have been shown in this research project to be more representative of highly effective principals than of ineffective principals. The lists of behaviors should not be considered comprehensive, but rather should be used as examples.

Community Services and Relations

> Reports instructional problems and achievements to the school constituency. Generates support among staff for school-community programs. Gathers public opinion data from the school constituency. Explains policies and procedures for parents of new students. Uses parents and other citizens as resource persons. Establishes communication with the school constituency for the purpose of assessing needs and setting broad instructional goals.

Evaluation, Planning, Development of Curriculum, and Instruction

> Analyzes information and issues before decisions are made about curriculum or instruction. Influences the direction of planning among both colleagues and outside groups. Involves teachers as collaborators in formative teacher evaluation. Involves teachers in the evaluation of programs. Establishes a plan for continuous evaluation of curriculum and

Source: Castleberry, Judy M. 1983. "Development of a Forced-Choice Principal's Behavior Rating Scale." Unpublished doctoral dissertation. Austin, TX: The University of Texas at Austin.

instruction. Provides for both short-range and long-range curriculum planning.

Financial Management

Plans in advance to prevent emergency buying of supplies. Forecasts multi-year needs of the school. Demonstrates familiarity with the projected budgetary needs of the school, including salary, operation, and maintenance costs. Buys wholesale when an appreciable savings is possible. Analyzes costs of alternatives for achieving program objectives. Analyzes school costs by student, by grade by total enrollment, by number graduating, and by number failing or dropping out.

Personnel Administration

Behaves in such a way as to build and maintain high morale of staff members. Communicates to staff personnel in a straight-forward manner without hidden meanings. Is impartial and objective in dealings with staff. Follows through on commitments to teachers and other personnel. Shares ideas and feelings with teachers and encourages them to do the same. Assigns non-teaching duties with fairness and good judgment.

Personnel Improvement

Leads faculty meetings and committee sessions in productive discussions. Stimulates teachers to keep abreast of current educational developments by setting an example of this practice. Arranges time for staff members to share new ideas, methods, and information. Is easily approachable by teachers for assistance in dealing with professional problems. Structures the role of the principal and the demands on time so that it is possible to pursue prioritized professional objectives as a principal. Plans for his/her own inservice training with clearly established

goals.

Pupil Personnel Administration

Provides leadership for staff efforts designed to improve counseling of students in

the school. Analyzes, assesses, and describes the value orientations of students

within the school. Establishes adequate control of the student body. Judges and

weighs each problem after hearing every side of the controversy. Develops

relationships of mutual understanding with students by demonstrating interest in

their welfare. Helps students develop positive self-concept.

Research and Development; Innovation and Change

Builds trust in various constituencies, increasing the validity of information

collected. Concentrates on changes needed to reach priority goals. Actively seeks

ideas to improve the school. Assumes initiative in bringing about change.

Provides the staff with information necessary to stimulate interest in change. Joins

in the effort of those pushing for appropriate change.

School Plant Management

Maintains an office area which is attractive and which projects a friendly

atmosphere. Plans the school's educational program to get maximum benefits from

the available physical facilities. Inventories the changing needs for equipment and

facilities to accomplish instructional goals. Encourages student responsibility for

the appearance of the school. Participates in the redesigning of instructional

facilities. Appraises the enrollment implication of population shifts in the

attendance area.

PRINCIPAL'S BEHAVIOR PROFILE

Relative Strength

Category of Responsibility		1	2	3	4	5	6
Community Services & Relations	T						
	P						
	S						
Evaluation, Planning, Curriculum & Instruction	T						
	P						
	S						
Financial Management	T						
	P						
	S						
Personnel Administration	T						
	P						
	S						
Personnel Improvement	T						
	P						
	S						
Pupil Personnel Administration	T						
	P						
	S						
Research & Development	T						
	P						
	S						
School Plant Management	T						
	P						
	S						

T–Mean of teacher ratings
P–Principal's self rating
S–Supervisor's rating

ABBREVIATED LISTING OF TASKS AND SUB-TASKS BY AREA

Task Area: INSTRUCTIONAL PLANNING

Task 2.1.1 Utilizes federal & state curriculum mandates in local planning
   Sub-Task 2.1.1.1: Identifies state & federal curriculum mandates
   Sub-Task 2.1.1.2: Develops strategies by relating them to state & federal agency actions
Task 2.1.2 Defines local instructional priorities by relating to state & federal curriculum trends
   Sub-Task 2.1.2.1: Analyzes state & federal trends as related to local priorities
   Sub-Task 2.1.2.2: Conducts district wide needs assessment
   Sub-Task 2.1.2.3: Develops strategies for adopting or rejecting trends
Task 2.1.3 Ensures that goals & objectives that satisfy local needs of the district are established
   Sub-Task 2.1.3.1: Implements a process for restructuring district goals & objectives
   Sub-Task 2.1.3.2: Directs the development of curriculum guides & plans
Task 2.1.4 Supervises & updates goals & objectives
   Sub-Task 2.1.4.1: Directs the use of district goals & objectives for instructional planning
   Sub-Task 2.1.4.2: Restructures goals & objectives
Task 2.1.5 Promotes the development of a sound educational philosophy
   Sub-Task 2.1.5.1: Implements a process for developing & reviewing district's philosophy
   Sub-Task 2.1.5.2: Uses the district's educational philosophy
Task 2.1.6 Provides for theory & research-based curriculum planning, development & Design
   Sub-Task 2.1.6.1: Develops a rationale for restructuring instructional programs
   Sub-Task 2.1.6.2: Develops a planning process for curriculum design & development
   Sub-Task 2.1.6.3: Prioritizes program development that offers diversity for all students
Task 2.1.7 Develops strategies for implementing new or revised curricula
   Sub-Task 2.1.7.1: Directs procedures for conducting curricula appraisal & development
   Sub-Task 2.1.7.2: Plans the use of change models in implementing curriculum change
   Sub-Task 2.1.7.3: Directs the implementation of instructional & curriculum development
Task 2.1.8 Monitors new and/or existing programs
   Sub-Task 2.1.8.1: Utilizes diagnostic & formative evaluation data in monitoring programs
   Sub-Task 2.1.8.2: Revises plans for improving instructional programs
Task 2.1.9 Ensures that all students' curricular needs are met
   Sub-Task 2.1.9.1: Observes & enforces laws & mandates relating to special populations
   Sub-Task 2.1.9.2: Provides for differentiated assessment of students in special populations
   Sub-Task 2.1.9.3: Directs the implementation of program to meet special populations' needs
   Sub-Task 2.1.9.4: Evaluates programs for special populations
Task 2.1.10 Implements drop-out prevention programs
   Sub-Task 2.1.10.1: Directs regular reviews of drop-out status and causes
   Sub-Task 2.1.10.2: Develops monitoring process to help students in trouble
   Sub-Task 2.1.10.3: Develops plans for reducing drop-out rate
   Sub-Task 2.1.10.4: Develops special programs for helping students at risk of dropping out

Task Area: STAFFING FOR INSTRUCTION

Task 2.2.1 Maintains adequate staffing levels
   Sub-Task 2.2.1.1: Monitors to maintain staff adequacy
   Sub-Task 2.2.1.2: Assesses needs for staffing changes
Task 2.2.2 Oversees recruitment procedures
   Sub-Task 2.2.2.1: Plans for systematic recruitment
   Sub-Task 2.2.2.2: Directs or coordinates recruitment efforts
Task 2.2.3 Provides for a screening process for most qualified candidates
   Sub-Task 2.2.3.1: Analyzes job descriptions
   Sub-Task 2.2.3.2: Assembles preliminary data
   Sub-Task 2.2.3.3: Identifies the most promising candidates
Task 2.2.4 Provides a process for selecting the most qualified candidates

Sub-Task 2.2.4.1: Organizes selection process
Sub-Task 2.2.4.2: Trains & guides selection personnel
Sub-Task 2.2.4.3: Directs in-depth data gathering
Sub-Task 2.2.4.4: Analyzes selection data
Sub-Task 2.2.4.5: Makes recommendation
Task 2.2.5 Provides staff orientation & induction for new staff
Sub-Task 2.2.5.1: Provides new personnel with orientation
Sub-Task 2.2.5.2: Provides induction programs
Task 2.2.6 Implements a personnel-reassigning placement system
Sub-Task 2.2.6.1: Plans for assignment, reassignment & balancing personnel
Sub-Task 2.2.6.2: Coordinates assignment & reassignment to meet high priority needs
Sub-Task 2.2.6.3: Balances staff to assure appropriate competencies needed
Task 2.2.7 Directs personnel operation to improve work force
Sub-Task 2.2.7.1: Oversees policy administration
Sub-Task 2.2.7.2: Provides an adequate wage & benefit schedule
Sub-Task 2.2.7.3: Directs staff retention activities
Sub-Task 2.2.7.4: Directs reduction in force
Sub-Task 2.2.7.5: Oversees minority staffing

Task Area: ORGANIZING FOR INSTRUCTION
Task 2.3.1 Understands instructional design
Sub-Task 2.3.1.1: Analyzes existing organizational structures for their instructional implications
Sub-Task 2.3.1.2: Identifies strengths and weaknesses in organizational structures
Task 2.3.2 Prioritizes instructional goals & objectives
Sub-Task 2.3.2.1: Proposes priority needs for changes in existing organizational structures
Sub-Task 2.3.2.2: Proposes organizational change anticipated by new programs or situations
Sub-Task 2.3.2.3: Criticizes proposed changes that can be expected to produce undesirable consequences
Task 2.3.3 Adopts efficient methods to facilitate delivery of curriculum
Sub-Task 2.3.3.1: Organizes decision-making groups for implementing delivery system changes
Sub-Task 2.3.3.2: Monitors implementation of delivery system changes to reinforce best efforts
Sub-Task 2.3.3.3: Stimulates consideration of innovative teaching strategies accommodated by changes
Task 2.3.4 Develops instructional resource management system
Sub-Task 2.3.4.1: Stimulates consideration of innovative teaching strategies accommodated by changes
Sub-Task 2.3.4.2: Organizes for the selection of new instructional materials
Sub-Task 2.3.4.3: Provides for systematic production of instructional media
Sub-Task 2.3.4.4: Organizes for efficient delivery of teaching and learning resources
Task 2.3.5 Develops goals & objectives guiding instructional philosophy
Sub-Task 2.3.5.1: Develops future projections for long-range organizational changes
Sub-Task 2.3.5.2: Organizes for systematic review & prioritization of long-range organizational futures
Sub-Task 2.3.5.3: Develops time lines & action proposals for selected long-range priorities
Task 2.3.6 Monitors instructional evaluation program
Sub-Task 2.3.6.1: Structures instructional program monitoring, focusing on structural & input factors
Sub-Task 2.3.6.2: Coordinates program monitoring at school, program and district levels
Sub-Task 2.3.6.3: Interfaces program monitoring with formal formative and summative evaluations
Task 2.3.7 Monitors student achievement
Sub-Task 2.3.7.1: Arranges for periodic reviews of achievement, drop-out rates, and other data
Sub-Task 2.3.7.2: Organizes feedback to teachers, principals, and supervisors, on student performance
Task 2.3.8 Maintains a system for instructional change
Sub-Task 2.3.8.1: Develops a need sensing/environmental scanning process to ensure need for changes
Sub-Task 2.3.8.2: Organizes for the systematic use of public opinion and suggestions for action
Sub-Task 2.3.8.3: Directs formal strategic planning processes when major changes are required
Sub-Task 2.3.8.4: Stimulates interest in, enthusiasm for, and creativity in approaching change process

Task 2.3.9 Maintains a system for instructional improvement
    Sub-Task 2.3.9.1: Coordinates the assimilation of new programs into the existing operations
    Sub-Task 2.3.9.2: Initiates the remodeling of instructional facilities for new & improved programs
    Sub-Task 2.3.9.3: Arranges for the systematic use of special personnel for supporting services

    Sub-Task 2.3.9.4: Organizes for parental and citizen involvement in the instructional program
Task 2.3.10 Ensures a wide range of learning styles
    Sub-Task 2.3.10.1: Organizes reviews of policy, & other practices restricting instructional diversity
    Sub-Task 2.3.10.2: Proposes organizational changes that offer more flexibility and variety
Task 2.3.11 Stipulates that students are appropriately grouped
    Sub-Task 2.3.11.1: Monitors existing & changing grouping practices to avoid rigid, segregating effects
    Sub-Task 2.3.11.2: Critiques policies & non-instructional operations for potential & negative effects
    Sub-Task 2.3.11.3: Promotes increasing sensitivity to the negative effects of homogeneity, etc.

Task Area: HUMAN RESOURCE DEVELOPMENT
Task 2.4.1 Exhibits a positive attitude towards staff & self development
    Sub-Task 2.4.1.1: Develops a district wide staff development program
    Sub-Task 2.4.1.2: Promotes & supports systematic budgeting
    Sub-Task 2.4.1.3: Models support for the staff development efforts
    Sub-Task 2.4.1.4: Creates a warm supportive, non-threatening climate of trust
Task 2.4.2 Keeps staff development practices & procedures current with trends
    Sub-Task 2.4.2.1: Reads current research & examines exemplary programs
    Sub-Task 2.4.2.2: Makes discriminating decisions regarding in-service programs
    Sub-Task 2.4.2.3: Provides for effective communication regarding trends
    Sub-Task 2.4.2.4: Allocates district resources for up-dating program development
    Sub-Task 2.4.2.5: Influences & interprets governmental actions relating to ISE
Task 2.4.3 Provides a systematic program of diagnostic evaluation
    Sub-Task 2.4.3.1: Recommends allocation of funds for instructional personnel evaluation
    Sub-Task 2.4.3.2: Gathers data for planning & implementing a diagnostic evaluation system
    Sub-Task 2.4.3.3: Establishes procedures for developing a diagnostic evaluation system
    Sub-Task 2.4.3.4: Provides training for personnel involved in the evaluative process
    Sub-Task 2.4.3.5: Implements a systematic program for instructional personnel evaluation
    Sub-Task 2.4.3.6: Employs a variety of information gathering techniques to collect data
    Sub-Task 2.4.3.7: Acts as role model for supervisory personnel
Task 2.4.4 Designs & administers staff development programs
    Sub-Task 2.4.4.1: Develops a needs assessment program
    Sub-Task 2.4.4.2: Directs the design of the staff development program
    Sub-Task 2.4.4.3: Administers the staff development program
Task 2.4.5 Ensures personnel professional growth opportunities
    Sub-Task 2.4.5.1: Reviews and/or develops staff development policies
    Sub-Task 2.4.5.2: Develops guidelines regarding participation of all personnel
    Sub-Task 2.4.5.3: Reviews budget allocation and cost estimates
    Sub-Task 2.4.5.4: Develops guidelines of professional growth for human resources personnel
Task 2.4.6 Formulates an evaluation process to determine in-service needs
    Sub-Task 2.4.6.1: Provides organizational support for summative evaluation
    Sub-Task 2.4.6.2: Analyzes staff development program evaluations
    Sub-Task 2.4.6.3: Disseminates evaluation findings systematically
Task 2.4.7 Uses evaluation data to redesign staff development
    Sub-Task 2.4.7.1: Identifies areas not met by staff development program
    Sub-Task 2.4.7.2: Redefines program goals for needed revisions on annual basis
Task 2.4.8 Coordinates staff development programs with program & staff evaluations
    Sub-Task 2.4.8.1: Makes arrangements for follow-up program & staff evaluations
    Sub-Task 2.4.8.2: Facilitates classroom instruction improvement
    Sub-Task 2.4.8.3: Identifies problems teaching personnel face as they apply training
    Sub-Task 2.4.8.4: Establishes a system for staff evaluation

Task 2.4.9 Provides for developmental differences
    Sub-Task 2.4.9.1: Initiates a tri-level staff development program
    Sub-Task 2.4.9.2: Relates human resource development to the district training needs
    Sub-Task 2.4.9.3: Identifies various needs of different categories of teaching personnel
    Sub-Task 2.4.9.4: Oversees that development needs of mid-career & master teachers are met

Task Area: EVALUATING INSTRUCTION

Task 2.5.1 Structures & applies unified policy framework
    Sub-Task 2.5.1.1: Designs framework of policy
    Sub-Task 2.5.1.2: Programs for implementation of policy
    Sub-Task 2.5.1.3: Plans for rigorous implementation of designs
Task 2.5.2 Develops a formative personnel evaluation system
    Sub-Task 2.5.2.1: Develops evaluative criteria
    Sub-Task 2.5.2.2: Selects instruments, sources, & procedures
    Sub-Task 2.5.2.3: Conducts evaluation to reflect both strengths & needs for improvement
Task 2.5.3 Develops a summative personnel evaluation system
    Sub-Task 2.5.3.1: Develops evaluative criteria
    Sub-Task 2.5.3.2: Develops procedural guidelines
    Sub-Task 2.5.3.3: Selects instruments, sources, & procedures
    Sub-Task 2.5.3.4: Implements with rigor & fidelity
Task 2.5.4 Coordinates a system of evaluation of instructional programs
    Sub-Task 2.5.4.1: Develops a comprehensive plan
    Sub-Task 2.5.4.2: Provides for instruments, sources, & procedures
    Sub-Task 2.5.4.3: Coordinates gathering, analyzing, & using of data
    Sub-Task 2.5.4.4: Arranges for dissemination, review, & follow-up actions
    Sub-Task 2.5.4.5: Analyzes & interprets data
Task 2.5.5 Studies information from evaluation reports to make recommendations
    Sub-Task 2.5.5.1: Reports results to personnel & community
    Sub-Task 2.5.5.2: Initiates actions

Source: Harris Ben M. and Yping Wan, eds. 1991. *Performance Criteria for School Executives' Instructional Leadership.* Austin, TX: Executive Leadership Program, Department of Educational Administration, The University of Texas at Austin.

Self Appraisal Instrument

TEACHER BEHAVIOR PROFILE

INSTRUMENT *

Instructions:

1. Review the eighty (80) statements of teacher behavior
   listed on the following pages.
2. Read each SET of four behaviors. Mark with an X the
   two (2) behaviors which better describe your teaching.
   Mark only two out of each set of four, even though none
   or all of the choices may seem appropriate.
3. Indicate the degree to which you believe each of the
   eighty behaviors (80) are important for teachers in
   your type of assignment (grade level, subject field,etc.).
   Check on the graphic scales at the right-hand side of
   each behavior. Place your check (✔) on the scale to
   indicate the level of importance of each behavior
   as you see it.

   NOTE: Ignore the numbers in parentheses at the far right in
   the column designated Beh. Cat. These are to be used
   for later analysis.

_____

* Adapted from Delmer Pearson, " Development of a Forced-Choice
Teacher Behavior Rating Scale". Unpublished PhD. Dissertation.
The University of Texas At Austin, December 1980. p. 240-45

Teacher Behavior Profile Instrument

Item	Behaviors	Choices	Importance	Beh. Cat.
1	Speaks quietly and slowly	_____	low high	(1)
2	Challenges students with difficult material	_____		(6)
3	Uses lots of different teaching methods	_____		(2)
4	Talks with a pupil after school about an idea the pupil has had	_____		(5)
5	Uses student answers	_____		(5)
6	Presents thought-provoking ideas	_____		(7)
7	Uses behavioral objectives	_____		(1)
8	Keeps the classroom quiet	_____		(4)
9	Treats students much like sons and daughters	_____		(8)
10	Amplifies student answers	_____		(5)
11	Individualizes instruction	_____		(6)
12	Uses contests and games	_____		(2)
13	Requests opinions	_____		(7)
14	Is helpful around the building	_____		(3)
15	Uses contracts or performance agreements	_____		(6)
16	Is an excellent public speaker	_____		(1)

Appendix D continued

Item	Behaviors	Choices	Importance	Beh. Cat.
17	Gives a direction or a threat and carries through with it	_____		(4)
18	Is imaginative	_____		(3)
19	Waits long enough for a student to responds to a question	_____		(7)
20	Disciplines in a quiet, dignified, positive, and fair manner	_____		(8)
21	Enjoys funny remarks made by students	_____		(8)
22	Is enthusiastic in manner	_____		(3)
23	Helps children understand difficult things	_____		(1)
24	Refers all incidents involving serious misbehavior to the office as soon as they occur	_____		(4)
25	Asks high-level questions	_____		(7)
26	Utilizes resource persons from the community	_____		(2)
27	Integrates student ideas into the curriculum	_____		(5)
28	Cooperatively establishes instructional goals with each child	_____		(6)
29	Describes things simply	_____		(1)
30	Concentrates on children's right answers	_____		(5)
31	Gives everyone a chance to to express himself	_____		(6)
32	Is a strong adult children can trust and turn to	_____		(8)

Appendix D continued

Item	Behaviors	Choices	Importance	Beh. Cat.
33	Speaks in a clear voice	_____		(1)
34	Is willing to try	_____		(3)
35	Respects cultural backgrounds	_____		(8)
36	Is responsible	_____		(4)
37	Uses the students' interests and background as a point of jumping off in presenting a subject	_____		(5)
38	Uses games as learning activities	_____		(2)
39	Insists that students stay in one place and work	_____		(4)
40	Asks simple questions	_____		(7)
41	Makes certain that assignments and directions are understood	_____		(1)
42	Enforces rules consistently	_____		(4)
43	Identifies students with learning problems and makes appropriate referrals	_____		(6)
44	Defends a student from verbal or physical assault by another	_____		(8)
45	Expects students to be ready with answers to questions	_____		(7)
46	Uses the textbook only as a guide or resource	_____		(2)
47	Meets any unusual classroom situation competently	_____		(4)
48	Is involved in self-improvement activities	_____		(3)

Appendix D continued

Item	Behaviors	Choices	Importance	Beh. Cat.
49	Uses exams as learning experiences	_____	⊔⎸⎸⎸⎸⎸⎸⎸⎸⎸⎸⎸⎸⊔	(6)
50	Outlines lesson content for students	_____	⊔⎸⎸⎸⎸⎸⎸⎸⎸⎸⎸⎸⎸⊔	(1)
51	Has artistic ability	_____	⊔⎸⎸⎸⎸⎸⎸⎸⎸⎸⎸⎸⎸⊔	(2)
52	Solicits students' ideas	_____	⊔⎸⎸⎸⎸⎸⎸⎸⎸⎸⎸⎸⎸⊔	(5)
53	Varies the degree of guidance given to students	_____	⊔⎸⎸⎸⎸⎸⎸⎸⎸⎸⎸⎸⎸⊔	(2)
54	Gives feedback on student questions	_____	⊔⎸⎸⎸⎸⎸⎸⎸⎸⎸⎸⎸⎸⊔	(5)
55	Recognizes that children must be given opportunity to use what they learn	_____	⊔⎸⎸⎸⎸⎸⎸⎸⎸⎸⎸⎸⎸⊔	(6)
56	Requests facts	_____	⊔⎸⎸⎸⎸⎸⎸⎸⎸⎸⎸⎸⎸⊔	(7)
57	Takes advantage of the "teachable moment" that is not a part of the lesson plan	_____	⊔⎸⎸⎸⎸⎸⎸⎸⎸⎸⎸⎸⎸⊔	(2)
58	Communicates with students accurately	_____	⊔⎸⎸⎸⎸⎸⎸⎸⎸⎸⎸⎸⎸⊔	(1)
59	Reads for pleasure	_____	⊔⎸⎸⎸⎸⎸⎸⎸⎸⎸⎸⎸⎸⊔	(3)
60	Does not invade a pupil's "life space" unnecessarily	_____	⊔⎸⎸⎸⎸⎸⎸⎸⎸⎸⎸⎸⎸⊔	(8)
61	Asks varied questions	_____	⊔⎸⎸⎸⎸⎸⎸⎸⎸⎸⎸⎸⎸⊔	(7)
62	Gives meaningful assignments rather than "busy work"	_____	⊔⎸⎸⎸⎸⎸⎸⎸⎸⎸⎸⎸⎸⊔	(4)
63	Uses exams as evaluative devices	_____	⊔⎸⎸⎸⎸⎸⎸⎸⎸⎸⎸⎸⎸⊔	(6)
64	Is a person who possesses curiosity	_____	⊔⎸⎸⎸⎸⎸⎸⎸⎸⎸⎸⎸⎸⊔	(3)

Appendix D continued

Item	Behaviors	Choices	Importance	Beh. Cat.
65	Tends to experiment	_____	⊔⊔⊔⊔⊔⊔⊔⊔⊔⊔⊔⊔⊔	(2)
66	Does not overreact to pupil behavior	_____	⊔⊔⊔⊔⊔⊔⊔⊔⊔⊔⊔⊔⊔	(8)
67	Schedules all activities carefully	_____	⊔⊔⊔⊔⊔⊔⊔⊔⊔⊔⊔⊔⊔	(4)
68	Becomes involved with children in extracurricular activities without remuneration or compensatory time	_____	⊔⊔⊔⊔⊔⊔⊔⊔⊔⊔⊔⊔⊔	(3)
69	Keeps bulletin board displays current and attractive	_____	⊔⊔⊔⊔⊔⊔⊔⊔⊔⊔⊔⊔⊔	(3)
70	Pays attention to students when they are working independently	_____	⊔⊔⊔⊔⊔⊔⊔⊔⊔⊔⊔⊔⊔	(6)
71	Lets students express their own ideas	_____	⊔⊔⊔⊔⊔⊔⊔⊔⊔⊔⊔⊔⊔	(5)
72	Changes plans if a lesson is not going well	_____	⊔⊔⊔⊔⊔⊔⊔⊔⊔⊔⊔⊔⊔	(2)
73	Asks frequent questions	_____	⊔⊔⊔⊔⊔⊔⊔⊔⊔⊔⊔⊔⊔	(7)
74	Writes and speaks effectively	_____	⊔⊔⊔⊔⊔⊔⊔⊔⊔⊔⊔⊔⊔	(1)
75	Listens to what students are saying	_____	⊔⊔⊔⊔⊔⊔⊔⊔⊔⊔⊔⊔⊔	(8)
76	Has lessons well planned	_____	⊔⊔⊔⊔⊔⊔⊔⊔⊔⊔⊔⊔⊔	(4)
77	Is stimulating	_____	⊔⊔⊔⊔⊔⊔⊔⊔⊔⊔⊔⊔⊔	(3)
78	Does not equate failure with laziness	_____	⊔⊔⊔⊔⊔⊔⊔⊔⊔⊔⊔⊔⊔	(8)
79	Asks questions that make students think	_____	⊔⊔⊔⊔⊔⊔⊔⊔⊔⊔⊔⊔⊔	(7)
80	Uses ideas of students	_____	⊔⊔⊔⊔⊔⊔⊔⊔⊔⊔⊔⊔⊔	(5)

Pearson's Teacher Behavior Summary Profile*

Instructions: Tally your choices (X) from the TBP Instrument on the appropriate category scale, using Behavior Category numbers shown for each item chosen.

Tally each choice on the appropriate category scale in the scale segment corresponding to your importance designation as checked (✓), estimating the importance value.

When all chosen behaviors are tallied, multiply numbers of tallies by importance (1–4) and sum products for each category.

Enter the sum of products at the right side of the category scale to produce a fraction ($^{14}/_{10}$, $^{3}/_{10}$, $^{40}/_{10}$, etc.)

Finally, convert the fraction by dividing the denominator into the numerator, carrying it to a single decimal place.

Each category scaled score is entered in the box to the far left. These scores will range from a high of 4.0 to a low of zero.

Behavior Category	Category Scales	Fractions	Scaled Scores
1. Clarity	Low 1 2 3 4 High	/10	
2. Variability	Low 1 2 3 4 High	/10	
3. Enthusiasm	Low 1 2 3 4 High	/10	
4. Task-Oriented	Low 1 2 3 4 High	/10	
5. Indirectness	Low 1 2 3 4 High	/10	
6. Opportunity to learn	Low 1 2 3 4 High	/10	

Pearson's Teacher Behavior Summary Profile*

Behavior Category		Category Scales				Fractions	Scaled Scores
7. Questioning techniques	Low 1	2	3	4	High	/10	
8. Relationships to students	Low 1	2	3	4	High	/10	

*Interpretations:

Your scaled scores are a composite estimate of your capability for each category of teaching behavior, weighted for its importance in your opinion. The lowest score of zero (0) simply means that no behavior in this category was chosen to describe your teaching. The highest score of 4.0 means that all behaviors in this category were chosen by you as descriptive of your behavior, and they were also rated as important.

Scaled scores at the lower levels should be reviewed, behavior by behavior, to determine those not chosen and those chosen but given a low importance level.

More sophisticated analysis procedures are available using the scoring procedures recommended by H. Delmer Pearson (1980) in the dissertation previously cited.

Personnel Use Only	
☐ Stu. Tchg.	NTE ☐
☐ Place. File	Core ☐
☐ References	Spec ☐
☐ Transcripts	Cert ☐

APPLICATION FOR EMPLOYMENT

Applicant's Full Name _____
　　　　　　　　　　　　　　(Last)　　　　　　　　　(First)　　　　　　　　(M.I.)　　　　　　　(Maiden Name)

Other Name(s) _____
(Please provide any additional information relative to change of name, use of an assumed name, or nickname, necessary to enable a check on your work or school record.)

Present Mailing Address _____
　　　　　　　　　　　　　(Street)　　　　　　　(City)　　　　　　　(State)　　　　　　(Zip)

Permanent Mailing Address _____
　　　　　　　　　　　　　(Street)　　　　　　　(City)　　　　　　　(State)　　　　　　(Zip)

Telephone Numbers:

Present: (　　)　　　　　　　　Permanent: (　　)　　　　　　　　Work: (　　)

Social Security Number _____ (Note: Completion of number is optional. Failure to submit social security number on this form will not prohibit employment consideration. Social Security number may be required on other forms prior to employment.)

My signature below authorizes the school division to conduct a background investigation and authorizes release of information in connection with my application for employment. This investigation may include such information as criminal or civil convictions, driving records, previous employers and educational institutions, personal references, professional references, and other appropriate sources. I waive my right of access to any such information, and without limitation hereby release the school division and the reference source from any liability in connection with its release or use. This release includes the sources cited above and specific examples as follows: the local Sheriff, information from the Central Criminal Records Exchange of either data on all criminal convictions or certification that no data on criminal convictions are maintained, information from the Virginia or other State Department of Social Services Child Protective Services Unit and any Locality to which they may refer for release of information pertaining to any findings of child abuse or neglect investigations involving me.

Furthermore, I certify that I have made true, correct and complete answers and statements on this application in the knowledge that they may be relied upon in considering my application, and I understand that any omission, false answered statement made by me on this application, or any supplement to it will be sufficient grounds for failure to employ or for my discharge should I become employed with the school division.

Date _____ Signature of applicant _____

MARK THE APPROPRIATE BOXES:

☐ New Application

☐ Previous Application on File

☐ Former Employee of the
　School Division

Are you a U.S. citizen?

☐ Yes　　　☐ No

If not, are you eligible to work in the U.S.?

☐ Yes　　　☐ No

INDICATE POSITION(S) DESIRED FOR WHICH YOU ARE ENDORSED

☐ Teacher　　　　　　☐ Administrator

☐ Guidance　　　　　☐ Supervisor

☐ Library/Media　　　☐ Psychologist

☐ Other (Explain)　　☐ Visiting Teacher/Social Worker

_____　　_____

List grade level(s) and/or subject area(s) in order of preference:

_____

PERSONNEL USE ONLY

_____

_____

_____

THE SCHOOL BOARD IS AN EQUAL OPPORTUNITY EMPLOYER

I. EDUCATIONAL AND PROFESSIONAL TRAINING (List chronologically.)

Level of Education	Name of School or University	State	Field of Study	Type of Degree	Year of Graduation	Dates of Attendance From...To
High School						
College or University						

II. STUDENT TEACHING EXPERIENCE (List chronologically and include any internships.)

Name of School	School Division City/County	State	Grade Level and/or Subject	Dates	Personnel Use

III. TEACHING EXPERIENCE (List chronologically all teaching experience. DO NOT INCLUDE SUBSTITUTE TEACHING.)

Name of School	School Division City/County	State	Position Held Grades and/or Subjects Taught (Specify)	Dates Mo./Day/Yr. (From...To)	Total years	Full Time (✓)	Part Time (✓)	Personnel Use
				Total				

IV. WORK EXPERIENCE OTHER THAN TEACHING (List chronologically and attach a sheet if necessary.)

Employer	City/County	State	Kind of Work	Dates of Employment	Personnel Use

V. MILITARY EXPERIENCE

Branch of Service	Occupational Specialist (MOS)	Inclusive Dates	Type of Discharge

THE SCHOOL BOARD IS AN EQUAL OPPORTUNITY EMPLOYER

VI. CERTIFICATION

A. If you have been issued a Virginia certificate, **please submit a photocopy** . . . .   Copy enclosed? No ☐   Yes ☐

Type of Va. Certificate: Provisional ☐   Collegiate Professional ☐   PG Professional ☐   Pupil Personnel ☐   VIE ☐

Year of Expiration of Virginia Certificate _____   Endorsement(s) _____

_____

Have you applied for a Virginia certificate? No ☐   Yes ☐   When _____   Check if statement of eligibility enclosed ☐

B. If you have been issued a certificate in another state, **please submit a photocopy.**   Copy enclosed? . . . . . . No ☐   Yes ☐

State _____   Expiration Date _____   Certification/Endorsements _____

State _____   Expiration Date _____   Certification/Endorsements _____

C. Have you taken the National Teacher's Examination? **(If yes, please submit a copy of your scores.)**

Core Battery: No ☐   Yes ☐   _____   Copy Enclosed? No ☐   Yes ☐
                                 Month   Year   CS   GK   PK

Speciality Area: No ☐   Yes ☐   _____   Copy Enclosed? No ☐   Yes ☐
                                 Month   Year   Subject   Score

VII. GENERAL INFORMATION

Month, Day, and Year Available for employment _____   Are you under contract? No ☐   Yes ☐

If yes, where? _____   Present Position _____

If presently employed, why do you wish to change? _____
If under contract, what type: Annual/Probationary ☐   Other ☐ (explain) _____   Continuing/Tenure ☐
If under contract have you checked and can you be released if you are offered another position? . . . .   Yes ☐   No ☐
If not under contract now, have you ever held a continuing contract in Virginia? . . . .   No ☐   Yes ☐

If yes, cite school division(s) and date(s) _____
Referral Source: Advertisement/Posting ☐   Employee ☐   Friend ☐   Other (Explain) _____

Have you ever been refused tenure or a continuing contract? (If yes, explain on back.) . . . . .No ☐   Yes ☐

Have you ever been discharged or requested to resign from a position? (If yes, explain on back.) . . . . .No ☐   Yes ☐

Have you ever been convicted of a violation of law other than a minor traffic violation? (If yes, explain on back.) ...No ☐   Yes ☐

Have you ever had a certificate or license revoked or suspended (If yes, explain on back.) . . . . .No ☐   Yes ☐

Are any criminal charges or proceedings pending against you? (If yes, explain on back.) . . . . .No ☐   Yes ☐

Have you been convicted of any offense involving the sexual molestation, physical or sexual abuse,
or rape of a child? (If yes, explain on back.) . . . . .No ☐   Yes ☐

VIII. REFERENCES

It is **the applicant's responsibility** to have the following information provided the School Division in order to be considered for employment:

A. The names of at least three reference sources must be provided and must include current employer if employed, or last employer if not currently employed.

B. Unless included in Placement File, applicants with work experience must provide recommendations from principals and/or superintendents from all contracted educational work experiences within the past three years. If experience was not within the past three years, provide references from last contracted experience.

Applicants who are beginning teachers registered with a college placement office must include references from their student teaching supervisor(s) and co-operating teacher(s) in the placement file or by listing names below.

C. As indicated above, ☐ a Placement File is being sent, &/or ☐ references are listed below:

Name of Reference	Position/Relationship	Mailing Address	Phone Number
1.			
2.			
3.			

THE SCHOOL BOARD IS AN EQUAL OPPORTUNITY EMPLOYER

IX. EXTRACURRICULAR ACTIVITIES

Indicate the number of years experience in the activities listed below. **Circle activities you are willing to coach/sponsor:**

Extra Curricular Activities	High School Experience	College Experience	Contract Experience	Extra Curricular Activities	High School Experience	College Experience	Contract Experience
Football				IM Director			
Basketball				Athletic Director			
Baseball				Athletic Trainer			
Softball				Forensics			
Track				Debate			
Cross Country				Drama			
Wrestling				Yearbook			
Gymnastics				Newspaper			
Field Hockey				Literary Magazine			
Golf				Student Government			
Tennis				Honor Society			
Volleyball				Clubs			
Soccer				Cheerleaders			

X. OTHER INFORMATION

To avoid conflict of interest, list any local school board member or employee relative(s) in the school division and cite relationship

_____

Estimate your total absence from work or school for the last three years and explain the reason(s)_____

_____

Explain any physical or mental conditions which would adversely affect your ability to perform the duties of the position you

seek; or if there are none, so state _____

In your own handwriting, provide any additional information you desire that will afford an additional understanding of your qualifications. Your goals, objectives, philosophy, and other background factors are of special interest.

_____

_____

_____

_____

_____

_____

_____

_____

_____

_____

ADDITIONAL REMARKS AND/OR EXPLANATIONS FROM SECTION VII GENERAL INFORMATION

_____

_____

(attach sheet if needed)

The Personnel Evaluation Standards

OUTLINE ON STANDARDS OF THE JOINT COMMITTEE
ON STANDARDS FOR EDUCATIONAL EVALUATION (1988).

P   PROPRIETY STANDARDS

P1   Service Orientation

P2   Formal Evaluation Guidelines

P3   Conflict of Interest

P4   Access to Personnel Evaluation Reports

P5   Interactions with Evaluatees

U   UTILITY STANDARDS

U1   Constructive Orientation

U2   Defined Uses

U3   Evaluator Credibility

U4   Functional Reporting

U5   Follow-Up and Impact

F   FEASIBILITY STANDARDS

F1   Practical Procedures

F2   Political Viability

F3   Fiscal Viability

A   ACCURACY STANDARDS

A1   Defined Role

A2   Work Environment

A3   Documentation of Procedures

A4   Valid Measurement

A5   Reliable Measurement

A6   Systematic Data Control

A7   Bias Control

A8   Monitoring Evaluation Systems

Source: The Joint Committee On Standards for Educational Evaluation. 1988. The
        Personnel Evaluation Standards: How to Assess Systems for Evaluating Educators.
        Newbury Park, California: Sage Publications.

The full text for the Personnel Evaluation Standards including explanations, rationale and
guidelines related to each individual standard is found in the published document.

Inquiries related to the standards may be addressed to:

The Joint Committee on Standards for Educational Evaluation
The Evaluation Center
Western Michigan University
Kalamazoo, Michigan 49008-5178

APT DEMOGRAPHIC SHEET

Name _____ ID Number _____

Mailing Address _____
                          (street and number)   (city, state, zip code)

Telephone Number: Work _____ Home _____

School District

County _____

District _____

School _____

College or University

Institution _____

Classification of Observer:
(Circle the numbers of all that apply.)

1. College supervisor of student teachers
2. Cooperating teacher of student teachers
3. Principal or assistant principal
4. District administrator
5. Experienced teacher
6. Field coordinator
7. Trainer of field coordinators

Classification of Teacher to Be Observed:
(Circle only one number.)

1. Student teacher
2. Provisional contract teacher
3. Annual contract T&I teacher

Age: 1. under 25   2. 25-35   3. 36-50   4. over 50

Sex: 1. female   2. male

Race: 1. black   2. white   3. other

Experience (educational employment including this year): _____ years

Certification:

1. Specialization code(s) _____ _____ _____ _____

2. Teaching on permit

3. Not certified in SC

Source: Stulac, Josef F., et al. 1982. *Assessments of Performance in Teaching: Observation Instrument (APT).* Columbia, SC: South Carolina Educator Improvement Task Force.

Directions

It is important that all information requested on the Demographic Sheet be provided. Do not leave any blanks or omit any items unless so instructed by the person conducting the session.

1. Print your first name, middle initial, and last name on the first line.

2. Enter your social security number on the blank beside 'ID Number'. If you choose not to give your social security number, the nine-digit number that is chosen must be different from all others and must be remembered and used on all APT forms.

3. Print your permanent mailing address on the second line.

4. Enter your telephone numbers on the third line.

5. School District Employees: Print the name of the county, district, and school in which you are employed under 'School District'. Do not complete the section under 'College or University'.

6. College or University Employees: Complete the section under 'College or University' but do not complete the section under 'School District'.

7. Student Teachers: Print the name of the county, district, and school to which you have been assigned for student teaching under 'School District'. Also print the name of the college or university in which you are enrolled under 'College or University'.

8. Classification of Observer: Circle all of the numbers that apply.

9. Classification of Teacher to Be Observed: Circle only one number.

10. Age, Sex, and Race: Circle only one number in each category.

11. Experience: The present school year is to be included when determining the total years of educational employment. Student teachers should write 'zero years'.

12. Certification: Individuals who are certified should enter the appropriate code(s) for their area(s) of certification from the list provided. Teachers who have not yet received a certificate but have met all requirements and applied for a certificate should record the code(s) for the certificate they anticipate receiving. Persons who are employed on an out-of-field teaching permit should record their certification code(s) and circle 'Teaching on permit'. Student teachers should record the code(s) for the area(s) in which they are preparing to become certified and circle 'Not certified in SC'.

APT SCHEDULE SHEET

Teacher _____ ID Number _____

School _____ Room Number _____ Subject _____

District _____

Orientation Session Attended _____
Date

APT Instrument and Forms Received _____
Date

SCHEDULE (To be completed by the teacher prior to observations)

1st Observation _____ ___/___
Date   Times

Planning Sheet _____ _____
Date   Time

2nd Observation _____ ___/___
Date   Times

Planning Sheet _____ _____
Date   Time

3rd Observation _____ ___/___
Date   Times

Planning Sheet _____ _____
Date   Time

OBSERVERS (To be completed by the evaluator prior to observations)

The dates verified are acceptable.

1st Observer _____

2nd Observer _____

3rd Observer _____

_____
Evaluator's Signature

CONFIRMATION
(To be completed by the teacher following observations and conference)

1st Observation _____ ___/___   Observer _____
Date   Times

2nd Observation _____ ___/___   Observer _____
Date   Times

3rd Observation _____ ___/___   Observer _____
Date   Times

Conference _____   Evaluator _____
Date

I verify that all observers completed my assessments as scheduled.

_____   _____
Teacher's Signature   Date

Comments _____

_____

APT PLANNING SHEET

Teacher's Name _____ ID Number _____

School _____ Room Number _____ Date of observation _____

Observer's Name _____ Observation time begins _____ ends _____

Grade Level _____ Subject _____

Please write in complete sentences so that PD 4 i can be rated using this information.

Objectives for the lesson (What the students will learn)	Instructional procedures and materials for each objective (What will be done to achieve the objectives and the equipment or materials to be used) Briefly describe or attach any handouts. Underline or list materials needed.	Assessment of each objective (How student progress will be measured)

Student Records can be seen by observer: (where) _____ (when) _____

Attach additional sheets if necessary
and label sections.

APT OBSERVATION SHEET

Teacher ID No. _____   Grade Level _____   Subject _____

Observer ID No. _____   Date _____   Time _____
(Write 'self' if prepared as self-evaluation.)

Scores: PD 1: _____ PD 2: _____ PD 3: _____ PD 4: _____ PD 5: _____ Total: _____

Directions: Use the *Assessments of Performance in Teaching: Observation Instrument* (APT Instrument) to complete this sheet. After reading the Planning Sheet and examining records (for PD 1) or observing the teaching demonstration (for PD 2-5), write a brief statement of evidence or lack of evidence after each observation. Then circle the letter in the column on the right if the skill or behavior was demonstrated or place an X over the letter if evidence did not support the demonstration. All observations must be scored. Write the total number of observation statements demonstrated for each Performance Dimension (PD) in the blanks above.

Observation	Evidence	Demonstration

PD 1: PLANNING

Observation		Demonstration
a. outcomes stated		a.
b. objectives compatible		b.
c. procedures stated		c.
d. students involved		d.
e. materials stated		e.
f. differences planned		f.
g. objectives assessed		g.
h. progress recorded		h.

PD 2: INSTRUCTION

a. began promptly	a.
b. objectives addressed	b.
c. needs accommodated	c.
d. interest stimulated	d.
e. approaches varied	e.
f. size varied	f.
g. active opportunities	g.
h. application opportunities	h.
i. information obtained	i.
j. progress provided	j.
k. physical arrangement	k.

PD 3: MANAGEMENT

a. behavior established	a.
b. firm enforcement	b.
c. procedural confidence	c.
d. instruction continued	d.

PD 3: continued

e. disruptions addressed	e.
f. codes enforced	f.
g. inattentive involved	g.
h. special assistance	h.
i. strategies adjusted	i.
j. patient, poised	j.
k. fair, impartial	k.

PD 4: COMMUNICATION

a. instructional plan	a.
b. logical sequence	b.
c. understandable level	c.
d. explanations restated	d.
e. illustrations demonstrated	e.
f. knowledgeable authority	f.
g. information accurate	g.
h. legible writing	h.

PD 4: continued

i. written communication	i.
j. oral communication	j.
k. speech quality	k.

PD 5: ATTITUDE

a. courtesy modeled	a.
b. positive reinforcement	b.
c. expression encouraged	c.
d. learning personalized	d.
e. supportive corrections	e.
f. reasons given	f.
g. value communicated	g.
h. enthusiasm communicated	h.
i. open-mindedness	i.
j. humor acknowledged	j.

APT CONFERENCE SHEET

Teacher Observed _____ ID Number _____

District _____ School _____

Conference Date _____

	PD 1	PD 2	PD 3	PD 4	PD 5
Performance Dimension Standard:	18	26	28	29	21
Total Credit from Observers:	____	____	____	____	____
Performance Dimension Demonstrated:	yes no	yes no	yes no	yes no	yes no

Analysis of Performance Dimension 1:

Strengths   Weaknesses

	credit from three observations			credit from two observations			credit from one observation			no credit from three observations	
	observer	self		observer	self		observer	self		observer	self
a.			a.			a.			a.		
b.			b.			b.			b.		
c.			c.			c.			c.		
d.			d.			d.			d.		
e.			e.			e.			e.		
f.			f.			f.			f.		
g.			g.			g.			g.		
h.			h.			h.			h.		

Analysis of Performance Dimension 2:

Strengths   Weaknesses

	credit from three observations			credit from two observations			credit from one observation			no credit from three observations	
	observer	self		observer	self		observer	self		observer	self
a.			a.			a.			a.		
b.			b.			b.			b.		
c.			c.			c.			c.		
d.			d.			d.			d.		
e.			e.			e.			e.		
f.			f.			f.			f.		
g.			g.			g.			g.		
h.			h.			h.			h.		
i.			i.			i.			i.		
j.			j.			j.			j.		
k.			k.			k.			k.		

Analysis of Performance Dimension 3:

Strengths   Weaknesses

credit from three observations			credit from two observations			credit from one observation			no credit from three observations	
	observer	self		observer	self		observer	self		observer	self
a.			a.			a.			a.		
b.			b.			b.			b.		
c.			c.			c.			c.		
d.			d.			d.			d.		
e.			e.			e.			e.		
f.			f.			f.			f.		
g.			g.			g.			g.		
h.			h.			h.			h.		
i.			i.			i.			i.		
j.			j.			j.			j.		
k.			k.			k.			k.		

Analysis of Performance Dimension 4:

Strengths   Weaknesses

credit from three observations			credit from two observations			credit from one observation			no credit from three observations	
	observer	self		observer	self		observer	self		observer	self
a.			a.			a.			a.		
b.			b.			b.			b.		
c.			c.			c.			c.		
d.			d.			d.			d.		
e.			e.			e.			e.		
f.			f.			f.			f.		
g.			g.			g.			g.		
h.			h.			h.			h.		
i.			i.			i.			i.		
j.			j.			j.			j.		
k.			k.			k.			k.		

Analysis of Performance Dimension 5:

Strengths   Weaknesses

credit from three observations			credit from two observations			credit from one observation			no credit from three observations	
	observer	self		observer	self		observer	self		observer	self
a.			a.			a.			a.		
b.			b.			b.			b.		
c.			c.			c.			c.		
d.			d.			d.			d.		
e.			e.			e.			e.		
f.			f.			f.			f.		
g.			g.			g.			g.		
h.			h.			h.			h.		
i.			i.			i.			i.		
j.			j.			j.			j.		

Verification that the conference was held and that the results of the evaluation were received by the teacher:

Teacher _____   Evaluator _____
                     (signature)   (signature)

American Association of School Personnel Administrators: Standards for School Personnel Administration

1. The basic function of the board of education is policy-making and review of the total educational program of the school district.

2. The superintendent of the school district provides the professional leadership necessary for the continuous development of the personnel program to meet the objectives of the school district.

3. The personnel administrator has a clear understanding of the goals, objectives and processes of the school system and the role which the personnel administration function has in accomplishing those ends.

4. Decision-making is regarded as the search for the most effective operational alternatives of action that can be implemented. Decision-making is recognized as a most significant activity within the educational organization.

5. Written personnel policies furnish guidelines for administrative procedures relating to personnel matters.

6. The personnel department is that specific section of the administrative structure established to carry out the personnel activities of the school system.

7. Personnel operations are conducted in a manner that provides for effective and friendly employee relationships and contribute to individual motivation and morale.

8.   To enhance the team effort and to facilitate efficient work performance, the personnel administrator ensures the systematic dissemination of information to the staff and public while still protecting the privacy of individuals and identifiable groups.

9.   A well-developed system of personnel accounting and research helps predict staff needs and enables the administration to make sound projections for current and future employment needs.

10.   The recruitment process provides present as well as potential employees with information on available positions and provides them the opportunity to compete for vacancies.

11.   The application form requests information necessary to facilitate screening; contributes to sound decision-making on recommendations for appointment, and is in conformity with local, state and federal laws and regulations.

12.   Decisions involving staff selection are based upon a carefully planned program of investigation, screening, appointment and follow-up support.

13.   Placement, assignment, and transfer of personnel is a basic administrative responsibility through which attempts are made to meet the needs of the educational program, implement affirmative action plans, provide balanced staffing, and meet the desires of individual employees.

14.   Orientation of teachers is a continuing process based upon a planned program designed to acquaint the teacher with his/her responsibilities toward the student, school, and community, and to acquaint the teacher with the resources in the school system and the community.

15.   There is a commitment by the board of education and administration to a planned, comprehensive program dedicated to the continuing professional development of personnel.

16. Appraisal of teaching performance is a cooperative process designed primarily to improve the quality of teaching.

17. The personnel evaluation and supervision system, while directed toward helping employees improve the quality of their performance, provides information which enables evaluators to make objective and fair decisions concerning termination, retention, or discipline when the employee's performance or conduct is marginal or clearly unsatisfactory, and rewards excellent performance.

18. The administrator appraisal process is designed to yield information which will enable evaluators to make objective, fair decisions which relate to the improvement of administrative capabilities and/or retention/dismissal in cases of marginal performance.

19. In the interests of promoting high morale and leadership effectiveness, the personnel department will use its influence to assure that individuals on the professional staff are recognized for excellence and promoted on the basis of competency, performance, qualifications, fitness for the job, and probability of future growth and development regardless of age, sex, religion, national origin, ethnic heritage, marital status, or handicap.

20. Collective bargaining, as a personnel function, will conclude in an equitable agreement which preserves the board's responsibility to make policy and the administrator's right to manage the school district for the citizens and children and at the same time provide adequate wages, hours and working conditions for its employees.

21. A fringe benefits program that meets the particular needs of the staff should be established or negotiated within the constraints of local and state laws and school district resources.

22. Regulations or agreements covering the various types of leaves, with or without pay, are established of negotiated and are fairly administered by the personnel department.

23.   Compensation plans that place the school board in a favorable, competitive position and salary policies that encourage professional growth and personal improvement in service are essential elements of personnel administration.

24.   A difference in procedures is made between grievances and complaints. A grievance is defined as an alleged violation, misrepresentation or misapplication of any of the specific provisions of the negotiated agreement which may end in binding arbitration, while a complaint is described as an alleged violation, misrepresentation of misapplication of any rule, order, regulation or policy of the board outside the negotiated contract which should not be subject to binding arbitration.

25.   Job descriptions and classifications include the duties to be performed, the immediate supervisor, educational preparation required, and personal qualifications needed for the position.

26.   Regulations governing resignations should provide an orderly termination of service with a minimum of disruption to the school system and inconvenience to the employees.

27.   The school district has written and publicized policies for reduction of staff when needed.

Source: American Association of School Personnel Administrators. 1988. *Standards for School Personnel Administration*. 4th ed. Sacramento, CA: American Association of School Personnel Administrators.

The full text of the Standards for School Personnel Administration including the 217 statements of policies and practices is available from the American Association of School Personnel Administration.

Inquiries related to the standards may be addressed to:

American Association of School Personnel Administrators
P.O. Box 19549
Sacramento, California 95819-0549
(916) 448-4657

Statement of Ethics for Administrators*

An educational administrator's professional behavior must conform to an ethical code. The code must be idealistic and at the same time practical, so that it can apply reasonably to all educational administrators. The administrator acknowledges that the schools belong to the public they serve for the purpose of providing educational opportunities to all. However, the administrator assumes responsibility for providing professional leadership in the school and community. This responsibility requires the administrator to maintain standards of exemplary professional conduct. It must be recognized that the administrator's actions will be viewed and appraised by the community, professional associates, and students. To these ends, the administrator subscribes to the following statements of standards.

The educational administrator:

1. Makes the well-being of students the fundamental value in all decision making and actions.

2. Fulfills professional responsibilities with honesty and integrity.

3. Supports the principle of due process and protects the civil and human rights of all individuals.

4. Obeys local, state, and national laws and does not knowingly join or support organizations that advocate directly or indirectly, the overthrow of the government.

5. Implements the governing board of education's policies and administrative rules and regulations.

6. Pursues appropriate measures to correct those laws, policies, and regulations that are not consistent with sound educational goals.

7. Avoids using positions for personal gain through political, social, religious, economic, or other influence.

8. Accepts academic degrees or professional certification only from duly accredited institutions.

9. Maintains the standards and seeks to improve the effectiveness of the profession through research and continuing professional development.

10. Honors all contracts until fulfillment or release.

---

* Approved by the American Association of School Administrators, Executive Committee, May 1976.

Steps in Designing a Pay System

STEP	PURPOSE	HOW IT IS ACCOMPLISHED
STEP ONE *Analyse Job Requirements*	To understand the types and levels of knowledge, skill, effort, and responsibility required of different jobs - the universal factors that pay decisions are based on. Job requirements must be clearly understood and defined in order to evaluate the differences between jobs.	If more information about existing jobs is needed, it can be obtained from supervisors or employees. Questionnaires or structured interviews are often used if a large data gathering effort is necessary. If sufficient information about jobs is already available, then job analysis is not a necessary step
STEP TWO *Develop Job Descriptions*	In salary planning, job descriptions are used as reference tools for evaluating job requirements. Job requirements are the basis for pay classification decisions and must be defined by management in written job descriptions.	Job descriptions can be developed from the job questionnaires or interviews described in Step One or by adapting models from other sources. Whatever the source of information, job descriptions should be developed in a uniform style and format and must describe the critical elements of jobs. These critical elements include the type and level of qualifications needed (knowledge, skills, and abilities required to perform the work) and the type and level of key job responsibilities (those responsibilities that are essential to successful performance of the job).

SOURCE: Cindy Holdway (1985). Designing Employee Pay Systems. Austin, TX:
         Texas Association of School Boards. Used with permission.

STEP	PURPOSE	HOW IT IS ACCOMPLISHED
STEP THREE *Evaluate Jobs and Establish A Job Classification System*	A job classification system determines the grades or levels of pay for different jobs. A pay grade represents jobs that are of a similar value to the organization. This value is determined by the relative levels of knowledge, skill, effort, and responsibility required, as well as how much those jobs are worth in the competitive market. Each job is evaluated and compared to other jobs of a similar nature in order to assure an internally equitable pay system. Job classification simplifies salary administration by grouping different jobs that are similar in the level of work performed, thus eliminating the need to set individual pay rates for every job in the organization.	Job classification systems can be established through formal or informal job evaluation procedures and by salary surveys. Informal job evaluation can consist of nothing more than administrative judgments of job comparisons. Formal procedures are not necessary when there are only a few jobs with clear distinctions. Formal procedures would include a structured process to evaluate and classify jobs systematically. These procedures range from simple job-ranking techniques to more sophisticated techniques of evaluating jobs against individual factors of knowledge, skill, effort, and responsibility. Written job rating plans are used for this purpose. Salary surveys can sometimes be used to classify jobs without an internal job evaluation process. Classifying job by salary surveys alone may be useful in small districts where there are common jobs and survey data is available for all. In larger districts where there are many different and unique jobs, both an internal job evaluation process and salary surveys will probably be necessary.

STEP	PURPOSE	HOW IT IS ACCOMPLISHED
STEP FOUR *Use Salary Surveys To Price Jobs*	For a pay system to be equitable and effective in attracting and keeping good employees, salaries must be reasonably competitive with the outside job market for those employees. Salary surveys are used to determine what common types of jobs are worth in a competitive market.	First, the appropriate job market for each group of employees must be determined. Job markets are identified by what types of organizations and what geographic area the employees tend to work in. For non-professional jobs such as custodial and clerical, pay should be compared with the local community. For professional and administrative jobs, pay should be compared with other school districts of a similar size or geographic area. Salary surveys may be obtained from government agencies, professional associations, private survey firms or conducted by the district.
STEP FIVE *Design the Pay Structure*	Once jobs are classified and competitive pay levels are determined, pay structures must be designed for all jobs in the district. The pay structure includes the salary range for each job grade. The range established the minimum and maximum rates of pay for each job and controls the pay differences between employees. This structure is necessary to provide guidelines for salary administration, and to provide management control over equity, competitiveness, and affordability.. Setting salary ranges properly will keep the district from paying too much or too little for jobs and will maintain equitable pay relationships between employees.	Using the job classification system and salary survey data as guidelines, equitable and competitive salary ranges are determined for each group of jobs. The proper spread of the salary range (i.D., the difference between the maximum rate and the minimum rate) must be determined as well as the proper increase between salary ranges for different job grades.

STEP	PURPOSE	HOW IT IS ACCOMPLISHED
STEP SIX *Design the System for Individual Salary Advancement*	The salary ranges set the parameters of pay for each job. All preceding steps in the process of designing a pay system are based on jobs - not on employees. Once the overall structure of pay for jobs is determined, the proper method of salary advancement for employees must be planned. The step determines how and why employees will advance within the salary range.	The nature of the jobs and the goals of the district should determine the method of salary advancement. Different pay systems may be designed for different types of employees. The system for salary advancement may be based on performance, on length of service, or on a combination of both. It may be designed in fixed step increments or in a more flexible manner with salary increases planned each year.
STEP SEVEN *Plan the Implementation of the Pay System*	Once the pay system is designed, an implementation plan must be determined to place current employees in the new system. The implementation plan must be both equitable and affordable.	The new salary ranges for be must be compared to the current salaries of employees. Decisions must be made about the initial salary placement of each employee and how to deal with salaries that fall above or below the new pay range. The cost of implementing the new system must also be analyzed. If these costs are unaffordable, a gradual transition plan may be necessary to improve pay practices over time.
STEP EIGHT *Monitor and Adjust the Pay System Over Time*	Competitive salaries and the effects of inflation will change over time. In order to keep the pay system competitive and equitable, adjustments must be made to salary ranges periodically. The goal of monitoring and adjusting pay systems is to remain competitive and to maintain the purchasing power of employee salaries.	Changes is salary surveys and changes in the Consumer Price Index are both used as monitoring tools in salary administration. Inflation rates, as measured by the Consumer Price Index, are often used in planning annual salary increases for employees. When inflation is high, salary ranges can go out of date very quickly. Therefore, salary surveys are also necessary tools for monitoring and adjusting salary ranges to keep the system competitive. Adjusting salary ranges and granting employe raises within the range are two separate activities - no usually of the same amount.

REFERENCES

AACTE Task Force on Teacher Certification. 1984. "Emergency Teacher Certification," Washington, DC: American Association of Colleges for Teacher Education.

Aft, Lawrence S. 1985. *Wage and Salary Administration: A Guide to Job Evaluation.* Reston, VA: Reston Publishing.

Alexander, William. 1974. "The Middle School Emerges," in *Middle School in the Making.* Robert R. Leeper, ed. Washington, DC: Association for Supervision and Curriculum Development.

American Association of Colleges of Teacher Education. 1979. "In-Service Education: Opportunities and Options," *Journal of Teacher Education* 30(January-February): 27–32.

American Association of Colleges of Teacher Education. 1985. "Alternative Certification Policies in the States," in *Teacher Education Policy in the States: 50-State Survey of Legislative and Administrative Actions.* Washington, DC: American Association of Colleges for Teacher Education.

American Association of School Administrators. 1971. *Profiles of the Administrative Team.* Washington, DC: American Association of School Administrators.

American Association of School Administrators. 1986. *Effective Teaching: Observations From Research.* Arlington, VA: American Association of School Administrators.

American Association of School Administrators. 1987. *A Continuous Professional Development System for School Executives: A 5-Year Project Proposal.* Arlington, VA: Advisory Committee for the National Executive Development Center and the Consortium of Pilot Sites, American Association of School Administrators.

American Association of School Administrators. 1990. "Big Cities Suffer Rash of Vacancies," *Leadership News* 76(December 15):1, 3.

American Association of School Personnel Administrators. 1982. *Strike Manual.* Seven Hills, OH: Association of School Personnel Administrators

American Association of School Personnel Administration. 1987. *Handbook on Teacher Absenteeism.* Foster City, CA: American Association of School Personnel Administrators.

American Association of School Personnel Administrators 1988b. *Standards for School Personnel Administration.* 4th ed. Foster City, CA: American Association of School Personnel Administrators.

American Association of School Personnel Administrators. 1988a. *The American Association of School Personnel Administrators Celebrates 50 Years.* Foster City, CA: American Association of School Personnel Administrators.

Andrews, H. A. 1985. *Evaluation for Excellence.* Still Water, OK: New Forums.

Andrews, Janet R. 1987. "Where Doubts About the Personnel Role Begin," *Personnel Journal* 66(6): 85–89.

Anrig, G. R. 1986. "Teacher Education and Teacher Testing: The Rush to Mandate," *Phi Delta Kappan* 67(6): 447–51.

Arvey, Richard D., and James E. Campion. 1982. "The Employment Interview: A Summary and Review of Recent Research," *Personnel Psychology* 35(2): 281–322.

Asia and Pacific Prcgram of Education. 1985. *Teacher Development for Better Pupil Achievement: Report of the Technical/Working Group.* ChiangMai, Bangkok, Thailand: Innovation for Development Working Group, UNESCO Regional Office for Education in Asia and the Pacific.

Association for School, College and University Staffing. 1985. *Teacher Supply/Demand 1985.* Madison, WI: Association of School, College and University Staffing.

Association for Supervision and Curriculum Development. 1986. *Improving Teaching: 1986 ASCD Yearbook.* Karen K. Zumwalt, ed. Alexandria, VA: Association for Supervision and Curriculum Development.

Association for Supervision and Curriculum Development. 1990. "Resolution Correction: Professional Development." *ASCD Update* 32(August): 4.

Augenblick, John. 1985a. "The Current Status of School Financing Reform in the States," in *The Fiscal, Legal, and Political Aspects of State Reform of Elementary and Secondary Education.* Van Miller and Mary P. McKeown, eds. Cambridge, MA: Ballinger Publishing.

Augenblick, John, ed. 1985b. Public Schools: *Issues in Budgeting and Financial Management.* New Brunswick, NJ: Transaction.

Ayers, Jerry B. 1988. "Another Look at the Concurrent and Predictive Validity of the National Teacher Examinations," *Journal of Educational Research* 81(3): 133–37.

Bacharach, Samuel B. 1990. *Education Reform: Making Sense of It All.* Boston, MA: Allyn and Bacon.

Bacharach, Samuel B., and Sharon C. Conley. 1986. "Education Reform: A Managerial Agenda," *Phi Delta Kappan* 67(9): 641–45.

Bacharach, S. B., D. B. Lipsky, and J. B. Shedd. 1984. *Paying for Better Teaching: Merit Pay and Its Alternatives.* Ithaca, NY: Organizational Analysis and Practice, Inc.

Bailey, M. D. 1985. "The Relationship Among Supervisor Competencies, Job Expectations and Position Types." Unpublished doctoral dissertation. Austin, TX: The University of Texas at Austin.

Bales, R.F. 1950. *Interaction Process Analysis: A Method for the Study of Small Groups.* Reading, MA: Addison-Wesley.

Baltimore City Public Schools. 1980. *Procedures for Evaluation of Teaching Staff.* Baltimore, MD: Baltimore City Schools.

Barber, Larry W. 1985. *Improving Teacher Performance: Formative Evaluation.* Bloomington, IN: Phi Delta Kappa.

Barth, Roland S. 1990. *Improving Schools from Within: Teachers, Parents, and Principals Can Make the Difference.* San Francisco: Jossey-Bass.

Belcher, David W., and Thomas Atchison. 1987. *Compensation Administration.* 2d ed. Englewood Cliffs, NJ: Prentice-Hall.

Bellon, J. J. 1984. "Evaluator Competencies Needed for Evaluating Teachers and Teaching," *Thresholds in Education* 10: 22–24.

Benne, K.D. 1990. *The Task of Post-Contemporary Education: Essays in Behalf of a Human Future.* New York: Teachers College, Columbia University.

Bennett, William J. 1988. *American Education: Making It Work.* Washington, DC: U. S. Government Printing Office.

Berk, R. A. 1988. "Fifty Reasons Why Student Gain Does Not Mean Teacher Effectiveness," *Journal of Personnel Evaluation in Education* 1(4): 345–63.

Berliner, D. 1986. "In Pursuit of the Expert Pedagogue," *Educational Researcher* 15 (Jan.-Feb.): 5–13.

Biklen, Douglas, Dianne Ferguson, and Alison Ford, et al., eds. 1989. *Schooling and Disability.* 88th Yearbook of the National Society for the Study of Education, Part III. Chicago: University of Chicago.

Black, John A., and Fenwick W. English. 1986. *What They Don't Tell You in Schools of Education About School Administration*. Lancaster, PA: Techonomic Publishing.

Blake, Robert R., and Jane S. Mouton. 1964. *The Managerial Grid*. Houston, TX: Gulf Publishing.

Bloom, Benjamin S. 1981. *All Our Children Learning*. New York: McGraw-Hill.

Blumberg, Arthur. 1989. *School Administration as a Craft*. Boston: Allyn and Bacon.

Blumberg, Arthur, and William Greenfield. 1986. *The Effective Principal: Perspectives on School Leadership*. 2d ed. Boston: Allyn and Bacon.

Boles, Harold W. 1975. "An Administrative Team?" *Journal of Educational Administration* 13(October): 73–80.

Bolton, Dale L. 1974. "Evaluating School Processes and Products: A Responsibility of School Principals," in *Performance Objectives for School Principals*. Jack A. Culbertson, Curtis Hensen, and Ruel Morrison, eds. Berkeley, CA: McCutchan Publishing.

Boyd, William Lowe. 1987. "Public Education's Last Hurrah? Schizophrenia, Amnesia, and Ignorance in School Politics," *Education Evaluation and Policy Analysis*, 9N2(Summer): 85–100.

Boyd, William Lowe, and H. J. Walberg. 1990. *Choice in Education: Potential and Problems*. Berkeley, CA: McCutchan Publishing.

Brandt, Ron. 1988. "On the High School Curriculum: A Conversation with Ernest Boyer," *Educational Leadership* 46(1): 4–9.

Brandt, Ron. 1990. "Restructuring: What is it?" *Educational Leadership* 47(7): 11–16.

Brauchle, Paul E., Joyce R. Mclarty, and James Parker. 1989. "A Portfolio Approach to Using Student Performance Data to Measure Teacher Effectiveness," *Journal of Personnel Evaluation in Education* 3(1): 17–30.

Bredeson, Paul V. 1985. "The Teacher Screening and Selection Process: A Decision Making Model for School Administrators," *Journal of Research and Development in Education* 18(3): 8–15.

Bredeson, Paul V. 1988. "The Use of Application Blanks as Pre-Screening Devices in Employee Selection: An Assessment of Practices in Public Schools," *Planning & Changing* 19(2): 67–78.

Bredeson, Paul V., and William E. Caldwell. 1988. "Personnel Screening and Selection: An Analysis of Legal Compliance in Schools," *The High School Journal* 71(2): 81–87.

Bridges, Edwin M. 1984. *Managing the Incompetent Teacher*. Eugene, OR: ERIC Clearinghouse on Educational Management.

Bridges, Edwin M. 1986. *The Incompetent Teacher*. Philadelphia: The Palmer Press.

Brophy, J., and T. L. Good. 1986. "Teacher Behavior and Student Achievement," in *Third Handbook of Research on Teaching*. 3d ed. M. Wittrock, ed. New York: Macmillan, 328–75.

Browne, Beverly A., and Richard Rankin. 1986. "Predicting Employment in Education: The Relative Efficiency of National Teacher Examinations Scores and Student Teacher Ratings," *Educational and Psychological Measurement* 46(1): 191–97.

Bryant, Miles T. 1988. "Teacher Evaluation and the Diminishment of Creativity?" *Planning and Changing* 19(1): 36–40.

Buffie, Edward G. 1989. *The Principal and Leadership*. Bloomington, IN: Phi Delta Kappa Educational Foundation.

Bunker, R. M. 1975. "New Teachers Have Special Problems," *Instructor* 85(August): 29.

Bureau of Business Practice. 1987. *Drugs in the Workplace: Solutions for Business and Industry*. Waterford, CT: Prentice-Hall.

Bureau of National Affairs. 1983. *ASPA-BNA Survey No. 45: Employee Selection Procedures*. Washington, DC: Bureau of National Affairs.

Bureau of National Affairs. 1988. *National Recruiting and Selection Procedures.* Washington, DC: Bureau of National Affairs.

Burke, Peter J., and R. G. Heideman, eds. 1985. *Career-Long Teacher Education.* Springfield, IL: Charles C. Thomas.

Burnham, J. G. 1989. "The Career Development Experiences and Career Patterns of Superintendents in the U.S.," Unpublished doctoral dissertation. Austin, TX: The University of Texas at Austin.

Burrup, Percy E., Vern Brimley, Jr., and Rulon R. Garfield. 1988. *Financing Education in a Climate of Change.* 4th ed. Boston: Allyn and Bacon.

Burry, Judith A., and Dale G. Shaw. 1988. "Teachers and Administrators Differ in Assessing Teacher Effectiveness," *Journal of Personnel Evaluation in Education* 2(1): 33–41.

Buser, Robert L., and Vernon D. Pace. 1988. "Personnel Evaluation: Premises, Realities, and Constraints," *NASSP Bulletin* 72(512): 84–87.

Buttram, Joan L., and Brian L. Wilson. 1987. "Promising Trends in Teacher Evaluation," *Educational Leadership* 44(70): 5–6.

California State Board of Education. 1988. *History-Social Science Framework of California Public Schools, K–12th Grade.* Sacramento, CA: California State Department of Education.

Campion, Michael A., Elliott D. Pursell, and Barbara K. Brown. 1988. "Structured Interviewing: Raising the Psychometric Properties of the Employment Interview," *Personnel Psychology* 41(2): 25–42.

Carter, D. S. G., and Ben M. Harris. 1990. "Assessing Executive Leadership Behavior for Continuing Professional Development," *Journal of Personnel Evaluation in Education* (in press).

Carter, David, B. Harris, H. Estees, J. Loredo, and Y. Wan. 1991. "Assessment Center Approach to School-Executive Diagnosis and Development," *Journal of Personnel Evaluation in Education* (in press).

Cascio, Wayne F., Ralph A. Alexander, and Gerald V. Barrett. 1988. "Setting Cutoff Scores: Legal, Psychometric, and Professional Issues and Guidelines," *Personnel Psychology* 41(1): 1–23.

Castetter, William B. 1986. *The Personnel Function in Educational Administration.* 4th ed. New York: Macmillan.

Castleberry, Judy M. 1983. "Development of a Forced-Choice Principal's Behavior Rating Scale." Unpublished doctoral dissertation. Austin, TX: The University of Texas at Austin.

Cavender, S. K. 1986. "A Study of Design Characteristics for Transfer of Training in In-Service Education Programs in Selected Schools." Unpublished doctoral dissertation. Austin, TX: The University of Texas at Austin.

Chen, Vivien, and L. Granger. 1988. "Arts Smarts: First Rate Arts Education Programs," *The School Administrator.* 45(November 1988): 8–11.

Clandinin, D. J. 1986. *Classroom Practice: Teacher Images in Action.* Lewes: Falmer.

Clark, D. L. 1989. "Seize the Initiative," *Agenda* 1(2). (A newsletter of the National Policy Board for Educational Administration)

Clark, R. W. 1988. "Who Decides the Basic Policy Issue," in *Critical Issues in Curriculum.* 87th Yearbook of the National Society for the Study of Education, Part I. Laurel N. Tanner, eds. Chicago: The University of Chicago Press.

Clarke, C. M., and P. L. Patterson. 1990. *Teachers' Thought Processes.* Washington, DC: American Educational Research Association.

Claughton, Stelle, and Jean Eisel. 1987. *A Practical Guide for Successful Teacher Recruitment.* Foster City, CA: American Association of School Personnel Administrators and Association for School, College and University Staffing.

Cohen, David K. 1988. "Teaching Practice: Plus Que Ça Change," in *Contributing to Educational Change.* Phillip W. Jackson, ed. Berkeley, CA: McCutchan Publishing.

Cohen, M. 1983. "Ineffective Schools: Accumulating Research Findings," *American Education* 18(Jan–Feb): 13–16.

Cohen, M. 1988. *Restructuring the Education System: Agenda for the 1990's.* Washington, DC: National Governor's Association.

Coil, A. 1984. "Job Matching Brings Out the Best in Employees," *Personnel Journal* 63(1): 54–60.

Coleman, Charles J. 1979. *Personnel: An Open System Approach.* Cambridge, MA: Winthrop Publishers.

Colosi, Thomas R., and Arthur Berkeley. 1986. *Collective Bargaining: How It Works and Why.* New York: American Arbitration Association.

Colton, David L. 1985. "Vision," *National Forum* 65(2): 33–35.

Commonwealth Secretariat. 1982. *In-Service Education of Teachers in the Commonwealth.* London: The Secretariat, Marlborough House, Pall Mall.

Conley, Sharon C., and Samuel B. Bacharach. 1990a. "From School-Site Management to Participatory School-Site Management," *Phi Delta Kappan* 71 (7): 539–44.

Conley, Sharon C., and Samuel B. Bacharach. 1990b. "Performance Appraisal in Education: A Strategic Consideration," *Journal of Personnel Evaluation in Education* 3(4): 309–19.

Cook, William J. 1988. *Bill Cook's Strategic Planning for America's Schools.* Arlington, VA: American Association of School Administrators.

Cooke, Dennis H. 1939. *Administering the Teaching Personnel.* Chicago: Benj. H. Sanborn & Company.

Cornett, Lynn, ed. 1987. "More Pay for Teachers and Administrators Who Do More: Incentive Pay Programs, 1987," *Southern Regional Education Board Career Ladder Clearinghouse* (December).

Couley, David T. 1987. "Critical Attributes of Effective Evaluation Systems," *Educational Leadership* 44(7): 60–64.

Craigmile, James, and R. Dean Kerr. 1974. "Improved Preparation of Educational Administrators Through Competency Based Programming," *UCEA Review* 16(10).

Crawford, S., and S. T. Halliwell. 1986. *Assessment Centre Approach to Selection: An Annotated Bibliography—Research Report 86-1.* Willowdale, Ontario: Canadian Forces Personnel Applied Research Unit.

Crehan, E. Patricia, and Peter P. Grimmett. 1989. "Teachers' Perspectives on Dyadic Supervisory Interaction." Presented at the Annual Meeting of the American Educational Research Association. San Francisco, CA. March 1989.

Cuban, Larry. 1988a. "Constancy and Change in Schools (1980's to the Present)," in *Contributing to Educational Change: Perspectives on Research and Practice.* Phillip W. Jackson, ed. Berkeley, CA: McCutchan Publishing.

Cuban, Larry. 1988b. "A Fundamental Puzzle of Reform," *Phi Delta Kappan* 69 (5): 340–44.

Cuban, Larry. 1990. "Reforming Again, Again, and Again," *Educational Researcher* 19(1): 3–13.

Culbertson, J. A. 1988. "A Century's Quest for a Knowledge Base," in *Handbook of Research on Educational Administration.* Norman J. Boyar, ed. New York: Longman.

Culbertson, Jack A., Curtis Henson, and Ruel Morrison, eds. 1974. *Performance Objectives for School Principals.* Berkeley, CA: McCutchan Publishing.

Cunningham, L. L., and J. T. Henges. 1982. *The American Superintendency, 1982: A Summary Report.* Arlington, VA: American Association of School Administrators.

Darling-Hammond, Linda. 1986a. "A Proposal for Evaluation in the Teaching Profession," *The Elementary School Journal* 86(4): 531–51.

Darling-Hammond, Linda 1986b. "The Futures of Teaching," *Educational Leadership* 46(3): 4–10.

Data Research, Inc. 1989. *1989 Deskbook Encyclopedia of American School Law*. Rosemount, MN: Data Research, Inc.

Data Research, Inc. 1990. *1990 Deskbook Encyclopedia of American School Law*. Rosemount, MN: Data Research, Inc.

Day, David V., and Stanley B. Silverman. 1989. "Personality and Job Performance Evidence of Incremental Validity," *Personnel Psychology* 42(1) Spring: 25–36.

DeKalb County Schools. 1975. *Performance-Based Certification/Supportive Supervision Project*. Decatur, GA: DeKalb County Schools.

DeMont, Roger A., and Larry W. Hughes. 1984. "Assessment Center Technology: Implications for Administrator Training Programs," *Planning & Changing* 15(14): 219–25.

Denver Public Schools. 1971. *Teacher Performance Appraisal*. Denver, CO: Denver Public Schools, Division of Personnel Services.

DiGeronimo, Joe. 1985. "Boredom: The Hidden Factor Affecting Teacher Exodus," *Clearing House* 59 (December): 178.

Dillon-Peterson, Betty. 1986. "Trusting Teacher to Know What's Good for Them," in *Improving Teaching, 1986 ASCD Yearbook*. Karen K. Zumwalt, ed. Alexandria, VA: Association for Supervision and Curriculum Development.

Dodl, N.R. 1972. *Florida Catalog of Teacher Competencies*. Tallahassee, FL: Florida State University.

Doherty, Edward J., and Laval S. Wilson. 1990. "The Making of a Contract for Educational Reform," *Phi Delta Kappan* 71(10): 791–96.

Doud, J. L. 1989. *The K–8 Principal in 1988: A Ten-Year Study*. Alexandria, VA: National Association of Elementary School Principals.

Doyle, Denis P., and Terry W. Hartle. 1986. *Excellence in Education: The States Take Charge*. Washington, DC: American Enterprise Institute for Public Policy Research.

Doyle, R. P. 1989. "The Resistance of Conventional Wisdom to Research Evidence: The Case of Retention in Grade," *Phi Delta Kappan* 71(3): 215–20.

Dreher, George F., Ronald Ash, and Priscilla Hancock. 1988. "The Role of the Traditional Research Design in Underestimating the Validity of the Employment Interview," *Personnel Psychology* 41(Summer): 315–27.

Drucker, Peter F. 1985. "Getting Things Done: How to Make People Decisions," *Harvard Business Review* (July–August): 22–26.

Duckett, Willard R., ed. 1982. *Observation and the Evaluation of Teaching*. Bloomington, IN: Phi Delta Kappa.

Duckett, Willard R., ed. 1983. *Teacher Evaluation: Gathering and Using Data*. Bloomington, IN: Phi Delta Kappa.

Duckett, Williard R., ed. 1985. *The Competent Evaluator of Teaching*. Bloomington, IN: Phi Delta Kappa.

Duke, D. L., and R. J. Stiggins. 1986. *Teacher Evaluation: Five Keys to Growth*. A joint publication of American Association of School Administrators, National Association and National Education Association. Washington, DC: National Education Association.

Dunkin, M.J., and B. J. Biddle. 1974. *The Study of Teaching*. New York: Holt, Rinehart, and Winston.

Dunn, R. and Dunn K. 1977. "Seeing, Hearing, Moving, Touching Learning Packages." *Teacher* 94(9) May/June: 48–51.

Duttweiler, Patricia Cloud. "Improving Teacher Effectiveness: Incentive Programs, Evaluation, and Professional Growth," *Education* 109(2): 184–90.

Edelwich, Jerry, and Archie Brodsky. 1980. *Burn-Out: Stages of Disillusionment in the Helping Professions*. New York: Human Services Press.

Educational Research Service. 1988. *Teacher Evaluation: Practices and Procedures*. Arlington, VA: Educational Research Service.

Eisner, E. 1985. *The Educational Imagination*. 2d ed. New York: Macmillan.

Elam, Stanley. 1989. "The Second Gallup/Phi Delta Kappa Poll of Teachers' Attitudes Toward the Public Schools," *Phi Delta Kappan* 70(10): 785–98.

Elbaz, F. 1983. *Teacher Thinking: A Study of Practical Knowledge*. New York: Nichols.

Ellet, C. D. 1987. "Emerging Teacher Performance Assessment Practices: Implications for the Instruction Supervision Role of School Principals," in *Instructional Leadership: Concepts, Issues, and Controversies*. W. D. Greenfield, ed. Boston: Allyn and Bacon.

Elliott, Ronald D. 1990. "The Challenge of Managing Change," *Personnel Journal* 69(March 1990): 40–49.

Ellson, Douglas. 1976. "Tutoring," in *The Psychology of Teaching Methods*, 75th Yearbook of the National Society for the Study of Education, Part I. N. L. Gage, ed. Chicago: University of Chicago Press.

Ellson, Douglas G. 1986. *Improving the Productivity of Teaching: 125 Exhibits*. Bloomington, IN: Phi Delta Kappa.

Engel, Ross A. 1986. "Creating and Maintaining Staff Morale: The Personnel Administrator's Role in a Time of Ferment in Education," *Clearing House* 60(November): 104–106.

English, F.W., and D. K. Sharpes. 1972. *Strategies for Differentiated Staffing*. Berkeley, CA: McCutchan Publishing.

Feistritzer, C. Emily. 1984. *The Making of a Teacher: A Report on Teacher Education and Certification*. Washington, DC: National Center for Education Information.

Feistritzer, C. Emily. 1985. *The Condition of Teaching: A State by State Analysis, 1985*. Princeton, NJ: Carnegie Foundation for the Advancement of Teaching.

Feistritzer, C. Emily. 1986. *Profile of Teachers in the U.S.* Washington, DC: National Center for Education Information.

Feistritzer, C. Emily. 1988. *Profile of School Administrators in the U.S.* Washington, DC: National Center for Education Information.

Fensch, Edwin A., and R. E. Wilson. 1964. *The Superintendency Team: Organization and Administration of a School System's Central Staff*. Columbus, OH: Charles E. Merrill Books.

Fitzwater, Ivan W. 1977. *Finding Time for Success and Happiness*. San Antonio, TX: Mandel Publications.

Flanders, N.A. 1970. *Analyzing Teaching Behavior*. Reading, MA: Addison-Wesley.

Florida Department of Education, Office of Teacher Education, Certification and Staff Development. 1984. *Teacher Education Internship Project, Final Report*. Tallahassee, FL: Florida Department of Education.

Frase, Larry E., and Conley, Sharon. 1990. "From Teacher Compensation to School Improvement—A Re-Examination," *National Forum of Educational Administration and Supervision Journal* 7(1): 77–86.

Fullan, Michael. 1982. *The Meaning of Educational Change*. New York: Teachers College Press.

Gael, Sidney, ed. 1988. *The Job Analysis Handbook for Business, Industry, and Government*. Vol. II. New York: John Wiley & Sons.

Gage, N. L. 1984. "What Do We Know About Teaching Effectiveness?" *Phi Delta Kappan* 66(2): 87–93.

Gage, N. L. 1985. *Hard Gains in the Soft Sciences: The Case of Pedagogy*. Bloomington, IN: Phi Delta Kappa.

Gage, N.L., and D. C. Berliner. 1989. "Nurturing the Critical, Practical, and Artistic Thinking of Teachers," *Phi Delta Kappan* 71(3): 212.

Gagne, R.M. 1976. "The Learning Basis of Teaching Methods," in *The Psychology of Teaching Methods*. 75th Yearbook of the National Society for the Study of Education, Part I. N.L. Gage, ed. Chicago: University of Chicago Press.

Galbraith, John Kenneth (1971). *The New Industrial State,* 2nd Ed. Boston: Houghton Mifflin.

Gall, Meredith D., and J. P. Gall. 1976. "The Discussion Method," in *The Psychology of Teaching Methods,* 75th Yearbook of the National Society for the Study of Education, Part I. N. L. Gage, ed. Chicago: University of Chicago Press.

Garman, Noreen B. 1982. "The Clinical Approach to Supervision," in *Supervision of Teaching.* Thomas J. Sergiovanni, ed. Alexandria, VA: Association for Supervision and Curriculum Development.

Gatewood, Robert D., and Herbert Feild. 1990. *Human Resource Selection.* 2d ed. Chicago: The Dryden Press.

Gatewood, Robert, James Lahiff, and Richard Deter. 1989. "Effects of Training on Behaviors of the Selection Interview," *The Journal of Business Communication* 26(1): 17–31.

Gaugler, B. B., D. B. Rosenthal, G. C. Thornton, and C. Bentson. 1985. "Meta-Analysis of Assessment Center Validity." Presented at the Annual Meeting of the American Psychological Association, Los Angeles, CA.

Gephard, William J., Robert Ingle, and Mary Caroll, eds. 1981. *Planning for the Evaluation of Teaching.* Bloomington, IN: Phi Delta Kappa.

Gerald, Debra E. 1985. *Projections of Education Statistics to 1992–93.* Washington, DC: National Center for Education Statistics.

Ginsberg, Rick, and Barnett Berry. 1989. "Influencing Superiors' Perceptions: The Fudge Factor in Teacher and Principal Evaluation," *Urban Review* 21(1): 15–34.

Gips, Crystal J., and Paul V. Bredeson. 1984. "The Selection of Teachers and Principals: A Model for Faculty Participation in Personnel Selection Decisions in Public Schools." Presented at the Annual Meeting of the American Educational Research Association, New Orleans, LA, April 23–27, 1984. ED 251-974.

Glatthorn, A.A. 1990. *Supervisory Leadership: Introduction to Instructional Supervision.* Glenview, IL: Scott, Foresman.

Glickman, Carl (1985). *Developmental Supervision.* Boston, MA: Allyn and Bacon.

Glueck, William F. 1982. *Personnel: A Diagnostic Approach.* 3d ed. Plano, TX: Business Publications.

Goldstein, William. 1986. *Recruiting Superior Teachers: The Interview Process.* Bloomington, IN: Phi Delta Kappa Education Foundation.

Goodard, Robert W. 1989. "Is Your Appraisal System Headed for Court?" *Personnel Journal* 68(1): 114–18.

Goodison, Marlene. 1985. "Pros and Cons of Paper and Pencil Tests for Teacher Assessment." Presented at the Annual Assessment and Policy Conference of the Education Commission of the States, June 1986. Boulder, CO. ED 276-747.

Goodlad, John, Roger Soder, and Kenneth A. Sirotnik, eds. 1990. *Places Where Teachers Are Taught.* San Francisco: Jossey-Bass.

Goodlad, John I., and Robert Anderson. 1962. *The Nongraded Elementary Schools.* New York: Harcourt, Brace, and World.

Graham, Patricia Albjerg. 1987. "Black Teachers: A Drastically Scarce Resource," *Phi Delta Kappan* 68(8): 598–605.

Grant, Philip C. 1988. "Why Job Descriptions Don't Work," *Personnel Journal* 67(1): 53–59.

Greenfield, T. Barr. (1976). "Theory About What? Some More Thoughts About Theory in Educational Administration," UCEA Review 17: 4–8.

Grootings, Peter, et al., eds. 1989. *New Forms of Work Organization in Europe.* New Brunswick, NJ: Transaction.

Gustavsen, Bjorn, and L. Hethy. 1989. "New Forms of Work Organization: An Overview," in *New Forms of Work Organization in Europe.* Peter Grootings et al., eds. New Brunswick, NJ: Transaction.

Haberman, Martin. 1989. "More Minority Teachers," *Phi Delta Kappan* 70(10): 771–76.

Haertel, Edward. 1986. "The Valid Use of Student Performance Measures for Teacher Evaluation," *Educational Evaluation and Policy Analysis* 8(Spring 1986): 45–60.

Hager, J. L., and L. E. Scarr. 1983. "Effective Schools–Effective Principals: How to Develop Both," *Educational Leadership* 40(5) Feb: 38–40.

Halcrow, Allan. 1987. "Should Business Alone Pay for Social Progress?" *Personnel Journal* 66(9): 58–73.

Hall, G., and S. Hord. 1987. *Change in Schools: Facilitating the Process.* Albany, NY: SUNY Press.

Halpin, Andrew W. 1959. *The Leadership Behavior of School Superintendents.* 2d ed. Chicago: Midwest Administration Center, University of Chicago.

Hammer, Edson G., and Lawrence S. Kleiman. 1988. "Getting to Know You," *Personnel Administrator* 33(5): 86–92.

Harris, Ben M. (1963). *Supervisory Behavior in Education.* Englewood Cliffs, NJ: Prentice-Hall, Inc.

Harris, Ben M. (1975), *Supervisory Behavior In Education,* 2nd Ed. Englewood Cliffs, N.J.: Prentice Hall, Inc.

Harris, Ben M. 1980a. *Improving Staff Performance Through In-service Education.* Boston: Allyn and Bacon.

Harris, Ben M. 1980b. *The Developmental Supervisory Competency Assessment System.* Rev. ed. Round Rock, TX: Ben M. Harris Associates. ED 224-092.

Harris, Ben M. 1985. *Supervisory Behavior in Education.* 3d ed. Englewood Cliffs, NJ: Prentice-Hall.

Harris, Ben M. 1986. *Developmental Teacher Evaluation.* Boston: Allyn and Bacon.

Harris, Ben M. 1987. "Resolving Old Dilemmas in Diagnostic Evaluation," *Educational Leadership* 44(7): 46–49.

Harris, Ben M. 1989. *In-Service Education for Staff Development.* Boston: Allyn and Bacon.

Harris, Ben M., and S. Burks. 1982. *Good Teaching Practices.* Austin, TX: Texas Cooperative Committee on Teacher Evaluation, Texas Classroom Teachers Association.

Harris, Ben M., and Jane Hill. 1982. *Developmental Teacher Evaluation Kit (DeTEK).* Austin, TX: Southwest Educational Development Laboratory.

Harris, Ben M., and Yping Wan, eds. 1991. *Performance Criteria for School Executives' Instructional Leadership.* Austin, TX: Executive Leadership Program, Department of Educational Administration, The University of Texas at Austin.

Harris, Ben M., and L. Wilson. 1990. "Preliminary Validation of Self-Reports," *Journal of Personnel Evaluation in Education.* (in press)

Harris, W.V. 1989. *Ancient Literacy.* Cambridge, MA: Harvard University Press.

Hart, L.A. 1989. "The Horse is Dead," *Phi Delta Kappan* 71(3): 237–42.

Haskvitz, Alan. 1987. "Profile of Dropout Teachers," *Thrust* (September), 24.

Hawley, Willis D. 1986. "Toward a Comprehensive Strategy for Addressing the Teacher Shortage," *Phi Delta Kappan* 67(10): 712–18.

Hawley, Willis D. 1989. "Policy Board Proposals Ignore Real Problems," *The School Administrator* 46(November): 8–11, 14–15.

Hemphill, John. 1964. "Personal Variables and Administrative Styles," in *Behavioral Science and Educational Administration,* 36th Yearbook of the National Society for the Study of Education, Part II. Daniel E. Griffiths, ed. Chicago: University of Chicago Press.

Herriott, Robert E., and Neal Gross. 1979. *The Dynamics of Planned Educational Change: Case Studies and Analyses.* Berkeley, CA: McCutchan Publishing.

Hersey, P. W. 1987. *How NASSP Helps Identify Develop Superior Principals*. Reston, VA: National Association of Secondary School Principals.

Hersey, Paul, and K. H. Blanchard. 1977. *Management of Organizational Behavior*. 3d ed. Englewood Cliffs, NJ: Prentice-Hall.

Hersey, Paul W. 1977. "NASSPs Assessment Center: From Concept to Practice," *NASSP Bulletin* 61(Sept): 74–76.

Hersey, Paul W. 1982. "The NASSP Assessment Center Develops Leadership Talent," *Educational Leadership* 39(5): 370–71.

Hersey, Paul W. 1986. "Selecting and Developing Educational Leaders," *The School Administrator* 43(3): 16–17.

Hewton, Eric. 1988. *School Focused Staff Development: Guidelines for Policy Makers*. London: The Falmer Press.

Hickman, Craig R., and Michael Silva. 1984. *Creating Excellence: Managing Corporate Culture, Strategy, and Change in the New Age*. New York: New American Library.

Higginbotham, Richard L. 1988a "Reflections from a Past President," *AASPA Bulletin* (April).

Higginbotham, Richard L. 1988b. "Reflections from a Past President," *AASPA Bulletin* (June).

Hilston, Charles R., ed. 1970. *The Principalship: Job Specifications and Salary Consideration for the '70s*. Washington, DC: National Association of Secondary School Principals.

Hirsch, E.D., Jr. 1987. *Cultural Literacy: What Every American Needs to Know*. Boston, MA: Houghton Mifflin.

Hodgkinson, Harold L. 1985. *All One System: Demographics of Education, Kindergarten through Graduate School*. Washington, DC: Institute for Educational Leadership. ED 251-101.

Hodgkinson, Harold L. 1987. "Changing Society: Unchanging Curriculum," *National Forum* 72(3): 8–11.

Hodgkinson, Harold L. 1989. *The Same Client: The Demographics of Education and Service Delivery Systems*. Washington, DC: Institute for Educational Leadership. ED 312-757.

Holcomb, John. 1983. "When Faculty Zeal Sputters, Here's How to Rekindle Enthusiasm Among Teachers," *The American School Board Journal* 170(March): 38–39.

Holdway, Cindy. 1985. *Designing Employee Pay Systems*. Austin, TX: Personnel Services of Texas Association of School Boards and Texas Association of School Administrators.

Holley, William H., Early Higgins, and Sally Speights. 1988. "Resumes and Cover Letters: What Do HR Managers Really Want?" *Personnel* 65(12): 49–51.

Holmes Group. 1990. "Holmes Group Leaders Seek to Place PDS Concept on Policy Agendas," *The Holmes Group Forum* 5(Fall): 1–28.

Honig, Bill. 1989. "The State Level: The View from California," in *Education Reform: Making Sense of It All*. Samuel B. Bacharach, ed. Boston: Allyn and Bacon.

Hopkins, Patricia. 1989. "Against the Odds: Recruiting Minority Faculty and Staff," Presented at the Annual Meeting of the Southwest Educational Research Association, January 1989. ED 306-685.

Hord, Shirley 1990. "An Investigation of Instructional Leadership Perceptions Among District Level Executives." Unpublished doctoral dissertation. Austin, TX: The University of Texas at Austin.

Hostetler, Karl. 1989. "Who Says Professional Ethics Is Dead? A Response to Myron Lieberman," *Phi Delta Kappan* 70(9): 723–25.

Hough, Leaetta M. 1984. "Development and Evaluation of the 'Accomplishment Record' Method of Selecting and Promoting Professionals," *Journal of Applied Psychology* 69(1): 135–46.

Howard, V. 1982. *Artistry: The Work of Artists.* Indianapolis, IN: Hacket.

Howarth, Christine. 1984. *The Way People Work: Job Satisfaction and the Challenge of Change.* Oxford: Oxford University Press.

Hoyle, John R., Fenwick W. English, and Betty E. Steffy. 1990. *Skills for Successful School Leaders.* 2d ed. Arlington, VA: American Association of School Administrators.

Huling-Austin, Leslie, et al. 1989. *Assisting the Beginning Teacher.* Reston, VA: Association of Teacher Educators.

Human Synergistics. 1984. *Educational Administrator Profile.* Ann Arbor, MI: Human Synergistics.

Hunter, J. E., and R. F. Hunter 1984. "Validity and Utility of Alternative Predictors of Job Performance," *Psychological Bulletin* 96(1): 72–98.

Hyman, Ronald T. 1986. *School Administrators' Staff Development Activities Manual.* Englewood Cliffs, NJ: Prentice-Hall.

Institute for Educational Leadership, Inc. 1986. *School Boards: Strengthening Grass Roots Leadership.* Washington, DC: Institute for Educational Leadership, Inc.

Jackson, Phillip W., ed. 1988. *Contributing to Educational Change: Perspectives on Research and Practice.* Berkeley, CA: McCutchan Publishing.

Jacobson, Stephen L. 1988. "The Distribution of Salary Increments and Its Effect on Teacher Retention," *Educational Administration Quarterly* 24(2): 178–99.

Janz, T. 1982. "Initial Comparisons of Patterned Behavior Description Interviews Versus Unstructured Interviews," *Journal of Applied Psychology* 67(5): 577–80.

Janz, T., L. Hellervick, and D. G. Gilmore. 1986. *Behavior Description Interviewing.* Boston: Allyn and Bacon.

Jensen, Mary Cihak. 1986. "Employment and Success as a Teacher: An Analysis of the Path from Measures of Academic Ability and Teacher Education." Doctoral Dissertation, University of Oregon.

Jensen, Mary Cihak. 1987. *How to Recruit, Select, Induct and Retain the Very Best Teachers.* Eugene, OR: ERIC Clearinghouse on Educational Management.

Johnson, Susan Moore, and Niall C. Nelson. 1987. "Teaching Reform in an Active Voice," *Phi Delta Kappan* 68(8): 591–98.

Johnson, William L., and K. S. Snyder. 1990. "Instructional Leadership Training Needs of Administrators," *National Forum of Educational Administration and Supervision Journal* 6(3): 80–95.

Joint Committee on Standards for Educational Evaluation (1981). *Standards for Evaluation of Educational Programs, Projects, and Materials.* New York: McGraw-Hill.

Joint Committee on Standards for Educational Evaluation. 1988. *The Personnel Evaluation Standards: How to Assess Systems for Evaluating Educators.* Newbury Park, CA: Sage Publications.

Joyce, B.R., and M. Weil. 1980. *Models of Teaching.* 2d ed. Englewood Cliffs, NJ: Prentice-Hall.

Joyce, Bruce R., R. H. Hersh, and M. McKibbin. 1983. *The Structure of School Improvement.* New York: Longman.

Joyce, Bruce R., and Beverly Showers. 1983. *Power of Research on Training for Staff Development.* Alexandria, VA: Association for Supervision and Curriculum Development.

Kennedy, B. L. (1989). *Critical Incidents in the School Superintendency.* Unpublished doctoral dissertation, The University of Texas at Austin.

Kimbrough, Ralph B. 1985. *Ethics: A Course Study for Educational Leaders.* Arlington, VA: The American Association of School Administrators.

Kindred, Leslie W., Don Bagin, and Donald R. Gallagher. 1990. *The School and Community Relations.* 4th ed. Englewood Cliffs, NJ: Prentice-Hall.

Kirst, Michael W. 1986. "Sustaining the Momentum of State Education Reform: The Link Between Assessment and Financial Support," *Phi Delta Kappan* 67(5): 341–45.

Klausmeier, Herbert J. 1987. *Local School Self-Improvement: Processes and Directions.* Bloomington, IN: Phi Delta Kappa.

Kleine, Paul F. 1982. "Teaching Styles," in *Encyclopedia of Educational Research.* 5th ed. Harold E. Mitzel, ed. New York: The Free Press.

Klimoski, Richard D., and Mary Brickner. 1987. "Why Do Assessment Centers Work? The Puzzle of Assessment Center Validity," *Personnel Psychology* 40(2): 243–60.

Kochan, Thomas A., and J. B. Chatykoff. 1987. "Human Resource Management and Business Life Cycles: Some Preliminary Propositions," in *Human Resource Management in High Technology Firms.* Archie Kleingartner and Carolyn S. Anderson, eds. Lexington, MA: Lexington Books.

Krupp, Judy-Arin. 1987. "Understanding and Motivating Personnel in the Second Half of Life," *Journal of Education* 69(1): 20–46.

Langlais, Donald E., and Mary R. Calarusson. 1988 "Improving Teacher Evaluation," *Executive Educator* 10(5): 32–33.

Lanier, Judith, and Joseph Featherstone. 1988. "A New Commitment to Teacher Education," *Educational Leadership* 46(3): 18–22.

Latham, Gary P., Lise Saari, Elliott Pursell, and Michael Campion. 1980. "The Situational Interview," *Journal of Applied Psychology* 64(4): 422–27.

Latham, Glenn. 1988. "Why Innovations Fail," *The National Elementary Principal* 68(September): 41–43.

Lawler, S. Dianne. 1990. "Issues and Trends in Kindergarten: Implications for Instructional Leaders," *National Forum of Applied Educational Research Journal* 3: 56–59.

Lawrence, Stephanie. 1987. "Has the Push for Workers' Rights Shaped Social Change?" *Personnel Journal* 66(9): 74–91.

Lawrie, John. 1990. "Assessment: Prepare for a Performance Appraisal," *Personnel Journal* 69(4): 132–36.

Ledvinka, James. 1982. *Federal Regulation of Personnel and Human Resource Management.* Boston: Kent Publishing.

Leifer, Aimee D. 1976. "Teaching with Television and Film," in *The Psychology of Teaching Methods,* 75th Yearbook of the National Society for the Study of Education, Part I. N. L. Gage, ed. Chicago: University of Chicago Press.

Leinhardt, Gaea. 1990. "Capturing Craft Knowledge in Teaching," *Educational Researcher* 19(March): 18–25.

Leonard, Patricia Y., et al. 1988. "Teaching in the Year 2000: Minority Recruiting Push to Span the Gap," *The School Administrator* 45(September): 33–40.

Levine, Sarah. 1989. *Promoting Adult Growth in Schools: The Promise of Professional Development.* Newton, MA: Allyn and Bacon.

Levy, Martin. 1989. "Almost-Perfect Performance Appraisals." *Personnel Journal* 68(4): 76–83.

Lewis, A.C. 1989a. "A Box Full of Tools But No Blueprint," *Phi Delta Kappan* 71(3): 180–81.

Lewis, A.C. 1989b. *Restructuring America's Schools.* Arlington, VA: American Association of School Administrators.

Lewis, Anne C. 1982. *Evaluating Educational Personnel.* Arlington, VA: American Association of School Administrators.

Lieberman, Myron. 1988. "Professional Ethics in Public Education: An Autopsy," *Phi Delta Kappan* 70(2): 159–60.

Lieberman, Myron. 1989. "A Reply to Karl Hostetler," *Phi Delta Kappan* 70(9) May: 726–27.

Lifton, Fred B. 1990. "Picking an Effective Negotiator," *AASPA Bulletin* (June/July): 2.

Likert, Rensis. 1967. *The Human Organization: Its Management and Value.* New York: McGraw-Hill.

Linn, Robert L., et al. 1989. "The Development, Validation, and Applicability of the Personnel Evaluation Standards," *Journal of Personnel Evaluation in Education* 2(3): 199–214.

Lipsky, David B. 1982. "The Effect of Collective Bargaining on Teacher Pay: A Review of the Evidence," *Educational Administration Quarterly* 18(1): 14–42.

Loehr, Peter. (1986) "Relationships Between Teacher Interview Scores and On-the-Job Performance: A Self-Initiated Study in Conjunction with Monitoring Equal Employment, Affirmative Action, and Equal Educational Opportunities." Presented at the Annual Meeting of The American Association of School Personnel Administrators, Houston, TX, October 1986. ED 277-118.

Loredo, Judith, Nolan Estees, and Yping Wan. 1990. "The DECAS Executive Diagnostic Assessment System: How It Works." Presented at the Annual Convention of the American Association of School Administrators, New Orleans, LA, February 1990.

Louis, K.S., and M. B. Miles. 1990. *Improving the Urban High School: What Works and Why*. New York: Teachers College, Columbia University.

Mace-Matluck, Betty. 1987. *The Effective Schools Movement: Its History and Context*. Austin, TX: Southwest Educational Development Laboratory.

Macy, Neil. 1988. "A Perspective on Due Process in Teacher Evaluation," *Journal of Personnel Evaluation in Education* 2(1): 53–57.

Madaus, George F., and Diana Pullin. 1987. "Teacher Certification Tests: Do They Really Measure What We Need to Know?" *Phi Delta Kappan* 60(1): 31–38.

Main, Alex. 1985. *Educational Staff Development*. London: Croom Helm.

Manese, Wilfredo R. 1988. *Occupational Job Evaluation: A Research-Based Approach to Job Classification*. New York: Quorum Books.

Margulies, Newton, and S. Black. 1987. "Perspectives on Implementation of Participative Approaches," *Human Resource Management* 26(Fall): 385–412.

Maurer, Steven D., and Charles Fay. 1988. "Effect of Situational Interviews, Conventional Structured Interviews, and Training on Interview Rating Agreement: An Experimental Analysis," *Personnel Psychology* 41(2): 329–44.

May, Leslie S., G. A. Moore, and S. J. Zammit, eds. 1987. *Evaluating Business and Industry Training*. Boston: Klower Academic Publishers.

Mayer, Richard E. 1989. "Models for Understanding," *Review of Educational Research* 59(1): 43–64.

McAfee, R. Bruce, and Paul J. Champagne. 1988. "Employee Development: Discovering Who Needs What," *Personnel Administrator* 33(February): 92–98.

McClure, Maureen W., John C. Weidman, and Laure M. Sharp. 1988. "Teaching Career Paths and Teacher Education Reforms," *Educational Administration Quarterly* 24(2): 200–21.

McCulloch, Kenneth J. 1981. *Selecting Employees Safely Under the Law*. Englewood Cliffs, NJ: Prentice-Hall.

McDaniel, Michael A., Frank Schmidt, and John Hunter. 1988. "A Meta-Analysis of the Validity of Methods for Rating Training and Experience in Personnel Selection," *Personnel Psychology* 41(2): 283–309.

McDonnell, Lorraine M., and Anthony Pascal. 1988. *Teacher Unions and Educational Reform*. Santa Monica, CA: RAND Corporation.

McGreal, Thomas L. 1983. *Successful Teacher Evaluation*. Alexandria, VA: Association for Supervision and Curriculum Development.

McIntyre, Kenneth E. 1974. "The Way It Was/Is," *The National Elementary Principal* 53(5): 30–34.

McLaughlin, Milbrey Wallin, R. Scott Pfeifer, Deborah Swanson-Owens, and Sylvia Yee. 1986. "Why Teachers Won't Teach," *Phi Delta Kappan* 68(6): 420–26.

McLogan, P. 1989. *Models for Excellence*. Arlington, VA: Association for Staff Training and Development.

Medley, Donald M., and Homer Coker. 1987. "How Valid Are Principals' Judgement of Teacher Effectiveness?" *Phi Delta Kappan* 69(2): 138–40.

Medley, Donald M., Homer Coker, and Robert S. Soar. 1984. *Measurement-Based Evaluation of Teacher Performance: An Empirical Approach.* New York: Longman.

Meek, Anne. 1988. "On Teaching as a Profession: A Conversation with Linda Darling-Hammond," *Educational Leadership* 46(3):11–17.

Melohn, Thomas. 1987. "Screening for the Best Employees," *Inc.* 9(1): 104–106.

Meyer, Herbert E. 1976. "Personnel Directors Are the New Corporate Heroes," *Fortune* 93: 84–140.

Michel, George J. 1990. "Educational Reform by the President and the Task Forces of the Johnson Administration," *National Forum of Applied Educational Research* 3: 60–65.

Michigan Association of School Boards Labor Relations Service. 1988. *Board Members' Guide to the Negotiations Process.* Lansing, MI: Michigan Association of School Boards.

Miller, R.D. 1988. "Let's Stop Tinkering with Reform," *The School Administrator* 45(September): 44.

Milstein, Mike, and Celia Karen Fiedler. 1988. "The Status and Potential for Administrative Assessment Centers in Education." Presented at the Annual Meeting of the American Educational Research Association, New Orleans, LA, April 1988. ED 296-479.

Mitzel, Harold E. 1983. *Encyclopedia of Educational Research.* 5th ed. Washington, DC: American Educational Research Association.

Monk, D. H., and S. L. Jacobson. 1985. "The Distribution of Salary Increments Between Veteran and Novice Teachers: Evidence from New York State," *Journal of Education Finance* 11(2): 157–75.

Moore, Kevin W. 1988. "The Most Important Things to Know About an Applicant," in *BBP Recruiting and Hiring Handbook.* Waterford, CT: Bureau of Business Practice.

Moore, Laurence V. 1988. "Maps to Good Match," *Personnel Administrator* (May): 102–5.

Moran, Sheila W. 1990. "Schools and the Beginning Teacher," *Phi Delta Kappan* 71 (3): 210–13.

Moses, J. L., and W. C. Byham, eds. 1977. *Applying the Assessment Center Method.* New York: Pergamon Press.

Mouton, Jane S., and R. R. Blake. 1984. *Synergogy: A New Strategy for Education, Training, and Development.* San Francisco, CA: Jossey-Bass.

Murphy, Joseph, ed. 1990. *The Educational Reform Movement of the 1980's: Perspectives and Cases.* Berkeley, CA: McCutchan Publishing.

Murphy, Kevin, and F. Welch, 1989. "Wage Premiums for College Graduates: Recent Growth and Possible Explanations," *Educational Researcher* 8(May): 17–26.

Muth, Rodney, and Jann Azumi. 1990. "The School Site Level: Involving Parents in Reform," in *Education Reform: Making Sense of It All.* Samuel B. Bacharach, ed. Needham Heights, MA: Allyn and Bacon.

Myricks, Noel, and Bernard Hodinko. 1975. "Changing Patterns of Due Process and Predetermination Rights of Untenured Faculty in Public Colleges and Universities," *NOLPE School Law Journal* 5(1).

Naisbitt, J., and P. Aburdene. 1990. *Megatrends 2000.* New York: William Morrow and Co.

National Advisory Council on Education Professions Development. 1969. *Leadership and the Educational Needs of the Nation: A Report to the President and Congress of the United States.* Washington, DC: U.S. Government Printing Office.

National Association of Elementary School Principals. 1986. *Proficiencies for Principals.* Alexandria, VA: National Association of Elementary School Principals.

National Association of Elementary School Principals. 1988. *Effective Teachers: Effective Evaluation in America's Elementary and Middle Schools.* Alexandria, VA: National Association of Elementary School Principals.

National Association of Elementary School Principals. 1990. *Principals for 21st Century Schools.* Alexandria, VA: National Association of Elementary School Principals.

National Board for Professional Teaching Standards. 1988. *President's 1987/88 Report.* Washington, DC: National Board for Professional Teaching Standards.

National Commission on Excellence in Education. 1983. *A Nation at Risk: The Imperative for Educational Reform.* Washington, DC: U.S. Government Printing Office.

National Education Association. 1986. *Irregular Teacher Certification Policies.* Washington, DC: National Education Association. ED 271-474.

National Research Council. 1989. *Summary Report 1988: Doctorate Recipients from U.S. Universities.* Washington, DC: National Research Council.

National School Boards Association. 1982. *The School Personnel Management System.* Alexandria, VA: National School Boards Association.

Neill, Shirley Boes, and Jerry Custis. 1978. *Staff Dismissal: Problems and Solutions.* Arlington, VA: American Association of School Administrators.

Nettles, Barry. 1989. "Developing a Recruiting Plan," in *New Personnel Administrators Academy Notebook.* Austin, TX: Personnel Services TASB/TASA and Texas Association of School Personnel Administrators.

Nettles, Barry. 1990. "Teacher Induction Texas Style." Presented at the Personnel Academy sponsored by the Texas Association of School Boards, Texas Association of School Administrators, and Texas Association of School Personnel Administrators. Austin, TX, July 17–18, 1990.

Nicholson, Everett W., and William D. McInerney. 1988. "Hiring the Right Teacher: A Method for Selection," *NASSP Bulletin* 72(511): 88–92.

O'Dell, C. *The ABCs of Teacher Evaluation.* Yreka, CA.: Mardell.

O'Neil, John. 1989. "Global Education: Controversy Remains, But Support Growing," *Curriculum Update* (January): 1–4.

Office of the Federal Register, National Archives and Recorders Administration. July 1, 1989. *Code of Federal Regulations Volume 29.* Washington, DC: U.S. Government Printing Office.

Ogle, Laurence T., and Nabeel Alsalam, eds. 1990. *Condition of Education 1990, Volume 1.* Washington, DC: U. S. Government Printing Office.

Orlich, Donald D. 1989. *Staff Development: Enhancing Human Potential.* Boston: Allyn and Bacon.

Owen, D. E. 1984. "Profile Analysis: Matching Positions and Personnel," *Supervisory Management* 29(11): 14–20.

Owens, William A. 1976. "Background Data," in *Handbook of Industrial and Organizational Psychology,* M. D. Dunnette, ed. Chicago: Rand-McNally.

Pajak, Edward. 1986. *Identification of Supervisory Proficiencies Project.* Athens, GA: University of Georgia.

Pajak, Edward. 1989(a). *The Central Office Supervisor of Curriculum and Instruction: Setting the Stage for Success.* Boston: Allyn and Bacon.

Pajak, Edward. (1989b). "A Report on the Nationwide Survey of Outstanding Supervisors and University Professors," A paper presented at the Annual Meeting of the Council of Professors of Instructional Supervision, at the Pennsylvania State University, (November 10–12).

Paperman, Jacob B., and Martin, Desmond D. 1980. "Human Resource Accounting: A Managerial Tool?" In *Contemporary Issues in Human Resources Management: Cases and Readings,* edited by Fred E. Schuster. Reston, VA: Reston Publishing Company., pp. 438–44.

Pearson, H. Delmar. 1980. "Development of a Forced-Choice Teacher Behavior Rating Scale." Unpublished doctoral dissertation. Austin, TX: The University of Texas at Austin.

Pennsylvania School Board Association. 1989. "Demographic Data Delivers Valuable Information for Decision Making," *PSBA Bulletin.*

Perry, Nancy C. (1981) "New Teachers: Do the Best Get Hired?" *Phi Delta Kappan* 63(2): 113–14.

Persson, Leonard N. 1982. *The Handbook of Job Evaluations and Job Pricing.* Madison, CT: Business & Legal Reports.

Peters, Stephen, and Naida Tushnet Bagenstos. 1988. "State-Mandated Principal Evaluation: A Report on Current Practice." Presented at the Annual Meeting of the American Educational Research Association, New Orleans, LA, April 1988. ED 292-889.

Peters, T. 1987. *Thriving on Chaos: A Revolutionary Agenda for Today's Manager.* New York: Alfred E. Knopf.

Peterson, Donovan, and Kathryn Peterson. 1984. "Guidelines for Administration: A Research-Based Approach to Teacher Evaluation," *NASSP Bulletin* 68(469): 30–46.

Peterson, K. D., Joseph Murphy, and Philip Hallinger. 1987. "Superintendents' Perceptions of the Control and Coordination of the Technical Core in Effective School Districts," *Educational Administration Quarterly* 23(1): 79–95.

Peterson, Kent D. 1985. "Obstacles to Learning from Experience and Principal Training," *The Urban Review* 17(3): 189–200.

Pigford, Aretha B. 1989. "How to Hire Teachers That Fit," *The School Administrator* 46(November): 38.

Pigge, Fred L. 1985. "Teacher Education Graduates: Comparisons of Those Who Teach and Do Not Teach," *Journal of Teacher Education* 36(July/August): 27–30.

Pittman, R. B., and J. R. Slate. 1989. "Faculty Evaluation: Some Conceptual Considerations," *Journal of Personnel Evaluation in Education* 3(December): 39–51.

Porter, Andrew C. 1988. "Understanding Teaching: A Model for Assessment," *Journal of Teacher Education* 39(4): 2–7.

Pounder, Diana G. 1989. "Improving the Predictive Validity of Teacher Selection Decisions: Lessons from Teacher Appraisal," *Journal of Personnel Evaluation in Education* 2(2): 141–50.

Pringle, P. G. (1989). "Relationship of General Administrative Skills to Superintendent Selection and Contract Renewal." Unpublished doctoral dissertation. The University of Texas at Austin.

Ramsey, R.D. 1984. *Management Techniques for Solving School Personnel Problems.* West Hyack, NY: Parker Publishing.

Rauth, Marilyn. 1990. "Exploring Heresy in Collective Bargaining and School Restructuring," *Phi Delta Kappan* 71(10): 781–90.

Rea, Peter, Julie Rea, and Charles Noonmaw. 1990. "Training: Use Assessment Centers in Skill Development," *Personnel Journal* 69(April): 126–30.

Rebore, Ronald W. 1982. *Personnel Administration in Education: A Management Approach.* Englewood Cliffs, NJ: Prentice-Hall.

Reddin, William J. 1970. *Managerial Effectiveness.* New York: McGraw-Hill.

Redfern, George B. 1980. *Evaluating Teachers and Administrators: A Performance Objectives Approach.* Boulder, CO: Westview Press.

Redfern, George B. 1984. "Using Job Descriptions as an Administrative Tool," *Spectrum: Journal of School Research and Information* 2(Winter): 21–26.

Reed, S., and R. C. Sautter. 1990. "Children of Poverty: The Status of 12 Million Young Americans (Special Report)," *Phi Delta Kappan* 71(10): K1–K12.

Richardson, M. D. 1988. "The Administrative Assessment Center: An Opportunity for Service." Presented at the Annual Meeting of the Kentucky Association of School Superintendents, Louisville, KY, June 1988 ED 301-930.

Richardson, Virginia. 1990. "Significant and Worthwhile Change in Teaching Practice," *Educational Researcher* 19(October): 10–18.

Rivlin, Alice M. 1971. *Systematic Thinking for Social Action*. Washington, DC: The Brookings Institution.

Robinson, Glen E. 1990. "Synthesis of Research on Class Size," *Educational Leadership* 47(7): 80–90.

Robinson, Virginia. 1985. *Making Do in the Classroom: A Report on the Misassignment of Teachers*. Washington, DC: American Federation of Teachers and the Council for Basic Education. ED 163-108.

Rosenholtz, Susan J. 1986. "Career Ladders and Merit Pay: Capricious Fads or Fundamental Reforms?" *Elementary School Journal* 86(4): 513–29.

Rosenshine, Barack. 1976. "Classroom Instruction," in *The Psychology of Teaching Methods*, 75th Yearbook of the National Society for the Study of Education, Part I. N. L. Gage, ed. Chicago: University of Chicago Press.

Russell, George H. 1988 "Minority Teachers—'Dinosaurs' of the Twenty-first Century?" *AASPA Research Brief* 1(1).

Rutherford, W. L. 1985. "School Principals as Effective Leaders," *Phi Delta Kappan* 67(1): 31–34.

Ryan, R. Lloyd. 1987. *The Complete Inservice Staff Development Program*. Englewood Cliffs, NJ: Prentice-Hall.

Ryans, D.G. 1955. *Characteristics of Teachers*. Washington, DC: American Council on Education.

Sackett, Paul R. 1987. "Assessment Centers and Content Validity: Some Neglected Issues," *Personnel Psychology* 40(1): 13–25.

Sandler, Len. 1990. "Two-Sided Performance Reviews," *Personnel Journal* 69(1): 75 78.

Schlechty, P.C. 1990. *Schools for the 21st Century: Leadership Imperatives for Educational Reform*. San Francisco: Jossey-Bass.

Schlei, Barbara Lindemann, and Paul Grossman. 1983. *Employment Discrimination Law*. 2d ed. Washington, DC: Bureau of National Affairs.

Schlesinger, A.M. 1986. *The Cycles of American History*. Boston: Houghton Mifflin.

Schmitt, Neal. 1983. "Validity of Assessment Ratings for the Prediction of Performance of School Administrators." Presented at the Meeting of the American Psychological Association, Anaheim, CA, August 1983. ED 236–777.

Schmitt, Neal, and S. A. Cohen. 1990. "Criterion-Related Validity of the Assessment Center for Selection of School Administrators," *Journal of Personnel Evaluation in Education* 4(October): 203–12.

Schmitt, Neal, R. Z. Gooding, Raymond Noe, and M. Kirsch. 1984a. "Meta-Analysis of Validity Studies Published Between 1964 and 1982 and the Investigation of Study Characteristics," *Personnel Psychology* 37(3): 407–22.

Schmitt, Neal, Raymond Noe, Ronni Merritt, and Michael Fitzgerald. 1984b. "Validity of Assessment Center Ratings for the Prediction of Performance Ratings and School Climate of School Administrators," *Journal of Applied Psychology* 69(2): 207–13.

Schuler, Randall S., and Stuart A. Youngblood. 1986. *Effective Personnel Management*. 2d ed. St. Paul, MN: West Publishing.

Schuster, Jay R., and Patricia K. Zingheim. 1987. "Merit Pay: Is It Hopeless in The Public Sector?" *Personnel Administrator* 32(10): 83–84.

Schwab, Richard L. 1990. "Reforming Teacher Education: Lessons Learned from a Five Year Program," in *Education Reform: Making Sense of It All.* Samuel B. Bacharach, ed. Boston: Allyn and Bacon.

Sclafani, S. B. 1987. "AASA Guidelines for Preparation of School Administrators: Do They Represent the Important Job Behaviors of Superintendents?" Unpublished doctoral dissertation. Austin, TX: The University of Texas at Austin.

Scribner, J. D. 1990a. "Reform, Reaction, Renewal: UCEA's Response to the National Policy Board Agenda." Presented at the Annual Meeting of the American Educational Research Association, Boston, MA, April 1990.

Scribner, Jay D. 1990b. "Liberating Educational Administration from Hedgehog Thinking: A Planning Proposal for the New Millennium." Annual Presidential Address presented to the University Council on Educational Administration, Boston, MA, October 1990.

Scriven, Michael. 1990. "Can Research-Based Teacher Evaluation Be Saved?" *Journal of Personnel Evaluation in Education* 4(September): 19–32.

Seidner, Constance J. 1976. "Teaching with Simulations and Games," in *The Psychology of Teaching Methods,* 75th Yearbook of the National Society for the Study of Education, Part I. N. L. Gage, ed. Chicago: University of Chicago Press.

Seidow, Mary D., et al. 1985. *Inservice Education for Content Area Teachers.* Newark, DE: International Reading Association.

Seif, Elliott. 1990. "How to Create Schools that Thrive in Chaotic Times," *Educational Leadership* 47(9): 81–82.

Sendor, Benjamin. 1987. "It's Okay to Set Affirmative Action 'Targets' " *The American School Board Journal* 174(7): 16–17, 40.

Shaffer, Garnett Stokes, Vickie Saunders, and William A. Owens. 1986. "Additional Evidence for the Accuracy of Biographical Data: Long-Term Retest and Observer Ratings," *Personnel Psychology* 39: 791–809.

Shaplin, Judson T., and Olds, H. F., eds. 1964. *Team Teaching.* New York: Harper & Row.

Shedd, Joseph B. 1988. "Collective Bargaining, School Reform, and the Management of School Systems," *Educational Administration Quarterly* 24(4): 405–15.

Sheive, Linda Tinelli, and Marian Beauchamp Schoenheit. 1987. "Vision and the Work Life of Educational Leaders," in *1987 ASCD Year Book.* Alexandria, VA.: Association for Supervision and Curriculum Development.

Shepard, Lorrie A., and Mary Lee Smith. 1990. "Synthesis of Research on Grade Retention," *Educational Leadership* 47(9): 84–88.

Showers, Beverly. 1985. "Teachers Coaching Teachers," *Educational Leadership* 43(7): 43–48.

Showers, Beverly, Bruce Joyce, and B. Bennett. 1987. "Synthesis of Research on Staff Development: A Framework for Future Study and a State-of-the-Art Analysis," *Educational Leadership* 45(3): 77–87.

Shulman, L. S. 1986. "Those Who Understand: Knowledge Growth in Teaching," *Educational Researcher* 5(2): 4–14.

Shulman, Lee S. 1987. "Assessment for Teaching: An Initiative for the Profession," *Phi Delta Kappan* 69(1): 38–44.

Shulman, Lee S. 1988. "A Union of Insufficiencies: Strategies for Teacher Assessment in a Period of Educational Reform," *Educational Leadership* 46(3): 36–41.

Sibson, Robert E. 1976. *The Executive Guide to Wage and Salary Administration.* Boston: American Management Associations.

Sizer, Theodore R. 1988. "A Visit to an 'Essential' School," *The School Administrator* 45 (November): 14, 18–19.

Slavin, Robert E. 1989. "PET and the Pendulum: Faddism in Education and How to Stop It," *Phi Delta Kappan* 70(10): 752–58.

Slavin, Robert E., N. L. Karweit, and N. A. Madden. 1989. *Effective Programs for Students at Risk*. Boston: Allyn and Bacon.

Smith, Stuart C., and J. J. Scott. 1990. *The Collaborative School: A Work Environment for Effective Instruction*. Eugene, OR: ERIC Clearinghouse of Educational Management.

Snyder, Mark, Ellen Berscheid, and Alana Matwychuk. 1988. "Orientations Toward Personnel Selection Decisions: Differential Reliance on Appearance and Personality," *Personality and Social Psychology* 54(6): 972–79.

Soar, Robert S., Donald M. Medley, and Homer Coker 1983. "Teacher Evaluation: A Critique of Currently Used Methods," *Phi Delta Kappan* 65(4): 239–46.

Soar, Robert, and R. Soar. 1976. "An Attempt to Identify Measures of Teacher Effectiveness From Four Studies," *Journal of Teacher Education* 27(Fall): 261–67.

Staub, Susan. 1989. "Can Texas Survive Collective Bargaining in Education?" Presented at the Distinguished Lecture Series, Texas Association of School Boards and Texas Association of School Administrators Joint Annual Convention, San Antonio, TX, September 1989.

Steffy, Betty E. 1989. *Career Stages of Classroom Teachers*. Lancaster, PA: Technomic Publishing.

Sternberg, Robert J., and J. Kolligian. 1990. *Competence Considered*. New Haven, CT: Yale University Press.

Stiggins, Richard J. 1989. "A Commentary on the Role of Student Achievement Data in the Evaluation of Teachers," *Journal of Personnel Evaluation in Education* 3(1): 7–15.

Stiggins, Richard J., N. Faires Conklin, and NJ. Bridgford. 1986. "Classroom Assessment: A Key to Educational Excellence," *Educational Measurement: Issues and Practice* 5: 6–17.

Stodolsky, S. 1988. *The Subject Matters: Classroom Activity in Math and Social Studies*. Chicago: University of Chicago Press.

Stolze, William J. 1989. "A Team Approach from the Start," *Nation's Business*. 10(November): 9.

Stone, Dianna L., and Eugene F. Stone. 1987. "Effects of Missing Application-Blank Information on Personnel Selection Decisions: Do Privacy Protection Strategies Bias the Outcome?" *Journal of Applied Psychology* 72(3): 452–56.

Street, S., and Ellett, C.D. 1986. "An Analysis of Policy-Based Responses to Educational Reforms for Teachers: Performance-Based Certification, Merit Pay, and Career Ladders." Presented at the 1986 meeting of the Southwestern Educational Research Association, Houston, TX.

Streifer, Phillip A. 1987. *Teacher Evaluation Systems: A Review of Critical Issues and the Current State of the Art*. Andover, MA: The Regional Laboratory for Educational Improvement of the Northeast and Islands. ED 295-336.

Strike, Kenneth A. 1988 "The Ethics of Teaching," *Phi Delta Kappan* 70(2): 156–58.

Stufflebeam, D. L., and D. M. Brethower. 1987. "Improving Personnel Evaluations Through Professional Standards," *Journal of Personnel Evaluation in Education* 1(2): 125–55.

Task Force on Teaching as a Profession. 1986. *A Nation Prepared: Teachers for the 21st Century*. New York: Carnegie Forum on Education and the Economy.

Taylor, G. Stephen, and Thomas W. Zimmerer. 1988. "Personality Tests for Potential Employees: More Harm Than Good," *Personnel Journal* 67(1): 60–64.

Teschner, W. P., Torstein Harbos, Bertilgran Henninghaft., eds. 1983. *In-Service Teacher Training Models, Methods and Criteria of Its Evaluation*. Strasbourg: The Council of Europe and Swets and Zeitlinger, Lisse.

Texas Education Agency. 1985. *Performance Criteria for the Texas Teacher Appraisal System*. Austin, TX: Texas Education Agency.

Thorndike, Robert L. 1984. *Intelligence as Information Processing: The Mind and the Computer*. Bloomington, IN: Phi Delta Kappa.

Thornton, G. C., and W. C. Byham. 1982. *Assessment Centers and Managerial Performance.* New York: Academic Press.

Thorson, John R., Roger K. Miller, and Jerry Ballon. 1987. "Instructional Improvement Through Personnel Evaluation," *Educational Leadership* 44(7): 52–54.

Toffler, A. 1990. *Powershifts.* New York: Bantam-Doubleday.

Tracey, William R. 1984. *Designing Training and Development Systems.* Rev. ed. New York: American Management Association.

Trachtenberg, Stephen. 1988. "Teacher Competency: How Do We Assess It?" *College Board Review* 149(Fall 1988): 24–27.

Troy, Leo. 1988. "Public Sector Unionism: The Rising Power Center of Organized Labor," *Government Union Review* 9(3): 1–35.

Tuthill, Doug. 1990. "Expanding the Union Contract: One Teacher's Perspective," *Phi Delta Kappan* 71(10): 775–80.

Tyler, Ralph W. 1981. "Curriculum Development Since 1990," *Educational Leadership* 38(9): 599–601.

U.S. Department of Justice, Immigration and Naturalization Service. 1987. *Handbook for Employers.* Washington, DC: U.S. Government Printing Office.

U.S. Equal Employment Opportunity Commission. 1979. *Job Discrimination: Laws and Rules You Should Know.* Washington, DC: U.S. Government Printing Office.

U.S. Equal Employment Opportunity Commission, Civil Service Commission, Department of Labor, and Department of Justice. 1983. *Adoption of Four Agencies of Uniform Guidelines on Employee Selection Procedures.* 43 Federal Register 38, 290-38, 315.

Ubben, G. G., and L. W. Hughes. 1987. *The Principal: Creative Leadership for Effective Schools.* Boston: Allyn and Bacon.

Ulmer, Dale. 1986. "Interactive Video for the Electronic Age," *Workplace Education* 4(March–April): 6–7.

Urbanski, Adam. 1990. "Restructuring Schools for Greater Choice: The Rochester Initiative," in *Education Reform: Making Sense of It All.* Samuel B. Bacharach, ed. Heedham Heights, MA: Allyn and Bacon.

Valente, William D. 1987. *Law in the Schools.* 2d ed. Columbus, OH: Merrill Publishing.

Vukovich, Eli. 1987. *Teacher Selection Process: Part I. How to Use References.* Foster City, CA: American Association of School Personnel Administrators.

Wagstaff, L.H., and K. S. Gallagher. 1990. "Schools, Families and Communities: Idealized Images and New Realities," in *Educational Leadership and Changing Contexts of Families, Communities, and Schools,* 89th Yearbook of the National Society for the Study of Education, Part II. Brad Mitchell and LuVern L. Cunningham, eds. Chicago: University of Chicago Press.

Walberg, Herbert J. 1986. "Synthesis of Research on Teaching," in *Handbook of Research on Teaching.* 3d ed. Merlin C. Wittrock, ed. Washington, DC: American Educational Research Association.

Walker, Billy D. 1987. "Introduction and Philosophical Foundations of Public School Finance." Presented at the School Finance Seminar. Dallas, TX, December 4, 1987.

Wallace, Marc J., and Charles H. Fay. 1988. *Compensation Theory and Practice.* 2d ed. Boston: PWS-KENT Publishing.

Watts, Gary D., and Robert M. McClure. 1990. "Expanding the Contract to Revolutionize School Renewal," *Phi Delta Kappan* 71(10): 765–74.

Watts, Larry R., and Harold C. White. 1988. "Assessing Employee Turnover," *Personnel Administrator* 33(4): 80–85.

Wayson, W.W. 1988. *Up from Excellence: The Impact of the Excellence Movement on Schools.* Bloomington, IN: Phi Delta Kappa.

Weaver, Timothy, 1983. *America's Teacher Quality Problem: Alternative for Reform.* New York: Praeget Special Studies.

Webb, L. Dean, John Greer, Paul Montello, and M. Scott Norton. 1987. *Personnel Administration in Education: New Issues and New Needs in Human Resource Management.* Columbus, OH: Merrill Publishing.

Webb, L. Dean, and Van D. Mueller. 1984. *Managing Limited Resources: New Demands on Public School Management.* Fifth Annual Yearbook of the American Education Finance Association. Cambridge, MA: Ballinger.

Weber, James R. 1987. *Teacher Evaluation as a Strategy for Improving Instruction: Synthesis of Literature.* Joint publication of the ERIC Clearinghouse on Educational Management and the North Central Regional Laboratory. ED 287-213.

Wendel, Frederick C., and Ward Sybouts. 1988. *Assessment Center Methods in Educational Administration: Past, Present, and Future.* Tempe, AZ: The University Council for Educational Administration.

Weston, David J., and Dennis Warmke. 1988. "Dispelling the Myths About Panel Interviews," *Personnel Administrator* 33(5): 109–11.

Wiersma, W., and T. Gibney. 1985. "Observation as an Approach to Measuring Teacher Competency," *Action in Teacher Education* 7: 59–67.

Wirt, Fredrick M., and M. W. Kirst. 1989. *Schools in Conflict: The Politics of Education.* 2d ed. Berkeley, CA: McCutchan Publishing.

Wise, Arthur. 1988. "The Two Conflicting Trends in School Reform: Legislated Learning Revisited," *Phi Delta Kappan* 69(5): 328–32.

Wise Arthur E., and Linda Darling-Hammond. 1985. "Teacher Evaluation and Teacher Professionalism," *Educational Leadership* 42(4): 28–33.

Wise, Arthur E., Linda Darling-Hammond, and B. Berry. 1987. *Effective Teacher Selection: From Recruitment to Retention.* Santa Monica, CA: National Institution of Education.

Wittrock, M.C. 1986. *Handbook of Research on Teaching.* 3d ed. New York: Macmillan.

Willy, Elaine P. 1982. *Prospects for Black Teachers: Preparation, Certification, Employment.* Washington, DC: ERIC Clearinghouse on Teacher Education.

Wochner, Raymond E., ed. 1976. *Competency-based Preparation of Educational Administrators: Tasks, Competencies, and Indicators of Competencies.* Tempe, AZ: Arizona State University.

Yankelovich, Daniel. 1981. "Who Rules in American Life: Search for Self-Fulfillment in a World Turned Upside Down," *Psychology Today* 15: 35–91.

Yarbrough, Donald B. 1989. "A Cognitive Psychological Perspective on Teacher Evaluation," *Journal of Personnel Evaluation in Education* 2(3): 215–28.

Young, I. Phillip, and Bruce R. McMurry. 1986. "Effects of Chronological Age, Focal Position, Quality of Information and Quantity of Information on Screening Decisions for Teacher Candidates," *Journal of Research and Development in Education* 19(4): 1–9.

Young, I. Phillip, and Will Place. 1988. "The Relationship Between Age and Teaching Performance." *Journal of Personnel Evaluation in Education* 2(1): 43–52.

Young, I. Phillip, and Dean Ryerson. 1986. *Teacher Selection: Legal, Practical and Theoretical Aspects.* Tempe, AZ: The University Council for Educational Administration.

Zedeck, S., A. Tziner, and S. E. Middlestadt. 1983. "Interviewer Validity and Reliability: An Individual Analysis Approach," *Personnel Psychology* 36(2): 355–70.

Zemke, Ron. 1985. "Is Performance Appraisal a Paper Tiger?" *Training* 22(12): 24–32.

INDEX